POLITICS
IN THE
NEW SOUTH

POLITICS

IN THE

NEW SOUTH

Republicanism, Race and Leadership in the Twentieth Century

RICHARD K. SCHER

Second Edition

M.E. Sharpe
Armonk, New York
London, England

First edition published 1992 by Paragon House.

Library of Congress Cataloging-in-Publication Data

Scher, Richard K.
Politics in the new South : republicanism, race, and
leadership in the twentieth century / by Richard K. Scher.—2nd ed.
p.   cm.
Includes bibliographical references and index.
ISBN 1-56324-847-6 (c : alk. paper). —
ISBN 1-56324-848-4 (p : alk. paper)
1. Southern States—Politics and government—1865–1950.
2. Southern States—Politics and government—1951–
I. Title
F215.S34   1997
320.975—dc20   96-30362
CIP
Printed in the United States of America

The paper used in this publication meets the minimum requirements of
American National Standard for Information Sciences—
Permanence of Paper for Printed Library Materials,
ANSI Z 39.48-1984.

BM (c)   10   9   8   7   6   5   4   3   2   1
BM (p)   10   9   8   7   6   5   4   3   2   1

Contents

List of Tables and Figures

Preface to the Second Edition

Like so many other books written by academicians, this one grew out of the classroom. A transplanted New Yorker, I knew little of the South when I arrived in Florida more than twenty years ago. What I thought I knew was not especially pleasing. In many respects I had a traditional easterner's view of the South and things southern, that is, detached and slightly superior. Even eight years as a schoolboy in Houston did little to shape my views into more sympathetic ones. And they were altogether reinforced during the civil rights movement, which occurred while I was a college student in New York, and in which I participated in a modest way.

But when I settled in Gainesville, it rapidly became apparent to me that my preconceived ideas were wrong. Not that Gainesville was typical of the South; university communities are seldom typical of anything. Having an interest in state and local affairs and politics, I immediately began to observe, study, read about, discuss, and even involve myself in southern politics.

I was delighted with what I found. Here was a style and rhythm and substance of politics unlike anything I knew about; it could not have been more different from New York City and State, with which I was already familiar. True, much of it seemed baroque, deceptive, anachronistic, quaint, silly, even crazy. Issues were cloaked under clouds of smoke and magnolia blossoms, distorted by mirrors, and overlaid by history and myths. People kept talking about tradition, place, time, and family as if they were real and as if they were a legitimate part of political life. They were. I just had to discover how they fit together.

Fortunately, I had two professionally rewarding experiences that got me on the right track for understanding and appreciating southern politics. One was my first chair, the inimitable (and indomitable) Manning J. Dauer. He took me under his wing, and seemed to want to make me his southern project. He succeeded. Under his tutelage and guidance I learned, and worked, and talked, and read, and wrote, and discussed, and worked, and read some more. He was an extraordinary mentor; without him, I would have become neither interested in nor aware and appreciative of the breadth, depth, and richness of southern politics.

The other experience was to meet two young academicians at my own stage of professional life: David Colburn, a historian from New England by way of the University of North Carolina at Chapel Hill; and James W. Button, political scientist, an upstate New Yorker who had lived in California and Texas. Neither of these other two gentlemen knew much about southern politics either. But we became interested together, and with each of them I engaged in major research. We learned together—to enjoy, to criticize, to analyze, to evaluate, to understand, to appreciate. I hope they learned half as much from me as I did from them.

Anyway, back to the classroom. By the late 1970s, Manning Dauer thought I was ready; that is, he felt I had learned enough to have advanced beyond the ignoramus stage and thought I was even asking some important questions. He asked me to prepare and teach a course on southern politics, aimed primarily at third- and fourth-year political science majors and a smattering of graduate students but broad enough to appeal to students from other departments and colleges. The first few semesters were rocky. I'm sure students in the initial classes wondered what this was all about. I certainly did. There is no question that I learned as much from the students, especially the native southerners in the classes, as they did from me.

Eventually, however, the course found its measure, and I am happy that it has. It has proven exceptionally popular. I always look forward to teaching it. But the longer I taught the course, the more obvious it became that a book of the type I have written seemed necessary, not just for students but for other individuals as well.

There is no shortage of writings on the South or on southern politics and public affairs. The extensive sources cited in this book are just a fraction, albeit a representative one, of the major available writings. But the problem, it seemed to me, was twofold. First, students of today's generation know little of the traditional South. They have heard of it, of course, but their actual knowledge is very limited. They may also be aware of something called the "new South," with its "new" southern politics; certainly they are barraged by the terms in the media during every election season. But they have very little idea what the new South and new southern politics really are. Just as important, they don't know where they came from, what it took to get from there to here, and what is the relationship between the old and the new. In short, they know little of historical perspective or political evolution.

The problem is not limited to students. For many people, traditional southern ways, including politics, are an increasingly dim memory. Even the civil rights movement seems remote. Pictures of Martin Luther King Jr.'s civil rights campaign in Birmingham, Alabama, in 1963, which I recently showed an audience, were thought to be from another country. Did that actually happen here, some asked? And what was so important about King and what he did, anyway?

It is a major theme of this book that the reality of the political past must be kept alive. Not to glorify or mythologize it—southerners have done too much of that already. But it is important for today's citizens—students and those outside the academy—to be aware of and sensitive to the past. Much of what happened in traditional southern politics is neither pleasant nor commendable. But if we want to know about the new South and new southern politics, we had better understand fully what life, and politics, used to be like in this region.

The second major problem I found in teaching and lecturing is that some of the most up-to-date works on southern politics are largely inaccessible to students and other nonspecialists. There is no denying the erudition and magisterial quality of Earl and Merle Black's recent *Politics and Society in the South* or their *Vital South,* and of Robert H. Swansborough and David M. Brodsky's detailed *South's New Politics,* among a number of others. These are invaluable works of scholarship. But they are certainly more sophisticated than most undergraduates can handle; they are also too technical for the interested nonspecialist to plow through. Even classics, including V.O. Key's essential *Southern Politics in State and Nation* or William C. Havard's *Changing Politics of the South,* as compelling and rewarding as they are even for neophytes, leave many modern readers wondering what's happened since they appeared.

This volume deliberately and specifically seeks a broad audience. It is designed to appeal to a wide range of readers. In some ways, the book is a text in that it encompasses a great deal of material and presents it in a way intended to attract and hold the interest of many different kinds of people. But it is also a scholarly book in that it seeks to address complex issues in a systematic way and to maintain rigorous standards of research, analysis, and interpretation. This eclectic approach was specifically chosen in order to bring this fascinating subject to many readers and to give each of them something to satisfy his or her particular curiosity.

More specifically, the book is meant to meet the needs of undergraduate and some graduate students, scholars in other fields, public school and community college teachers, journalists, government and public officials, and the interested lay public for an approachable, accessible book on twentieth-century southern politics. It tries to show the sweep of what southern politics was, and what it has become, by focusing on three areas: the rise of Republicans, the entrance of blacks into mainstream southern politics, and political leadership, specifically southern governors. It is particularly concerned with how these major aspects of modern southern political life have addressed the traditional major problems of the South—race and poverty. Although it is deliberately broad and longitudinal in scope, by focusing on a limited range of topics it avoids superficiality. It is, I hope, analytical enough to appeal to my professional colleagues but sufficiently nontechnical and jargon free to appeal to a broad range of other interested readers as well.

The book has been substantially edited and fully updated for the second edition. Each chapter has been fully revisited and reworked. References and bibliography have been augmented. While the first edition was available on the market for but a brief period, comments and reactions and suggestions from colleagues and reviewers have proven most helpful in making changes in this updated version. Particularly helpful were the thoughts of Larry Moreland at the Citadel and Wayne Bailey at Stetson University. The contribution of Evelyn Fazio, editor of the book's previous publisher and now publisher at M.E. Sharpe, must be heralded; her interest, enthusiasm, unflagging support, and dedicated professionalism prompted me to make the book the best it could be. My editor at M.E. Sharpe, Patricia Kolb, and Elizabeth Granda, could not have been more helpful and positive—although I still don't know if either has ever been south of the Bronx.

Like many other books, mine has too many intellectual debts to catalogue. The support and encouragement and insights of the late Manning J. Dauer must be gratefully recognized at the outset; the stamp of his influence is on virtually every page. The late Ruth O. McQuown, professor of political science and associate dean of the College of Liberal Arts and Sciences at the University of Florida, was a constant inspiration; Ruth did not simply study and teach southern politics; she lived it. James W. Button repeatedly heard about each page, aside from reading various parts and the whole manuscript, with an extraordinarily positive attitude and constant sensitivity, concern, and good humor. His help has been without peer. My former chair, Ken Wald, has been unflagging in his enthusiasm for the project, both in his prodding me to finish the first edition before the end of the century and in his insistence that I revise it for a second one. Jon Mills, former Speaker of the Florida House of Representatives and currently professor of law and director of the Center for Governmental Responsibility, University of Florida, gave invaluable material from an insider's standpoint. John Hotaling, a former lobbyist and currently free-lance journalist and political consultant, gave me a feel for real-world politics on the street, where the rubber meets the road. Members of the electronic and print media, who often call to get my thoughts on developments in southern and Florida politics, stimulated my thinking through the probing questions. My students, consciously or not, have aided their process of structuring the work, gathering the data, sharpening my thinking, and refining the text. While there have been literally hundreds passing through my classroom and office who have assisted in ways they probably can't imagine, four stand out for their invaluable help—Matt Adler, Richard Alexander, Dr. Warren Heyman, and Amie Singer. The organizers and participants in the very worthwhile Symposium on Southern Politics, held biennially at the Citadel in Charleston, South Carolina, have been exceedingly generous with their time and criticisms and encouragement as they allowed me to try out different parts of the book on various panels.

To all of these people, a hearty thank you! They helped enhance the book's strengths and minimize its defects (the leftovers of which are mine, not theirs).

Most important, however, have been my children, and especially my wife Miriam, who saw the genesis of this book and nurtured me and it through to its conclusion. Without her and them, to whom the work is lovingly dedicated, neither the first nor the second edition would ever have been started or completed.

POLITICS
IN THE
NEW SOUTH

1

Introduction: Seeking the New South

I have a deep affection and respect for the South. It's the land of my forefathers and the region of so many historically significant events that shaped our nation's development.
—John Warner, senator from Virginia

The last vestiges of regionalism should be hung onto like a Doberman with a sweater. When it goes away, it won't ever come back.
—Dan Baird, southern singer

Forget? Hell!
—Southern slogan often seen on bumper stickers

After all these years, is there yet a "new" South? Have the ghosts of the past finally been laid to rest? Is America's wayward region now a full partner and participant in the life of the nation? Has all been forgiven? Or is the new South mainly an illusion, perhaps even a public relations gimmick, in which traditional values, behaviors, beliefs, and attitudes persist in spite of the obvious transformations and convulsions that have occurred during this century?

Is there also a "new" southern politics? Has the character of the region's traditional politics been so altered that something qualitatively different has emerged? Or can we continue to see some of its past patterns still alive beneath the glitz and glitter and high-tech modernisms so loudly trumpeted about the new politics of the South?

3

These are not trivial questions. At least since the end of the Civil War, if not earlier, journalists, scholars, politicians, visionaries, and other students of southern affairs have debated, sometimes acrimoniously, whether a new South could emerge. While there has never been agreement on the specific character of a new South, most suggested that it would be a region freed of the historical burden of slavery and defeat in the Civil War, humiliation during Reconstruction, and subsequent guilt about its peculiar position in American history. It might also mean a reduction, even elimination, of its traditional characteristics of poverty, illiteracy, racism, lack of opportunity, and, ultimately, despair, to become more like the rest of America, particularly in the promises it held out.

The likelihood of this transformation has also been a matter of considerable debate. For some observers, the emergence of a new South was both inevitable and desirable. Henry Grady and the disciples of the "new South creed" late in the nineteenth century, as well as more recent students of the South such as H. Brandt Ayres and Thomas Naylor, were strong advocates of regional progress that permitted the South to transcend its past and become fully integrated into the life of the nation. Others, such as the Vanderbilt agrarians, were rueful of what progress might mean to the traditional verities of southern life. And still other writers, from the acerbic H.L. Mencken to the encyclopedic regionalists Howard Odum and Rupert Vance to the eminent political scientist V.O. Key, wondered about the conditions under which the South might develop social and political institutions capable of coping with its traditional, massive problems.

The literature on the new South and a new southern politics dwarfs the imagination. It is virtually impossible for any one person to have read, let alone digested, the numerous studies, books, essays, articles, tracts, and divinings prepared by a host of scholars, journalists, pundits, muckrakers, defenders, travelers, onlookers, and other interested participants and bystanders during the late nineteenth and early twentieth centuries. But while there is no shortage of facts, information, and interpretation, neither is there a clear picture of what the new South really is, when it arrived, what it looks like, or, indeed, if it is anything other than a figment of the imagination. The same could also be said about the putative existence of a new southern politics.

Part of the problem arises from the sheer mass of material; a coherent picture could hardly emerge from such a disparate and wide-ranging literature. Contributing also to the confusion is what is meant by "new." To some extent the question is analogous to the half-full or half-empty glass of water problem, in that the criteria for determining what is new have not always been agreed upon or even made explicit. Thus a certain vagueness, even subjectivity, is inevitable. The same point also applies to the concept of "South." Volumes have been written just trying to define it, to determine its perimeter.

This book seeks to enter the long and rich discussion of the existence of a new South and new southern politics. The South itself and its politics have, during the course of this century, undergone a tremendous number of pressures and tensions, changes and developments. The story of political change, but continuity also, in the twentieth-century South is a fascinating one. Indeed, it sheds light not only on the perpetuation of regional politics in the United States but illuminates and underscores changes and developments in the larger context of American politics as well.

Seeking the New South: A Grand Tradition

As we suggested at the outset, students of the South have searched for something new in its politics or other social institutions for a hundred years and more. Thus a grand tradition of writing about the South has developed on this topic. It is a varied, rich, and virtually inexhaustible literature, one into which any student of southern affairs can, and should, dip. No matter where one looks, one is likely to be informed, provoked, delighted, even entertained by the extraordinary material available.

It is not the intention of this section of the introduction to review this literature, for two reasons. There is too much for a short review, and for most readers it is unnecessary. Nonetheless, even the most casual of readers needs to know something of this grand tradition of seeking the new South and a new southern politics.

For our purposes this quest began with the young Henry Grady, the Atlanta journalist and editor, and his band of followers who ascribed to the new South creed. Grady, writing late in the nineteenth century, surveyed the post-Reconstruction South and found a region mired in poverty, defeat, and despair. He was particularly appalled at the colonial status of the region and felt it was victimized by northern and midwestern commercial and industrial interests. The result was a tremendous burden on the economy of the South, a vast waste of human and other natural resources, and political institutions that had atrophied to the point of uselessness.[1]

For Grady and other new South advocates, the solution was clear. Industrialization of the region would allow it to revive and throw off its colonial yoke. Grady spent a great deal of time in the North and Midwest, speaking with business and commercial groups, extolling the virtues of the South, and seeking outside investment to begin the industrialization process. Whether he realized that in many respects this approach to southern improvement could make matters worse rather than better is problematic. On the other hand, he and his followers not only established a pattern for other writers about the new South throughout this century but set in motion an enormous wave of southern politicians and businessmen who sought to continue his recruitment efforts during the ensuing decades. They can still be seen today in the efforts of governors, mayors, businessmen, planning directors, Chamber of Commerce leaders, heads of downtown redevelopment authorities, and a variety of southern visionaries to seek outside capital to improve the southern economy and southern life generally.[2]

Searches for an understanding of southern politics and speculation about the rise of a new southern politics could also be found late in the nineteenth and well into the twentieth century. However, the grand tradition in political science on these matters really began in 1949, with the publication of V.O. Key's magisterial *Southern Politics in State and Nation*. Few books have had the impact that Key's did, and continues to have, on both those who study and write about southern politics and those who practice it. It remains a seminal work, not only for those interested in southern politics but for those concerned about American politics generally.[3]

Key's book was written on several levels. At the most basic, it was an overview of the nature of southern politics in the first half of this century. In a series of brilliant, often amusing, case studies, Key illuminated the major features of one-party politics found in the eleven southern (i.e., formerly Confederate) states. On another level, Key discussed the implications of one-party politics for democratic theory, focusing specifically on the adequacy of the fundamentally undemocratic political institutions of the South for coping with the major problems of the region, especially race. Finally, Key's book represented a major essay on normative theory, in that he addressed the relationship between one- and two-party politics to institutionalizing democratic, accountable government in the region.

Of these levels, the second is most relevant to this text and, indeed, to many other scholars writing after him. Key's essential point was that the political institutions of the South—especially, but not exclusively, the one-party system—failed to provide an effective means of dealing with the region's major problems. Race, in his mind, was the most critical of all; for him, it was the fundamental axiom of southern politics. The reason stemmed from the presence of a vast black population and hostile white racial attitudes that generated an array of political behaviors and structures that were designed to keep blacks out of politics and a segregated society intact. One-party politics dominated by a small but powerful group of white elites ensured that traditional racial practices remained untouched. One-party politics further allowed the continued reelection of southern senators and representatives to Washington, D.C., who, through the congressional seniority system, reached sufficient levels of power to keep the federal government from interfering in southern racial affairs. One-party politics also ensured that popular political activity in the region was carefully controlled: while blacks were political victims and objects of manipulation, white participation—especially by the vast numbers of poor or poverty-stricken whites—was also sharply limited.

Key was less concerned with finding a new southern politics than in analyzing the old politics entrenched in the region since before the turn of the century. He explicitly noted the conditions needed to bring about a new, more democratic politics in the region. He argued that until a two-party system developed that would allow real political discussion and conflict to occur, and thereby permit the integration of blacks (and poor whites) into the political system of the South, little change could be expected. Two of his followers, Alexander Heard and Donald Strong, wrote companion volumes that are essentially searches for the origin of a two-party South.[4]

Key missed the mark in some aspects of his analysis of southern politics. He thought it likely, for example, that the Republican Party, as it developed in the region, would become the more moderate of the two parties on racial issues. In fact, the opposite occurred.

Nonetheless, it is virtually impossible to overstate the impact Key had on the study of southern politics. His work spawned a host of successive studies, articles, and books. Texts by William C. Havard, Neal Peirce, Jack Bass and Walter DeVries, Alexander Lamis, and Robert H. Swansborough and David M. Brodsky are explicitly modeled on Key's work in that they follow a state-by-state case study approach focusing on developments in the South's party system, especially the growth of a second party and its implications for a more open southern politics. Each of these works examines, explicitly or implicitly, the emergence of a new southern politics. So does *Politics and Society in the South* by Earl and Merle Black, which seeks to move away from the state-by-state approach and focus primarily on the new southern electorate; the Blacks' 1992 work, *Vital South,* pursues this line of inquiry for presidential politics. It, too, is ultimately rooted in the Key tradition, insofar as it is primarily concerned with the relationship between race and party politics in the new South.[5]

The present text is also a part of the grand tradition of southern political analysis begun by Key. Like the Blacks' books, it avoids the state-by-state approach characteristic of many other works, and it seeks to incorporate a scope of analysis broader than the other major texts on this subject. Nonetheless, any writer on southern politics in the twentieth century cannot avoid Key's shadow; it is simply too long and far reaching for that. The real issue for the modern student of southern politics is not to hide his debt to Key but to strive to reach the standards of scholarship, understanding, and insight that he set decades ago.

Of the South

While what is meant by "the South" might seem self-evident, in fact it is not. Literally volumes have been written attempting to define what the South is, where it is, and what it is like. Our purpose in this section, however, is much more limited—to specify the region under consideration and whose political odyssey we will explore. To do so, we must really identify three different "Souths": geographical, sociological, and political.

While it would seem to be the easiest to identify, there is almost no agreement on what is meant by the geographical South. Historically, anything south of the so-called Mason-Dixon line, which ran between Pennsylvania and Maryland and was first surveyed in the mid-1760s, was considered the South. The Civil War helped identify the South as the eleven Confederate states that seceded from the Union and rebelled against the national government. But the matter of what is "the South" remained ambiguous, largely because of several border states such as Missouri and Kentucky that did not join the Confederacy but that in other ways appeared to be very southern. Complicating matters further is the fact that in the twentieth century the U.S. government, through its Census Bureau, has tended to take a broad view of the geographic South. It has included the eleven Confederate states and added to them Delaware, Maryland, West Virginia, Kentucky, and Oklahoma; in recent years, the Census Bureau has often added Washington, D.C., to its list of southern states.[6]

Recent analysts have sought other ways of defining the South, or at least of putting it into a different context. Perhaps the most significant of these efforts has been the identification in recent years of the Sunbelt, of which the South is a part. Geographically, the Sunbelt supposedly extends from the Atlantic to the Pacific, bordered on the northern edge by Virginia in the East and California in the West. While the South can still be identified as a subregion within the Sunbelt, in fact it tends to lose much of its identity as it merges into this vast, disparate belt of growth-oriented America. Yet another attempt to delineate the southern region (as distinct from a discrete South) has been put forward by Joel Garreau. He bases his analysis on cultural similarities and geographic interdependence rather than state boundaries; indeed, the concept of state as a subunit of American life loses its meaning entirely in his conception.[7]

The issue of subregions has also produced considerable ambiguity in any identification of a geographical South. Southerners and nonsoutherners alike are accustomed to speak of "deep" South and "border" or "rim" South states. The former term generally refers to the five so-called black-belt states (Alabama, Georgia, Louisiana, Mississippi, and South Carolina) where cotton was king and the plantation economy abounded. ("Black belt" does not actually make reference to the large population of African descendants in these states, but rather to the kind of soil characteristic of the cotton belt.) The "border" or "rim" South are the remaining states that surround those of the black belt: Arkansas, Florida, North Carolina, Tennessee, Texas, and Virginia. Lumping all of them under this one rubric suggests a homogeneity (geographic and otherwise) that is simply not present; in fact, they are all very different states.[8]

To try to clarify this problem, the Census Bureau subdivided "its" South into three distinct subregions: South Atlantic (Delaware, Maryland, Washington, D.C., Virginia, West Virginia, North Carolina, South Carolina, Georgia, and Florida); East South Central (Kentucky, Tennessee, Alabama, and Mississippi); and West South Central (Arkansas, Louisiana, Oklahoma, and Texas). For some purposes this division helps, because it tends to group together states that have similar geographic and other characteristics. But for other purposes it obfuscates; for example, comparability of data between census subregions and the more traditional subregions of deep and border states is virtually impossible.

For the purposes of this text, we have chosen the most simple and conventional way of defining the geographic South. It refers to the eleven Confederate states—Alabama, Arkansas, Florida, Georgia, Louisiana, Mississippi, North Carolina, South Carolina, Tennessee, Texas, and Virginia. For the purpose of subgroupings, we shall also use the standard "deep" and "rim" or "border" categories mentioned above. There are several reasons for making these choices, but the most important involve tradition and convenience. These categories are very common in other writings, especially the literature in political science begun by Key. They tend to fit the grand tradition of writings on the South. Thus, they enhance comparability as well as the contribution of this book to the richness of discourse on the South.

But arriving at a geographical definition of the South solves only part of our problem, because, as any southerner knows, the South is much more than just a place. There is a psychological-sociological South as well, whose identity has perhaps been best explored recently by the eminent southern social scientist John Shelton Reed. In much of his writing, Reed concerns himself with two major issues: What constitutes the South, or at least "southernness"? And, why, in an age of seeming cultural homogenization and leveling in American life, do these qualities seem to persist?[9]

The answer to these questions, Reed feels, has to do with the continuing sense of group self-consciousness, interdependence, and self-identification that characterizes southerners, even today. He argues that southerners are distinctive because they form a sort of modern-day ethnic group whose members can identify themselves, who feel a sense of compatriotism or even "kinship" with other members of the group, and who can be (and are) identified as a unique group by southerners and nonsoutherners alike.[10] Thus, according to Reed, the South is much more than a geographic entity; it, like being southern, is really a state of mind. It is precisely this quality that enables Yankees to live in Atlanta or Richmond without becoming southern, but it is also the reason why southerners and southernness can exist not just in Shreveport and Savannah but in New York or New Delhi, Milwaukee or Marrakech.

This is by no means the end of the matter. Reed does not, for example, pursue very far the question of why this cultural identity tends to persist. We shall have occasion to address this issue, but perhaps for the moment we can indicate, following Raymond Gastil's helpful analysis, that the reason has to do with the complex interaction between individuals and their cultural milieu. Thus it is possible to become southern and for southern culture to persist even in the face of massive immigration from other parts of the country.[11]

The writings of Reed, Gastil, and others can help us further understand what we mean by South and southern for the purpose of this book. From a sociological standpoint, there is no incompatibility between our definition of the South as the eleven traditional, Confederate states and the idea that the South and southern refer to groups of people with a common heritage and sense of identity, who recognize and feel a sense of kinship with one another and who can be identified by nonsoutherners. Thus our concern in this work is not just with people and institutions *in* the South, but *of* the South as well.

We have one further South to identify—the political South. This is our greatest concern in this text and, in a sense, it is the easiest to pick out. As C. Vann Woodward observed, the common heritage of the eleven Confederate states strongly shaped the politics of the South during the twentieth century—the legacy of slavery; rebellion and defeat in the Civil War; the burdens of Reconstruction; and the aftermath of 1876 in which the South became a one-party system largely isolated from the rest of the nation, in exchange for which it was left alone to deal with its racial problems. All of these shared experiences have united the southern states into a political region in spite of the many differences that characterize the individual states.[12] This heritage also permits us to examine the eleven Confederate states to find out what has been their major political characteristics during this century and to assess the extent to which they have changed and been maintained.

There are many possible aspects of the political South on which we could focus. The one that clearly stands out, however, and that has been noted by Woodward, Key, and virtually every other observer of the southern political scene during this century, is the long existence of the one-party system. It has clearly been the dominant feature of the region's political landscape for well into the latter part of this century. And just as Key noted that race was at the heart of southern politics and nurtured the one-party system, so the existence of the one-party system influenced and shaped virtually every phase of southern political life for decades, and in some respects continues to do so even today.

Beginning late in the nineteenth century, most significant political activity that occurred in the region took place within the context of a single party, the Democratic Party, hence the terms one-party or solid South. Party labels might not always appear (for example, in purely local elections), but nonetheless everyone knew that candidates were really Democrats. Sometimes renegade Democrats might win elections (for example, Sidney J. Catts, elected governor of Florida in 1916, opposing the regular Democratic nominee). In Tennessee, Republicans were actually elected to the governorship in 1910, 1912, and 1920. And, at least early in the century, candidates could be found on southern ballots running under the Populist label, or even the Socialist Party.

But these were exceptions. Overwhelmingly, the political identity of the South throughout much of this century came from a simple fact: only Democrats won elections. Republican strength was generally weak except in a few mountainous regions of eastern Tennessee, southwestern Virginia, western North Carolina, northern Alabama and Georgia, and central Arkansas. Third parties in the South generally met the same fate as they did elsewhere in the nation. They seldom survived one election and were likely to disappear before the next one came along.

It was not unusual for voters to find in a general election that there were no candidates for public office listed on the ballot other than Democrats. Even if there were, they were often merely token opponents, not to be taken seriously. Indeed, as Key and others have noted, the real electoral contests in the one-party South took place in the Democratic primaries, for the winner of these elections was essentially assured of victory in the general election. The latter was often just a charade: while politicking in the primary could reach ferocious proportions (although often primaries were dreary affairs), the victorious Democratic candidate often did not bother to campaign at all for the November election, or did so in a peremptory way, since he need not fear the results.

At the level of presidential politics, the eleven southern states consistently gave their electoral support for the Democratic nominee in every election between 1900 and 1948, except for 1928 when the Roman Catholic governor of New York, Al Smith, ran and lost five border South states (Florida, North Carolina, Tennessee, Texas, and Virginia) to Republican Herbert Hoover. Beginning in 1948, when the so-called Dixiecrats broke away from the Democratic Party and ran separate candidates in the South, the solid South began to break down. Indeed, as we shall see, Democratic presidential candidates have had trouble winning southern states in the years since 1948.

But the solidly Democratic South continued, alive and well, in state and local politics long after 1948. Democratic candidates for governor, senator, representative, and members of state legislatures continue to do well in electoral contests. Many observers of southern politics have thought that by this late in the twentieth century the South would have a fully developed two-party system, perhaps one dominated by Republicans. By the mid-1990s, especially following the midterm elections of 1994, Republican strength did finally equal, and in some states actually exceed, that of the Democrats; our point for now, however, is that this development was a long time in coming.[13] How and why it did so is a matter for later chapters.

Origins of the One-Party South

The end of Reconstruction brought with it the decline of the Republican Party in the South. For more than half a century thereafter it remained a largely impotent political force in the region. Reconstruction, to be sure, saw Republicans assume positions of power in southern politics. A substantial number were black; most were white; all were supported by carpetbaggers, northern Republicans, and of course the army of occupation. The degree to which southerners, and the South, suffered under Reconstruction is a matter of historical dispute. What is incontrovertible were the resentment and ill feelings that defeated southerners felt toward former slaves who were suddenly thrust into positions of political power, toward the carpetbaggers and white southern Republicans willing to cooperate with northern Republicans, and of course toward the army encamped in their midst.

The presidential election of 1876 offered the South a way out. By agreeing to support Republican Rutherford B. Hayes during a bitter dispute over whether he or Democrat Samuel Tilden would win the election, southerners in one swoop forced the removal of the army and the carpetbaggers and began to subvert the power of blacks and Republicans. These changes did not happen instantly, of course, but once Hayes had been inaugurated, the end of Reconstruction loomed.

Bourbon "Redeemers" assumed office in the South (the name refers to their efforts to "redeem" the South) in increasingly greater numbers once Hayes became president, but they moved slowly in order to avoid alienating still-powerful northern Republicans. All southerners, and especially those in political office, wanted to avoid provocation; at stake was a possible return of the army of occupation.[14] They sought to return political power to the hands of conservative southerners, in whom it could be trusted, as new state constitutions were written and political institutions created following those imposed during Reconstruction. For obvious reasons, blacks were not among those who could be entrusted with political power; indeed, they increasingly became objects of scorn and derision.

Those attempting to build new constitutions and political institutions in the South following the election of 1876 were aided by the abandonment of southern blacks during the 1880s by Republicans and other northerners (especially liberals) who had supported and protected them until then. There are many reasons why this occurred, but as Woodward has shown, the growth of an imperialist American foreign policy and the strong belief that nonwhite peoples throughout the world (including the South) had to be colonized by whites made continued support of southern blacks impossible.[15]

Thus, as the 1880s wore on, political power in the South continued to shift away from Republicans and blacks and back toward Bourbon redeemers and other conservative southern Democrats. Indeed, because of attitudes toward blacks and the role Republicans played prior to and during the Civil War, and most especially during Reconstruction, southerners increasingly viewed both groups as politically illegitimate. Efforts to remove them entirely from the political process proceeded apace as Democrats reasserted their role and power in public affairs and became less concerned that the army might return.

The death of populism in 1896 essentially gave the coup de grace to southern Republicans. Southern populism had created a working alliance between poor whites and blacks during the severe economic crisis of the late 1880s and 1890s. This was potentially a powerful coalition, one that posed a threat to increasingly entrenched Democrats. But conservative Democrats and their allies fought back by intimidation of blacks, electoral fraud, and exploiting racism. Their clear message to southern whites was not only that blacks were the enemy and the cause of their economic distress but that Democrats would stop at nothing to maintain their newly gained positions of power. It was a cynical, brutal strategy, but it worked.

White populists like Tom Watson of Georgia became disillusioned with their former black allies, whom they thought had abandoned them; Watson, and others, became vicious racists.

Moreover, the national Democratic Party moved to take over the populist agenda in 1896. It nominated William Jennings Bryan before the Populist Party convention (which also nominated Bryan) could meet, and Bryan's famous Cross of Gold speech, first delivered before the Democrats, stole the free silver issue from the heart of populism which was dear to the hearts of many southerners. But once the national Democratic Party co-opted populism, the movement no longer had a future in the South. Indeed, it rapidly ceased to be an independent political force. Increasingly, the Democratic Party was the only real forum for political activity in the region, and it was controlled by a relatively small group of conservative economic and political elites.

Thus, following the presidential election of 1896, the one-party Democratic South was well entrenched. By then virtually all vestiges of the hated Republicans had been swept from state politics; no self-respecting southerner dared proclaim himself a Republican, except in a few mountainous areas. Blacks, who not only had been slaves but also Republicans (insofar as they had any political affiliation following the Civil War), had become objects of discrimination and hatred. Indeed, by 1896 every southern state was well along in its institutionalization of "Jim Crow" laws, designed to force blacks into secondary citizenship and ensure the existence of a segregated society. Populism was merely a slogan and a memory, one that left a bitter taste in the mouth of many southerners.

The Democratic Party in the South, then, offered the only real mechanism or instrument of political activity and power, since all the alternatives had vanished or been banished. The relatively small groups of conservative businessmen, agriculturists, and industrialists who controlled the southern Democratic Party carefully limited the extent of even white participation. Their power became the basis of most of the undemocratic, often authoritarian and repressive, impulses of southern politics that followed. For many decades to come there was little change. The institutionalization of a one-party system was complete.

Toward the New South: Design of the Book

In our investigation of southern politics, we shall be deeply concerned with changes and continuities in the one-party system. But we shall also study other political characteristics of the South as well. Indeed, having established an intellectual context for the present work, and having indicated how the term "South" is to be understood, let us turn to the specific focus of the book.

Virtually all writings on southern politics, as we noted before, that came after Key's *Southern Politics* have been very significantly influenced by it. This influence is both a strength and a weakness: the former, because it has helped create a massive literature on party politics in the South; and the latter, because until the recent appearance of the Blacks' text, scholars have not ventured very far from the research scope and methods Key initially laid out.

In fact, to make a very broad point, the recent literature on southern politics suffers from two major weaknesses. First, it is time bound. With the exception of Key, who covers nearly five decades of political life, most of the texts confine themselves to relatively narrow time periods—a decade or less. Thus it is difficult to assess, in such a brief slice, how much change and continuity have actually occurred. Second, scholars have tended to limit their discussion of southern politics to party and electoral politics. There are a number of reasons for these limits—the obvious importance of parties and elections; the shadow of Key; and the ready adaptability of available data sets to modern, especially quantitative, political science research techniques.

This observation is not meant as a criticism of the rich findings that scholars have produced. But, as Key himself recognized, southern politics involves more than just party and electoral matters. Thus additional political variables need to be considered if we are really to examine the questions of whether southern politics has evolved from an old to a new form, how it happened, and what the differences are.

In the present volume, three major characteristics or variables of southern politics have been selected for discussion to take account of this gap in the literature and provide readers with a fuller picture of the movement from old to new politics in the region. These characteristics are political organization, political participation, and political institutions. Each constitutes an important element in analyzing politics.

The first characteristic, political organization, involves party and electoral politics, focusing specifically on the rise of the Republican Party (and consequent two-party politics) in the South. Second, we shall investigate political participation by considering the entry of blacks into mainstream southern politics, looking especially at the civil rights movement and its legacy for and impact on southern politics. Finally, we shall examine political leadership in the South by investigating gubernatorial politics—political institutions—analyzing both the changing nature of the executive office in the region and the quality of leadership southern governors have provided.

These are not the only variables or characteristics that could have been chosen. As Key noted, legislative politics, judicial politics and law enforcement, interest groups, and state-local relations are worthy topics of study. Studies of individual policy areas, such as education, public finance, and environmental protection, would also help illuminate the movement from old to new southern politics.

But clearly any book, if it is not to be an encyclopedia, must have its limits. These three areas were chosen for a number of reasons, but one supersedes all other considerations. Anyone, including the most casual observer, who examines southern politics will conclude that these three areas of political activity have involved the most extraordinary upheaval in the most recent decades. The term "revolution," while often overused, certainly applies to each. Alterations in traditional party politics, black politics, and executive leadership in the South have been not just dramatic; they have been fundamental. Thus our investigation of them will help us trace the movement from old to new politics and provide a meaningful picture of modern southern politics.

This book will often explicitly, and deliberately, delve into historical materials. An accurate picture can only be drawn with reference to the past. Small slices of time make research manageable. But they can also give a distorted view of the significance of any set of developments that may have occurred. We will take a broad view of events that have occurred in southern politics during this century, although for obvious reasons the emphasis will be on the most recent decades. In this way we will be able to understand, and assess, the richness and diversity, continuities and changes, in southern politics.

Readers concerned primarily with methodological issues might feel uncomfortable with this approach. Many political scientists are not experienced in historical research and are often suspicious of the somewhat particularistic approach common to much historical analysis. Broadening the time frame can also lead to possible overgeneralizations of interpretation or a blurring of details that can illuminate critical moments in southern politics.

The response to these concerns is that this book is deliberately eclectic. It seeks to paint as full a picture as practicable about the political life of a major region of this country. It is further designed as an overview; specific studies can always be consulted for other views and refinements. Moreover, previous research by the author, as well as years of classroom and lecturing experience, have conclusively demonstrated the value of combining historical with present-centered research techniques.

A final response to possible objections about the breadth of the text concerns the specific focus or "window" through which we shall examine party politics, the entry of blacks into politics, and gubernatorial leadership.

Obviously, a mechanism must be found for handling and organizing the wealth of available material, and not surprisingly Key has pointed the way to do so.

Writing in 1949, Key noted that perhaps the major problem with southern politics was that its political institutions were inadequate in the sense that they were unable to cope with the region's massive problems. He provided a lengthy list, including such obvious matters as lack of opportunity, inferior public services, and a host of inequities, but in his view, two stood out as fundamental—race and poverty. Other observers and scholars writing about the South, before and after Key, have reached the same conclusion.

Thus, our investigation of the rise of a new southern politics devolves into a very straightforward question: Have political institutions in the South become adequate to deal with the region's long-standing, deep-rooted problems of race and poverty? Have the rise of a southern Republican Party, the recent entrance of blacks into the mainstream of southern politics, and changes in gubernatorial leadership—each of which demonstrates a substantial change in southern politics—created a political milieu in which a meaningful attack on these traditional problems has been able to take place? In other words, has the new southern politics really made a difference in the South?

There are any number of ways in which these questions can be answered. Use of relevant empirical data can help address them. But we shall also look at the issues raised by these questions in terms of democratic theory: Specifically, to what extent have key variables in adequate democratic government been enhanced through the changes in southern politics discussed in the following chapters? The key variables chosen for discussion in our final chapter are accountability, equality, and legitimacy. Thus the fundamental questions Key raised nearly a half-century ago are still appropriate today. They form the basis for our discussion in the ensuing chapters and conclusion after we have completed our twentieth-century political odyssey.

The Plan of the Book

We are now ready to begin our exploration of politics in the South with an eye toward finding the emergence of a new South and a new southern politics. The chapters are arranged into groupings that can help the reader follow the presentation of data and the development of the argument.

Part I contains two chapters. The first examines the socioeconomic context or foundation of southern politics during this century, focusing on the extent and persistence of the classic southern problems—race and poverty. The second chapter outlines some of the major features of old style politics in the South by illuminating the most significant dimensions of political life, and their consequences, in the early decades of this century.

Part II (on political organization) investigates political parties in the South, especially the varying fortunes of the Republican Party and the rise of a two-party South. Part III (on political participation) analyzes the rise of black political involvement in the South, focusing specifically on the civil rights movement and its impact on the region.

Part IV (on political institutions) is an investigation of the variety and impact of political leaders in the South, with reference to governors, their politics, and the types of leaders they have been and have become.

The final part, consisting of one chapter, seeks to pull together major themes developed in the text, specifically addresses the question of the adequacy of modern southern political institutions to deal with the region's long-standing problems, and tries to inform the reader about the nature of the new South and new southern politics.

Part I

The Traditional South

2

Race and Poverty in the Twentieth-Century South

*The South presents right now the Nation's No. 1
economic problem. . . .*
—President Franklin D. Roosevelt, 1938

Franklin D. Roosevelt wrote these words on July 5, 1938, after receiving a report from his National Emergency Council entitled *The Economic Conditions of the South.*[1] Roosevelt, who considered himself something of an adopted southerner, stressed that the economic conditions of the region were damaging not only to it but to the nation as a whole. He felt that real economic recovery from the Depression could not be complete until the backward South began to catch up the rest of the nation. Indeed, his administration believed that the South had enormous economic potential that could benefit the entire nation, yet remained essentially untapped.

The report of the National Emergency Council brought to public attention conditions that had actually existed for a long time. That the South was poor was obvious, especially to the vast majority of citizens who lived there. What was less well known was just how far behind the rest of the nation the South really was. The council studied fifteen indicators: economic resources, soil, water, population, private and public income, education, health, housing, labor, women and children, land ownership and use, credit, natural resources, industry, and purchasing power. On every measure, the South lagged woefully behind the rest of the nation.

In this chapter we shall look briefly at the extent of persistent southern poverty during this century as well as at changes and improvements that eventually occurred. We shall concern ourselves especially, but not exclusively, with the racial dimension of southern poverty. We will first examine some of the causes of southern poverty, focusing on its roots in the southern economy, particularly manufacturing and especially southern agriculture. We will then look at southern demography, illiteracy, and poor public health as a way of understanding southern poverty, and its persistence, throughout the century.

These materials are included in the text because students of twentieth century southern politics must understand the context of extreme poverty and harsh socioeconomic conditions in which "old-time" southern politics took place and from which changes toward a new southern politics occurred. The discussions that follow should not be understood merely as the rehashing of a dead past. Rather, they represent human tragedies and a waste of human resources from which the South has only recently emerged.

Socioeconomic Problems of the South

What was the matter? What problems existed in the South that Roosevelt felt required national attention?

The simplest and most direct answers to these questions are that too many poor people lived in the region; that the amount of available wealth was less than in other parts of the nation; that the wealth present was poorly distributed (with most of it concentrated in too few hands); and that there seemed to be very little way, given the overall structure of the southern economy and a host of other conditions, that any significant change could take place.

A few facts taken from the council's report illustrate the extent of the problem.[2] In 1938 the South was still heavily rural and agricultural, and while the population was increasing, it was rising most rapidly in the poorest areas. Southern farmers in 1929 had an annual income approximately 40 percent of farmers elsewhere. Southern schools educated one-third of the nation's children with one-sixth of its educational resources. Illiteracy was four times as great in the South as in the Northeast. Health problems resulting from poor economic conditions were rampant; about half of all southern families lived in housing considered inadequate by the standards of the day. The tenant and sharecropping system of farming left millions of people in poverty. But there was neither sufficient credit nor capital in the South to make extensive changes in agriculture or to improve the weak business and manufacturing sectors that existed.[3]

But to say that the economic problem of the South was a result of too many poor people, and not enough opportunity, is to describe a symptom, not a cause. The structure of the southern economy and its relation to the rest of the nation caused the regional difficulties.[4] Even before the Civil War, but certainly since the end of Reconstruction, the southern economy was little more than a colony of the North. Little economic development beneficial to the region, or its inhabitants, could occur under such circumstances.

Southerners in the late nineteenth century understood all too well how precarious their economic situation really was and how much it depended on the North. The editor Henry Grady of Atlanta poignantly noted the tragedy that colonial economic status held for the South:

> I attended a funeral once in Pickens County in my state. This funeral was particularly sad. It was a poor fellow like most Southerners. . . . They buried him in the midst of a marble quarry; they cut through solid marble to make his grave; and yet a little tombstone they put above him was from Vermont. They buried him in the heart of a pine forest, and the pine coffin was imported from Cincinnati. They buried him within touch of an iron mine, and yet the nails in his coffin and the iron in the shovel that dug his grave were imported from Pittsburgh. They buried him by the side of the best sheepgrazing country on the earth, and yet the wool in the coffin bands and the coffin bands themselves were brought from the North. The South didn't furnish a thing on earth for that funeral but the corpse and the hole in the ground.[5]

Grady and his "new south industrialists" set out to change this dependency by spending large amounts of time pleading with financial interests in the North and Midwest to invest capital in the South. They felt only through this kind of investment could the South develop its potential resources, throw off its colonial status, and reduce its crushing burden of poverty.

Grady and some of his followers partially succeeded in bringing outside investment to the South. But in some respects their efforts actually made matters worse, not better. For example, many manufacturing plants established in the South were headquartered elsewhere. Thus money they made tended not to stay in the region, where it could have been reinvested to create more jobs and higher wages, but rather flowed out to company headquarters. It took government programs beginning in the 1930s, World War II, a rapid in-migration of people and flow of money after the war, the rise of indigenous systems of credit and capital, restructured agricultural and labor systems, and a modernizing national economy to help finally remove the shackles of southern economic colonialism.[6]

There were a host of other problems that contributed to southern economic shortcomings and thus to the perpetuation of poverty. Let us briefly turn our attention to three major ones—the character of traditional southern industry; population and cultural forces; and the nature of the southern agricultural system.

Manufacturing and Industry

Manufacturing began to come South following the end of Reconstruction, in part as a function of the rapid development of American industrial power elsewhere in the nation. Cotton mills were among the first to spring up. Many moved from New England because of cheap construction and labor costs and proximity to cotton markets. Later lumber, pulpwood, and mineral-extracting industries also came south, along with more textile and apparel factories, furniture manufacturing, tobacco processing, and others.

Several major problems with southern industrial development emerged late in the nineteenth and early twentieth centuries. Some of them lingered until after World War II.

Much, even most, of southern industry at this time was highly exploitive of human and natural resources. It primarily processed raw materials or produced goods for shipment to markets outside the South. Little care was given to protecting the environment. Conservation was not a matter of public or private policy. The result was wasting and polluting water, devastation of forests and coal fields, strip mining, and, ravenous, essentially unregulated, drilling for oil and mining of other minerals.

More painful were the human costs of this industrial development. Southern industry provided almost exclusively low-skill, low-wage jobs. Much of it was physically dangerous to workers, whether in mines, mills, or factories. Little protection for workers existed, and virtually no unionization occurred; in fact, unions were prevented from coming south through public and private policy and by violence when necessary. Workdays were long and tedious, with little or no time off. Women and children were also pressed into service, usually for wages lower than those paid to adult males. The whole system resembled the sweatshops of the Northeast and Midwest a generation and more earlier.

The problem was that the South had no muckrakers to write about industrial conditions or to stir up public concern for workers' plight. The South's agricultural laborers were, after all, generally worse off than industrial workers.[7] The middle class was small and politically largely inert. State governments, which might have attempted some form of business regulation, were for the most part in the hands of conservative businessmen and wealthy elites whose sympathies lay with the factory owners, not the workers. They, after all, were the ones seeking to expand industrial development, not inhibit it by forcing rules and regulations on it.

Related to this point was the "foreign" ownership of southern industry. As late as 1960, only twenty-five of the top "Fortune 500" firms in the United States were located in the South.[8] As we noted, absentee ownership generally meant a flow of capital out of the South, largely in the form of corporate profits. But it also meant that distant owners of southern factories and industries would be less concerned about the welfare of their employees, and their impact on the quality of life in the communities where they were located, than if they had been locally or even regionally owned.

Associated with the problem of absentee ownership of industry was the lack of availability of southern capital and credit. Southern banks, in the first half of this century, were almost insignificant in the financial life of the nation. They lacked the capital to finance agricultural or business ventures in the South of the magnitude that might establish a solid, indigenous economic base. Instead, they worked with banks elsewhere in the nation to raise capital for local needs. Southern banks were also charged high rates of interest by outside banks, which both discouraged southern investment and contributed to the outflow of capital from the region.[9]

Perhaps, though, the most serious impediment to southern industry was in railroad freight differentials. In general, southern manufacturers had to pay higher rates to ship finished goods north than manufacturers in those areas had to pay to ship goods in their own territory or to the South. Indeed, southeastern manufacturers had to pay freight rates nearly 40 percent higher than their northern counterparts had to pay. The result was that it was more economical, from a manufacturing standpoint, to ship raw materials to the North and re-import finished goods into the South than to try to make them in the South and market them elsewhere.[10]

Under these conditions, manufacturing in the South could neither flourish nor grow. It was not until 1945 that the Interstate Commerce Commission abolished the discriminatory freight rates. After World War II, in-migration of people and capital helped begin the process of building a stronger southern economy by creating new local markets and means of production. Until that occurred, however, manufacturing in the South was literally the prisoner of outside forces.[11]

Southern Demographics

The characteristics of the southern population for much of this century also contributed, in several ways, to the extent and persistence of regional poverty. First, as Charles Roland has noted, for much of this century relatively few southerners lived in cities. In 1900 the region's population was only 15 percent urban; in 1930, 31 percent; in 1960, 53 percent.[12] Cities, as many scholars have observed, are essential elements in economic growth and cultural development. But southern cities were often little more than overgrown towns and villages and lacked the complexity, dynamism, energy, and cultural pluralism associated with big-city life. As a result, southern cities lacked a critical mass of citizens, skills, and capital needed to serve as engines driving forward economic and other social institutions.[13]

Another basic demographic problem that inhibited southern economic development was the lack of basic education and skills among the population. For much of this century, the South suffered from a "brain drain." Roosevelt's Emergency Council noted the tendency for educated men and women, or those wanting an education, to move out of the South. The public school systems in the region were generally considered inferior to those elsewhere in the nation on virtually any measure used for comparison—per-pupil expenditures, quality of teaching faculty, adequacy of facilities, range and availability of school curricula, or richness of library and other instructional resources. Southern universities, with few exceptions, were also regarded as second-rate compared to those in the Northeast, Midwest, and Far West. As a result, the South lacked a pool of manpower capable of developing sophisticated industry and a complex economy. Working in the fields, textile mills, mines, and sawmills required little or no skill or education.

Related to this point was the presence of a huge underclass of blacks. They were the least educated, and had the fewest and least developed technical skills, of the entire southern population. Cultural forces, moreover, prevented them from having access to better education or developing better job skills. They constituted a tremendous waste of human resources, since they were relegated to the lowest rungs of the economic ladder.

Indigenous cultural forces related to demography also acted as constraints on the southern economy. At least three were important. First, as just suggested, were southern attitudes toward blacks. The cultural emphasis on racial segregation and discrimination extended so far that southerners actually blamed blacks for the economic woes of the region: they translated blacks' lack of opportunities and skills into feelings that blacks were shiftless and worthless workers, an anchor dragging the entire region down to their level.

A second set of attitudes involved blaming the North—Yankees and the federal government—for southern economic woes. Many white southerners thought that whatever hardships and problems blacks had not created for the South, northerners had accomplished. The Civil War, and in particular Reconstruction, had ruined the South and forced it into a position of subordination. The result was that southerners were the victims of their own countrymen, who systematically sought to exploit them and squeeze out southern resources for their benefit.

A third powerful cultural force that prevented southern economic growth was the dominance of business progressives in southern politics. Composed of economic elites and elements of the emerging middle class, they were especially interested in retaining economic power in their own hands rather than in seeking out or creating investment opportunities for more southerners, or in finding ways to expand and improve the southern economy to benefit all southerners, black and white. These business progressives cooperated fully with northern bankers and economic venturists. Even if they were not the owners of southern factories, they were important investors and local managers and operators. They profited greatly from this arrangement, but the region as a whole did not. Indeed, it is no exaggeration to say that southern business progressives sold out the southern economy, even though they were in the best position to help it.[14]

These cultural forces tended to act as inhibitors of southern economic development. In particular, they helped foster southern attitudes of fatalism, especially regarding regional conditions, and scapegoatism. Because of these attitudes, southerners often seemed disinclined to expend energy in seeking to overcome the poverty of their region; if it was inevitable, caused by blacks, Yankees, and other forces beyond their control, why try? The widespread acceptance of these attitudes permeates a good deal of southern writing, especially that of William Faulkner and Flannery O'Connor. Their stories are filled with people resigned to their fate, seemingly unwilling or unable to muster the strength to try to change the direction of their often miserable lives, but instead propelled along toward a destiny they do not challenge.

Beginning before World War II, but assuredly seen in the years following it, demographic changes in the South had a profound impact on the economy of the region and on the lives of the people living there. In 1940 only 32 million people lived in the southern states, roughly 24 percent of the nation's population of 132 million. By 1990, the southern population had more than doubled, to nearly 71 million, some 28 percent of the national population of 249 million. The rate of growth of the southern population between 1940 and 1990 was 122 percent; for the entire nation, the figure was 88 percent.

These aggregate figures mask some important differences within the southern states. Growth patterns have not been uniform. Texas and Florida have experienced explosive growth: between 1940 and 1990 the Sunshine State grew by 582 percent, and Texas, by 165 percent. Florida was the least populous southern state from 1900 to 1920; by 1960 it was the second most populous, as it remains today.

In contrast, both Arkansas and Mississippi experienced a net loss of population between 1940 and 1960. Following 1960 they, too, began to grow, albeit slowly. Between 1960 and 1990 Arkansas's population grew by only 32 percent, and Mississippi's by a mere 18 percent. As of the 1990 census, they remain the least populated southern states.[15]

But even these figures are not meaningful unless we examine them against the fundamental shifts that occurred in the southern black population during this century. In 1900 the South was 38 percent black; by 1990, it was only 19 percent black, although during that time the absolute numbers of southern blacks grew from 7 to nearly 14 million.[16]

What happened? The answer is that millions of blacks moved out of the South to the cities of the Northeast and Midwest. While the process began early in the century (approximately 700,000 blacks left the South between 1900 and 1920), in fact this was merely a trickle compared to what happened later. Between 1920 and 1940, about 1 million blacks left the South; from 1940 to 1960, 2.5 million; and from 1960 to 1980, about 1.5 million. Thus a total of about 5.7 million blacks are estimated to have left the South during the first eighty years of this century. The sheer size of this out-migration achieves even greater significance if the reader recalls that in 1980 the entire black population of the South was only slightly more than 12 million.[17]

Out-migration of blacks was not uniform across the South. Black-belt areas of Louisiana, Mississippi, Alabama, Georgia, and South Carolina were the most affected. Out-migration of blacks was somewhat less pronounced in rim South states. Texas and Florida seem to have been the least affected and may actually show a net gain of black population by in-migration throughout the century.

Why did so many blacks leave the South? There were both push and pull factors. Racial discrimination and the impact of economic hardship on blacks served to push them out of the region. But during World War II many blacks left to find jobs in war industries elsewhere in the nation. Later, especially after the war, the growth of public social services in northern, midwestern, and western states, as well as expanding job opportunities there, acted as a pull for blacks out of the South, where public services were minimal, opportunities few, and discrimination widespread.

The out-migration of blacks from the South had a substantial impact on the economy of the region, and indeed of the nation. As Ray Marshall and Virgil Christian have documented, blacks who left the South were, generally speaking, somewhat better educated and had somewhat greater job skills than those who stayed behind. Thus, the pool of blacks remaining in the South were the least capable of filling the new, nonagricultural jobs that opened in the South after World War II; between 1950 and 1967, these constituted some 6.6 million jobs. Most of these new jobs were filled by whites, especially recent in-migrants who brought higher levels of education and job skills with them.

But the blacks who out-migrated were not skillful or educated enough to compete for skilled jobs elsewhere in the nation. The result was the creation of a vast pool of underskilled, underemployed blacks both in the South and in northern and midwestern cities. As Marshall and Christian conclude, "The South's policy of deliberate underdevelopment of her human resources had come home to roost."[18]

Thus demographic changes in the South greatly influenced regional economic development. For skilled, educated whites who came south after the war, there were jobs available. For the blacks who stayed, there were relatively few jobs available, and those that were available were generally low paying and offered little job security. The southern blacks who migrated to other parts of the nation faced—perhaps unexpectedly—segregated housing and racial discrimination. But they also, and inadvertently, contributed to the growing national, as well as regional, economic gulf between blacks and whites that has proven to be so intractable.

Southern Agriculture

Agriculture in the South for much of this century was both a symptom and a cause of regional poverty. The agriculture industry has, of course, long been a major pillar of the southern economy: in 1929, 21 percent of personal income in the South came from agriculture, compared to 9 percent nationally; as late as 1950, 12 percent of personal income in the South still came from agriculture, compared to 7 percent for the whole nation.[19] But it was not a healthy industry. Indeed, southern agriculture for much of this century was notable for its backwardness, lack of productivity and diversity, and incapacity to provide the millions of agricultural workers in the region with resources to rise above the level of peasants and serfs elsewhere in the world.[20]

There are many reasons for the traditional problems of southern agriculture. They include lack of capital for investment; poor farming techniques that exhausted and wasted natural resources, including land; poor technology and an unskilled work force without access to advanced technologies or able to use them; cultural inhibitions against change; and a maldistribution of land ownership. But for the sake of brevity we shall focus our discussion on two major factors: the unique southern system of land ownership, agricultural employment, and farm credit; and the longtime reliance on a cash crop agricultural economy centered on cotton and, to a lesser degree, tobacco. These two factors were so central to the problems of southern agriculture that they encompass virtually all its other ills.

The Tenant-Sharecropper System

At the heart of the southern agricultural system from the end of the Civil War until well into this century was the tenant-sharecropper system. A number of observers of southern agriculture have argued that this system, alone, was the single greatest problem with this regional industry.

The origins of the tenant-sharecropper system largely explain the problems it created. After the Civil War, there was a vast labor surplus in the South. There was also an abundance of land that could be cultivated, left over from the collapse of the plantation system. Added to these was a lack of indigenous capital for investment, low levels of economic development, widespread poverty and unemployment, and substantial national and international markets for cotton and tobacco.

The result of these forces was the development of the tenant-sharecropper system. In theory, it seemed promising. Landowners needed workers to farm their lands. There were hordes of workers looking for employment, both blacks and whites. The idea of the tenant-sharecropper system was that individuals willing to work the land would raise cash crops for the landowner. In exchange for their labor, they were supposed to receive a share of the profits from the sale of the crops raised. Thus, it would seem, there would be work and cash for everyone.

But the system did not work. In fact, rather than creating a mutual system of dependence in which everyone benefited, the tenant-sharecropper system actually created one of mutual dependence in which everyone involved in the agricultural industry—tenant, landowner, storekeeper, banker—lost. Instead of eliminating regional poverty, it created and perpetuated it.

What was the matter? It must first be noted that the tenant-sharecropper system was more than just an economic organization. It was a whole social system, one based on traditional southern attitudes and beliefs involving social status and racial discrimination. As such, it was really as much a mechanism of social control as of economic production.

How did the system work in this fashion? It was actually a complex social arrangement that carefully defined one's place in southern society, one's relationship with other parts of society, and one's status and power. As Rupert Vance and others have shown, the tenant system was actually a ladder comprising an entire social network: it began on the bottom with the casual wage hand, and by gradations rose to regular wage hand, sharecropper, share tenant, standing renter, cash renter, manager, part owner, mortgaged owner, full owner of a small farm, landlord, and large planter.[21]

There was some mobility in the system, more for whites than for blacks. But often the farmer's position on the ladder was a function of forces outside his immediate control. Thus, for example, good prices for cotton might enable a sharecropper to purchase a mule or tools to become a tenant, or a tenant might be able to buy, or become part owner, of a piece of land. But low prices or a failed crop would cause a net loss for the farmer, throwing him into debt and often off the land if he could not pay. They would also result in mortgage foreclosures for landowners who could not pay off loans because of their lack of cash, in bankruptcy for shopkeepers dependent on farmers and owners for sales, and in bank losses and closings. Thus, depending on the quality and size of the crop produced, as well as market prices resulting from national and international demand and commodity availability, all individuals involved in the tenant-sharecropper system could move up or down the status ladder.

The farmer's position on the tenancy ladder was also a function of available land. When it was plentiful, it might be possible for a wage earner, cropper, or tenant to move into a previously undeveloped area, work the land for a cash crop, and possibly even become an entrepreneur. But by early in the twentieth century, the "frontier" in the Southeast was largely closed, except for sections of Florida and west Texas. Both these areas lacked transportation facilities. Moreover, because of poor farming techniques, a great deal of land in the South had become wasted or was of such poor quality that agricultural production was small. Consequently, there were too many farmers seeking to work a limited amount of land, some of which was virtually exhausted anyway.

How extensive was the tenant system in the South? In 1910, the first year for which reliable data are available, fully 50 percent of all southern farms were operated by tenants and croppers.[22] But there was wide variability: in the black-belt, cotton-belt states of the deep South the percentage was above 60 percent; in Virginia and Florida tenant farming was less common.

The Depression, as we shall examine shortly, had a disastrous impact on southern agriculture. One of its major effects was to greatly increase the extent of tenancy; this result might have been expected, given the collapse of farm prices and decline of farm credit. By 1930, some 72 percent of farms in Mississippi were tenant or cropper operated, followed closely by Georgia, Louisiana, South Carolina, Arkansas, and Texas. Overall in the South some 56 percent of farms were tenant operated in 1930.

There was actually a decline of tenancy during the 1930s, followed by a sharp drop-off after 1940. The reason for the decline was not that small farmers could not manage during the Depression years. Rather, two factors reduced the number of tenants. The first was that the Depression in the South was so bad that it forced many on the lowest rungs of the ladder off the land completely, for there was no longer any hope for them to remain as farmers: they moved to towns and cities or out of the South altogether. The other reason is that the Depression had an especially great impact on black farmers: of those forced off the land, a disproportionate number were black.[23]

Why didn't the tenant-cropper system work? Why did it actually perpetuate, instead of alleviate, poverty?

The root of the problem lay in two factors—the cash crop system of agriculture and a surplus of farmers. In the former case, crops were grown without regard to regional utilization or consumption, but rather with a view toward sales in distant markets. The result was that in spite of the vast amount of crops raised, the South was not agriculturally self-sufficient, in terms of its need for food.

Moreover, there were not only too many farmers; there was too little capital to go around. It took money to grow cotton. But most southern farmers had nothing to mortgage for bank loans to raise a crop. Most, indeed, had no collateral other than next year's harvest. As a result, farmers often had to mortgage their yearly earnings before their crop had been grown, harvested, and sold. They mortgaged the crop to landowners and to merchants from whom they had to buy supplies. Landowners themselves, rich in land but often poor in cash, also had to mortgage themselves to merchants and bankers; they, too, were betting on future harvests to make money and pay off debts. Southern merchants were mortgaged to banks, but these, in turn, lacking sufficient capital, were borrowers from banks outside the region.

Thus a huge, rigid lien-and-credit system in the South arose that linked the tenant and cropper to landlord, merchant, and banker and that, in turn, linked them to him. If times were good and prices high, the system could function. But when times were bad, and crops failed or cotton and tobacco prices fell, the whole system collapsed. As James Street concludes, "Thus large and small farmers and their suppliers alike were subject to a high degree of economic risk through the costly and precarious credit structure."[24]

Because of the risks involved, the costs of credit were both differential and high. The highest burdens were put on the tenants and croppers themselves, followed by the small landowners. In the case of the farmers, it was not unusual to have a lien placed on the entire future crop, with accompanying substantial interest charges. Even in the best of times farmers had to pay high rates to landowners and merchants. In bad times, they became so indebted that it was often impossible to break free. Thus many were forced to move to other farms or off the land altogether. Since there was a surplus of farmers, the landowners could be assured of finding another tenant to continue working the land.

But the nature of crop production in a cash crop system assured that "good times" would not last very long. The better the market for cotton and tobacco, and the higher the prices, the greater the incentive for farmers to produce as much as possible. The effect was, of course, to drive prices down, create surpluses that might take years for markets to absorb and thus keep prices low, and also to exhaust and erode the farmland itself. Thus, as farmers planted next year's crop, so also did they sow the seeds of their own economic distress.

But why did the future cash crop have to form the basis of the credit system? Why not diversify commodity production and create other bases for extending credit? The answers to these questions are based as much on cultural forces as on economic considerations.

In the first place, even though the risks of cash crop production were well known, landowners, merchants, and bankers were willing to take them. They knew the vagaries of the cotton culture, but they also knew that cotton always had a market. A bad crop, or a weak market, in one year could potentially be made up the next. There was very little incentive for land-owners, merchants, and bankers to change to other systems of extending credit; besides, without a wholesale commitment to new forms of production, no other collateral existed in the region besides next year's crop.

There were other factors as well that prevented diversification from occurring. To diversify would have required large amounts of capital to tide over the army of southern farmers while the change took place. Southern banks lacked the capital needed to float the necessary long-term loans necessary for these modifications. The money was available, of course, but only from banks outside the South, which would have charged very high interest fees to southeastern banks. It simply wasn't worth it to them.

Also, the South for much of this century lacked the transportation facilities needed to get perishable goods to market. Cotton (if it did not get wet or catch on fire) could not spoil while waiting to be shipped. Once tobacco was cured, relatively little could happen to it while sitting in a warehouse. Before refrigerated warehouses and trains were widely available in the South, perishable goods could not withstand lengthy storage, especially given the humidity and heat of southern summers. Southern creditors did not like the idea of lending cash on the basis of time-bound crops; it injected yet another uncertainty into an already precarious economic system.

Finally, there was no effort by farmers to make changes. It was to the advantage of the individual farmer not to fight the system, but to exploit it; his only hope for getting out of debt was to raise a large crop successfully and get it to market while prices were high. If his crop failed, and he had to leave his plot of land, there was substantial likelihood (unless he was black) that he could find another landlord willing to take him on as a tenant. From the farmer's standpoint, this was the bright side, the one that kept him devoted to the system. But there was a dark side as well. Given the farmers' indebtedness, and the fact that second chances were seldom available, farmers were caught in a terrible bind from which they could not escape. Virtually no matter what they did, or how well or poorly they farmed, they were ultimately doomed to economic hardship and poverty.

It is for this reason that the whole system of tenant-cropper farming, based on liens and credit, was one of social control. Those holding the mortgages were in positions of power—bankers, successful merchants, large landowners. They could dictate what happened to marginal owners, merchants, and farmers; they held the future of vast numbers of people in their hands. Compounding this power, of course, was racial discrimination: blacks were in the most precarious position of all. Thus, through economic sanctions and manipulation southern elites could reinforce social and racial structures, keeping poor people in line and determining the circumstances, if any, under which they could continue to farm. Not infrequently, these elites jerked the chain, the farmer and his family would have to leave, a new tenant or cropper would come, and the cycle would repeat.[25]

Occasionally farmers would protest. In the late nineteenth century a populist movement in the South sought ways of easing credit and making money more available. During the twentieth century various populist and demagogic politicians appeared on the scene, attempting to rally poor farmers behind them in protest against big landowners and banks. Seldom, however, were they successful in alleviating the burden of the poor farmer. The system itself had to collapse before real relief was possible.

The federal government tried to offer some help to southern tenant farmers. During the New Deal, programs were passed to try to limit crop plantings, indeed to pay farmers not to produce staple crops. But those programs, as well intentioned as they were, in some respects made things worse for southern croppers. The reason is that crop quota systems, soil conservation measures, and price support mechanisms worked for large farms but not for tenants. Their impact, indeed, was to prompt croppers to produce larger, not smaller, cash crops (especially cotton) and, when the price failed to rise, to drive still more farmers further into debt or off the land.[26]

After 1940 farm tenancy in the South declined rapidly. The war, and the subsequent transformation of southern agriculture into technologically based agribusiness, helped speed this process. By 1954, only about 27 percent of southern farms were tenant operated, compared to a national average of 24 percent. Still, Mississippi at this date had 46 percent of its farms tenant operated. South Carolina, North Carolina, Georgia, Louisiana,

Alabama, and Arkansas were still above 30 percent. By 1969, however, the U.S. and southern figures had reached virtual parity (13 and 12 percent, respectively). While it is not possible to say that the tenant system in the South has completely disappeared, as any visitor to the rural South quickly recognizes, it is now largely a historic curiosity.

King Cotton

The second major problem with southern agriculture during this century was its heavy reliance on "King Cotton" as the principal element in its agricultural economy. To a lesser extent the problems extended to tobacco and corn as well, but cotton was fundamental to southern agriculture. Indeed, the "cotton economy" in some respects seemed to symbolize the entire region and its poverty. Moreover, cotton (and tobacco) production were inextricably linked to the tenant-sharecropper system of farming.[27]

For much of this century, more acreage in the South was devoted to cotton than to any other crop, except on brief occasions for corn. The farm value of cotton exceeded that of other agricultural commodities from the region, especially in the first half of this century. Cotton was an important factor in the economic development of such key southern commercial centers as Memphis, New Orleans, and Savannah. It has been fixed in southern lore as the quintessential southern crop: "cotton farmer" or "cotton picker," terms often used in disparaging ways, refer not just to occupations but to lifestyle, social position, and political status.

Cotton is an especially labor-intensive crop to grow. When little or no mechanization was present, as was often the case under the tenant system, the labor was backbreaking. Before a new crop can be planted, the soil must be prepared by chopping the old plants back into the ground. Once the new plants appear, the chopping has to continue as weeds grow. But the most difficult task is the harvest. Before the advent of mechanical pickers (available only to wealthy farmers with large holdings), cotton bolls had to be picked by hand. Workers dragged heavy sacks behind them as they made their way up and down the rows in the unforgiving southern sun. Cotton bolls are hard to remove from the plant, causing both fatigue and occasionally physical injury. In the hot, dusty fields, the harvest was carried out by as many workers as could be pressed into service—necessitating the use of children and even the elderly and infirm—because the bolls had to be removed before the autumn rains came.

Prior to mechanization, it took roughly 30–40 man hours to harvest one acre of cotton (approximately the same as it took to harvest three acres of corn in Iowa). It took about 155 man hours to produce a single bale of cotton (roughly 500 pounds), assuming only mule power and limited mechanization; complete mechanization reduces the figure to 10–12 man hours.[28]

Cotton could be grown on very small plots of land. It might not have been very efficient to do so, and small plots prevented the use of machines to help, but it was possible for farmers to eke out an existence by planting cotton on relatively small areas of ground. Because of this, cotton production actually contributed to the maintenance of the tenant-cropper system. If larger holdings were needed to make the cash crop profitable, there might well have been economic pressure to modify the tenant system. But because of the nature of the crop, this pressure was absent.

Cotton farming was also extremely wasteful of natural resources because of both the crop itself and southern farming methods. Cotton tends to leach the soil of needed nutrients very rapidly. In the nineteenth century, as harvests declined in quality and quantity, land was often abandoned as it wore out. Later such wastage was no longer practical, but still farmers seldom took care, or did not know how, to preserve or replenish the soil. As a result, in many cotton-growing areas of the South production of cotton fell off because of poor farming techniques.

Of course, the tenant and cropper system did not provide an incentive for improved farming methods. If a farmer was certain that he would be working the same land over a long period of time, it would clearly be in his interest to practice sound farming. But the tenant-cropper system promoted the opposite, because the only way the farmer could possibly make any money was to raise the maximum possible amount of cotton from his land and hope for a good market price.

Thus the small southern cotton farmer was doomed whatever he did. To practice conservation required cutting down the crop, or growing something else, for which the market, and market price, could be uncertain. To exploit the land, as he was inclined to do, was to ruin it. It was a vicious cycle from which few farmers could break free, or even break even.

What happened to cotton farming in the South? Why did it eventually decline in overall importance? Why did it finally become a "distress industry"?[29]

Between the turn of the century and World War I, cotton farming in the South seemed to improve, even prosper. International markets for cotton grew rapidly, especially in Europe, which were largely filled by southern cotton. New marketing techniques were developed that could forecast future needs. And cottonseed, which previously had been discarded, was found to have important commercial values: it could be used for oils, livestock feed, and some other purposes and thus became an element in the cash crop economy.

But the upsurge did not last long. The first major problem to appear was the boll weevil. It first showed up in southern Texas in 1892 and spread so rapidly that by 1922 all areas of the cotton belt were infested. By 1909 and 1910 it seriously affected cotton production in Louisiana. Between 1910 and 1928, the average crop loss from the boll weevil was 12 percent; in 1921, it was estimated that the insect ruined 30 percent of the crop. One of its most serious effects was to completely eliminate from production several of the finest long- and medium-staple varieties of cotton that commanded the highest market prices; they had to be replaced with the less desirable short-staple plants.

A major effect of the boll weevil, in conjunction with the post–World War I collapse of cotton prices and soil exhaustion, was to drive many farmers off the land. Even during the war cotton did not enjoy the agricultural boom of other commodities, since access to European markets disappeared during hostilities. As a result, cotton prices fell, farm income declined, and the amount of farm tenancy rose. Also, after the war other nations began to export cotton plentifully, especially India, China, the Soviet Union, and Brazil. The U.S. share of the international cotton market (virtually all of which was southern in origin), which had been about 75 percent in 1891, fell to less than 50 percent by 1933. Thus the beginning of the century that had seemed so promising for southern cotton farmers had by the mid-1920s turned completely sour.

During the Depression of the 1930s another major problem emerged—an enormous cotton surplus. It might have been expected that, with a decline in demand because of the worldwide economic collapse, southern cotton production might have fallen off. Instead, it did the opposite. In 1937 production reached 19 million bales in the South, a figure not approached again until the 1980s; in 1920, 13 million bales were produced, and in 1930, 14 million. The tenant system, and its frenetic system of production, caused the increase.

The Roosevelt administration sought to curtail the amount of cotton produced through the Agricultural Adjustment Act of 1933, followed by the Soil Conservation and Domestic Allotment Act of 1936, passed after the AAA was declared unconstitutional. But these pieces of legislation did not touch the basic problem—namely, the tenant system. Large landowners were paid not to plant crops, but not small tenants and croppers who made up the bulk of southern producers.[30] Even after the new AAA was passed in 1938, and in spite of its stronger system of acreage allotments, production quotas, and parity payments, production declined only slightly, and prices scarcely responded upward. The reason was the huge glut of surplus cotton left over from the previous overproduction that could not be easily absorbed by national or international markets.

There were many effects of this sharp decline in the cotton economy. Hundreds of thousands of southerners were affected. As Vance, Street, and others have shown, the effect of the "sickness" of King Cotton was psychological and well as economic.[31] But perhaps the easiest way to comprehend the collapse of the southern cotton economy is to point to its decline in value: in 1930, the farm value of cotton produced in the South was half ($587 million) of what it had been in 1929, $1.1 billion; by 1939, it was $459 million. It was not until the onset of World War II that farm values of cotton increased again.

Actually the market value of cotton suffered tremendously after the first two decades of this century. While there was always fluctuation, in general it rose between 1900 and 1920, from about 10 cents per pound at the dawn of the century to 34 cents twenty years later. During the 1920s the price of cotton began to fall fairly steadily, until by 1929 it was 19 cents. Then it collapsed totally, reaching 6 cents in 1932 and 9 cents in 1938. By 1955 the price of cotton was about what it was in 1920 (36 cents); in 1968, it was 22 cents (about what it was in 1917, and again in 1945). In 1980 it was 75 cents a pound, but in 1981, only 55 cents. These are absolute figures and do not take inflation into account. Not only, then, have cotton prices been unstable; they have not remained at high enough levels long enough for any but the largest producers to have any resilience or slack to withstand the next drop.

The conclusion is inescapable: except for a promising period early in the century, most cotton farmers in the South were relegated to a position of economic deprivation and poverty. King Cotton never produced the economic or social benefits that many southerners thought, and hoped, it would.

Continuing Problems with Southern Agriculture

The reader should not infer that the demise of the tenant system and the decline in importance of cotton as a mainstay of the southern economy have meant the end of problems in southern agriculture. Poverty and other forms of economic distress continue to accompany this regional industry, especially for the small farmer dwarfed by huge agricultural combines. As one Georgia farmer is said to have remarked, "I'd rather have two tickets on the *Titanic* than be farming today."[32]

What continuing problems remain? Why is southern agriculture still a source, and symptom, of regional poverty? There are a number of answers to these questions. Let us begin by noting that southern agriculture was very slow to participate in the technological, economic, and managerial transformation of American agriculture that began during the 1930s.[33]

Were an ancient Egyptian or Old Testament farmer suddenly transported to an average American farm in 1900, he would have felt very much at home. The basic principles of production and technology would all have been familiar—hoes, rakes, plows, flails, and draught animals.

But beginning around 1930, as Luther Tweeten points out, and accelerating at the onset of World War II, American agriculture began to change rapidly. No longer would the Old Testament farmer have felt at home on the modern farm. The change was, at bottom, fundamentally one of exchanging labor for capital—new technologies, new management techniques, the use of economies of scale, and vertical integration of production, transportation, distribution, and marketing functions.

There were important costs to these changes: farms became bigger and fewer in number, causing many small farmers to lose, or have to sell, their land. The number of agricultural jobs also fell. But food production became much more efficient. In 1910 the labor of one farm worker in America could feed seven people; by 1965, thirty-seven; and by 1978, forty-five, besides himself.[34]

This is not the place to discuss the reasons for these dramatic changes in agriculture. What we must note, however, is that southern agriculture was slow to participate in this transformation. The result was that it lost ground to much of the rest of the nation. As agriculture elsewhere was becoming more efficient and economically sound, southern agriculture was lagging behind. In some respects, and in some states, especially Florida and Texas, it has now caught up. But continuing problems remain.

Why did the South lag behind the American agricultural revolution? Several factors were important.

Perhaps most important factor was the lack of indigenous capital. The transformation of American agriculture took vast sums of money that were simply unavailable in the South. Related to this point, however, was the fact that from the standpoint of the structure of the southern labor force there was little incentive to move away from labor-intensive to capital-intensive agriculture. As long as there was a surplus of unskilled labor in the region, it was cheaper to pay low wages than to invest in machinery or technology. Only after the labor surplus began to disappear, as it did after World War II, did economic incentives appear in the South to make capital investments in agriculture.

Moreover, because the tenant-cropper system was a form of social control, there was little incentive for dominant southern elites to promote systemic change. Indeed, it was clearly in their interest not to do so. The tenant-cropper system, as we noted, began to die by the late 1930s and onset of World War II. But while it existed, it provided an effective mechanism for ensuring that the southern labor surplus—both poor whites and blacks—could be held in check and manipulated by white leaders.

There was also little technical assistance available to most southern farmers to help transform agriculture, even if they had the resources and desire to do so. States provided some help through county agricultural extension agents, and universities carried on research and offered some services through extension programs. But most of the beneficiaries of these services were large producers, not small farmers. And, as we noted earlier, the major thrust of federal programs designed to improve southern agriculture was also more geared to big farmers than to tenants and croppers.[35]

Finally, Street argues the controversial point that the South was the slowest region to experience an agricultural transformation because of the inertia, even indolence, of its traditional, conservative culture. Southern farmers seemed not to want, and even to resist, change. As a group they were suspicious of it, often apathetic, and uncertain that they could make a positive impact on their lives or destiny by making changes. As a result, they resisted modernization, and it took World War II, with its broadening effect on southern culture, to make southern farmers somewhat more accepting of agricultural changes.[36]

Nonetheless, eventually southern agriculture began to take a similar form to developments elsewhere in the nation. Even as the number of farms declined, their size increased significantly, generally making them more efficient. Crop diversification finally became a part of southern agriculture, lessening its dependence on just a few cash crops. Corporate farming and agribusiness have also become common in the South, resulting in huge agricultural combines that link and coordinate all phases of agricultural activity from the initial planting through harvesting, processing into food, and distribution to wholesale and retail markets.

While in general southern agriculture has become economically stronger as a result of this transformation, there have been some major costs to it. In addition, some major problems remain in southern agriculture, suggesting that it has a long way to go before providing an economically viable undertaking for everyone engaged in it.

At the macrolevel, the transformation of southern agriculture has had a profound impact on southern life and culture. As farms grew, became mechanized, and declined in number, opportunities for agricultural employment lessened. Workers and their families were forced off the land, into cities, or out of the region altogether. Moreover, as Jim Hightower notes, these changes were accompanied by a restructuring of the rural South. Many small towns, merchants, and shopkeepers who traded with small farmers also went into decline, or disappeared altogether, as the farmers left.

It is easy to overromanticize about the disappearance of the small-town, rural South. The fact is that often these were places where life was ugly, brutish, and short. On the other hand, the changes in southern agriculture did cause tremendous disruptions, even tragedies, in people's lives, often as a result of circumstances completely beyond their control. Thus the costs in terms of human lives of this transformation were considerable.

Moreover, if we examine some aspects of the distribution of resources created by agricultural sales in the South, we see that serious inequities remain. By the early 1980s, the South had about 30 percent of the nation's farms, but only about 25 percent of the value of agricultural products sold.[37]

But in fact this figure is deceptive because of Texas, which in 1982 had 27 percent of the total value of agricultural sales in the South.[38] Eliminating Texas from the calculations shows that southern farms accounted for only 18 percent of the national value of agricultural sales, in spite of the large percentage of the nation's farms located in the region.

These figures suggest that the average southern farm may not be doing very well, economically speaking. In fact, in 1978 the value of sales from an average southern farm was only 80 percent of the national average.[39] Only Florida farms exceeded the national figure. In Tennessee—not the poorest southern state, but the one that continues to have a large proportion of small farms—the value of agricultural sales from the average farm ($14,694) was only 43 percent of the southern figure and 34 percent of the national figure. Thus not only has there been a maldistribution of the sales value of agricultural products between the South as a region and the whole United States, there is a serious imbalance across the region as well.

But the situation is actually worse than this if race is factored in. The Agricultural Census collects data on the poorest farms in the nation—that is, those whose sales total less than $2,500 per year. In 1974, 55 percent of black-operated farms were in this category. By 1978, fully 63 percent of all black-operated farms in the South had incomes less than $2,500; for the entire nation, the figure was 50 percent. In Alabama and Mississippi, more than 70 percent of black-operated farms were in this category.

By 1982, some improvement had taken place, at least for white farmers. About one-third of southern farms operated by whites had sales under $2,500. The figure for black farms was still about 50 percent, although it was higher in some states—Alabama, 59 percent; Louisiana, 54 percent; Mississippi, 62 percent. Thus, even as white southern farmers were having trouble keeping up with farmers elsewhere in the nation, black-operated farms appeared to be backsliding rapidly.

It might be objected that many of these farms are not really commercial endeavors but mainly truck farms used for family subsistence or as an economic supplement to another form of activity. To satisfy this objection, we can look at the next category of farms—that is, sales under $5,000. In 1978, 49 percent of white-operated farms in the South, and 76 percent of black farms, were in this category.[40] In Alabama and Mississippi, more than 80 percent of black farms had sales less than $5,000.

By 1982, there was a sharp decline in the percentage of southern black farms with such low sales: it fell to 65 percent. However, this change was not due to an economic boom for black farmers; it occurred because about 20,000 southern black farms disappeared between 1978 and 1982. Moreover, 79 percent of black Mississippi farms, and 77 percent of Alabama's, still had agricultural sales under $5,000; Florida had the least—54 percent.

Data from the 1992 Agricultural Census indicates that with some exceptions southern agriculture continues to struggle economically. The region still has about 30 percent of the nation's farms, but only 25 percent of the sales value of agricultural goods (18 percent, without Texas). In 1982, there were 32,432 black farms in the South. By 1992, the figure was down to 17,877, a drop-off of more than 14,500 farms, or 45 percent. In 1992 blacks operated or owned only 3 percent of southern farms; southern agriculture, at least from the managerial and ownership side, is increasingly a white industry.

In 1992, the market value of agricultural sales from an average southern farm was 87 percent that of the nation;[41] but if Florida is eliminated from the calculation because its average sales figure ($149,586) was two to three times that of other states, the figure falls to 78 percent. More revealingly, if average net cash returns from agricultural sales are compared, the average southern farm reached only 80 percent of the national figure ($12,661 compared to $15,801). Eliminating Florida ($32,356) from the calculations reduces the southern percentage to 69 percent. In Tennessee net cash from sales for an average farm was only $5,622 in 1992, only 44 percent of the southern figure and 35 percent of the national one. In South Carolina ($7,792) the figures were 61 percent and 49 percent, respectively.

In 1992, 28 percent of southern farms had agricultural sales under $2,500; 61 percent had sales under $10,000. In Alabama, 91 percent of black farms had sales of less than $10,000; in Texas the figure was 86 percent, in Mississippi 82 percent, and in South Carolina 80 percent. The overall southern figure of black farms selling under $10,000 in agricultural products was 75 percent.

Clearly, then, southern agriculture continues to face not only an economic problem but a racial one as well. Black farming—opportunities in which are extremely limited—in the South constitutes little more than a route to hardship and poverty. Census figures document that black-operated farms tend to be the smallest and have the lowest levels of agricultural sales in the South. Black farms have disappeared faster than white farms, creating enormous human problems. As long as this racial inequity continues to exist, it cannot be said that the transformation of southern agriculture has been beneficial for black farmers.

One final measure of southern agriculture must also be noted—the contribution that farms of less than $5,000 in sales made to total agricultural sales in the region. In other words, even though there appear to be many farms with low sales, do they not, in the aggregate, contribute significantly to total agricultural sales in the region?

The answer is no. By 1982, only about 2 percent of all agricultural sales came from all farms selling less than $5,000 in commodities; the national figure was 12 percent, down from 18 percent in 1978. In 1992 the total market value of agricultural sales from farms selling under $10,000[42] annually accounted for only 3 percent of total regional sales. This means that a very small number of farms in the South account for nearly all the sales; conversely, a huge block of farms (actually a substantial majority of farms) contribute virtually nothing to total agricultural sales. These figures underscore our previous point that there is a very serious maldistribution of money from agricultural sales in the South. The figures are similar, moreover, to those in so-called developing nations where peasant farming is dwarfed by huge agricultural combines and aggregations.[43]

In sum, while southern agriculture is overall healthier than it was for most of this century, major problems continue in the distribution of money from agricultural sales and in the difficulty that small—especially black—farmers face in attempting to remain economically viable. Except in Florida, North Carolina, Arkansas (in each of which sophisticated corporate agribusiness dominates—even overwhelms—the industry), and a few other places, southern agriculture seriously lags behind the rest of the nation. Southern agriculture may no longer be the major source of southern poverty, as it once was. But for too many southerners, white and black, it continues to fail to provide a decent living.

Southern Poverty

That the South was the nation's poorest region was common knowledge well before the dawn of the twentieth century. Roosevelt's National Emergency Council, however, documented the extraordinary extent of human suffering and deprivation that existed during the bleak Depression years.

Southerners, the council reported, spent a disproportionate share of their income on basic life necessities—food, clothing, shelter. Farm families, in particular, could not afford money for clothes: many spent less than $1.00

per year on coats and comparable amounts on shoes and hats. Only one of four white village residents had a car. Over half of all southerners needed new housing; the proportion in rural areas was greater. Less than 1 percent of poor southern farmers had running water or indoor toilets, virtually none had electric or gas cooking facilities, and less than 2 percent had electricity. In the urban South these percentages were higher, but not by very much. Most rural southerners subsisted on a diet of fatback, corn bread, and molasses, resulting in a host of dietary and health problems. As the council grimly concluded, "The South's people want and need houses, radios, butter, beef, vegetables, milk, eggs, dresses, skirts and shoes. They want and could use the many thousands of things, little and big, that men and machines make to bring health and good living to people."[44]

In 1937, the average annual personal income in the South was $314, compared to $604 nationally. "Prosperous" southern farm people had an annual income of $186 per person, compared to $528 elsewhere.[45] But for the majority of southern farmers, who as we have seen were tenants or croppers, incomes were much lower. Many families on cotton farms had to survive on an annual per capita income of $73; the range was $38 annually to $87 (the former figure represented about 10 cents each day). Urban incomes were somewhat higher, of course. Nonetheless, the council concluded that many southerners, especially farm families, lived "in poverty comparable to the poorest peasants in Europe."[46]

There are many ways to demonstrate the extent and persistence of poverty in the South. Perhaps the most direct and meaningful way is to compare per capita income in the South, and southern states, with that of the rest of the nation during this century. Table 2.1 (a and b) presents these data for selected years. It shows per capita income in absolute dollar figures between 1929 and 1994 for the United States, the South, and individual southern states. It also expresses the regional and state per capita income as a percentage of the U.S. figure. It also aggregates the figures by border and deep South states and expresses them as a percentage of the U.S. figure.

The table documents that per capita income in the South continues to lag behind that of the entire nation. Although not shown in the table, per capita income in the South in 1900 was only 52 percent of the nation's; in 1920, it was 61 percent. The table shows that it began to fall, relative to the nation, during the Depression. By 1980, it was 85 percent of the U.S. figure. In 1990 the figure was the same (85 percent), and by 1994 it had risen to 87 percent. Obviously the South has improved, relative to the nation, during this century, but it has taken a long time to approach national levels.

But the aggregate figures mask some important facts about the distribution of wealth in the South. Every state did make substantial gains during

Table 2.1a

Southern per Capita Income, 1929–1960

Area	1929 Per Capita Income	%	1940 Per Capita Income	%	1950 Per Capita Income	%	1960 Per Capita Income	%
United States	705		592		1,496		2,216	
South	374	53*	343	58	1,032	69	1,596	72
Alabama	322	46	278	47	880	59	1,493	67
Arkansas	306	43	254	43	825	55	1,376	62
Florida	525	74	507	86	1,281	86	1,946	88
Georgia	349	50	336	57	1,034	69	1,637	74
Louisiana	414	59	360	61	1,120	75	1,662	75
Mississippi	287	41	216	36	755	50	1,205	54
North Carolina	333	47	323	55	1,035	69	1,558	70
South Carolina	269	38	301	51	893	60	1,372	62
Tennessee	375	53	334	56	994	66	1,544	70
Texas	480	68	430	73	1,349	90	1,931	87
Virginia	434	62	458	77	1,228	82	1,842	83
Rim South	409	58	384	65	1,119	75	1,700	77
Deep South	328	47	298	50	936	63	1,474	66

Source: U.S. Census of Population and *Statistical Abstracts.*
*Percents are of U.S. figure.

Table 2.1b

Southern per Capita Income, 1970–1994

Area	1970 Per Capita Income	1970 %	1980 Per Capita Income	1980 %	1990 Per Capita Income	1990 %	1994 Per Capita Income	1994 %
United States	3,943		9,521		18,666		21,809	
South	3,194	81	8,093	85	15,911	85	19,054	87
Alabama	2,913	74	7,488	79	14,903	79	18,010	82
Arkansas	2,869	73	7,268	76	13,784	73	16,898	77
Florida	3,692	94	8,996	94	18,788	100	21,677	99
Georgia	3,318	84	8,073	85	17,123	91	20,251	92
Louisiana	3,068	78	8,458	89	14,281	76	17,651	80
Mississippi	2,596	66	6,580	69	12,571	67	15,838	72
North Carolina	3,218	82	7,819	82	16,275	87	19,669	90
South Carolina	2,963	75	7,260	76	15,106	80	17,695	81
Tennessee	3,082	78	7,720	81	15,905	85	19,482	89
Texas	3,576	91	9,545	100	16,749	89	19,857	91
Virginia	3,653	93	9,392	99	19,537	104	22,594	103
Rim South	3,348	85	8,457	89	16,840	90	20,030	91
Deep South	2,972	75	7,572	80	14,797	79	17,889	82

Source: U.S. Census of Population and *Statistical Abstracts.*
*Percents are of U.S. figure.

this century in both absolute dollar amounts and its percentage of the U.S. figure. But only one state (Texas) actually surpassed the national average by 1980; it was closely followed by Virginia and Florida. In 1990, only Florida and Virginia exceeded the U.S. figure; by 1994, only Virginia was above the national norm; Florida fell in rank due to regional economic dislocations in the early 1990s.

On the other hand, as late as 1980, no other southern states came within 10 percent of the U.S. figure. Louisiana and Georgia were closest, but South Carolina and Arkansas had per capita income figures only three-fourths that of the United States, and Mississippi's per capita income was barely more than two-thirds that of the nation (69 percent). In 1960, Mississippi's per capita income was just over 50 percent of the national average; in Arkansas and South Carolina, the figure was slightly more than 60 percent. In 1929, these three states were also the poorest, as measured by per capita income.

Moreover, Texas, Florida, and Virginia skew the aggregate southern figures upward. Leaving them out of the calculations for the South as a whole reveals that, in fact, throughout the century the southern figures are on average 5 percent less than those shown. If the states are ranked by per capita income, in 1980 the southern states occupied bottom positions: Mississippi (50); South Carolina (49); Arkansas (48); Alabama (47); Tennessee (44); North Carolina (41). Only two states, Texas (18) and Virginia (22) were in the top half. None was in the top ten. Eight were in the bottom fifteen and four were at the very bottom.

The 1990 figures show much the same. In 1994, per capita income in Mississippi was still less than three-quarters that of the entire United States. Indeed, because of economic downturns in the early 1990s, Florida and Texas—two of the wealthiest southern states—lost ground relative to the rest of the nation. In 1993, only one southern state (Virginia, 13), ranked near the top ten of all states in per capita income; Florida ranked twentieth. Arkansas (49) and Mississippi (50) were at the very bottom; five southern states ranked fortieth or below (Mississippi, Arkansas, Louisiana, South Carolina, Alabama); nine states ranked thirtieth or below.[47]

An additional problem for the South is that while in percentage terms the region has improved itself relative to the nation, in terms of the gap in absolute dollars between southern and national figures things have gotten worse. In 1929, the dollar gap was $331. By 1980, it was $1,428, and in 1990, $2,755 ($2,755 in 1994 as well). In Mississippi, South Carolina, Arkansas, and Alabama, the gaps exceeded $2,000 in 1980; by 1990 the gap between Mississippi and the national figure was $6,095, while in Arkansas the gap was $4,882; Louisiana, $4,385; Alabama, $3,763; South Carolina, $3,560; and Tennessee, $2,761.[48] Indeed, the 1980 dollar gap in Mississippi was greater than its per capita income in 1970. In 1929, the per capita difference between the richest and poorest southern states was $256; in 1980, it was more than ten times that ($2,965). In 1990, the difference was $6,966, and in 1994, $6,756; in 1980, Mississippi's per capita income ($6,580) was virtually the same as the high-low gap in 1990.[49]

These figures do not bode well for the South. Only Virginia, Florida, Texas, and North Carolina show evidence of catching up to the rest of the nation. Texas and Louisiana, moreover, were hard hit by the collapse of oil prices in the 1980s, and other southern states experienced a substantial economic downturn in the early 1990s, raising questions of whether they can sustain their levels of per capita income relative to the rest of the country. Other southern states are not doing well relative to the rest of the nation. There is a real question of whether four of them at the very bottom will ever really catch up. The South remains the country's poorest region.

These aggregate figures additionally do not differentiate among the population by race. Blacks have traditionally occupied the lowest rung of the socioeconomic ladder in the South. It was not unusual for black farmers to earn less than half of what white farmers received, and nonagricultural black workers also received only a fraction of the wages whites were paid.[50]

According to figures derived from the 1980 census, the per capita income of all southern blacks was only 51 percent of that for whites.[51] The range was from 44 percent in Mississippi to 58 percent in Tennessee.[52] By 1990, per capita income of southern blacks had fallen to 47 percent of whites.[53] The range was from a low of 39 percent in Mississippi to a high of 54 percent in Texas.[54] Thus it is clear that the per capita income numbers previously cited for the South have little to do with blacks. Their situation was actually far worse than that of their white counterparts.[55]

Moreover, as Carl N. Degler has shown, the improvement of per capita income figures in the South following the 1930s was actually not as great as the numbers suggest. The reason has to do with the migration of blacks out of the South in the middle decades of this century. Once they were gone, they were no longer included in the calculations of per capita income figures; thus at least some of the "rise" in southern per capita figures resulted from the fact that those representing the lowest numbers were no longer present to depress the figures downward, and much of the "improvement" was simply an arithmetic "rebound."[56]

Finally, if we look at the percentage of southerners who live below the poverty line, we find that the figures suggest a continuing core in dire economic straits.[57] While there are more poor southern whites than blacks (about 1 million more), as late as 1979 the rate of poverty among southern blacks was about three times that of whites: 34 percent to 11 percent. Table

Table 2.2

**Rates of Poverty, White and Black Persons and Families,
United States, the South, and Southern States, 1989**

Area	% White Persons in Poverty	% White Families in Poverty	% Black Persons in Poverty	% Black Families in Poverty
United States	9	6	29	26
South	10	7	34	31
Alabama	11	7	37	33
Arkansas	13	9	42	38
Florida	9	6	31	28
Georgia	8	4	30	27
Louisiana	12	9	45	41
Mississippi	12	8	45	41
North Carolina	8	5	25	27
South Carolina	8	5	32	29
Tennessee	11	8	33	30
Texas	14	10	30	27
Virginia	6	4	22	20
Rim South	10	7	31	28
Deep South	10	7	38	34

Source: U.S. Census of Population, 1990.

2.2 shows black and white poverty rates in the South as of 1989 at both personal and family levels. The proportions have changed little since 1979. It indicates that while about 10 percent of southern whites live below the poverty line, 34 percent of southern blacks do. In the deep South states, 38 percent of southern blacks continue to live in poverty, and in two of the states (Louisiana and Mississippi), poverty rates among blacks are about 45 percent. Figures for family poverty are only marginally better. Among whites, only in Georgia, North Carolina, South Carolina, and Virginia do per capita rates of poverty fall below national levels; but among blacks, only in Virginia is this true.

If figures are aggregated and race disregarded, the South continues to show greater rates of poverty than the nation as a whole. In 1993, the U.S. rate of poverty (measured by individuals) was just over 15 percent. In the South the rate was 18 percent, from a high of 25 percent in Mississippi to a low of 10 percent in Virginia. In 1990–91 nearly twice as many persons in the census South could be expected to be poor in an average month, a two-month period, or a twenty-four-month period compared to people in other parts of the country.[58]

The conclusion is inescapable. Southerners are more likely to be poor than persons in other parts of the country. Black southerners continue to lag significantly behind white southerners on measures of income, and their poverty rates are more than three times those of whites in the same region. Southern poverty continues to be a problem.

The Correlates of Poverty

Poverty does not exist in isolation. It is inevitably accompanied by a host of social ills that bring misery to people's lives as well as tremendous waste in human resources. Two in particular are of concern here—lack of education and poor public health.

A full discussion of the problems of southern education goes beyond the scope of this text. However measured, it has been seriously lacking in comparison to education elsewhere. Expenditures for schools and higher education have been significantly lower than in the rest of the nation, at least on a per capita basis. Teachers' salaries, library facilities, faculty credentials—in all these measures southern schools and colleges have been lower, and of lesser quality, than elsewhere. Indeed, it has only been within the past fifteen years or so that southern universities and colleges have been considered approaching the quality of institutions of higher education in other parts of the country.

By other objective measures southern education has been lacking. Throughout this century southerners had fewer years of completed schooling than Americans elsewhere. More important, there were large gaps between southern whites and blacks: in 1940, the gap was 3.6 years; in 1960, it was still 3.6 years. By 1980, southerners had virtually caught up to the rest of the nation in years of completed schooling, and the black-white gap had lessened considerably.

Illiteracy figures are also revealing. In 1900, while the United States as a whole had an illiteracy rate of 11 percent, in the South it was 29 percent; in Louisiana it was nearly 40 percent. By 1970, the national illiteracy rate had been cut to 1 percent; the mean for the South was 2 percent, but in Louisiana it was nearly 3 percent, and in several other deep South states it was above 2 percent.[59] In 1969, 7 percent of all applicants for the armed forces failed the entrance examination, but 14 percent of southerners failed. These figures, too, suggest continuing problems with the basic education of southerners.

Public health, like education, has shown improvement, but lingering problems remain. Traditional diseases such as hookworm and malaria have been largely obliterated. Dietary diseases such as pellagra, caused from an unbalanced diet and eating too much corn, have also disappeared.

But other health problems that are related to the existence of poverty, poor living conditions, low levels of education, and inadequate public health facilities persist. The South continues to have higher rates of deaths from diseases that are associated with these social and economic conditions than elsewhere in the nation: typhoid and paratyphoid fever, dysentery, diarrhea, gastritis and appendix complications, pregnancy complications, tuberculosis, and syphilis, to name only a few.[60] Moreover, there continues to be a wide gap between southern whites and blacks in the percentage dying from these diseases; in every case, blacks die at a higher rate, sometimes as much as 200 percent higher.

Perhaps most tragic are the statistics dealing with stillborns and infant mortality. Both conditions are positively correlated with low levels of education, poverty, and poor public health facilities. The South has had significantly higher rates of deaths from them than other parts of the country, especially when whites and blacks are compared. As late as 1975, the southern black stillbirth rate was nearly twice that of southern whites (19 and 11 per thousand, respectively); in 1978, black infant mortality rates in the South were about twice that of southern whites (24 and 13 per thousand, respectively). By the 1990s, infant mortality rates among southern whites were slightly higher than national averages,[61] while for the first time infant mortality rates among southern blacks were lower than those nationally.[62] However, mortality rates among southern blacks continued to average about twice that of southern whites.

Finally, on another important public health indicator southerners continue to lag behind the nation. In 1993, about 18 percent of southerners lived without health insurance, compared to 15 percent nationally; the range was from 13 percent in Virginia to 24 percent in Louisiana. On a three-year average from 1991 to 1993, about 18 percent of southerners had no health insurance, compared to 15 percent nationally; the range was from a low of 13 percent in Tennessee to 22 percent in Louisiana.[63]

Conclusion

These bare-bone figures illuminate some serious, ongoing problems for the South. While poverty and its correlates have decreased in the region, and in general the population is better off than it was during much of this century, continuing, persistent poverty remains a part of southern life. And just as the economic system of the South has improved for most southerners, so have many southerners been left behind as the new South economic engine runs in high gear. In both cases, those left out, those at the lowest end of the socioeconomic ladder, are more likely to be black than white.

Economic and social conditions do not always determine political activity. But it would be foolish to ignore the impact they have on it. Thus, as we begin our survey of the rise of a new Southern politics, we must keep in mind that the political transformations have taken place against a backdrop of socioeconomic changes that are inconsistent and irregular in their impact on southern life. Moreover, we must also keep in mind the fundamental question V.O. Key asked more than forty years ago: Have the political changes really helped alleviate the traditional problems of poverty and racial discrimination that have so permeated, and dominated, southern politics during this century?

Chapter 3

Race, Democrats, and Old Style Southern Politics

Issues? Why, son, they don't have a damn thing to do with it.
—Comment of a north Florida county judge, 1949

The "it" to which the Florida politician referred was getting elected to office. In fact, he seemed quite astonished that his interviewer would think otherwise. In his mind, and in the minds of many southerners for much of this century, issues seemed to play a very limited part in electoral politics. Of much greater importance were such factors as where a candidate lived, for how long, the particular faction to which he belonged, and how dominant elites (including, in this case, the local "courthouse gang") viewed him.

But the truth is that in some ways the judge was wrong. Issues could, and did, emerge in southern politics. Indeed, as Dewey Grantham has shown, just because the South had a one-party system did not mean that nothing happened in the political arena.[1] True, personalities could become exceedingly important, especially in the absence of clearly defined policy positions. And geographic-sectional factional fights were frequently vicious. But issues did surface in politics, and enormous controversies erupted over competing political ideas. It is also true, however, that the range of political issues was often seriously constrained in the South, certainly compared to political discussion elsewhere in the nation. Issues in the South ultimately seemed to rest on, and devolve from, a single, fundamental axiom of southern political life—race. With very few exceptions, other issues were secondary to this one.

The purpose of this chapter is to investigate the reason why race played such a crucial role in southern politics during much of this century. More specifically, we need to explore the relationship between race and one-party politics, meaning the long-term dominance of the Democratic Party. Establishing this linkage will indicate why issues were infrequently found in the region's politics, or alternatively were subsidiary or correlates of the more fundamental matter of race.

Thus, in this chapter we shall look at old style politics and political culture[2] in the South. What were they like? What were the dynamics of politics in the region for much of this century? And, most crucially, what were their implications and consequences, not just for democratic theory but for the citizens of the South, both black and white?

We must immediately clarify the term "old style." In using it, we refer to politics in the region between roughly 1900 and 1960. These are somewhat arbitrary but convenient dates. By 1900 the one-party system was well established and Democratic dominance assured for the next five decades. By the 1950s, some substantial changes in the region could be observed and felt. Postwar migration patterns and economic development were well under way. The civil rights movement, while in many ways still nascent, had nonetheless already become a force to be reckoned with, and not (as many whites believed or hoped) simply ephemera associated with a few "uppity" blacks. In the 1950s also, stirrings of southern Republicanism could be found. And the election of John F. Kennedy in 1960 signaled the beginning of a politically active period in Washington, D.C., that would eventually leave an indelible stamp on the traditional customs of the South. Thus, 1960 marks an end period of an old South politics soon to be irreversibly altered.

Southern Blacks, Southern Whites

The political position of southern blacks in the first decades of this century was largely a function of patterns of race relations established after Reconstruction. It was precisely the social position of the southern black community that underscored and reinforced one-party politics and influenced both the style and content of white political activity. To grasp the connection between race and one-party politics, then, we must briefly examine the nature of race relations in the South during the first six decades of this century.[3]

The major influence on the relations between southern blacks and whites following Reconstruction was the legacy of slavery and blacks' role after the Civil War. Blacks had been brought to the South forcibly, as slaves, and were regarded as property, not as human beings. Conditions facing slaves varied considerably, but even as it was in the interest of slave owners to maintain the health of their slaves, it is also true that slavery, as a reality, meant bondage and physical deprivation. Far more critical was the emotional and cognitive deprivation caused by the psychological and social boundaries that slavery established between whites and blacks. Whites were taught as children that blacks were morally, intellectually, and biologically inferior and suited only for menial work. Social interaction was decidedly unequal; southern whites established and enforced the rules. Blacks, too, learned as children that their role was one of inferiority and deference; to deny or protest was to invite serious trouble.

Freeing the slaves did not necessarily change race relations very much. Blacks were no longer property or chattels, strictly speaking. But the psychological and social attitudes that marked white-black interaction under slavery did not simply disappear with the Emancipation Proclamation. Moreover, at the end of the Civil War, blacks in many parts of the South suddenly found themselves placed in positions of political power, propped up by northern whites—carpetbaggers and the army of occupation. Southern whites, who already resented blacks because (to many whites) they caused both the war and the southern defeat, became even more hostile at finding their former "property" in positions of public leadership and responsibility. Thus, once Reconstruction ended, southern whites, led by conservative Democrats, moved to disenfranchise blacks. But this political discrimination was really a manifestation of a larger issue: southern whites wished to relegate blacks to social and economic roles as similar to those of slavery as they could. Thus so-called Jim Crow laws[4] ensured that blacks would know, and stay in, their place; to violate their position, as under slavery, meant risking the imposition of very severe sanctions.

As the twentieth century dawned, the social position of southern blacks was generally precarious. They existed in a milieu determined by white laws, rules, attitudes, and expectations. They completely depended on the white community for their survival, yet the most they could hope for was that the rules defining this dependence would be more paternalistic than draconian.[5]

Moreover, the position that whites defined for blacks was underscored by the extreme poverty and ruralism of the South. While whites, too, suffered from the region's economic stagnation, blacks occupied the lowest rung of the economic ladder. The combination of crushing poverty and racial attitudes permitted, even encouraged, whites to engage in scapegoatism. Because of their alleged shiftlessness, laziness, immorality, and biological inferiority, the argument ran, blacks actually constituted a drain on the southern economy that was largely responsible for the region's defeat in the Civil War, its poverty, backward industry, and other shortcomings.[6]

The agricultural economy of the South also kept blacks dependent on whites. The tenant and sharecropper system, which developed after the war, held both races in economic bondage.[7] But there seems no doubt that blacks suffered more from the system than did whites. To make matters worse, there were few, if any, other economic opportunities open to rural southern blacks besides agriculture.

Blacks were also widely dispersed throughout the southern countryside, with a relatively small percentage living in urban places. Their dispersal allowed whites to exploit their dependence still further, permitting the practice of dividing and conquering the southern black community. In urban places blacks had somewhat more economic opportunity and independence and exhibited somewhat greater social coherence. It was no accident that the civil rights movement later began in, and was largely sustained by, urban black southerners.

Southern poverty underscored the psychological attitude that whites held toward blacks and helped define the system of social status in the region. Blacks were not only useful as economic scapegoats; they also could be seen as social inferiors. No matter how serious the economic plight of southern whites (and for the vast majority at the beginning of this century it often involved starvation, malnutrition, and related conditions of poverty), they still held a higher social position than blacks. They were, then, able to feel and act superior, even if appearances were deceiving.

In a sense, this hierarchy permitted whites certain psychological feelings of satisfaction, even arrogance, in spite of their living conditions and in spite of black experience in the Civil War and Reconstruction. White elites wanted poor whites to maintain the illusion of higher social position than blacks. They further wanted poor whites to feel that their economic problems were a function of shiftless blacks and Yankees, not their own political leaders and institutions. If poor whites began to think otherwise, there was always the danger that class consciousness and economic deprivation would again overcome racial antagonism to create a potent political alliance, as occurred during the rise of southern populism late in the nineteenth century.[8]

Theoretically, Jim Crow laws and the racial attitudes that gave rise to them defined how blacks and whites were to live together in one region. In fact, however, it should not be assumed that race relations were uniform across the South. There was considerable variation. In the border South and in those areas where relatively few blacks lived, relations could be fairly benign. But where blacks were numerous (perhaps even outnumbering whites, as in parts of the deep South) and where the traditions of slavery were kept alive most strongly, relations were likely to be much more hostile. Indeed, race relations in the early twentieth century South can be viewed on a continuum, whose boundaries can be seen as "benign paternalism" at one end, and "terror and violence" at the other. It is this latter dimension that has attracted the most public attention: as John Hope Franklin shows, more than 2,500 southern blacks were lynched in the late nineteenth century, and more than 1,100 in the new century prior to World War I.[9]

But even when lynchings did not occur and night riders did not appear, the social, economic, and psychological position of blacks remained vulnerable. To make matters more discomfiting for blacks, the boundaries separating the races were semipermeable: contact between the races was inevitable. The problem for blacks was that because of their vulnerability, these interactions were at best ambiguous and at worst life threatening. Even in places where race relations tended toward the benign-paternalistic end of the spectrum, blacks could seldom expect decent treatment or respect. Rather, they had to hope that these interactions were not moments marked by anything worse than embarrassment or further loss of dignity.

There was a certain irony in these relations. Whites, especially poor whites, were in some ways as dependent on blacks as blacks were on whites, particularly as a justification or excuse for the misery of their lives. For middle- and upper-income whites, blacks served as menial labor for business and industry. In the ultimate irony, black maids and nannies ran southern white homes and even raised white children. The upscale southern white woman was very dependent on her black domestics to maintain her position on the pedestal and to perpetuate the illusion of her helplessness.[10] Yet southerners, even if they were aware of these ironies, could not act on them. The racial codes were too rigid and fixed to permit action.

Blacks in Southern Politics

The psychological attitudes and social position of southern whites toward blacks defined the place of blacks in the political system. Just as blacks were economic and social scapegoats, so they were also political scapegoats and objects of discrimination. Jim Crow laws that relegated blacks to the lowest rungs on social and economic ladders also forced them into second-class political status. Indeed, blacks were frequently denied even the most basic rights of citizenship, including access to the ballot and equal justice under the law. The constitutional niceties of habeas corpus requirements or a trial by a jury of peers were not respected by vigilantes, a lynch mob, or many southern judges and law enforcement officers.

But to say that blacks were second-class citizens, or denied access to political resources, does not mean that they played no political role at all. In fact, they became significant political actors in two ways. First, some blacks actually did participate in politics. Relatively few were allowed to register to vote; those who did were likely to be found in the border South and/or in urban places where racial attitudes were somewhat more moderate than in the rural or deep South. But even where blacks could vote, in general they did so only at the behest of whites. In this sense, they were politically manipulated by the white community. It was not too unusual to find blacks rounded up on election day, brought to polling places, and "voted" by supervising whites. Sometimes certain rewards would be forthcoming— some money, whiskey, possibly even the promise of a road or a few jobs. This kind of participation, of course, was nothing more than a charade and mockery of democracy. On the other hand, it was fairly common; Boss Ed Crump in Memphis, for example, regularly voted "his" blacks, even bringing them from West Memphis, Arkansas (across the Mississippi River), on election day.[11]

But the more important way in which blacks played a role in southern politics during the first decades of this century was as a foil for white politicians. In this sense, blacks became objects of derision, discrimination, loathing, even fear. They were the fodder on which southern politicians could unleash their racist cannons. And while it is well recognized that southern demagogues like Theodore Bilbo and Gene Talmadge became masters at race-baiting and using racial hatreds to build mass followings, these were not the only politicians to engage in these tactics. Even restrained, dignified, southern politicians often attacked blacks, blamed them for the ills of the region, and used them as excuses for doing little or nothing once in office.

This latter point brings us to the heart of the issue. Blacks as political scapegoats allowed white politicians to engage in "smoke-screen" politics. That is, since it was possible, indeed legitimate and necessary, to blame blacks for the ills of the South, the politician need not then bother with serious discussions of public problems. Issues were of little or no significance, since the causes of southern problems were not a colonial economy and maldistribution of resources leading to poor education, ignorance, poverty, and disease. Rather, they were the consequence of a large black population that sucked energy and resources from whites in the region. Even if efforts were made to solve problems, in the view of white politicians, the effect of a parasitic, enervating black population would simply undermine solutions. There was no reason, then, to waste resources by trying.

The matter went even further. Issues were potentially dysfunctional to white politicians. The reason is that issues have a way of stirring people up, causing them to pay attention, ask questions, or be concerned about what public officials were really doing. Thus it was clearly in the interest of southern politicians, whether of the demagogic or courtly variety, to feed the white population a continuing big lie about the real causes of southern distress. To the extent that their constituency was poor, frustrated, ignorant, and racially bigoted, they could continue to make the lie as vivid and outrageous as they wished. It would continue to be credible.

Southern politicians also recognized that public policies aimed at improving public welfare (such as better schools) might have to include blacks. Such an idea was unacceptable, not only because of the expense but because it might lead to increased levels of equality between the races. This strategy, for example, was fundamental to James Vardaman's famous defense of avoiding public expenditures for black schools: "Why squander money on [black] education when the only effect is to spoil a good field hand and make an insolent cook?"[12]

This attitude gave southern politicians the perfect excuse for doing nothing. But an excuse to do nothing was exactly what entrenched, conservative Democrats and the elites they represented actually wanted. Southern politicians understood for decades the danger for them in the theory of rising expectations: better to do nothing than something. As long as the majority of whites remained willing to blame blacks for southern problems, no change was needed and no public enterprise in the form of (potentially expensive) public policy was necessary. The result was that those in power were able to "govern" for their own, not the public's, benefit.

It was precisely for this reason that ruling Democrats feared the populist or other troublemaker who occasionally appeared on the southern political scene. The populist, heir to the late-nineteenth-century movement, introduced ideas into political discussion that were heretical and dangerous to entrenched Democrats, because populists often talked to the public about economic inequalities. They protested the exploitation wrought by banks, railroads, and utilities and occasionally even addressed the issue of "public," as opposed to purely "private," interests.

In short, populists represented the introduction of issues, or at least excitement and popular ferment, into political rhetoric and discussion. They were a threat to conservative ruling elites. There was always fear by entrenched Democrats that their constituents, poor and ignorant as they were, might listen to the populist message and vote for it. There was even the potential that the old populist coalition of poor whites and blacks might be resurrected, thereby endangering the status of Democratic elites.

Thus throughout the South, whenever populists appeared, it was not unusual to find a vigorous, rapid response by ruling Democrats. Efforts to defeat the populist in an election were common and even involved electoral fraud. But when such strategies could not be used, or failed to work, they would seek to isolate the populist in office or, alternatively, to co-opt him. In either case, the effect was generally the same. Populist figures, such as James E. and Miriam ("Pa" and "Ma") Ferguson in Texas, Jeff Davis and Sid McMath in Arkansas, and "Big Jim" Folsom in Alabama, often built substantial personal followings, but they seldom accomplished very much. Ruling Democrats had too many resources to ensure that they did not.

Thus the presence of southern racial attitudes in politics sharply limited the range, scope, and depth of political activity. Other factors were important, too; for example, the extensive poverty of the region prevented serious attention to issues or problem solving, because states could not pay for measures designed to alleviate poverty even if they wanted to.

Issues did exist, as Grantham argued. But they were largely defined by white elites and ruling politicians; the exception was if a populist or other gadfly came along to stir things up. Issues as serious discussion of public problems, solutions, and alternatives, were rare. More likely they involved disputes over personality or style among leaders. They might also reflect geographic rivalries and local patriotism. Occasionally they might involve important economic cleavages among elite groups. Or they could involve conflict among different political organizations and factions. All of them could, and did, become acrimonious.

Ultimately, however, racial attitudes and relations defined what politics could be or what types and levels of political rhetoric and activity were legitimate. Blacks-as-scapegoats permitted white politicians to engage in politics-by-mirrors. By distracting the public through loud racial appeals, entrenched elites had freedom to use the public weal to advance their own private interests, rather than the public interest.

Race and One-Party Politics

We have already alluded to the close relationship between race and the maintenance of the one-party system for so many years. More than one party would mean a broadening of political rhetoric and activity and a possible competition for voters, a situation that would threaten the position of dominant southern white elites. An even more frightening scenario, but one not inconceivable if more than one party existed, involved the possibility of appealing to, and seeking out, black support in order to ensure victory.[13] Such a scenario extended beyond the realm of legitimacy in old style southern politics and was neither thinkable nor practical.

But as V.O. Key points out, there was also a critical geo-political linkage between race and the one-party Democratic system. The basis of one-party dominance, he observed, was in well-defined areas of the South. In particular, he found that the rulers of the Democratic party generally came from black-belt areas of southern states, so-called because they had formerly been the sites of plantations and massive cotton farming. As a corollary, they were also the residence of a substantial black population; in some delta counties of the deep South, in fact, blacks actually constituted a majority of the population, or close to it.[14]

Given this demographic configuration, entrenched white elites (many of whom were heirs of the planters and later constituted the business and commercial class of southerners) had to maintain strict control over political participation. Allowing blacks into the political process might threaten their ruling status. But there was another problem for delta whites—the so-called hill country whites. These were often small, dirt farmers and residents of small, up-country towns whose economic interests seldom paralleled those of large planters, businessmen, and other substantial commercial interests. Indeed, even before the Civil War there was friction between delta and hill country whites, and it did not diminish following Reconstruction or as the new century began.[15]

Maintenance of one-party politics, then, became a matter of survival for black-belt whites, permitting domination of both blacks and up-country whites.[16] Not surprisingly, it was often from up-country areas in southern states that the occasional political protest in the form of a populist, demagogue, or some other character, would come.

If racial feelings and attitudes in the South had been less entrenched, or if they had been more diverse, it is likely that cracks in the one-party system would have appeared before they did. But deviation from a standard litany on race was not possible for much of this century if a candidate hoped to succeed to office. Even among "genteel" southerners, many of whom found the extremist racial language unseemly and violence against blacks repulsive, there was little incentive to speak out or attempt to instigate change. To be a real southerner meant to share prevailing racial views, or at least keep quiet if one's views were different. Indeed, white extremists could, and did, retaliate against even middle-class whites who were seen as "nigger lovers," and smear campaigns and violence were directed against those suspected of "moderation."[17]

The close relationship between racial attitudes and the one-party system can further be shown by noting what happened to it once blacks began to leave the South: it continued. Beginning in the second decade of the twentieth century, blacks started to migrate from rural areas to urban places in the South as well as to the North and Midwest.[18] But the rapid decline in the proportion of blacks in the South did not, by itself, significantly alter the existence of one-party politics.[19] Racial attitudes and beliefs persisted in spite of the declining threat supposedly presented to white southerners by a large black population. Other demographic changes, regional economic development, and the rise of other political forces inside and outside the South had to occur before the one-party system began to erode in any significant way.

Other Bases of One-Party Politics

Race and the survival instinct of dominant white elites were not the only factors helping to maintain the one-party system in the South. Other forces also contributed, of which three are very important.

Most obvious was the political skill of southern white elites. Conservative Democrats maintained control of southern political and governmental machinery for more than fifty years. Even given the undemocratic, often repressive, way in which they retained control, this was no mean accomplishment. Southern white elites were able to maintain control because they had a virtual monopoly on political resources and were dominant in economic resources as well. But saying this does not really address the question of how they managed dominance over such a long period, especially considering that opposition did arise from time to time and internecine party warfare in the form of factional disputes occasionally threatened the existence of the whole enterprise. What, actually, did they do?

First, these elites sharply limited access to political resources, as we have noted, to carefully controlled situations. As E.E. Schattschneider observed, this control allowed ruling elites to determine the overall shape and scope of political conflict. In other words, they seldom let matters get away from them,[20] and they learned to deal with opposition. Elite response could range from a relatively benign co-optation to electoral fraud. The effect was usually to defuse external opposition, or, if necessary, simply to outlast or survive it, as the bankers and businessmen in New Orleans and Atlanta did with Huey and Earl Long, and Gene Talmadge.[21]

Next, ruling Democrats had sanctions at their disposal that could help them maintain control. Electoral fraud was but one such technique. Economic reprisals, even violence, were also a part of their political arsenal, and even while the more genteel southerners might privately abhor violence, exploiting the vulnerability (economic and otherwise) of southern whites and blacks was very much within the realm of political acceptability.

In addition, Democratic elites understood the mass psychology of poor, frustrated white southerners. Preying on, and actually perpetuating, the racial fears and hatreds of poverty-ridden, ill-educated southerners served the purpose of making this population believe that the ruling elites actually served their best interests. Indeed, this strategy continued to work until pressures from blacks inside the South, public opinion from outside, and the federal government forced overt racist practices to stop.

Widespread, extensive poverty and ruralism in the South also served to perpetuate the one-party system. The narrow-based, essentially colonial agricultural economy (grounded in sharecropping, tenancy, and credit liens) kept millions of southerners, white and black, in a perpetual state of poverty that could literally last their entire lives. The one-party system provided no opportunities or channels for significant political protest activity by impoverished citizens.

Finally, an important aspect of southern political culture also helped foster and maintain the one-party system. As Daniel Elazar and Earl and Merle Black point out, southerners traditionally have been suspicious of collective action to promote the public good.[22] In Elazar's terms, they represent both traditionalistic and individualistic types of political culture. Southerners have looked unfavorably on governmental activity or the intrusion of the public sector into individual lives. In practical, political terms, they have held low-tax, low-service attitudes toward government and politics. Only the most modest levels of collective action (in the form of public services) were to be permitted or encouraged. More abstractly, southerners have sought to constrain the scope and powers of the state; in the grand agrarian tradition of Thomas Jefferson and John C. Calhoun, they have seldom recognized the desirability, or legitimacy, of state action that transcends individual liberty or behavior.[23]

This set of attitudes acted as a disincentive for the establishment of two political parties. Where political and governmental activities were decentralized, and minimized, as was the case in the South, there was little reason to try to create a competing system of party politics. The effects of this competition might well have included enlargement or expansion of the range and scope of government. Neither was acceptable to southern elites.

One-Party Politics in the South

Since we began this chapter we have repeatedly referred to the one-party South. But in a very real sense, as V.O. Key demonstrated, the term "one-party" is misleading. One-party politics really means "no-party" politics. Since virtually all political activity takes place within the context of a single political party, the term "party" loses most of its significance, at least as it is generally understood in American politics.[24]

Key described this nonparty as, for the most part, "merely a holding-company for a congeries of transient squabbling factions, most of which fail by far to meet the standards of permanence, cohesiveness, and responsibility that characterize the political party."[25] The operative word is "faction." It refers to cliques or groupings of voters and candidates, usually with little structure and fewer organizing principles. Not infrequently, they were geographically or personality based. Some factions in southern politics, Key to the contrary notwithstanding, were remarkably long lived, particularly those existing around an exciting or dominant personality, such as Gene Talmadge or Huey Long, or populist opposition to entrenched elites. More commonly, however, factions within the southern Democratic Party were relatively transient, lasting no more than a campaign or two, since they usually had little structure or leadership and offered neither emotional ties nor incentives and rewards to voters to maintain loyalty.

Factions, to be sure, were mechanisms—in some cases, organizations— that moved political activity along. They could serve as devices for organizing voters, at least to limited degrees. They could help recruit candidates for office and provide a way for campaigns to be carried out. In a general sort of way, they could even help both like-minded and uncertain voters orient themselves toward the political process, since factions could represent different approaches to politics or at least help differentiate one set of personalities from another.

Couid it therefore be said that the factional system of southern politics represented a multiparty system, if only in miniature? The answer appears to be no. Factions were not based on proportionate systems of legislative representation, a critical variable in the maintenance of multiparty systems. Factions in the southern Democratic Party did not provide many of the functions we generally associate with political parties in this country. They were not broad aggregations of disparate population groups; in fact, rather than serving as "big tents"[26] in which a wide variety of people were welcome, they operated more as private clubs, designed to keep people out and suspicious of all except those who were members. They did not serve to integrate marginal groups into the political system. They rarely served as instruments of socialization, except perhaps to acceptable members of dominant groups. And they did not provide the educational function characteristic of American parties, which give information, cues, and assistance to voters. Nor did they provide voters with all-important symbolic attachments, the sense of belonging and self-identification, that parties can give.[27]

Thus the political party can, at least potentially, aid the individual in carrying out the responsibilities of citizenship. It can also increase his sense of belonging and attachment to the political system and raise his level of efficacy and satisfaction. But virtually none of this was true of the factional system of old style southern Democratic politics. Indeed, the emphasis was on keeping people out of politics, not on making them feel a part of the system.

The Varieties of Old Style Factional Politics in the South

One of the common misperceptions about southern politics, especially old style politics, is that it was essentially uniform, even monolithic, across the region. The "gothic politics" referred to by Robert Sherrill and others represents a kind of stereotype in which the fundamentally pernicious, undemocratic, even authoritarian politics of the states was only slightly relieved and exonerated by the parade of colorful characters who crossed the southern political stage.[28] Sometimes southerners themselves fueled the stereotype fires and even came to believe that they represented the reality of southern politics. Many southerners, and other Americans, came to believe, for example, that Robert Penn Warren's famous novel (and, later, successful movie), *All the King's Men,* represented a true portrayal of the region's typical politics.[29]

There is some truth in the portrayals of southern politics and politicians offered by Sherrill and Warren. Sherrill, in particular, writes with the hauteur of the northern liberal and seems anxious to convey his sense of the serious deficiencies and pathology of the southern political scene just after midcentury. But his exclusive focus on the exciting and colorful cast of southern demagogues leads him inevitably to his antipathy to all that is "southern" in the region's politics. It cannot be denied that the figures he wrote about loomed large in the region and sometimes dominated the southern political stage. But to leave the reader with the impression that gothic politics, as he discusses it, encompassed the whole of southern politics is seriously misleading.

Warren's analysis is far more penetrating and sensitive than Sherrill's. He does not titillate the reader through the antics of zany, reprobate southern politicians. Rather, he explores the morality of political power, especially the inevitable corruptibility of those seeking to use and aggrandize it. Indeed, in Warren's view, corruption extends beyond the actual practitioners of power (in this case, a fictionalized Huey Long–type figure named Willie Stark) to include innocents and ingenues who nonetheless associate themselves with, and are inevitably ruined by, the powerful. To Warren, an adherent of the Jeffersonian-agrarian tradition of southern politics, the centralization of authority, and its inevitable degradation, were blights on the South. But in many respects Warren's portrayal of southern politics was also misleading: Willie, Jack, Ann, and the other book characters no more represented the range of southern politics than did the cast Sherrill portrayed.

The most useful attempt to grasp the full spectrum of southern political activity in the first half of this century was provided by V.O. Key. Writing at midcentury, Key provided a way to overcome the illusion that the South was politically homogeneous.

Key categorized southern politics based on the degree of factionalism within the states' Democratic Parties.[30] He posited that states could be placed on a continuum based on the number and longevity of Democratic factions they contained. The ends of the continuum were represented, on one end, by "relative stability," and on the other by "discontinuity and impermanence." To the extent that a state had relatively few but ongoing factions within the Democratic Party, it would be placed toward the "relatively stable" end of the continuum. To the extent that there was a shifting constellation of factions, often lasting no longer than an election or two, the state would represent a discontinuous, multifactional system.

Determination of the extent of factionalism and placement on the continuum were accomplished by examining the number of candidates for the governorship, although Key used other statewide offices on occasion.[31] Key focused on the governorship because for much of this century governors in most southern states had four-year terms and could not succeed themselves. Thus for every election a host of candidates would appear in the primary, each representing particular factions. In some states, relatively few candidates would appear, and their organizational bases might carry over from one election to the next. This situation evidenced a rather stable factional system. In other states, there might be ten or more candidates for governor in the Democratic primary, and their constituency or organizational bases might change considerably from one election to the next. These states, then, represented a more fluid, and discontinuous, style of factional politics.

Unifactional States

Unifactional states were those that, over time, tended to be dominated by a single ruling faction whose organizational base was relatively stable. Two southern states—Virginia and Tennessee—were characterized by this form of factional politics. In a sense, they were exceptions to the general proposition that factional politics invariably meant discontinuous and unstable politics. Indeed, quite the opposite was true. In both states the Democratic Party was led by political machines that lasted for decades and whose legacy could still be felt long after their organizational apparatus had collapsed.

Key referred to Virginia as an oligarchy, and a "political museum piece."[32] The description was apt. The ruling faction of Virginia was composed of the heirs of Virginia's plantation class—political aristocrats and patricians who took their political ancestry very seriously. For decades the machine was headed by Harry F. Byrd, former governor and longtime U.S. senator. It was firmly embedded in the political traditions and fabric of the state. Politics in Virginia was "for gentlemen, by gentlemen." Intensely conservative, and unresponsive, even oblivious, to public needs, the machine was fundamentally concerned with ensuring its own continuity and limiting the role of government as much as possible.

The machine in Tennessee was somewhat different. It was not based on the social structure and tradition of the state but on the political skill of Edward Crump, a Memphis-based boss reminiscent of his counterparts in eastern and midwestern cities. In truth, Tennessee factional politics even before Crump frequently had the style, flavor, and scandals of old-time urban machines. Crump, who virtually ruled western Tennessee, formed a working alliance with eastern Tennessee Republicans (a small but noisy minority in the state) to control state politics. Based on a mutually satisfactory arrangement of exchanging patronage for votes, the Crump machine lasted for nearly two decades, until its final collapse in the early 1950s.

Unifactional politics did provide stability to state government, especially in Virginia. Indeed, though, machine politics in the South may have carried continuity and stability to excess. In both states machine interests were the exclusive concern of politics; the public's interest was ignored. The machines carefully controlled access to political resources and sharply regulated participation. Opposition was dealt with firmly, even ruthlessly. Factional politics in Virginia and Tennessee frequently seemed more akin to autocratic feudal baronies than to twentieth-century democracies.

Bifactional States

Louisiana, Georgia, and in some respects Alabama represented southern bifactional politics. In these states, over time, politics seemed to polarize between two major factions. In the case of Louisiana and Georgia, polarization resulted from the impact of compelling political personalities whose impact could still be felt long after they were gone. In Alabama, two factions crystallized around geographic and socioeconomic cleavages that sharply divided the state.

The dominant personalities of Louisiana and Georgia were Huey Long and Eugene Talmadge. But others were also important, especially Huey's brother Earl and Gene's son Herman. The old populist, Tom Watson of Georgia, also gave rise early in this century to a cult of personality that seemed to set the pattern for much of what happened later in the state.[33]

Long and Talmadge were very dissimilar kinds of personalities and politicians. Long, the crafty populist, fashioned a powerful organization whose goals were often aimed at improving the public welfare and attacking entrenched social and economic interests, such as banks and oil and gas corporations. His methods, however, were frequently at odds with democratic norms. Long was immensely popular among Louisiana's poor rural and small-town populations, and despised by the monied interests of New Orleans. But he built his power on more than popularity; his political organization, based on patronage and strong-arm tactics, extended deep into the parishes (counties) of Louisiana.

Watson, and especially Talmadge, were classic southern demagogues, powerful personalities who could arouse a rural, poor, ignorant population to a frenzy.[34] Unlike Long, who seldom exploited racial issues, Talmadge used race as his major political currency. He was a race-baiter of the first rank. But also unlike Long, Talmadge never built a powerful, stable, statewide organization. He lost virtually as many elections as he won. And unlike Long, he had virtually no public agenda. His interest in public office seemed to focus exclusively on railing against blacks, Atlanta aristocrats, and Yankees.

The bifactional politics of Louisiana and Georgia were fundamentally personality based. Elections, issues, and voting patterns ultimately resolved themselves into referenda on these personalities: voters were pro- or anti-Long, pro- or anti-Talmadge. As noted, this same factional pattern continued through the brother and son, respectively, who became their political heirs.

But bifactional politics in these states also exhibited important geographic and sectional cleavages, specifically an urban versus rural tension.[35] Both Long and Talmadge sought their support among the rural populations; in Georgia, the county unit system assured that rural counties would determine the outcome of statewide votes.[36] Hostility toward and suspicion of urban centers and urban life were long features of southern culture. Talmadge, in particular, raised them to an art form.

Alabama never exhibited the cult of personality in politics that these other states did, at least not until the ascent of George Corley Wallace in the 1960s. On the other hand, Alabama also demonstrated an urban-rural cleavage as well as a more fundamental sectionalism that pitted southern and northern counties of the state against the midstate, black-belt counties. This sectional dispute reflected a tension between have-nots and "big mule" industrialists and planters. Thus a kind of class-centered politics tended, over time, to polarize Alabama into two major factions. Occasionally, in fact, a major protest movement developed around a populist candidate who sought to take on the big mules. This was precisely the origin of Alabama's famous populist governor, "Big Jim" Folsom. While it has not always been recognized, protest was also the basis of the initial career of Wallace.[37]

Multifactional States

Grouping the remaining southern states under the rubric of "multifactional states" is somewhat unfair. They differed substantially in their political complexion and style. Each certainly possessed a unique political heritage and culture that defies easy comparisons with other states. On the other hand, they shared some key political similarities. Most important, factional politics, over time, were dominated neither by a single, long-lived organization nor by a bipolar alignment centered around personalities or class cleavages. Rather, each demonstrated some degree of impermanence in the constellation of factions, and it was often difficult to trace organizational or ideological continuity, over time, among them.

This argument should not be pushed too far. In these states personalities did emerge who had a significant, and in some cases long-lasting, impact on their state's politics: Jeff Davis and Hattie Carraway in Arkansas, "Pa" and "Ma" Ferguson in Texas, James Vardaman and Theodore Bilbo in Mississippi, and Ben Tillman and Cole Blease in South Carolina are just a few major figures who cast long shadows over their states. Important cleavages emerged over time, especially delta or black-belt–up-country splits. Urban-rural conflicts were also common, and on occasion divisions between social classes could be seen, especially when highlighted by the emergence of a populist or demagogic figure.

But we still refer to these states as multifactional because they did not demonstrate a consistent pattern or set of alignments in their factional behavior. Factions tended to shift, to arise and disappear from one election to the next, sometimes without giving birth to a new one whose heritage could be traced. Politics in these states, then, tended to have less stability and continuity than in unifactional and bifactional southern states.

North Carolina was the most stable of the multifactional states. Its political culture was long dominated by southern progressivism, whose cause was taken up early in this century by North Carolina's business community.[38] While it was not monolithic and the state was often wracked by sectional cleavages and disputes, factions centered in the business community provided the impetus for strong gubernatorial leadership and a more progressive approach to public policy than existed in other southern states.[39]

Arkansas was also dominated by a business elite, but it was much less cohesive or forward-looking than North Carolina's. Political discussion in Arkansas was almost totally devoid of issues, except for those rare occasions when populists such as Jeff Davis or Hattie Carraway and Sid McMath forced them onto the political agenda; the same could also be said for the demagogic Orval Faubus, who came later. Rather, business elites in Arkansas seemed more concerned with discussing the qualifications of various officeholders and seekers than with their programs; frequently this emphasis was just a smoke screen for internecine factional infighting.

Moreover, a structural nicety of Arkansas government—a two-year guber-natorial term, with a traditional (but not constitutional or legal) limitation of two terms—added to the fluid, revolving-door quality of its politics and fueled additional discussion of contenders' qualifications.

Texas had a much richer factional politics than either of these states, a reflection of its vast size and diversity. Cultural cleavages reflecting sec-tional differences—the "western" style of the panhandle, "southern" east Texas, and "Hispanic" south Texas—resulted in a host of factional align-ments. Social class and economic tensions also arose among these areas, as well as among the populism of the central hill country, cattle ranching and other forms of big agriculture in the panhandle, and the massive oil, gas, real estate, and financial interests of urban Texas. There was, at times, some permanence to a liberal-conservative ideological split that took place within the Democratic Party in Texas. On the other hand, populist-progressive-liberal factions seemed unable to take firm root and instead died out rapidly, leaving the field open to fundamentally conservative, monied business interests.

In neither South Carolina nor Mississippi did political life approach the richness of Texas. Both demonstrated some continuity of cleavage across low-country–up-country lines. But the real continuity of politics in these two states came from race and poverty. With the possible exception of Georgia and Alabama, in no other states was race the all-pervasive, monu-mental issue that it was in these two. Indeed, virtually no other public questions arose except for race; on the other hand, the crushing poverty of South Carolina and especially Mississippi obviated any real possibility that government programs to aid the needy population might be created. To push the point a bit further, the extreme poverty forced race to the center stage and allowed demagoguery and scapegoatism to flourish; both states had more than their share of both. Yet the demagogues seldom left perma-nent organizations or factional legacies beyond the attitudes they fostered in their personal followings and a feeling among subsequent politicians that they had to equal or surpass the demagogues in racial vilification.

Florida, according to Key, represented the most extreme example of a multifactional state. He referred to it as "kaleidoscopic," another apt de-scription. Extremes of geography and economic diversity underscored the tendency of Florida politics to break up into a host of impermanent factions. This tendency was further exacerbated by the extraordinary population boom of the state. Beginning in the 1920s, but really accelerating after World War II, Florida rapidly changed from the least populous to the sec-ond most populated southern state (after Texas). Rapid population expan-sion almost invariably meant a rootless, shifting, impermanent form of politics in which newcomers had few ways to orient themselves and virtually no ongoing political organizations with which to affiliate. Florida, as virtually any citizen or observer of the state quickly recognizes, may well be the last "frontier" state east of the Mississippi River; it is decidedly a post–World War II state whose political institutions and behaviors have yet to stabilize and mature. Its expansion assuredly has contributed to the instability of its politics, and continues to do so. Moreover, a unique feature of Florida government, the Cabinet, further served to fragment state politics. To give some indication of the extent to which a multiplicity of factions characterized Florida politics, we need only note that in the Democratic gubernatorial primary in 1932, there were eight candidates; fourteen in 1936; eleven in 1940; and, as late as 1960, ten. As Key points out, these were not so much elections as they were lotteries.[40]

The Consequences of One-Party Politics

This brief survey of old style, one-party politics in the South should convince even the most skeptical of observers of the considerable variety and texture of its political life. Even though serious discussion of public problems played little or no role in southern politics, there was often a great deal of both smoke and fire. The stakes involved in a gubernatorial or senatorial election, or even lesser offices, for example, mattered a good deal, because for the winning faction the rewards in terms of prestige, power, and access to public resources in the form of patronage could be considerable.

What about the consequences for this type of politics for the South? What difference did it make for the political life of the South and for the region's citizens? There were a number of very important consequences.

Most obviously, factional politics tended to foster an emphasis on personality and style over serious discussion of issues. We have already noted that dominant elites tried to keep real issues out of the political arena. But other practical considerations obtained as well. For example, let us suppose, as was often the case, that a primary election contained five, six, or more candidates. Under those circumstances, a major goal of the candidate is to differentiate himself from the others, since name recognition or some other form of visibility would be the likely key to victory or at least assure participation in a runoff; the likelihood of any one individual, from a group of political unknowns, receiving a majority in the first primary was remote.[41] Therefore, pursuing a strategy involving colorful antics, even demagoguery, rather than a bland presentation of self, or a serious discussion of issues, would likely be the best way to build a solid base of support, especially if the electorate was poor, ignorant, and largely indifferent to politics.

Factional, one-party politics tended also to split states geographically along sectional and local lines. There was often a tendency to line up behind a candidate who came from one's home county or section of the state, especially if there was little information about candidates or a lack of issues to provide voters with a sense of identification with the candidate. While undoubtedly this situation served to reinforce a sense of local pride and patriotism, it also balkanized state politics and constrained political discussion from moving much beyond local, parochial interests to include larger questions of the state's interest.

Factional politics also constrained the emergence of powerful leadership, especially in the governor's office. Frequently the governor was little more than a mouthpiece for a dominant faction or factions. Often he was in office more to protect factional interests and reward the winning faction with patronage, appointments, contracts, and other forms of state largesse than to address public issues or solve public problems. Many of the states' governors were colorless, almost invisible figures closely tied to business communities. But it is of interest that some of the nosiest, most colorful southern governors were among the least effective, from a political standpoint. Often they were isolated by other political figures who owed them little or no political allegiance; others were co-opted by dominant factions and in some cases bought off by the possibility of future financial or political gain. Still others, especially the demagogues, proved so politically inept that they failed to govern effectively.[42]

Some qualifications on the preceding paragraphs are necessary. Perhaps the most important is the subregional variation between border South and deep South states. Race and poverty were more entrenched in the deep South states than elsewhere. In a very real sense, they acted as a constraint, even a tourniquet, on the possibility of an open, responsive political system. It is no accident that southern demagogues were much more common in the deep South states than elsewhere; the poverty, the size of the black population, and the depth of racial hostility among a poor, ignorant white population encouraged the race-baiting scapegoatism characteristic of demagogic politics.

This observation was less true in the border states. In some rim states of the South, especially parts of North Carolina, Texas, and Florida, race was scarcely a concern at all. And with the exception of Arkansas, the border South states were more economically advantaged than deep South states. Thus more political possibilities arose in the border than in the deep South states. Political discussion was somewhat freer, the political agenda somewhat more complex, a willingness to mobilize state resources to provide public services somewhat stronger; Arkansas and Virginia, it should be noted, do constitute exceptions to this conclusion.

But to continue the point made before, relatively few demagogic political figures emerged in the border South states prior to 1960. Those who did appear generally did so later on, with the onset of the civil rights movement and its southern reaction, called massive resistance. Moreover, while political leadership in the South in the first half of this century was notoriously weak, some able chief executives emerged, such as Charles Aycock, Austin Peay, and Millard Caldwell, to name only three. These individuals, as well as others who could be mentioned, were governors in border South states; there is not a comparable list from deep South states.

Unfortunately, the operative phrase earlier is "political possibilities." While border South states were freed from some of the constraints of their deep South neighbors, public officials seldom took advantage of them. The actual performance of government, in terms of how it aided the population, was scarcely better than in deep South states. While this book does not examine governmental outputs, even a cursory examination of such matters as per capita expenditures for public education, colleges and universities, public health programs, and other social services indicates that southern states in the first half of this century ranked at or near the bottom of all the states.[43] Moreover, there were only marginal differences in the level of public services between border and deep South states, differences that can probably be accounted for by the relative wealth of the states and a somewhat less oppressive political culture, rather than by fundamentally different approaches to politics and public issues.[44]

The Isolation of the South

These were not the only consequences of the one-party Democratic system in southern politics. Ultimately, perhaps the most important was the contribution it made to the political isolation of the South throughout the first half of the twentieth century. Indeed, without this isolation the South would not have been able to exist as a unique political region for so many decades.

A major payoff for the South at the end of Reconstruction was that the federal government withdrew its armies, which had been propping up blacks and Republicans in public office. As carpetbaggers withdrew and northern liberals turned their attention elsewhere, southern Democrats were left to handle internal affairs as they wished. Southern elites had carte blanche to deal with, or solve racial matters in their own way. Southerners were fearful late in the nineteenth century that armies could always be sent back, but by the turn of the century the message from Washington was that the federal government would not interfere with southern racial policies. Indeed, in *Plessy v. Ferguson,* it actually endorsed them.[45]

But the problem for the South was that there was never any assurance as to how long Washington would look the other way or allow overt discrimination to continue under the guise of "separate but equal." Especially was this true whenever public outcries over lynchings occurred, as for example happened in 1915 when a Georgia mob executed Leo Frank, an innocent white Jew. Even the most unreconstructed southerner recognized that while the federal government and northern media might not pay too much attention to the mutilation and lynching of an occasional black, they would not long sit idly by if whites were also victimized. Moreover, the possibility existed, remote though it may have seemed early in the century, that the Supreme Court would reverse *Plessy* or that a president would choose to attack segregation through executive orders.

Congress provided the necessary safeguards for the South, especially after the institutionalization in Congress of the seniority system early in the twentieth century.[46] For the first few decades of the twentieth century, while southern senators and representatives were building up seniority, no assaults on segregation in the South occurred. Even during the progressive administrations of Teddy Roosevelt and Woodrow Wilson, Washington paid little attention to Jim Crow laws or practices; Wilson, in fact, actually strengthened segregationist practices within the federal government.

The liberalism of the New Deal began to raise potential problems for the South, however, since it was conceivable that federal relief programs desperately needed in the South might require a modification of southern racial practices. There was even danger to southerners inside the White House. While the president seemed relatively indifferent to the political problems of southern blacks (although not their economic plight), Eleanor Roosevelt and some of the liberal advisers around the president were not.

To be sure, there were sufficient numbers of southerners inside Congress to ensure that the president would have to bargain with them for passage of New Deal programs. This situation alone might have provided southerners with the necessary congressional power to block possible assaults on segregation. But by the 1930s, southern representatives and senators had built up sufficient seniority to acquire important chairmanships in Congress that would enable them to control the flow of legislation and, hence, of public policy. Indeed, southerners continued in the following decades to amass enormous seniority, chairmanships, and corresponding power: by 1960, southerners held 65 percent of major Senate chairmanships and 60 percent of key ones in the House.[47]

The extraordinary hold by the South on the legislative life of the nation was a direct result of the one-party system. Because of it, senators and representatives were virtually assured of reelection as long as they wished. Many often ran unchallenged in primaries. It was much more common that they retired from office, or died while serving, than that they were defeated in an election. As any "right-thinking" southerner could understand, it was much safer for the South to continue to return the same senators and representatives to Congress and exploit the seniority system than to send a new face and risk giving up a potentially powerful chairmanship or other committee slot.

All these factors ultimately isolated the South, in a political sense, from the rest of the nation. It allowed a single position to exist on the critical issue of race, at least in terms of how the South represented itself to the nation at large. And because of the power of southern members of Congress, no intervention into the internal, racial life of the region was possible. Indeed, even after the 1954 *Brown* decision,[48] southerners in Congress blunted any real or meaningful intervention by the federal government for some years thereafter.

Thus the one-party system served to build a political wall around the region, one that allowed Jim Crow laws and practices to continue. The cost to the South was disassociation with the larger political life of the nation; the South could agree to, or accept, no national programs that required even partial dismantling of the Jim Crow system. From the southern standpoint, the one-party system thus became the ideal mechanism to use for its last stand. It proved to be remarkably resilient. The wall did not come tumbling down, and the political isolation of the South did not end, until it was assaulted from within and without during the civil rights movement.

Old Style Politics and Southern Society

What role, then, did old style, one-party southern politics play in the life of the region? The answer is that politics was for the few, not the many. For most of the southern population in the first decades of this century, politics was at best irrelevant and at worst pernicious. It offered nothing to blacks except exploitation and subjugation. For whites it offered occasional entertainment, but ultimately disappointment and disillusionment. Neither political leaders nor political structures possessed the capacity or the will to act on their behalf. Rather, they cynically sought their support by pointing at (black and/or Yankee) scapegoats or offering promises they could not deliver. Some leaders tried, in good faith; sometimes, most notably in North Carolina, some promises were actually kept. But for the most part in the South, political organizations and institutions failed to recognize or respond to public needs, and leaders neither offered a positive vision of the future nor tried to seek it.

Ultimately, the hopelessness and despair of much of southern life were reflected in the extraordinary political apathy that pervaded the region. It is of interest that in fictionalized portrayals of southern life (for example, the novels of Faulkner and the stories of Flannery O'Connor), the characters, many of whom are dirt poor, ignorant, frustrated, and desperate, did not look to politics as a way out of the misery of their lives, or even for help. Some found help in religion; some in alcohol; some in violence; some in a combination of these. But politics, for these all-too-real fictional characters, was for other people, people different from them. Politics in the South did not speak to the needs of the people most in need and those in the worst circumstances.

In fact, in many respects politics made matters worse, not better, for the southern population. Our concern, it will be recalled, is with the impact that southern politics had on the traditional regional problems of race and poverty. Old style politics ameliorated neither. Indeed, it exploited, and therefore exacerbated, racial issues. Because of racial and prevailing norms on social questions, politics did little to alleviate the crushing burden of southern poverty either. Thus, if we are to examine the causes of serious southern problems during the first decades, even first half, of this century, we are forced to list politics prominently among them. It would be quite some years before politics could be moved to the list of southern solutions.

Part II

Toward the Two-Party South:
The Rise of
Southern Republicanism

4

Out of the Closet: Southern Republicans and Presidential Elections

I do not know where he got them [1,100 South Carolina votes for Calvin Coolidge, 1924]. I was astonished to know that they were cast, and shocked to know that they were counted.
—Senator Cole Blease, South Carolina Democrat, 1924

Senator Cole Blease's mock surprise and feigned anger are typical of the conventional wisdom many traditional southerners had about the presence of Republicans in their region. From the late 1890s until sometime after World War II, it was difficult to find people who admitted to being Republicans or voting for GOP candidates. There are even historical anecdotes of reasonable credibility in which average southerners, stumbling across a genuine Republican, are astounded that the specimen resembled other human beings.

And yet Republicans, Republican votes, even Republicanism,[1] were present in the South. Their strength and numbers were not consistent throughout the region; sometimes they could barely be seen, while in other areas they were actually a voting majority and could elect Republicans to office. Because of the history and tradition that developed in the South about Republicans during and after Reconstruction, however, they were loathed by dominant Democrats. As a result, many southerners chose to ignore the Republicans around them.

How extensive were Republicans in the South between 1900 and 1994?

79

If they were not simply an optical illusion or figment of the imagination, where and how powerful were they? Does the rapid growth of the Republican Party in the South since 1960, and its frequent success at the polls, indicate that a sharp break with the past has been made? In other words, has the contemporary South become truly a two-party system, in contrast to the one-party structure dominated by Democrats that characterized southern politics for much of this century?

These are essential questions, fundamental to an understanding of how much traditional southern politics has changed during this century. Answers to these questions are a necessary, but not sufficient, part of the evidence concerning the existence of a new southern politics. In this chapter, we shall look at traditional Republicans in the South, focusing most of our attention on presidential Republicans. In the next chapter, our concern will be with Republicanism at the state and local level and the extent to which its rise demonstrates the possible emergence of a two-party system.

A New View, and the Conventional One

These two chapters will argue that Republicanism in the South was somewhat more widespread than is often recognized. It was strong in only a few places, but it was present in many. This crucial point has not always been fully understood. One reason is that many southerners and students of the South have not believed that Republicans lived in the region, so naturally they did not find many. Also, many true Republicans declined to identify themselves publicly and have only "come out of the closet" fairly recently.

Moreover, Republicanism might well have become a potent force throughout much of the South decades earlier than it did were it not for a series of historical events and circumstances that hindered its development considerably. Its present viability, then, does not necessarily represent a real break with the past but rather is the outgrowth of an evolutionary process, perhaps an inevitable one.

But Republicanism in the contemporary South has not quite developed as many previous students thought it might, and there may well be outer limits to its ultimate regional strength. This outcome, along with some structural problems, raises serious questions about the long-term prospects for southern Republican dominance. Consequently, we may have reason to question just how much politics in the contemporary South can be characterized as a two-party system.

Still, what of the traditional views? For much of this century were not most voting southerners "yellow dog Democrats"? This term, apparently Georgian in origin, refers to citizens who would vote for the Democrats no matter who was running, even if it was an old yellow dog. The answer is that in most places in the South, Democrats were consistently elected to virtually all offices. Even if all voters did not behave so blindly as the term "yellow dog Democrat" implies, allegiance to the Democratic Party was, over time, remarkably constant. And if we look only at public utterances and professions of political faith, we might wonder whether there were any Republicans at all in the eleven southern states.

But this point is exactly the rub. The evidence will show that Republicans, and Republicanism, were present, although certainly not uniformly across time and space. Sometimes, and in some places, they were just a mirage, sometimes merely a faint zephyr, and occasionally strong enough to uproot dominant Democrats.

Thus private political attitudes and behaviors did not always match public ones. As Will Rogers noted more than once, not infrequently southerners voted for the Democratic presidential candidate but secretly hoped the Republican would win and were happy when he did. Something else, then, was operating at election time besides historical attachments, unthinking sentimentality, or blind party loyalty. Perhaps it was a willingness (even if unarticulated or furtive) to respond to the Republican candidate and/or his message and to chart a different, even independent, political course. The result, astonishing as it may have been to Blease and other southern Democrats, was that significant numbers of votes were cast for Republicans, especially but not exclusively at the presidential level, and these were actually counted.

An interesting research question requiring investigation is the extent to which the form or mechanics of voting may have influenced Democratic loyalty and voting totals. In times of limited literacy, when many voters marked ballots corresponding to the donkey symbol of the Democratic Party rather than because they read the names of candidates, or when the secret ballot did not exist because voters had to mark their ballots more or less in full view of local officials and fellow citizens, or when electoral fraud was common, the option of voting Republican may not have existed. It may well be that with the introduction of voting machines in the South, higher rates of literacy, and a more-or-less protected secret ballot, it was both psychologically and practically easier for a citizen to vote Republican. Data to investigate these matters may not exist (although there are related studies of the effect of election mechanics on voters),[2] but it is worth some informed speculation.

We shall not, however, be able to engage in such speculation here. Let us instead begin our survey of southern Republicans, focusing first on their place in regional political life at the turn of the century.

Republicans in the Late-Nineteenth-Century South

At the end of the Civil War, there were relatively few Republicans in the South, and these were relegated to a few areas, most of them in the high-lands. The Democratic Party had been the ruling one of the Confederacy, and Republicans were seen as the party of Lincoln, of the Union, of the enemy, of defeat. When the South surrendered in April 1865, there was a great deal of ambiguity, even fear, in the region about its future, politically and otherwise, as southerners waited to see what terms the North would impose on them.

And yet, as the stillness settled over Appomattox Courthouse, it was not necessarily obvious that the Republican Party would become the ruling party of the region. Mixed signals came from Washington about the politi-cal future of the South. Lincoln's own plans for the postwar South were apparently moderate; had he survived, and been able to resist the Radicals, the political history of the South might have been much different.

Whatever Lincoln might have done was undone at Ford's Theatre. After his death, he was succeeded by Andrew Johnson, a Tennessean and for-merly a conservative Democrat who had joined Lincoln in 1864 in order to ensure that Republicans remained in the White House. Johnson's approach to the South after the war was also a moderate one. He only insisted that southerners "organize loyal state governments, renounce the right of seces-sion, repudiate Confederate debts, and ratify the Thirteenth Amendment abolishing slavery."[3]

Johnson also wanted to pardon southern leaders to create a sense of goodwill and end the acrimony. Perhaps most significant, Johnson wanted to establish rule by conservative elites in the South. He felt their dominance would ensure stability and loyalty. He further wanted to avoid any kind of radical race policy that might allow former slaves to assume positions of responsibility or in other ways be any more disruptive of the traditional social order in the region than the war already had been. In political terms, Johnson's plans meant that the political leaders of the postwar South would be Democrats, the heirs of the Bourbons, not Republicans.

In designing these plans, Johnson acted alone, ignoring Congress, im-portant groups, members of the Republican Party, and much of the northern media that wanted a more punitive course of action against the South. He may have misunderstood their strength and mood; in fact, they were in-censed by his moderate course and eventually brought impeachment pro-ceedings against him. The result was a victory for Radical Republicans, both in and out of Congress. Even though Johnson was not convicted, he ceased to be the architect of federal policy toward the South. Instead, the

Radicals in Congress directed it. The result has become known as the period of southern Reconstruction.

Contemporary scholarship has shown that Reconstruction was neither as harsh nor as radical as many southerners at the time believed.[4] Nonetheless, it did serve the purpose of providing an opportunity for mythmaking about the period and the creation of a long tradition (still carried on in some areas and in some social circles) of bereavement and grief about the loss of the glorious, noble South, its citizens, and its way of life. These myths and traditions have served southerners and southern politicians well as a means of self-identification and self-justification. They assuredly perpetuated the siege mentality characteristic of the region until well into the twentieth century.

Reconstruction did not revolutionize the southern social order. In reality, it never approached the extremes of the Radical architects behind it or of the southern complaints about it. From a political standpoint, however, Reconstruction did have very important effects. Republicans replaced Democrats in public office. These included carpetbaggers from the North, scalawags (an imprecise term referring to southerners, including Democrats, willing to serve with Republicans), and blacks.

The Republican governments, the first of which did not appear until 1868, were propped up by the Republican-dominated federal government, northern Republican money, and the presence of an army of occupation. Without question these imposed Republican governments, staffed in part by former slaves, were the prime causes of the antipathy and resentment southerners felt toward the GOP for so long afterward.

Even as the Republican governments were established, the seeds of their destruction were sown. Conservative Democrats, the heirs of the antebellum ruling elites, were unwilling to sit idly by, powerless. Instead, they began the so-called redemption of the South through which the Republican governments were eventually discarded.[5]

In some areas of the South, Redeemers cooperated with Republicans at first and later challenged them successfully in elections: by 1870, Democratic Redeemers were in control of Tennessee, North Carolina, and Georgia. In other areas, Democrats resorted to violence and intimidation in order to restore Democratic rule. This period saw the origins of the Ku Klux Klan, which had as a major purpose the violent disruption of political activity by blacks, Republicans, and other Reconstructionists.[6]

Northern interest in Reconstruction was fully on the wane by the mid-1870s, and by 1877 all of the southern states had been fully "redeemed." It was in the spring of that year that the great bargain was struck which not only signaled the end of Reconstruction but established the southern primacy of the Democratic Party, and sealed the fate of the Republican Party for decades.

The so-called southern strategy of the national Republican Party did not begin in 1964, as is sometimes supposed, but following the election of 1876. It started with the disputed election of Republican Rutherford B. Hayes over Democrat Samuel Tilden. In order for Hayes to win enough Electoral College votes to be named president (Tilden won the popular vote), Republicans had to solicit southern electors. In exchange for their support of Hayes, southerners were promised an end to Reconstruction. The result was not simply a withdrawal of the army of occupation but a recognition by northern Republicans that southerners would be allowed to govern themselves.

There were several consequences. One was the final collapse of any remnants of the imposed Republican governments that, as we have noted, were virtually defunct by then anyway. Remaining northern political support of southern blacks was largely abandoned. Thus southerners could solve racial issues undisturbed by Washington; as a result, blacks promptly became, if not again slaves, then second-class citizens. And it meant that southern Democrats were permitted to control the region's federal patronage (money, projects, appointments) even under a Republican presidency. This arrangement served further to solidify the power of entrenched conservative Democrats in the South, because they were able to control the distribution of public goods and resources.

Despite the election of 1876 and the end of Reconstruction, Republicans did not completely disappear from the political scene. While outbreaks of violence against, and persecution of, blacks were not unusual in the years immediately following the Reconstruction period, similar outbursts did not occur against white Republicans. Conservative Democrats feared that were they to move rapidly and vigorously against Republicans, the bargain following the 1876 election might be forfeited, the armies might return, and Reconstruction would be renewed. Also, there was no particular need to persecute Republicans. Those who remained were essentially powerless or proved cooperative with Redeemers and other emerging conservative, largely business-oriented Democratic elites.

By 1896, populism was essentially dead as a major protest movement in the South. The dominance of a conservative Democratic Party assured that there was no room in southern politics for populism or for Republicans either. Indeed, while the GOP began to atrophy even as Reconstruction was drawing to an end, by the dawn of the new century it had virtually disappeared as a major political organization. But an anomalous situation persisted: Republican candidates could still (although not always) be found on the ballot, and voters cast ballots for them, especially at the presidential level. While the party was merely a historical relic, clearly Republicanism was not.

Republicans in This Century: V.O. Key and His Followers

V.O. Key provided a systematic overview of Republican fortunes in the South between the end of populism and the conclusion of World War II.[7] He noted the difficulty in finding bona fide Republicans in the South and especially emphasized the absence of Republican organization, at least any organization that resembled a political party.

Key castigated southern Republican Party leaders at state and local levels, arguing that in too many cases they were bureaucratic or palace politicians more concerned with maintaining their own positions, going to national conventions, meeting visiting dignitaries, and influencing patronage than in building a party organization, recruiting voters, and contesting elections. While he felt that the situation was changing by the end of the 1940s, there were still too many Republican leaders who treated their work in the party as a hobby instead of a serious business. Without identifiable, healthy organizations, Key felt, Republicans could not become a vital political force in the region.[8]

In spite of these difficulties, Key did succeed in identifying three persistent groups of Republicans. The first, and the most common, were the so-called presidential Republicans. These "political schizophrenics,"[9] as he termed them, were almost all registered Democrats who would seldom, if ever, admit to voting Republican. But in the existential moment, occurring every four years, of voting for president, they would likely vote for the Republican nominee. However, when it came to state and local offices, they usually reverted to the Democratic Party.

Key admitted that it was difficult to calculate how many presidential Republicans there were in the South. But he devised a rough approximation by comparing the number of votes received by a Republican presidential candidate with those for a Republican governor or senatorial candidate; the "excess" of votes for president would give an approximation of the number of presidential Republicans.[10]

There are some problems with this mode of calculation. It ignores the fact that there is a tendency for more voters to cast ballots for president than for other offices, thereby inflating the number of presidential Republicans. Also, sometimes (especially but not exclusively in the deep South) there were no Republican candidates for governor or senator, either because none had been nominated[11] or because no contest occurred for either seat in the presidential election year. Under these circumstances, it would not be possible to calculate the number of presidential Republicans voting.

In spite of these difficulties, Key did account for the continuing presence of often substantial votes for Republican presidential nominees in the region. Using this method of calculation, he concluded that Texas, Arkansas, and Florida had the most presidential Republicans because they had relatively weak Democratic loyalties, few attachments to old South myths about Republicans, and (particularly in the case of Texas and Florida) fairly diverse populations, including recent immigrants from the North and Midwest. Tennessee, North Carolina, and Virginia had relatively few presidential Republicans because at least in parts of those states Republicans actually constituted vital political forces and did not need to remain in the closet. The deep South states had the fewest presidential Republicans, not because the Democratic Party was well organized or disciplined but because anti-Republican feelings ran deepest there.

The next group of Republicans identified by Key were mountain Republicans.[12] These were individuals who lived in isolated areas of southern highlands: the Ozarks of Arkansas, the northern counties in Alabama and Georgia, and the Smokies of eastern Tennessee, western North Carolina, and southwestern Virginia. The important point about mountain Republicans is that they were not closet or schizophrenic Republicans. Rather, they openly declared themselves Republican and voted not only for Republican presidential candidates but for those contesting state and local offices as well. In some areas, they won with surprising frequency.

Mountain Republicans for the most part had inherited their partisanship from previous generations. In some cases, their manifestation of Republicanism preceded the Civil War. In certain highlands areas, white farmers had little in common with their low-country, black-belt fellow citizens. Many actually opposed both slavery and the economic system it engendered. When the political and economic forces leading to the Civil War began to crystallize and quicken, they opted not to participate and stayed with the party of Lincoln.

In some instances, mountain Republicans actually opposed secession. The most famous case was in Winston County, in mountainous northern Alabama. There the farmers established the Free State of Winston, when, in 1861, they withdrew from Alabama in protest over the state's secession. Winstonians desired to be neutral during the coming war, but an incursion of Confederate cavalry shortly after their declaration of independence put an end to the insurrection.[13]

The incident reveals the extent of political independence in this mountainous region and the population's desire not to participate in what it saw as a "rich man's war." Moreover, the fact that their independence was not recognized by fellow Alabamans left deep scars which nearly one hundred years later still had not healed. These feelings helped perpetuate the existence of mountain Republicans, as well as other feelings of political revolt that persisted in the area. Comparable examples occurred in other mountainous areas of the South.[14]

Not all mountain Republicans had their roots in armed insurrection, but all had them in political protest or revolt stemming from issues leading up to the Civil War. They consistently retained their identity as Republicans and just as consistently repudiated Democrats. In eastern Tennessee, mountain Republicans regularly elected representatives to the state legislature. It was their strength, in fact, that enabled them to bargain with Ed Crump in Memphis as he established his statewide machine in Tennessee. In western North Carolina and southwestern Virginia, the Republican strongholds were similarly potent, and while they did not always send representatives to state government, they were frequently able to frighten the ruling Democratic hierarchy, including the Byrd machine in Virginia. In North Carolina, mountain Republicans might have been more successful except that the legislature managed to keep them well gerrymandered to minimize their potential strength.

The last major group of Republicans identified by Key were black Republicans.[15] Their presence in the GOP was solely a historical legacy, a result of their presence in the Republican Party during Reconstruction.

There were not many black Republicans. The vast majority of blacks had no partisan affiliation, for they were not able to participate in politics. Nor did white Republicans in the South necessarily welcome blacks: their attitudes on racial questions did not differ significantly from those of their Democratic fellow southerners. During much of this century, southern Republicans were plagued by the question of whether they should be lily-white or black-and-tan. In some states, such as South Carolina, white Republican leaders seemed to recruit only middle-class blacks such as doctors, lawyers, and college presidents. In others, a few blacks were permitted to join as tokens in a symbolic recognition of the Republican heritage as the party of Lincoln. In Mississippi, by contrast, blacks actually formed the backbone of the Republican Party for a period during the 1920s, 1930s, and into the late 1940s. As late as 1947 one estimate held that about 85 percent of the Republican vote cast in Mississippi came from blacks, although this only amounted to fewer than 5,000 individuals.[16]

As Key correctly observed, for the most part the Republican Party in the South did not speak to the needs of black citizens. Unless one was middle class or especially interested in attending national party conventions, there was no reason for blacks to seek membership in the party. Moreover, beginning in 1932 in the North, and by 1936 throughout the nation, blacks moved away from the Republican Party and switched to the Democratic Party of Franklin Delano Roosevelt.

Yet some residual attachment to Republicanism persisted among some southern blacks until well after World War II. Often these were older, conservative, middle-class individuals who were frequently the focus of criticism by fellow blacks. On occasion, even today, a southern black Republican will campaign for public office.[17] Their success record, however, has been virtually nil, for they have trouble building winning constituencies in either black or white populations.

Key's followers Alexander Heard and Donald Strong were able to identify several other important aggregations of Republican voters in the South during the first half of this century. One of these consisted of scattered counties that had deep populist roots and because of disillusionment with the Democratic Party never turned to it as did many other populist enclaves. Examples include Sampson County in eastern North Carolina, Chilton County in central Alabama, and two parishes in north-central Louisiana, one of which was actually the birthplace of Democrat Huey Long. These counties were surrounded by areas that voted strongly Democratic and on the basis of demography resembled their neighbors. Yet they persisted in maintaining their traditional independence and fighting spirit. They voted heavily for Republican candidates, presidential and otherwise.[18]

Another important group of southern Republicans were those who tended to oppose the Democratic Party because of traditional religious or nationalistic inclinations. Germans in south-central Texas were liberals opposed to slavery and secession, and during the Civil War they were treated by Confederates in much the same way as mountain Republicans. Originally Democrats, many switched to the Republican Party before the Civil War and retained that affiliation subsequently.

Some counties in coastal North Carolina and Georgia also exhibited long-term Republican tendencies. In the former case, it was probably because residents were economically distinct from the plantation counties found elsewhere in the lowlands, and they also enjoyed considerable federal patronage from Republican administrations. In Georgia, the explanation appeared to be religious: the strong Lutheran and Scots Presbyterian communities in the areas around Savannah apparently felt antipathy toward the heavy Catholic influence in the Democratic Party, especially in the election of 1928.[19]

Another source of Republicanism that Heard was able to identify at the close of the first half of this century was immigration into the South. It was especially noticeable in Texas and Florida. We shall return to this point later on, but it is of interest that the impact of immigration of the growth of southern Republicans was felt at a relatively early date.[20]

Urban areas were a final source of Republican strength in the South. Donald Strong first identified these centers of Republican concentration by examining the vote for Dwight D. Eisenhower in 1952 and again in 1956. It turned out that while the general did very well throughout the South, the core of his appeal was in urban counties. By working backward, Strong was also able to show that the roots of Eisenhower's appeal actually extended in these urban counties to 1936.[21]

Strong does not suggest or imply that all southern urban counties by 1956 were majority Republican, either in registration or in votes cast. Nonetheless, it was clear that in many, if not most, urban areas, especially mushrooming suburbs, significant Republican growth was developing. In 1956, in a number of these counties a majority of votes were actually cast for Eisenhower. These counties, moreover, were not limited to border South states (where they might well have been anticipated) but included urban counties in Alabama, Louisiana, and Georgia as well.[22]

Key, Heard, and Strong studied Republicans at a time when it appeared that significant cracks were beginning to appear in the solid South. The Dixiecrats had just completed their revolt from the Democratic Party, with consequences still uncertain in the early 1950s. Moreover, it was clear that immigration, urbanization, and changing economics and demography were laying the groundwork for a breakdown of traditional Democratic affiliations and a possible growth of Republicanism. These scholars were sensitive to the changes occurring around them, and they speculated on what they might mean for the future of Republicanism in the South.

Key was deeply concerned about the organizational weakness of the Republican Party in the South. Reflecting a view of parties that permeated much of his other scholarly writing, Key felt that without vigorous leadership and solid organizational work, the party would continue to flounder in the region. He feared that there were not enough party members willing to do the very basic, difficult, time-consuming, often tedious tasks needed to construct effective party organizations at the grass-roots level. He even pointed to national Republican leaders who showed more interest in developing state and local organizations than did many southern party officials and members.

On balance, however, Key was hopeful about Republican prospects in the region. Reflecting his views on normative democratic theory, Key was convinced of the need for a vigorous two-party system in the South, because only through the give-and-take of a true two-party system would the region begin to face squarely its serious racial and other problems.

Key's hopefulness was underscored by the work of Heard and Strong. All felt that increasing levels of education and economic development would aid the growth of Republicanism. These efforts included a diversification of the southern economy, a rise in commerce and industry, and a declining reliance on staple-crop agriculture. Their feeling was that most of the growth of the southern Republican Party would occur among white, middle-class urbanites and suburbanites of the border states. Traditional southern antipathies toward Republicans were a little less severe in the border South than in the deep South. More fundamentally, all felt that middle-class urban and suburban whites would desert the Democratic Party as it became more liberal on social and economic issues. As urbanization continued and agriculture declined in relative importance, and as a blue-collar southern industrial workforce emerged, they would enter the Democratic Party. This connection, in their minds, would force a liberalization of the party that would be unacceptable to many middle-class white southerners.

At the same time, the Democratic Party would become somewhat more hospitable toward blacks. The result would be that a new, southern Republican Party would attract disaffected Democrats living largely in urban areas, especially of the border South, as well as middle-class white immigrants who brought their Republicanism along with their furniture.[23]

The South Votes for the President: 1900–1960

Between 1900 and 1952, there were only two occasions when the Republican presidential candidate won a majority of the votes cast in at least one southern state—1920 and 1928.[24] Otherwise, Democratic presidential nominees consistently won the region during these years, underscoring the region's nickname as "the solid South" (see Table 4.1 a–d).

In 1920, Tennessee, a border South state with a long history of Republican strength, cast its electoral college votes for Warren G. Harding, the Republican candidate and eventual winner. In an otherwise triumphant Republican year, the party failed to crack any of the other ten states, although in Alabama, Arkansas, Florida, Louisiana, and Virginia, Harding did manage to get more than 30 percent of the vote; in North Carolina, he got more than 40 percent.[25]

The presidential election of 1928 was unusual because the Democratic Party nominated the first Roman Catholic for the presidency, Governor Al Smith of New York. The combination of Catholicism, antiprohibitionism, and New York proved unattractive to the conservative, dry, Protestant South. Five border states—Florida, North Carolina, Tennessee, Texas, and Virginia—all voted for Herbert Hoover, the Republican nominee. Arkansas may well have also, except that the Democratic vice-presidential nominee, one Joseph T. Robinson, was from that state; still, Hoover got 39 percent of

Table 4.1a

Southern Presidential Vote, 1900–1912 (percent)

Region	1900		1904		1908		1912		
	Republican	Democratic	Republican	Democratic	Republican	Democratic	Republican	Democratic	Progressive*
South Total	29	69	23	72	26	70	10	73	15
Deep South									
Alabama	35	61	21	73	24	71	8	70	19
Georgia	28	67	18	64	31	55	4	77	18
Louisiana	21	79	10	89	12	85	5	77	12
Mississippi	10	88	6	91	7	90	2	89	6
South Carolina	7	93	5	95	6	94	1	96	3
Mean	20	78	12	82	16	79	4	82	12
Rim South									
Arkansas	35	64	40	55	37	57	21	55	17
Florida	19	71	22	68	22	63	8	70	9
North Carolina	46	54	40	60	46	54	12	59	28
Tennessee	45	53	43	54	46	53	24	53	22
Texas	31	63	22	72	22	74	9	73	9
Virginia	44	55	37	62	38	61	17	66	16
Mean	37	60	34	62	35	60	15	63	17

*Theodore Roosevelt.

Table 4.1b

Southern Presidential Vote, 1916–1932 (percent)

Region	1916		1920		1924		1928		1932	
	Republican	Democratic	Republican	Democratic	Republican	Democratic	Republican	Democratic	Republican	Democratic
South Total	20	76	30	68	24	71	40	60	16	85
Deep South										
Alabama	22	76	32	67	25	70	49	51	14	85
Georgia	7	80	29	71	18	74	43	57	8	92
Louisiana	7	86	31	69	20	76	24	76	7	93
Mississippi	5	93	14	84	8	89	17	82	4	96
South Carolina	2	97	3	96	2	97	9	91	2	98
Mean	9	86	22	77	15	81	28	71	7	93
Rim South										
Arkansas	29	66	39	59	29	61	39	60	13	86
Florida	18	69	31	62	28	57	57	40	25	75
North Carolina	42	58	43	57	40	59	55	45	29	70
Tennessee	43	56	51	48	44	53	56	44	33	67
Texas	17	77	24	59	20	74	52	48	11	88
Virginia	32	67	38	61	33	63	54	46	30	69
Mean	30	66	38	58	32	61	52	48	24	76

Table 4.1c

Southern Presidential Vote, 1936–1948 (percent)

Region	1936		1940		1944		1948		
	Republican	Democratic	Republican	Democratic	Republican	Democratic	Republican	Democratic	Dixiecrat**
South Total	16	84	21	82	34	76	22	77	37
Deep South									
Alabama	13	86	14	85	18	81	19	—***	80
Georgia	13	87	15	85	17	82	18	61	20
Louisiana	11	89	14	86	19	81	18	33	49
Mississippi	3	97	4	96	6	94	3	10	87
South Carolina	1	99	4	96	5	88	4	24	72
Mean	8	92	10	90	13	85	12	32	62
Rim South									
Arkansas	18	82	21	78	30	70	21	62	17
Florida	24	76	26	74	30	70	34	49	16
North Carolina	27	73	26	74	33	67	33	58	9
Tennessee	31	69	32	67	39	61	37	49	13
Texas	13	87	19	81	17	71	25	65	9
Virginia	29	70	32	68	37	62	41	48	10
Mean	24	76	31	74	31	67	32	55	12

**Strom Thurmond.
***Harry Truman was not on the ballot.

Table 4.1d

Southern Presidential Vote, 1952–1960 (percent)

Region	1952		1956		1960		1900–1960 Totals	
	Republican	Democratic	Republican	Democratic	Republican	Democratic	Republican	Democratic
South Total	46	54	44	50	43	50	27	68
Deep South								
Alabama	35	65	40	56	42	57	26	70
Georgia	30	70	33	66	37	63	22	72
Louisiana	47	53	53	40	29	50	21	73
Mississippi	40	60	25	58	25	36	11	78
South Carolina	49	51	25	45	49	51	11	82
Mean	40	60	35	53	36	51	18	75
Rim South								
Arkansas	44	56	46	53	43	50	32	63
Florida	55	45	57	43	52	49	32	61
North Carolina	46	54	49	51	48	52	38	59
Tennessee	50	50	49	49	53	46	42	55
Texas	53	47	55	44	49	51	27	67
Virginia	56	43	55	38	52	47	39	58
Mean	51	49	52	46	50	49	35	61

the vote in Arkansas.[26] Hoover received 49 percent of the vote in Alabama, but did badly in most of the rest of the deep South.

The 1928 election was also one of the first in which the Republicans tried to implement a southern strategy for winning the election. They recognized early that Smith might well prove unacceptable to southern voters and campaigned to secure the votes of disaffected southern Democrats. They were only partially successful. As I.A. Newby observed, just because Smith was unacceptable to the border South did not mean that those states were ready to turn Republican or that a two-party system was imminent there or in other parts of the region.[27] Attachment to the Democratic Party, even in the somewhat less doggedly Democratic border South, did not end merely because Smith was the nominee.

Conceivably things might have been different in the South, and the effects of Hoover and the southern strategy more noticeable, if the Depression had not ensued, followed by Franklin Delano Roosevelt, the New Deal, and later World War II. Separately and collectively, these forces pushed southerners solidly back to the Democratic Party for the next four presidential elections.

It was not until 1948 that a serious challenge was again mounted against the Democrats. This time it came not from the Republicans but from internal dissension within the Democratic Party itself. It was the first real breakdown in the solid South, as four deep South states—Alabama, Louisiana, Mississippi, and South Carolina—voted neither for Harry S Truman nor Thomas E. Dewey, but for the States' Rights Democratic Party, better known as the Dixiecrats.

A break with the national Democratic Party by some southern states had not been unexpected. In 1944, the national party had begun to pay attention to civil rights following race riots in Detroit and New York in the summer of 1943, as well as the discovery of discrimination against blacks outside the South, including in the armed forces.

Moreover, President Truman, from the border state of Missouri, surprised and disappointed many traditional southerners. He did not share their views on race or on other southern issues. Early in 1948, he pressed for enactment of legislation following the recommendations of the Commission on Civil Rights, which he had previously appointed. In the same year he issued an executive order forbidding racial discrimination in the armed services.[28] The Democratic Party also included a liberal civil rights plank in its 1948 platform, one that Truman seemed to embrace as he launched his reelection campaign.[29]

Truman's actions were viewed with a great alarm in many parts of the South. It appeared to southern traditionalists that what they most feared was about to happen—the end of the bargain of 1877. The reason was that a president sympathetic to civil rights, as well as a civil rights plank in the Democratic platform, might force a federal presence in what had been essentially purely southern affairs since 1877. Accordingly, in a number of southern states discussion took place about what to do at the Democratic convention if a strong civil rights plank were adopted and whether an alternative to Harry Truman could be found. When the convention did adopt strong civil rights language, the Mississippi delegation and half the Alabama delegation walked out. All the remaining southern delegates except thirteen of the thirty-two from North Carolina supported Senator Richard B. Russell of Georgia for the presidential nomination; those thirteen stayed with Truman.[30]

The delegates who walked out, as well as others, met in Birmingham, Alabama, in the middle of July. They called themselves "States' Rights Democrats," although the press promptly called them "Dixiecrats." They nominated for president, Governor J. Strom Thurmond of South Carolina, and for vice-president, Governor Fielding Wright of Mississippi, in addition to adopting a "declaration of principles."

Thurmond and Fielding won three of the deep South states with substantial majorities, and the fourth with a large plurality. Georgia was the only deep South state that the Dixiecrats failed to carry, because Senator Richard Russell chose to stay with Truman and the regular Democrats.

The Dixiecrats were less successful in the border South. In Tennessee, Boss Ed Crump of Memphis initially opposed Truman. However, by 1948, he was having problems of his own, and the moderate wing of the party (headed by Senator Estes Kefauver) eventually prevailed, supporting Truman and ultimately causing Crump's downfall. In North Carolina and Virginia there was fear of a Republican rather than Dixiecrat takeover, and in both states the Democratic Party (including the Byrd machine in Virginia) worked hard for Truman. In Arkansas, Florida, and Texas the stridency of Dixiecrats seemed to have little appeal and offered few incentives to abandon the Democratic, or even the Republican, party; indeed, in these states Dewey actually outpolled Thurmond.[31]

The emergence of the Dixiecrats represented a threat to continued Democratic hegemony in the South. The results of the 1948 presidential election indicated that southerners had become divided on their loyalty to the Democratic Party. There was no agreement, based on the relative strength of the three candidates, on whether the South should abandon the party, turn Republican, or establish a third presidential party. But there was certainly no firm evidence that the South was ready to become Republican. The most that could be said was that there was an indication, most notable in the deep

South, that the unwavering allegiance southerners had maintained to the national Democratic Party was badly shaken.

The 1952 presidential election again pointed to the dilemma of southerners. Adlai Stevenson represented what seemed to be a decidedly liberal turn for the Democrats. The urbane, literate, cosmopolitan (and divorced) nominee had little appeal for southerners. On the other hand, many southerners believed that the federal government was bluffing on civil rights, for Truman had not pushed it during his second administration. And they knew that they still had their congressional delegations to protect them.

It is interesting to speculate on what southerners might have done in 1952 if the Republicans had nominated Dewey again or, more probably, the conservative Robert Taft of Ohio. Instead, the GOP nominated the popular war hero, General Dwight D. Eisenhower. He was regarded as something of a moderate, with an affiliation for the South, having grown up in Texas and Kansas.

Eisenhower, in spite of his personal popularity, did not provide southerners with a needed incentive, or reason, to fully abandon the Democratic Party. As Table 4.1 shows, he was only able to capture four border states: Florida, Tennessee, Texas, and Virginia; to these he added Louisiana in 1956, when Stevenson was again the Democratic nominee. Indeed, his overall electoral performance in southern states, as measured by the percentage of the vote he received, was scarcely better for his second term than for his first.

Eisenhower's failure to "realign" the South suggests the degree to which traditional political affiliations and attachments persisted within the region. Following the split in the Democratic Party in 1948 and its nomination of Stevenson in the next two elections, there appeared to be every reason why southerners would eventually abandon the Democrats once and for all. The problem for the Republicans was that while a popular moderate Republican might be acceptable in some border states, he still was not acceptable in the heart of the South; only a renegade Democrat could win there. What the Republicans needed was a candidate who could appeal both to dissident Democrats and emergent Republicans; Eisenhower could not do so. Alternatively, had the GOP somehow co-opted Dixiecrats in 1952 and 1956 as the Democrats had the populists in 1896, the modern political history of the South might have been a good deal different.[32]

There is an additional point, as well. On May 17, 1954, the U.S. Supreme Court announced its *Brown* decision, declaring segregated dual school systems unconstitutional.[33] One of the effects of this decision in the South was to bring traditional southerners together, in a sense resurrecting their siege mentality, as they sought to stave off what they thought would be a federal assault on their racial practices and other southern ways. But, as Newby and others show, their efforts had to be confined within the southern Democratic Party, for it had been the South's primary defense for nearly eight decades. The early and mid-1950s were no time for the South to adopt Republicanism; rather, Democratic wagons had to be circled, to make a last stand.[34]

But the failure of Eisenhower and the Republicans to appropriate southern presidential politics in 1952 and 1956 should not be overemphasized. Political culture, traditions, and habits die very hard, especially in the South. Another way of viewing these results is that Eisenhower received some 8.3 million votes in the South,[35] and won four, later five, states. Following the breakup of the solid South in 1948, border South states began to abandon the Democratic Party with some regularity. They had, after all, less attachment to the Democratic Party than did deep South states. They had also been among the states willing to chuck the party in 1928. These elections offer further evidence for the points established earlier in the chapter: there was significant Republicanism in the South prior to 1960, and were it not for some unique historical developments in the second quarter of this century, it is likely that Republicanism in the South might have flowered more rapidly than it did, assuredly at the presidential level.

If 1948 represented the first real sign of a breakup in the solid South and the 1950s a transitional period in southern presidential politics, the 1960 election was the last hurrah for traditional southern affiliations with the Democratic Party at the presidential level. It was the last time a liberal, non-southern Democrat won a substantial popular and Electoral College vote in the region.

At the outset of the presidential campaign in 1960, John F. Kennedy's claim on southern votes was insubstantial. A Boston Catholic, member of the "eastern establishment," graduate of Harvard, Massachusetts representative and senator, he had a moderate to liberal congressional record. Very little in his background suggested that he could win in the South.

But Kennedy was aided by a number of factors. His primary victory over Hubert Humphrey in the border state of West Virginia proved that he could win in a traditional, relatively conservative state. Shortly after his nomination, he defused the Catholic issue by his highly publicized, forthright appearance before a ministerial association in Houston. Most significantly, he had Lyndon B. Johnson as his vice-presidential running mate. Johnson, the Senate majority leader, was a man of considerable popularity and prestige not only in his native Texas but throughout the South. He was well-known to be a protégé of the "Dean" of the Senate, Richard B. Russell of Georgia. Kennedy had added Johnson for a variety of reasons, not the least of which was that he would ensure Kennedy's victory in Texas, a state crucial to his successful campaign.

Kennedy was also assisted in that the Republican nominee, Richard M. Nixon, had never been especially popular in the South. Nixon seemed not to be well known there, as he had largely been under wraps in the Eisenhower administration and the general had made no effort either to anoint or support him as his successor. Moreover, Kennedy seized the campaign agenda from Nixon by pointing to defense deficiencies and a "missile gap" that allegedly had developed during the Eisenhower-Nixon years; these were topics appealing to hard-line, traditional southerners during a period of intense cold war with the Soviet Union. Additionally, it was by no means clear to southerners that Kennedy and the Democrats represented a greater civil rights problem to the South than did Nixon and the Republicans. The GOP had adopted a pro–civil rights plank, and both candidates seemed to take a moderate, supportive, but go-slow approach to civil rights issues.[36]

In 1960, only three border South states voted for Nixon—Florida, Tennessee, and Virginia. Nonetheless, the outcome was actually closer than these results indicate. Kennedy won the popular vote by less than 500,000: he received 5.2 million votes in the South, and Nixon, 4.7 million. He won the crucial state of Texas by less than 50,000 votes out of 2.2 million cast. And the core of his popular support actually came in the deep South states, including a 175,000-vote edge in Catholic Louisiana.[37] Nixon received 43 percent of the vote regionwide but actually won a slight majority of the popular vote in the six border South states (3.71 million to Kennedy's 3.69 million).[38] Thus, even though Kennedy won the South in 1960, it was really the end of the line for the southern Democratic presidential express. With very idiosyncratic exceptions, it was not to be seen again.

Several tentative conclusions can be briefly drawn from this discussion of presidential elections in the South between 1900 and 1960. Most obviously, even a cursory glance through Table 4.1 reveals that Republicanism was clearly present in the South prior to 1960. It was most apparent in the border South states, even from very early in the century. But prior to 1932, it was noticeable in the deep South states as well, especially Alabama, Georgia, and Louisiana. Twice prior to the 1950s it actually broke through, resulting in state victories for Republican presidential nominees.

The period 1932 through the end of World War II represented a setback for Republicanism at the presidential level. But as early as 1944, a Republican resurgence could be found in the border South. It accelerated in 1948 and reached substantial strength by the 1950s. The same resurgence was not noticeable in the deep South states prior to the 1950s, undoubtedly because of the presence of a Dixiecrat alternative in 1948. And while these deep

South states seemed more reluctant than their border South neighbors to give up their affiliation with Democratic presidential nominees, by the time of the Eisenhower candidacies even these states began to vote in significant numbers for him. By 1960, the same trend continued: it was just a matter of time before deep South states followed their border South neighbors in abandoning the Democratic nominee in favor of someone else, including even a Republican contender.

The South Votes for the President: 1964

Southerners were somewhat ambivalent about the candidacy of Lyndon Johnson in November 1964. On the one hand, there was tremendous pride in having a Texan occupy the White House, ready to run again. He was the first southerner since Woodrow Wilson to be president. Southerners seemed to relish the way in which Johnson and his wife Lady Bird established a southern and Texan ambiance in his administration.

But Johnson had also publicly endorsed the unfinished legislative program of the martyred Kennedy and had worked assiduously to assure the passage of the 1964 Civil Rights Act as the great monument to him. Many analysts felt that it was precisely because Johnson was a southerner that he was able to convince enough state officials and members of Congress, including many from the border South, to endorse and support the legislation for it to become law.

At the sidewalk level, however, many southerners, especially in the deep South, seemed to resent Johnson. The term "traitor" was heard applied to him. By the summer of 1964, the civil rights movement was in high gear. Never before had regional, national, and international attention to the problems of southern blacks been more rapt. Traditional southerners understandably felt besieged, and even dismayed, as they saw their fellow southerner in the White House aiding in the assault on southern racial practices.[39]

The Republican Party and its presidential nominee, Senator Barry Goldwater of Arizona, designed a campaign strategy that overtly sought to appeal to disaffected southerners as well as others throughout the country who thought the Kennedy-Johnson brand of liberalism had gone far enough. They took an unyielding, intensely conservative position on issues such as foreign policy, communist expansion, and national defense. On domestic issues, including civil rights, Goldwater and the Republicans resurrected John C. Calhoun and the Dixiecrats' states' rights positions. They argued that too much power and authority had been centralized in the federal government and it was time to move the balance back toward state and local governments.

Goldwater himself had voted against the Civil Rights Act of 1964. While he was a member of the National Association for the Advancement of Colored People (NAACP) and claimed to be supportive of the civil rights goals of blacks, he was unwilling to use federal authority to force desegregation on the South. From the standpoint of traditional southerners, Goldwater's message seemed to be a reaffirmation of the bargain of 1876.

The Goldwater candidacy received very substantial support in the deep South (see Table 4.2 a and b). He easily won all five of the states. He received an incredible 87 percent of the vote in Mississippi, and his weakest showing was in Georgia, where he still got 54 percent. Goldwater did not win any of the border South states. Nonetheless he received well over 40 percent of the vote in all but Texas (Johnson's home state), where he got 37 percent. But he nearly won Florida and Virginia, which gave him 49 and 46 percent, respectively.

Although Goldwater was soundly trounced at the national level, many analysts thought the southern results represented a very favorable trend for the GOP. For the first time since 1948, deep South states totally abandoned the Democratic Party. And while the border South appeared, on one level, to vote completely differently from the deep South, in fact the strong Goldwater showing in all the states but Texas indicated that even a fellow southern Democrat could not undo the nascent regional base of the GOP. The possibility that the South might even become majority Republican, at least in presidential politics, began to be considered seriously. And certainly the results of the election indicated to Republican planners and politicians that investing in a southern strategy could provide very generous returns.

A Detour for Southern Republicanism: 1968

By 1968 the political mood in the country had changed a good deal. Whereas in 1964 it seemed hopeful and progressive, in 1968 it was disillusioned, disquiet, cynical. Traditional values, mores, and attitudes were under attack, both on and off college campuses. The nation seemed sharply divided over international events, especially the Vietnam War, and national politics, including civil rights and Johnson's expensive efforts to build the Great Society through his War on Poverty. Political rhetoric had grown shrill, and not since the Great Depression had such deep cleavages marked the population. Perhaps the climax came in the spring 1968, when President Johnson, sensing unhappiness and bitterness in the land, announced he would not seek reelection.[40]

Johnson's renunciation of the White House shredded the Democratic Party. At their 1968 convention in Chicago, Democrats nominated Vice-

Table 4.2a

Southern Presidential Vote, 1964–1980 (percent)

Region	1964 Repub-lican	1964 Demo-cratic	1968 Repub-lican	1968 Demo-cratic	1968 American Indepen-dent*	1972 Repub-lican	1972 Demo-cratic	1976 Repub-lican	1976 Demo-cratic	1980 Repub-lican	1980 Demo-cratic	1980 Indepen-dent**
South Total	55	46	32	29	40	71	28	44	56	50	47	3
Deep South												
Alabama	70	—	14	19	66	72	26	43	56	49	47	1
Georgia	54	46	30	27	43	75	25	33	67	41	56	2
Louisiana	57	43	28	24	48	66	29	46	52	51	46	2
Mississippi	87	13	14	23	64	78	20	48	50	49	48	1
South Carolina	59	41	38	30	32	71	28	43	56	49	48	2
Mean	65	36	25	25	51	72	26	43	56	48	49	2
Rim South												
Arkansas	43	56	31	30	39	69	31	35	65	48	48	3
Florida	49	51	41	31	29	72	28	47	52	56	39	5
North Carolina	44	56	40	29	31	70	29	44	55	49	47	3
Tennessee	45	56	38	28	34	68	30	43	56	49	48	2
Texas	37	63	40	41	19	66	33	48	51	55	41	3
Virginia	46	54	43	33	24	68	30	49	48	53	40	5
Mean	44	56	39	32	29	69	30	44	55	52	44	4

*George Wallace.
**John Anderson.

Table 4.2b

Southern Presidential Vote, 1984–1992 (percent)

Region	1984 Republican	1984 Democratic	1988 Republican	1988 Democratic	1992 Republican	1992 Democratic	1992 Independent*	1964–1992 Totals Republican	1964–1992 Totals Democratic
South Total	62	38	59	42	44	42	14	52	41
Deep South									
Alabama	61	38	60	40	48	41	11	52	38
Georgia	60	40	60	40	43	44	13	50	43
Louisiana	61	38	55	45	41	46	12	51	40
Mississippi	62	37	60	40	50	41	9	56	34
South Carolina	64	36	62	38	48	40	12	54	40
Mean	62	38	59	41	46	42	12	53	39
Rim South									
Arkansas	61	38	57	43	36	53	11	48	46
Florida	65	35	61	39	41	39	20	54	39
North Carolina	62	38	58	42	43	43	14	51	42
Tennessee	58	42	58	42	43	47	10	50	44
Texas	64	36	56	54	41	37	22	51	45
Virginia	62	37	60	40	45	41	14	53	40
Mean	62	38	58	42	42	43	15	52	43

*H. Ross Perot.

President Hubert Humphrey as the presidential candidate, amid tremendous acrimony and violence. The Republicans, meanwhile, met in Miami and chose for their nominee Richard Nixon, the political phoenix who beat out his rivals George Romney, Nelson Rockefeller, and Ronald Reagan.

Nixon had openly courted southerners for the nomination. He understood fully the implications of the 1964 election, both for the South and the nation. In perhaps his most famous move, he reached an agreement with Senator Strom Thurmond of South Carolina, who had become a Republican in 1964, under which Nixon would receive southern Republican support for the nomination in exchange for increasing military spending, appointing strict constructionists to the Supreme Court, reducing federal pressures on school desegregation, and selecting a southerner for vice-president (Spiro Agnew of Maryland was the eventual choice).

Had the 1968 presidential election been a two-man race, Nixon would undoubtedly have done very well in the South. He assuredly would have been able to retain and expand his 1960 support in border South states and make significant inroads in the deep South by capturing the Goldwater "white-backlash" constituency. There was little to suggest that Hubert Humphrey had solid appeal anywhere in the region, especially not in the deep South.

Unfortunately for Nixon, his southern strategy was undermined by the serious presidential bid of Governor George Corley Wallace of Alabama. Wallace ran a modern populist campaign aimed at the disaffected American "little man" who was confused and angered by the turmoil of contemporary American life. He ran against bureaucrats, against Wall Street, against the media, against social engineers, against Democrats and Republicans.

Wallace's personal magnetism and dynamism made him an appealing candidate. He was especially, but not exclusively, popular in the South, where he remained a folk hero to many traditionalists who recalled the way he stood up to the federal government and civil rights activists, resisted desegregation, and sought to retain traditional southern ways. His critics scoffed that he was a Dixiecrat demagogue and opportunist. But to both Democratic and Republican strategists looking toward the South, it was clear that he was a force to be reckoned with.

In fact, as election day approached, much of Wallace's early national support eroded. But in the South he remained strong. He won five states: Alabama, Arkansas, Georgia, Louisiana, and Mississippi. In a three-man race he won more than 60 percent of the vote in both Alabama and Mississippi. In every southern state except Florida, Texas, and Virginia he received over 30 percent of the vote. He clearly inherited and expanded the Goldwater constituency of four years earlier.

The Democratic nominee did very badly in the South. Humphrey won only Texas, getting 41 percent in a state rent by political schisms. He received more votes than Nixon only in Alabama, Mississippi, and Texas, although in the two deep South states Wallace virtually doubled their combined total. Only in border South states Florida, Texas, and Virginia did Humphrey win more votes than Wallace. In all the southern states Humphrey got only 29 percent of the vote: he did slightly better in the border South (thanks to Texas), 32 percent, than in the deep South, 25 percent.

In spite of the fact that Wallace stole the deep South Goldwater constituency from him, Nixon did not have a weak showing. He won five states: Florida, North Carolina, Tennessee, and Virginia in the rim South, and South Carolina in the deep South; Republican Strom Thurmond was a boost to his candidacy there. Only in the deep South states of Alabama, Louisiana, and Mississippi did Nixon receive less than 30 percent of the vote, but of course Wallace swamped both Humphrey and him there. Nixon got 32 percent of the southern presidential vote: 25 percent in deep South states, and 39 percent in border South states.

Under the circumstances, this was not a bad southern Republican presidential outcome at all. Wallace clearly hurt Nixon in the deep South, but in the border South the Republican "drop" from 1964 percentages was fairly small: Florida and Tennessee, about 7 percentage points; North Carolina, 4; Virginia, 3. In Texas, it actually rose 3 points. Only in Arkansas was there a substantial drop, 12 points.

Thus by 1968 the transformation of southern presidential politics begun in 1948, and climaxing in 1964, was actually complete. By 1964, it was clear that the deep South had left the Democratic Party at the presidential level. In 1968, it was equally clear that even if border South voters would not support a Dixiecrat, they preferred a Republican over a Democrat. The issue raised, then, was no longer whether the South was solid for the Democrats, but whether, at the presidential level, the Democratic Party had any real future in the region at all.

But wasn't Wallace, or his modern Dixiecrats, a possible alternative for the South? Couldn't the region have abandoned both parties, in favor of a third? The answer to both questions is no. Wallace's appeal was primarily in the deep South. By election day 1968, his support waned outside of this area. There was no evidence that he had a sufficiently large regional base to create a permanent third party that had a realistic chance of dominating the southern states.

Moreover, the Republican Party shrewdly took a lesson from history and began to co-opt much of the Wallace position on civil rights, the Supreme Court, and states' rights, just as the party had moved after 1960 to adopt much of the old Dixiecrat position on these issues. By 1972, this process was largely complete. Thus the party had almost eliminated the need for southerners to support a Dixiecrat; they could feel perfectly at home in the GOP, whether they were deep or border South residents. And, of course, the problem of Wallace for the Republicans eventually became moot, anyway: Arthur Bremer took care of that on a Maryland parking lot in the spring of 1972, when he shot and paralyzed the Alabama governor.

The result of these developments was that following the 1968 election, southerners and the Democratic Party had completed their parting of the ways in presidential politics. In contrast, the Republicans had found a home. The following presidential elections in the South were largely the "natural" outcome of what happened in regional presidential politics during the 1960s.

Playing Out the Southern String:
Presidential Elections, 1972–1996

The resounding triumph of Richard Nixon in 1972 throughout the South was a thorough affirmation of the growth of presidential Republicanism in the region. It was also both a decisive repudiation of the Democratic Party and its liberal candidate, George McGovern, and an indication of the disarray into which the party had fallen.

By the time of the November election, Nixon was rapidly approaching the zenith of his "imperial presidency."[41] The Democratic Party, convulsed with reform, had restructured itself to ensure the inclusion of blacks, women, and young people in such a way as to affect its ideological position. The result was that it moved sharply to the left and seemed deliberately to ignore its moderate and conservative wings.

This strategy was not designed to appeal to southerners. One of its critical effects was to alienate many traditional public officials, county chairs, party leaders, and organizations in the South and elsewhere who were essential to creating the grass-roots support needed to conduct a successful presidential campaign. They felt McGovern and the national Democratic Party had bypassed them completely in its reorganization.

The effect of their estrangement from the party, as well as their view of McGovern as unacceptable and unelectable, was that throughout the South they refused to work on behalf of their own nominee. Many, in fact, chose to back Nixon, and it was not unusual throughout the South to find "Democrats for Nixon" organizations composed of public officials, party functionaries, and private citizens who were prominent Democrats.

Nixon's national victory was the most one-sided presidential election in American history up to that time.[42] In the South, McGovern was completely routed. Nixon won every state, usually by more than landslide proportions. His greatest victories came in the deep South: Alabama, Georgia, Mississippi, and South Carolina each gave him more than 70 percent of the vote, and Louisiana was not far behind (66 percent). In the border South, his performance ranged from 66 percent in Texas to 70 percent in Florida.

As might have been predicted from the 1968, there was virtually no difference in results between the border and deep South states in 1972. The GOP presidential candidate swept both areas handily. Perhaps the major outcome of the 1972 election, as far as southern presidential politics were concerned, was the decreasing difference in voting patterns between rim and deep South states. The South was once again solid—only now it was for the GOP.

On the surface, the prospective election of 1976 looked totally different from four years earlier. A debased Richard Nixon had resigned the presidency in summer 1974, as a result of his involvement in the Watergate scandal. He was replaced by Gerald Ford, who was appointed vice-president following the departure of Spiro Agnew, who also left in disgrace. It was the Republican Party, rather than the Democrats, who seemed in total disarray and popular disfavor this time.

Jimmy Carter was the Democratic presidential nominee. He had been governor of Georgia from 1970 to 1974, where he had distinguished himself for his progressive views on race relations following the flamboyant, erratic Lester Maddox. Carter captured the nomination by taking advantage of modification of rules within the Democratic Party, which allowed a greater role for public officials and party leaders in the nomination process, an increased reliance on presidential primaries as a way of selecting party nominees, and assiduously working to build strong grass-roots organizations that would help him capture those primaries.[43]

Carter deliberately ran as an outsider, someone not a part of the Washington establishment. He claimed not to be tainted by the excesses of the imperial presidency and the corruption of the Nixon-Agnew administration. In contrast, the Republican nominee, President Ford (who had to withstand a substantial challenge on the right from California Governor Ronald Reagan to secure the nomination), was saddled with a host of problems. He was unfairly portrayed by the media as a bumbler. Although he occupied the office, he had been appointed, not elected, to it. He carried the burden of a disgraced administration and had exacerbated his problem by pardoning Nixon. Thus he had none of the advantages of incumbency and, more important, no legitimate claim on the White House. For Ford and the Republicans, victory seemed all but impossible.

For our purposes, the interesting point is not that Carter won all but one of the southern states. Rather, it was that Ford did as well as he did. In the border South states, he won Virginia, nearly captured Florida and Texas, and had a strong showing in North Carolina and Tennessee. Only in Arkansas did Ford do badly, getting only 35 percent of the vote. Overall, he averaged 44 percent in these states.

In the deep South states, Ford also had a credible showing, averaging 43 percent of the vote. While he could not approach the level of Goldwater in 1964, he did much better than Nixon had done in 1968. He came very close to winning Mississippi. Only in Georgia—Carter's home state—did Ford do poorly.

Thus, although the GOP lost the White House in 1976, the results of the election did not constitute a serious setback for the Republican Party in the South, at least as far as presidential politics was concerned. Table 4.2 a and b shows that differences between the rim and deep South states continued to be slight, as in 1972. More important, the bedrock of southern support for Republican presidential candidates appeared not to have slipped in 1976, in spite of the heavy cloud hanging over the party, Ford's tenuous claim on the White House, and the presence of a native son Democratic candidate. Democrats may have won this battle, but clearly Republicans held their own.

The next three presidential elections constitute overwhelming evidence of the claim that Republicans secured on the southern vote; 1992 proved to be a small exception, and it may be that 1996 is a larger one, suggesting that no party has a lock in the region, in spite of obvious GOP presidential strength.

Any thoughts held by the Democratic Party that their fortunes might improve at the presidential level after 1976 were quickly dashed in 1980. Even the presence of a serious third-party challenge in 1980 by Representative John Anderson could not stop the Republican presidential juggernaut, for Anderson seemed to bleed votes from the Democratic nominee, incumbent President Carter, rather than the Republican candidate, as had happened in 1968.

Southerners loved the 1980 Republican nominee, conservative Ronald Reagan, former governor of California. The verities he espoused and homilies he gave were dear to the hearts of southern traditionalists: strong families, simple religious fundamentalism (more convincing than Carter's mystical appeals to love and faith), old-fashioned patriotism, a powerful military, a hard-line anticommunist foreign policy, conservative economic policies, and maintenance of traditional social institutions and roles. To the new middle-class white southerner and the transplanted white-collar northerner or midwesterner now living in a new southern city or suburb, he promised tax relief, an end to inflation and budget deficits, and policies geared to help them. For southern blue-collar industrial workers and farmers, he promised an "America first" policy and better times ahead.[44]

Reagan's appeal, popular disapproval of President Carter, and frustration over such foreign problems as the Iranian hostages, produced a Republican victory. Carter won only a single southern state, his native Georgia, but even there the GOP nominee gained 8 points over the 1976 total. Anderson captured enough votes in the South, especially the border states, to cost the president victory. Leaving Georgia out of the calculations, Carter averaged only 47 percent of the vote in the deep South and 44 percent in the border South.

Reagan did not score an overwhelming popular victory in the South, but it was a convincing one. Outside of Georgia, he got 50 percent of the vote in the deep South states and 52 percent in the border states. In each state he ran ahead of both 1976 and 1968 totals, the other two presidential elections involving peculiar circumstances. If he did not reach Nixon's 1972 levels, it was no sign of GOP political weakness. Carter was, after all, an incumbent president and a native southerner; for there to have been a rout would have required a more anemic Democratic Party than existed and a candidate completely unacceptable to southerners.

The rout did occur in 1984. The Democratic Party this time was badly divided, as Vice-President Walter Mondale withstood a serious challenge from Senator Gary Hart. Reagan, the incumbent, chose largely to ignore Mondale and campaigned against the Carter legacy. Even this slight against their fellow southerner did not drive southern voters toward the Democratic nominee. They supported Reagan handsomely.

Reagan carried the South, and nation, in a landslide.[45] He received 62 percent of the vote throughout the South. Only in Tennessee did he receive less than 60 percent. He showed equal strength in both deep and border South states.

The presidential election of 1988 was more of the same, as far as the South was concerned. The Republican nominee, Vice-President George Bush, won 59 percent of the vote in deep South states and 58 percent in the border states. While his totals were not quite as impressive as Reagan's, very few candidates had ever reached that level of popularity. Moreover, he was consistently strong throughout the South, showing no weakness in any state in the region. He captured all of the region's electoral votes, as Reagan had before him.

This latter point is crucial as the South faces future presidential elections. The heart of the Bush victory came in the eleven southern states. The region supported him over Governor Michael Dukakis of Massachusetts more strongly than any other region of the country, whether measured by percentage of the popular vote or number and percentage of Electoral College votes.[46]

This level of support suggests that the South may have reached the point where it was once again politically out of step with the rest of the country in presidential politics. Whereas earlier in the century, it had supported Democratic presidential candidates more strongly than other regions, it did so in 1988 with the Republican candidate.[47]

Whether there was a movement toward a more fluid, uncertain electoral result, and a loosening of the Republican lock on the southern presidential vote, can be seen by viewing the results of 1992 and anticipating those of 1996, as the Democratic Party sought to find more acceptable presidential candidates not only in the South but in the nation at large.

On the surface, the 1992 election looked like the Republican lock on the South had been broken. The Democratic Party nominated Governor Bill Clinton of Arkansas for president and Senator Al Gore Jr. of Tennessee for vice-president. While not abandoning key constituencies or principles of the national party, candidate Clinton rapidly moved it toward a more centrist posture.

Given the moderating influence of Clinton, and two candidates from the border South, it is clear that the national Democratic Party in 1992 put together its own southern strategy aimed at capturing the White House after a twelve-year hiatus. Strategists argued that unless Clinton won at least some southern states and made significant inroads toward attracting the party's traditional base among the white middle class, which it had lost to the Republicans during the Reagan and Bush years, the Democrats were doomed to another defeat.

In the early 1990s, Democratic prospects were not good.[48] President Bush, triumphant in 1988, had increased his standings in the polls following what was seen as a success in the Persian Gulf War. Some polls had Bush's approval ratings hovering around 90 percent, virtually unheard of figures previously. Democrats seemed dispirited and even more internally quarrelsome than usual. The GOP looked unbeatable in 1992.

A number of factors coalesced over a period of roughly twenty months to turn matters around. Clinton proved to be an energetic, appealing candidate. He—like Carter before him—ran as an outsider, willing and able to relieve Washington gridlock. His folksy, earnest ways and moderate but optimistic political message helped him overcome doubts about his character, in the South and elsewhere.

In addition, President Bush squandered his vast political standing. Following the Persian Gulf War, the president seemed to lack focus and direction; his administration wandered aimlessly and seemed out of touch with increasingly hostile attitudes that citizens—including southerners—felt toward Washington generally and his administration particularly. He was regarded as lacking vision, a concept he himself seemed not to grasp. His attempt to run as a Texan seemed artificial and disingenuous.

A further aid to the Democrats was the entrance, departure, and reentry of Texan H. Ross Perot into the presidential race. Perot, a peppery billionaire, ran a populist campaign designed to attack Washington insiders and gridlock; the irony that he was in reality a prominent Washington player and a billionaire and could hardly play the populist card convincingly seemed not to bother the public. His populism—a very different kind from the abrasive, negative, nativist populism of George Wallace and, later, Pat Buchanan—was based on a simplistic can-do, let's-fix-it approach to public issues and a clarion call to citizens to take back their government from the politicians.

Perot seemed as much motivated by a desire to see President Bush defeated as to advance his own candidacy. He largely ignored Clinton. The effect of his campaign was electrifying. Disaffected Democrats and Republicans (the evidence is that there were more of the latter than the former) and independents flocked to his campaign. Perot won no states but captured 19 percent of the vote nationally, the highest third-party percentage since Bull Moose–Progressive Teddy Roosevelt's 27 percent in 1912. His total in the South was 14 percent, although he won nearly 20 percent in Florida and 22 percent in Texas.

Table 4.2b shows the full result of the 1992 presidential election in the South. Governor Clinton won two deep South states—Georgia and Louisiana—and two border South states—Arkansas and Tennessee, residences of the presidential and vice-presidential candidates, respectively. Most revealing, however, is to compare Democratic votes in 1992 with those of 1988. They are virtually identical: in 1988 Democrats, with a liberal northeastern presidential candidate, won 42 percent of the southern vote, and in 1992, with a moderate southern governor as the nominee, they again managed only 42 percent. While these figures are somewhat higher than the 38 percent they received during the Reagan landslide of 1984, they are not as high as they were in 1980, when the Democrats lost the White House with another southerner (47 percent).

Conversely, George Bush won only 44 percent of the southern vote. He did, however, capture seven southern states (Alabama, Mississippi, South Carolina, Florida, North Carolina, Texas, and Virginia), including the two big southern prizes, Texas and Florida. In several states—notably Florida and North Carolina—his winning margins were razor-thin, about 100,000 (out of 5.3 million votes cast) in the former, and 20,000 (out of 2.6 million) in the latter.

What do these data tell us about the Republican lock on the southern presidential vote?[49] Perhaps the most revealing statistic is that 14 percent of southerners voted not for a Dixiecrat alternative but for a rich populist running as an outsider. John Anderson, another non-Dixiecrat third-party candidate, managed only 3 percent in his 1980 bid. The conclusion seems inescapable that southerners found the plain-speaking, folksy Perot nearly as appealing as voters everywhere else; their concern with gridlock and Washington insiders (viewed as a combination of the Perot and Clinton votes totaling 56 percent in the South) were not too far behind national figures (62 percent).

Bush, whose southern performance was nowhere near his 59 percent in 1988, nonetheless won a plurality of the southern popular vote (44 percent) and a clear majority of the southern states. And this plurality was achieved in spite of the fact that he ran a weak, ineffective, aimless national campaign, was beset by a terrifically dynamic southern Democrat who ran a flawless campaign, and an eccentric but appealing independent whose goal was to unseat the president, and faced a public increasingly disenchanted with the status quo in Washington. While the Republicans may well have run out of steam nationally, their performance in the South indicated that even in an off GOP year they could continue to expect to win, even if not by the extraordinary totals of 1984 and 1988. Moreover, if one assumes that a third to a half of the Perot vote came from disaffected Republicans and he had not been on the ballot, it is entirely likely that Bush's totals would have approached, even exceeded, 50 percent of the popular vote in the South.

Conversely, the Democrats' 1992 southern strategy was only partially successful. They won only four southern states, two of which were the home states of their candidates. Georgia, with thirteen Electoral College votes, was their biggest prize, but Clinton won with only a 14,000 vote plurality out of 2.3 million votes cast. True, Democrats had broken the lock that the GOP had held on the South since 1980. But with the exception of the very close votes in Florida and North Carolina there was little evidence that a Democratic southern strategy would, at least in the short run, produce significant results for the party in the region.

Yet conditions and circumstances can change, as they did in 1996, and perhaps again in 2000. President Clinton, after a lackluster first two years in office, by the start of election year 1996 had improved his political standing considerably, in the South and elsewhere. Republicans, in spite of their overwhelming congressional victories in 1994, seemed unable to consolidate their gains; indeed, the national party was fraught with division, ranging from the overexposed (and increasingly disliked) U.S. House of

Representatives Speaker Newt Gingrich (of Georgia); a massive influx of Christian Coalition conservatives into the party (by early 1996 this group was the single largest identifiable group within the national GOP);[50] a divisive Republican primary season that ended with the success of Senate Majority Leader Bob Dole, who subsequently resigned from the U.S. Senate to try to move his presidential campaign forward; a national Republican political agenda increasingly seen as out of touch with the majority of Americans; and the long shadow of Pat Buchanan, whose nativist and culture-war rhetoric made mainstream Republicans uncomfortable.

In short, the southern outlook for Democrats is not hopeless. While it is unlikely they will return to the success they had for most of this century, they might be able to divide and conquer, pick off a few southern states from the Republicans, and keep their presidential chances alive in the region. This outcome assumes, of course, that the party continues to nominate acceptable moderates, not northeastern liberals. And it further assumes that the Republicans, now burdened with the responsibility of governance instead of merely playing an opposition role, remain fractured, nominate lackluster candidates, and continue their politics-as-public-morality way of presenting themselves. As this book is written, they show every evidence of doing so; the result may well be to undermine the remarkable gains they made in southern presidential politics during the 1980s.

Conclusions

What can we conclude about southern voting patterns for presidential candidates? Several observations are in order at this point.

Most obviously, the South has largely abandoned the Democratic Party at the presidential level. There is a real question as to the ability of Democratic presidential candidates to win a majority of votes in the southern states. The term "solid South" has come full circle, but in an inverted way: it now refers to the region's support of conservative Republican candidates, just as it formerly supported Democratic candidates.

In this connection, Republican success in the South has largely paralleled that of Republican success throughout the nation. Only six times since 1944 have the Republicans lost the presidency (1948, 1960, 1964, 1976, 1992, 1996). In three of those years a majority of the southern states voted for the Democratic candidate, although in 1964 the region was badly split, with six border states for Johnson and five deep South states for Goldwater. In 1992, only four southern states gave Clinton a plurality (and none but Arkansas a majority). In 1996, two southern states gave Clinton a plurality (Florida and Tennessee) and two a majority (Arkansas and Louisiana). In the future, some southern states may buck this national trend. Up to now, however, as the nation as voted, so has the South. Indeed, the more recent the presidential election, the more emphatic has been the South's support of the national trend.[51]

Looking backward over the twentieth century, it is fair to conclude that presidential Republicanism in the South may have developed more rapidly than it did had the Depression not occurred or been as severe as it was, or if Franklin D. Roosevelt and the Democrats had not saddled the GOP with it. Historical "ifs," while intellectually amusing, are often of dubious value. Nonetheless, a quick perusal of Table 4.1 suggests the validity of the point. We have already noted that in the South there had been a noticeable Republican presidential vote early in the century. In the border South and Alabama, there was a significant Republican presidential vote through 1924; Republican candidates averaged 30 percent of the vote in these states during these years. In 1928, Republican Herbert Hoover won 51 percent of the votes in these seven states. Overall, between 1900 and 1928, the Republican nominee received a third of all votes cast in presidential elections in the border South and Alabama.[52]

These are sufficient figures to justify use of the phrase "significant Republican presidential vote." The problem for the Republicans was that whatever core support they may have had in the region evaporated because of the Depression, FDR, and World War II. While support for Republican presidential nominees began to creep upward in 1944 and 1948, it was not until the Eisenhower candidacy that the Republican nominee reached levels comparable to those of 1928. Thus had American history taken a different turn, substantial presidential Republicanism in the South might have made its appearance even decades earlier than it finally did.

How much support currently exists for Republican presidential nominees in the South? Registration figures are of little value in answering this question, since Democrats continue to outnumber Republicans in the region, as measured by registration, yet Republican presidential candidates have dominated recent elections.

We can estimate a core of Republican presidential support in the region by taking an average of the vote for the GOP nominee in recent elections. We can safely make our calculations using presidential elections from 1972 onward. The 1950s are too distant to provide any real insight into present-day strength, and the 1960s, we have argued, represent a period of confusion and transition as traditional southern voters began to discard Democratic affiliations, but did not yet feel fully comfortable in the GOP. By 1972, however, any lingering hesitations and doubts seem to have been overcome, and since then there is a fairly consistent pattern of Republican support.

Table 4.3 reports the result of this analysis. It shows the average vote for

Table 4.3

Southern Republican Presidential Base, 1972–1992 (percent)

	1972	1976	1980	1984	1988	1992	Mean
Deep South	72	43	48	62	59	46	55
Rim South	68	44	52	62	58	42	54
South Total	70	44	50	62	59	44	55

Republican presidential nominees from 1972 to 1992, broken down by sub-region as well as for the entire region. On the basis of these data, GOP presidential candidates have averaged about 55 percent of the vote over these six elections, representing virtually landslide proportions. No significant differences now exist, moreover, between border and deep South states.

Care must be taken in viewing these results. There is some interstate variation. This figure also includes, but is not limited to, so-called swing voters—that is, voters whose party preference at the presidential level shifts from one presidential election to the next and whose votes are up for grabs. Analysts of southern politics estimate that this swing vote might consist of 30 percent or more of southern voters.[53]

Republican presidential election strategists might be surprised if they simply assume that this large vote is theirs for the taking, without having to work for it. On the other hand, this functional Republican presidential majority in the South is potentially huge. Republican presidential candidates won every southern state in the three presidential elections of 1980, except for Georgia (Carter's home state) in 1980. In 1992, they managed to win seven southern states, in spite of Democrats' winning the White House. Even with the likelihood of defectors and the possibility of a revamped Democratic Party, these findings suggest that the GOP has a very strong hold on southern voters in forthcoming presidential elections. It may be that the most the Democrats can hope for is to crack the solid South; it seems unlikely that they will break it asunder in the near future.

What about the effect of possible third-party candidates on future GOP prospects? In the case of center-left candidates, such as John Anderson in 1980, the answer seems to be that it would scarcely affect Republican chances at all. To the extent that Anderson played a role in the outcome of the election in the South, he appeared to take votes away from Carter, the Democrat. The same would probably hold true again, should the situation arise.

In the case of a center-right populist or Dixiecrat, however, such as George Wallace in 1968, there is more room for conjecture. Wallace clearly hurt the conservative Nixon in the deep South, although he did not affect the outcome of the election. Yet as long as the Republican Party continues to nominate conservative candidates for president and stand for conservative, traditional policies that southerners (both old residents and recent arrivals) find acceptable, the GOP would appear to retain its solid base. If for some reason southerners see the Republican Party taking a more moderate or even liberal course, or if it nominates presidential candidates not acceptable to southerners, such as someone not from the Sunbelt or whose toughness and conservatism are suspect, then southerners might again look for alternatives, especially if a Dixiecrat were to appear. Given the kind of presidential candidates that the GOP has put forward since 1972, however, this seems unlikely to happen.[54]

And what of the Democratic Party? Has it been banished from the South forever, at least at the presidential level? Is it placed in the position of hoping for a few southern crumbs, even if it nominates southerners or candidates acceptable to the South? To answer these questions, we must look at why southerners stopped voting for its presidential candidates. There are many possible explanations, but the most basic is this: southerners do not feel they left the party but rather the party left them.

The process began in 1944 and 1948, with an increasing emphasis in the party on civil rights. Later, Democratic presidential candidates Stevenson, McGovern, Mondale, and Dukakis were perceived as liberal, not just on civil rights but on other social and economic issues. Moreover, they seemed not tough enough on those issues dear to southerners: patriotism and nationalism, family values, religion, strong defense, anticommunism. They appeared to favor centralization of power in Washington at the expense of state and local discretion.

Initially, southerners were concerned that through the Democrats' insistence on civil rights, the bargain struck by the election of 1876 was abrogated. Therefore, they no longer needed to have, nor could they maintain, any loyalty to the party. Once that break occurred, southerners found less and less reason to support Democrats at the presidential level, for they stood for things, and said things, that seemed unacceptable, whereas Republicans appeared to take up causes they favored.

True, southerners voted for Kennedy and Carter, and in some measure for Clinton. But the 1960 election represented the end of an era, the last gasp of the solid Democratic South. And Carter was one of their own, although he barely won against an opponent with few claims to the presidency. Indeed, there is a lesson in the Carter candidacy for the Democratic Party. It must not assume that southerners will automatically support a fellow southerner for president. Rather, that candidate must somehow strive to represent and convey those values, messages, policies, and positions that have made recent Republican nominees popular in the region and, conversely, Democratic nominees unpopular. Failure to do so will assuredly mean continued defeat for Democratic presidential candidates in the future. It is on this basis that the weak Clinton showing in the South can be understood; Clinton may have been a southerner, but he was still a Democrat. This is the continuing burden that all Democratic presidential nominees will continue to have for the foreseeable future.

5

Johnnies Come Lately: Southern Republicanism in State and Local Politics

[The GOP] scarcely deserves the name of a party. It wavers somewhat between an esoteric cult on the order of a lodge and a conspiracy for plunder in accord with the accepted customs of our politics.
—V.O. Key, 1949

V.O. Key's sardonic remark was directed at the ineptitude he observed in the southern Republican Parties at midcentury. Party leaders seemed less concerned with organizing or contesting and winning elections than with dabbling in party politics as a hobby, attending national conventions and meetings, and perhaps benefiting from whatever patronage came their way. Key's observation was apt: in most of the southern states, the Republican Party scarcely existed at all.

Although, at the time Key wrote, southerners were beginning to abandon the Democratic Party and vote for Republican presidential candidates, the same could not be said at the state and local levels. Indeed, with very few exceptions, Republican candidates had virtually no chance to win these elections. In a surprising number of instances, the party declined even to put forward candidates to oppose Democrats. Often those who were on the ballot campaigned in what can most charitably be described as a pitiful manner. As far as state and local politics were concerned at midcentury, the South was still solidly Democratic.

And yet in spite of this well-known point, at the state and local level evidence of Republicanism could be found in the South. What has not been well recognized is that even though the Republican Party, as an organization in most of the South, was feeble, voters willing to cast ballots for Republicans could be found—not in every place, or at all times, but enough so that a modification of the conventional wisdom has to be made. Republicans may have been scarce, but Republicanism was much more common than has previously been thought.

Moreover, even as Key wrote, the winds of change could be felt. Within a few years, Republican candidates became more numerous, campaigned more seriously, and even began to win elections. How this happened and to what extent Republicans became a vital political force in the region even at the state and local level are our concerns now.

In this chapter we will first examine electoral results for the governorship, U.S. Senate and House of Representatives, and state legislature. We will then account for the fortunes of contemporary southern Republicanism, suggest something of its direction and limits, and finally discuss its prospects within the context of the so-called two-party South.

State and Local Elections, Southern Style

Political scientists have long recognized that citizens look upon state and local elections differently from presidential contests. Presidential elections are usually conceived to involve great issues or directions in the country: war and peace, the fate of nations, the place of our nation in the international community, the role and place of government in our society, and overall direction of national domestic policy. On occasion, including in recent elections, they can also involve substantial questions of public values, private morality, and appropriate standards of ethical behavior.

Elections at the state and local level can also be concerned with important public questions. Even in the South, as we observed in chapter 3, campaigns and other forms of political discussion could become heated debates over issues. But the issues reflected in state and local elections often involve immediate solutions to pressing problems close to home.[1] Sectional, local, even neighborhood concerns replace the abstractions of presidential contests. Personalities and style, while not at all absent from national contests, are magnified in importance in state and local elections.[2] Regional, statewide, intrastate, and even local factional considerations, economic self-interests, and the preservation of particular traditions, beliefs, and subcultures are overtly manifest in these contests.

In the South, state and local elections took on an additional purpose, one closely related to this latter point. Election of governors and other state executives, senators and representatives, state legislators, even local officials, became important for preserving the southern way of life, especially race relations and states' rights. Earlier we noted how important the congressional seniority system was to southerners as a way of ensuring that the federal government would continue to honor the agreement of 1877. As a result they repeatedly returned incumbent senators and representatives to Washington, D.C. But other state and local officials were also expected to act as conservators of these same traditional southern values, through both word and deed. If they did not have the political longevity of U.S. senators and representatives, their duty as southern officials nonetheless made it incumbent on them to help protect the state and region from outside interference and to ensure the preservation of southern ways.

Regional self-interest and self-protection were not the only factors separating these contests from presidential ones. The timing of these elections was also important. Southern gubernatorial elections frequently were held on off-years to prevent national issues from influencing their outcome; it was also easier for competing elites to influence, even control, the outcome if political participation did not rise because of the presidential campaign. Alabama, Mississippi, and Virginia have throughout this century held gubernatorial elections on off-presidential years, while Florida began to do so in the mid-1960s. Arkansas, Georgia, South Carolina, Tennessee, and Texas have held at least some of their gubernatorial elections on off-years.

Additionally, half the elections for U.S. House of Representatives (barring special elections), some U.S. Senate elections, many state legislative and other state executive races, and numerous local contests occur in off-presidential years. "Presidential" issues may or may not infuse these contests, depending on when they are held.

Complicating the timing of state and local elections in the South have been primaries. As we noted in chapter 3, these were traditionally the most important elections in the South because much of the time the general election results were a foregone conclusion. Often southern primaries occurred in the late spring, although in recent years there has been a trend toward having them in the late summer, closer to the general election. But purely local elections—primary and otherwise—can and do occur virtually anytime during the year.

Another very significant characteristic of state and local elections, in the South and elsewhere, is that they have much less visibility than those for president. More citizens turn out in presidential elections than for purely state and local ones. Fewer cues, and less information, are available to voters about state and local contests. Often voters do not even know there is an election or have incorrect information about the candidates. Even among those who are aware, the salience of state and local campaigns and issues is often lower than for presidential ones.[3]

The effect is generally to depress voter turnout in state and local elections. The South, as we noted earlier, has had low rates of electoral participation anyway. In primaries, however, and in state and local elections in off-presidential years, turnout figures of less than 20 percent of the registered voters (usually only a fraction of those even eligible) were not unusual in the region.[4]

Given the small turnout in southern elections, the advantage clearly went to organized groups and interests, entrenched ruling elites, courthouse gangs and cliques, and the like. Clearly, this system worked to the disadvantage of fringe or minority political groups, including Republicans. The system is not the sole reason why Republicans had so much trouble winning elections at the state and local level in the South for much of this century, but it assuredly was a major factor.

There were other factors as well. The collective memory and set of attitudes that many southerners held toward the Republican Party and its role in the Civil War and Reconstruction were expressed at least as much toward Republicans in state and local elections as in presidential elections. Often there would be no Republican candidate on the ballot for state and local offices, or the candidacy would be merely a token, owing to party weakness and lack of organization. More important, most southern voters were convinced that only Democrats could ensure the continuation of traditional southern ways; Republicans were identified with the ignominious defeat of the South, Yankee interventionism, and the perpetuation of southern problems. And, as Cole Blease seemed to imply, if matters started to get out of hand and a Republican candidate appeared too strong, state and local officials, since they were all Democrats in control of election machinery, could simply fail to count Republican ballots.[5]

For these and other reasons, Republicans seldom saw victory in state and local elections in the South during much of this century. Where they occurred, they tended to be very localized. If the victory was statewide, prior to 1960 voters were likely to return to "normalcy" and throw the pretender out in the next election, to be replaced by a Democrat. The solid South was not limited to presidential elections. At the state and local level it was not simply solid, it was all but monolithic for the first six decades of this century.

Republican Penetration in the South: A Note and Method

All these factors notwithstanding, there were still Republicans and Republicanism in the South. Nor were either irrelevant or insignificant to politics in the region, states, or local areas, in spite of the difficulty of locating them. Our task is to identify the extent of Republican support at the state and local level, to show its evolution during this century, and finally to discuss just how far Republicanism extended, and currently penetrates, into the political life of the region.

To study the extent of Republican penetration throughout the fabric of southern political life, we must examine a significant number of elections over a long period of time. Because state and local elections are different from presidential ones, we would err if we examine one without the other. Likewise, if we chose a limited time frame, we would undercut our effort to examine trends and developments during this century. Furthermore, choosing the wrong time frame could seriously distort our conclusions.

To avoid these difficulties, we shall examine all southern elections for governors, senators, and representatives, and sample those for state legislatures, between 1900 and 1994.[6] Purely local elections, such as those for county and city governments, and judicial races have been omitted, in part because of unreliability of data and in part because so many are non-partisan.[7] However, there is every reason to think that U.S. House of Representatives and state legislature elections can be considered essentially local elections rather than state ones because of the preponderance of primarily local concerns that figure into their outcome. Thus our survey will be able to provide us with a glimpse of Republicanism at the local level, as well as at state and regional levels.[8]

How can we study the extent of Republican penetration into the political fabric of the South? Many studies look at voter registration figures and compare them with electoral outcomes. We shall take a somewhat different course in this investigation.[9]

For our purposes, we are interested only with the amount, depth, and extent of Republican voting in the South: When were citizens willing to vote Republican, where did this happen, for what offices, and over what time period? Voters' registration histories are of little concern to us here. Rather, we must ask about the extent to which southern voters were willing and able to cast a ballot for a Republican candidate, especially when given a choice of a Democratic one, and what were the chances of success of the Republican candidate.

We can call this approach a measure of "functional" Republicanism.[10] To demonstrate the extent of functional Republicanism in the South, three measures have been adopted: The first is the extent to which Republicans appeared on the ballot to challenge Democrats. Without GOP candidates, even the most fervent Republicans would be frustrated in their desire to vote for the party of their choice. When Republicans lacked the degree of political organization and mobilization needed to provide a challenge to Democrats, especially if this happened frequently, we can conclude that the extent of Republican penetration was small. On the other hand, when Republicans consistently put forward candidates, we can conclude that at least some reasonable levels of Republican penetration in the form of recruitment, support, and voter mobilization occurred.

Our second measure is the percentage of the vote that Republican candidates received in elections. More specifically, we are looking for a baseline figure that, if Republican candidates could achieve consistently, would demonstrate a core of support which could not be ignored, which represented a solid base, and which could potentially be augmented into a winning figure.

Many political scientists use 40 percent of the vote for this baseline figure of support. We shall use 30 percent instead, on the premise that a party which can gain at least 30 percent of the vote over time, and for a variety of offices, shows a significant, vital amount of support. This level, while perhaps not sufficient to result in victory, is nonetheless not trivial and is worthy of notice. While it is possible, even if uncommon, for a candidate receiving 40 percent of the vote in an election to be victorious, it is highly unlikely for a candidate to win with 30 percent. Thus the capacity of Republican candidates to receive, over time, at least 30 percent of the vote represents a meaningful measure of the party's vitality and support in the South.

Our final measure is the most obvious—victories. Our measure of the extent of functional southern Republicanism would be incomplete without looking ultimately at whether GOP candidates could actually win elections, which ones, where, and how often.

Southern Republican Candidates for Governor, 1900–1960

In the first six decades of this century,[11] Republican governors were elected three times in the South: 1910, 1912, and 1920. They were all elected in Tennessee and in general followed periods of Democratic scandals and disorganization. No other Republican candidates for governor were successful during this period in other southern states, and indeed it was extremely unusual if a candidate other than a Democrat was elected.[12]

Equally significant is the lack of Republican gubernatorial candidates on the ballot. Table 5.1 presents data on the percentage of elections in which no Republican gubernatorial candidates appeared. Throughout the South, GOP challengers were on the ballot in about one-third of gubernatorial elections. In the deep South states, it was very rare for a GOP candidate to be on the ballot. In fact, between 1900 and 1965, Georgia voters never saw a Republican gubernatorial candidate. In Mississippi and South Carolina they seldom appeared. Only in Alabama did a Republican gubernatorial candidate appear regularly.

In the border South, GOP candidates were much more common. Interestingly, in Tennessee, where three Republicans were elected governor early in the century, GOP gubernatorial candidates failed to appear in about a third of the contests between 1945 and 1960. This finding suggests their election early in the century failed to result in a significant Republican beachhead, a matter to which we will return.

Table 5.1 also shows the percentage of elections in which Republican gubernatorial candidates received 30 percent or more of the votes between 1900 and 1960. Overall in the South, they achieved this percentage about 20 percent of the time. In the deep South states, however, it simply did not occur in the first six decades. In the border South states prior to the New Deal, GOP gubernatorial candidates received 30 percent or more nearly half the time; between 1931 and 1960, about a third of the time.

Table 5.1 demonstrates that in general, Republican candidates for governor did not fare well in the South during the first six decades of the century. Only in a few of the border South states (North Carolina, Virginia, and to some extent Tennessee) did they make a significant electoral showing. Moreover, there is no evidence of an evolutionary strengthening of the candidates' performance over time. Indeed, following the New Deal, except in a few instances, they actually did worse.

Southern Republican Candidates for the U.S. Senate, 1914–1960

Data for southern GOP senatorial candidates begin in 1914, when senators were first popularly elected. Overall, they show a pattern similar to those of gubernatorial candidates. In contrast to the success of Republican gubernatorial candidates in Tennessee early in the century, no GOP challengers were elected to the United States Senate during this period.[13]

Table 5.2 shows that during this period GOP senatorial candidates were on the ballot only slightly more than half the time in the South. In the deep South states, Republican challengers for the U.S. Senate seldom appeared between 1914 and 1960. Prior to 1946, they were never on the ballot in Louisiana, Mississippi, and South Carolina. They were rare in Georgia. Only in Alabama were Republican senate candidates fairly common.

In the border South, GOP Senate contenders were more numerous than in the deep South states, but they were still uncommon; indeed, overall they

Table 5.1

Southern Vote for Republican Gubernatorial Candidates, 1900–1960 (percent)

	% No Republican Candidate on Ballot				30% or More of Vote			
	1900–15	1916–30	1931–45	1946–60	1900–15	1916–30	1931–45	1946–60
South Total	32	36	39	37	23	24	16	19
Deep South								
Alabama	0	25	0	0	0	0	0	0
Georgia	100	100	100	100	0	0	0	0
Louisiana	0	25	75	50	0	0	0	0
Mississippi	100	100	100	75	0	0	0	0
South Carolina	100	100	67	100	0	0	0	0
Mean	60	70	68	65	0	0	0	0
Rim South								
Arkansas	0	13	14	0	22	0	0	25
Florida	0	0	25	0	0	25	25	20
North Carolina	0	0	0	0	75	100	75	75
Tennessee	0	0	14	33	100	100	43	33
Texas	0	0	0	13	0	13	14	0
Virginia	25	0	0	0	75	50	25	67
Mean	4	2	9	8	45	48	30	37

Table 5.2

Southern Vote for Republican Candidates for the U.S. Senate, 1914–1960
(percent)

	% No Republican Candidate on Ballot			30% or More of Vote		
	1914–30	1931–45	1946–60	1914–30	1931–45	1946–60
South Total	51	59	55	21	8	16
Deep South						
Alabama	17	20	50	17	0	17
Georgia	88	83	100	0	0	0
Louisiana	100	100	50	0	0	0
Mississippi	100	100	86	0	0	0
South Carolina	100	100	83	0	0	0
Mean	81	81	74	3	0	3
Rim South						
Arkansas	29	29	80	29	0	0
Florida	17	57	40	17	0	0
North Carolina	0	0	30	100	80	60
Tennessee	0	17	0	71	17	33
Texas	0	60	0	17	0	43
Virginia	71	60	57	0	0	29
Mean	20	37	35	39	16	28

were less common than GOP gubernatorial candidates. Only in Tennessee and North Carolina did they appear rather frequently. In Arkansas and Florida they were on the ballot less often after 1930 than before. Texas had an unusual case in 1952, when one person ran as the candidate of both major parties.

Table 5.2 also shows that GOP senatorial candidates, in general, had trouble getting more than 30 percent of the vote during this period. Only in Alabama, among the deep South states, and Tennessee and North Carolina in the border South, did the candidates noticeably show this level of strength.

Of particular interest is the fact that there was a general decline in Republican senatorial support over the 1914–1960 period. The trend is more noticeable in the border than in the deep South, of course. Between 1931 and 1945 GOP senatorial candidates won at least 30 percent of the vote in only 8 percent of the contests. Between 1946 and 1960, they received 30 percent of the vote in only 16 percent.

There are several possible explanations for this finding. One is the general southern disaffection with Republicans that occurred as a result of the

Depression, during the New Deal, and through World War II. But another major reason has to do with the importance of senatorial seniority to the South. Southern Democrats were able to steer major federal projects to the South during the Depression, and later during the war, as a result of the seniority they built up.[14] Later, this same seniority served southerners as protection against increasing pressure by the federal government on civil rights. Thus, as time passed during the first sixty years of the century, Republican challengers were less able to make a case that they could represent the South better in the Senate than could Democrats. The longevity of Democratic senators helped insulate the South and ensure it would be free of federal interference over a long period of time.

Southern Republican Candidates for the U.S. House of Representatives, 1900–1960

Although southern Republican candidates did not have much success in statewide races during this period, in more localized races, where aggregations of Republicans could make their voting strength felt, they did much better. In particular, Republicans consistently won seats in the U.S. House of Representatives and showed electoral strength in other ways as well.

In the deep South, no Republican was elected to the U.S. House during the entire period. Even the pockets of Republicanism in the mountain areas of Alabama and Georgia were not sufficiently strong to elect a representative. Gerrymandering of congressional districts by Democratic state legislatures also served to dilute whatever strength was present.

In the border South, Republicans were elected to the House of Representatives throughout the time period. Tennessee had by far the most Republican victories (65), followed rather distantly by Virginia (25) and North Carolina (14). Each of these states, it will be recalled, had significant areas of Republican strength, especially in the mountainous regions. By the period after World War II, each of the border states except Arkansas sent Republicans to the House of Representatives. Texas actually sent its first Republican to Washington in 1920, while Florida did not do so until 1954. These states sent nine and four Republicans, respectively, to the House of Representatives between 1900 and 1960.[15]

Table 5.3 indicates the percentage of elections in which Republican challengers for the House of Representatives failed to appear on the ballot. Between 1900 and 1960, the percentage of elections which GOP candidates failed to contest actually increased, from 53 percent to more than 70 percent. In the border South the change was dramatic. Prior to 1930, GOP contenders failed to appear only about one-third of the time; but after 1930, over half the time. During the Depression–New Deal–war years, Republican challengers for the House of Representatives appeared less than 10 percent of the time in the deep South. Republican contenders were most common in North Carolina, Tennessee, and Virginia among the border South states, and in Alabama among the deep South states.

Care must be taken in interpreting these figures. They represent the percentage of total elections for U.S. House of Representatives that Republicans failed to challenge. In fact, in some areas of the states where Republicans were numerous, they challenged particular congressional seats on a regular basis. In overwhelmingly Democratic districts, Republican challengers may never have appeared throughout the entire time period.

Geographic dispersion of Republicans was also important in the level of support that candidates for the House of Representatives achieved. Table 5.3 shows that in the deep South, Alabama, Georgia, and Louisiana were the only states where Republican candidates for the House received at least 30 percent of the vote between 1900 and 1960. In Alabama most of this support came early in the century and declined after 1930. It was never strong in Georgia or Louisiana.

In the border South states, North Carolina, Tennessee, and Virginia again showed the most consistent support for Republican House candidates. After World War II, Florida also showed a significant number of elections in which Republican House candidates did well. In general, however, support for Republican House candidates was stronger prior to 1930 than afterward.

Southern Republican Candidates, 1900–1960: A Summary

Several important conclusions can be drawn from the data and discussion. First, Republicanism was not uniformly distributed across the South. It was far more extensive in the border South than in the deep South states. Republicans were more likely to be present on the ballot, secure more than 30 percent of the vote, and actually win in border South states than in the deep South. Only in Alabama, in fact, could it be said that Republicanism was more than a mirage during this period.

But even within the border South there was considerable variation. Tennessee, North Carolina, and Virginia, with their local aggregations of Republicans, proved the most fertile ground for Republican appeals. Republicans in Florida began to do well after World War II. Although the GOP showed signs of strength early in the century in Arkansas, it seemed to ebb sharply after 1915. Republican strength in Texas during the entire period appeared to resemble its deep South neighbors, especially following 1930.

Table 5.3

Southern Vote for Republican Candidates for the U.S. House of Representatives, 1900–1960 (percent)

	% No Republican Candidate on Ballot				30% or More of Vote			
	1900–15	1916–30	1931–45	1946–60	1900–15	1916–30	1931–45	1946–60
South Total	53	60	73	70	20	18	11	16
Deep South								
Alabama	42	56	73	74	17	21	2	3
Georgia	89	91	89	96	4	2	1	3
Louisiana	47	98	98	80	4	2	2	6
Mississippi	94	97	98	88	0	0	0	0
South Carolina	86	93	98	88	0	0	0	0
Mean	72	87	91	85	5	5	1	2
Rim South								
Arkansas	27	51	84	84	44	15	6	6
Florida	61	29	63	52	0	13	5	32
North Carolina	9	6	19	19	68	73	49	50
Tennessee	23	38	39	53	51	39	32	34
Texas	41	34	80	78	10	7	0	8
Virginia	34	40	46	38	38	32	31	44
Mean	33	33	55	54	35	30	21	29

For which offices did Republican candidates do best in the South? Comparing the means presented in the tables suggests that Republicans were most likely to contest the governor's race. Overall, GOP candidates for the governorship were the most likely to achieve at least 30 percent of the vote, although this is really only true in the border South. And of course Republicans did win three governorships, all in Tennessee.

This result might have been anticipated. Governors in the South during this period either served only one four-year term or had to face reelection every two years. Thus there were frequent occasions for Republicans to mount a statewide challenge. The congressional seniority system, as well as the infrequency of senate elections, discouraged significant Republican challenges for this office. Moreover, the governorship dealt directly with the operation of state administrative and political machinery, including patronage, which interested Republicans greatly. It is also the most visible statewide office. There was considerable incentive, then, for Republicans to focus their resources on the governorship, even if their prospects for victory were slight.

True, there were more victories for Republican House candidates than for the governorship. But Republican success in House races resulted more from local aggregations of Republican voters than from party strength. And the percentage of elections in which southern Republicans failed even to mount a challenge was greater for House contests than for gubernatorial races. Similarly, in general Republican contestants for the governorship were more likely to get at least 30 percent of the vote than were those for the House.

Finally, the tables clearly demonstrate the devastating impact that the Depression, Franklin D. Roosevelt and the New Deal, and World War II had on Republican fortunes in the South. Prior to 1930, there was a significant amount of Republicanism in the South, especially in the border states. But Republicans were less likely to be on the ballot, or to receive at least 30 percent of the vote, after 1930 than before. After World War II southern Republicanism began its recovery. But by 1960 it had barely returned to pre-1930 levels.

Thus the wrenching social and economic upheavals of the 1931–45 period had an impact on state and local southern Republican fortunes similar to the one they had on southern Republican presidential politics. Indeed, it took another revolution—civil rights—coupled with rapid immigration, a changing economy, and other nationalizing forces[16] to decisively undercut southern allegiance to the Democratic Party, and to reinterest southerners in the Republican Party.

Southern Voting for Republican Presidential and State and Local Candidates Compared, 1900–1960

How well did southern Republican candidates for state and local offices fare in comparison to GOP presidential nominees during this period?

Given the visibility and importance of the presidency and presidential elections, we might expect that GOP presidential candidates would do better than those for state and local offices. In general, this expectation is borne out. True, there were more "victories" for state and local Republican candidates in the South than for presidential ones, but a comparison on this measure is specious because of the enormous differences in the elections and the offices.

The most meaningful comparison is the ability of the respective candidates to gain at least 30 percent of the vote. Although the data are not shown for presidential votes, investigation reveals that on this measure presidential nominees always did better than state and local Republican candidates in the South. This finding was even true during the 1931–45 period, when southern Republican strength atrophied considerably. After World War II, overall Republican fortunes improved, especially in the border states. However, except for North Carolina, where state and local Republicans did fairly well, even in the border South Republican state and local candidates received 30 percent or more of the vote less than half the time that GOP presidential candidates did.

There are some individual exceptions. Republican House of Representative candidates could, and did, outpoll the presidential nominee at times, whether victorious or not. It would not, however, be correct to say that overall GOP state and local candidates ran more strongly that Republican presidential hopefuls. On balance, in fact, the opposite was true.

What about presidential coattails? Did the presence of a presidential campaign influence in any way the relative success of Republican state and local candidates in the South?

Comparing data for presidential and nonpresidential election years reveals that there was a very slight positive impact on state and local Republican candidates during presidential elections. In particular, Republican challengers were somewhat more likely to appear on the ballot during presidential elections than during off-years. And Republican candidates were somewhat more likely to get at least 30 percent of the vote when there was a presidential election.

These conclusions hold for both deep and border South states. However, one important proviso is necessary: in those states where Republicanism was more than a mirage—Tennessee, North Carolina, Virginia, to some extent Alabama, and, in the latter period, Florida—GOP candidates were less adversely affected in off-year elections than where Republicanism was pitifully weak. In those latter states a presidential election was critical to whatever meager chances of success a Republican candidate might have against a Democrat.

The Rise of Modern Southern Republicanism

In the years following 1960, southern Republican strength at the state and local level continued to develop. There was not, however, a quantum leap forward. Rather, the rise of modern southern Republicanism for state and local offices was largely an evolutionary process that proceeded by fits and starts and was not uniform across the region. We can see this most clearly by dividing the post-1960 years into three periods—1962–78, the 1980s, and the 1990s (see Tables 5.4, 5.5, 5.6).

For governors and senators, the change has been most emphatic. The tables show a steady growth in Republican strength from the 1960s into the 1990s. Whereas earlier in the century it was rare for GOP candidates to contest elections, especially in the deep South, Tables 5.4 and 5.5 show that by the 1980s they regularly challenged for the governorship and U.S. Senate. Only in Louisiana, Georgia, and Arkansas were there senatorial elections without GOP challengers. Similarly, the two tables show that Republican gubernatorial and senatorial candidates now receive over 30 percent of the vote in about 90 percent of elections, up sharply even from the period 1962–78. Where it counts the most, namely in electoral victories, Republican candidates for governor and senator have also done very well. In the 1980s, in fact, they won upward of 30 percent of these contests, and in the 1990s they failed to win governorships only in Arkansas, Georgia, Florida, and North Carolina.[17] By the mid-1990s, Republicans held a majority of southern governorships (seven of eleven states), and thirteen of twenty-two senatorial positions.[18]

Data from elections for the U.S. House of Representatives from the 1960s into the 1990s indicate a steady rise in Republican fortunes (see Table 5.6). Across the region, even by the 1990s, about 10 percent of all House races were uncontested by the GOP.[19] Only in Louisiana was there a sizable percentage of House seats in which Republicans failed to put forward a candidate.

Although in general GOP House candidates ran far more strongly than they did prior to 1960, they did not, overall, do quite as well as gubernatorial and senatorial candidates. Throughout the region, Republican House

Table 5.4

Southern Vote for Republican Gubernatorial Candidates, 1962–1994 (percent)

	% No Republican Candidate on Ballot			30% or More of Vote			% Republican Victories		
	1962–78	1980–88	1990–94	1962–78	1980–88	1990–94	1962–78	1980–88	1990–94
South	16	0	0	72	95	100	19	30	47
Deep South									
Alabama	40	0	0	20	100	100	0	50	100
Georgia	20	0	0	60	100	100	0	0	0
Louisiana	40	0	0	60	50	100	20	0	0
Mississippi	20	0	0	80	100	100	0	0	100
South Carolina	20	0	0	80	100	100	20	50	100
Mean	28	0	0	60	90	100	8	20	60
Rim South									
Arkansas	0	0	0	67	100	100	22	25	0
Florida	0	0	0	100	100	100	20	50	0
North Carolina	0	0	0	100	100	100	25	67	0
Tennessee	20	0	0	100	100	100	40	50	50
Texas	0	0	0	71	100	100	14	50	50
Virginia	0	0	0	100	100	100	60	0	100
Mean	3	0	0	83	100	100	30	40	33

Table 5.5

Southern Vote for Republican Candidates for the U.S. Senate, 1962–1994 (percent)

	% No Republican Candidate on Ballot			30% or More of Vote			% Republican Victories		
	1962–78	1980–88	1990–94	1962–78	1980–88	1990–94	1962–78	1980–88	1990–94
South	20	7	9	56	88	86	20	35	59
Deep South									
Alabama	29	0	0	43	100	100	0	33	50
Georgia	29	0	50	14	67	50	0	33	50
Lousiana	67	67	0	0	33	50	0	0	0
Mississippi	50	0	0	33	100	100	17	67	100
South Carolina	0	0	0	86	100	100	29	33	50
Mean	35	13	10	35	80	80	9	33	50
Rim South									
Arkansas	17	0	50	50	100	50	0	0	0
Florida	0	0	0	100	100	100	17	50	50
North Carolina	0	0	0	100	100	100	33	67	100
Tennessee	0	0	0	100	100	100	57	0	100
Texas	0	0	0	71	100	100	50	33	100
Virginia	14	0	0	57	67	100	29	67	50
Mean	5	0	8	80	95	92	31	36	67

Table 5.6

Southern Vote for Republican Candidates for the U.S. House of Representatives, 1962–1994 (percent)

	% No Republican Candidate on Ballot			30% or More of Vote			% Republican Victories		
	1962–78	1980–88	1990–94	1962–78	1980–88	1990–94	1962–78	1980–88	1990–94
South	38	27	10	47	61	79	23	34	40
Deep South									
Alabama	28	34	14	35	48	67	32	31	38
Georgia	48	30	0	37	46	84	9	14	37
Louisiana	60	67	31	28	32	50	10	32	40
Mississippi	53	19	6	36	66	53	18	28	6
South Carolina	31	13	17	56	80	88	17	47	50
Mean	44	33	12	38	54	70	17	30	36
Rim South									
Arkansas	53	25	0	33	60	83	22	35	41
Florida	30	20	6	53	58	90	25	34	58
North Carolina	19	5	0	70	87	94	25	31	45
Tennessee	27	20	11	63	57	77	41	34	40
Texas	35	32	13	44	58	77	10	29	32
Virginia	22	16	12	67	84	78	42	62	40
Mean	31	20	8	55	67	83	28	38	43

candidates in the 1990s received 30 percent or more of the vote in about 80 percent of elections, compared to nearly 90 percent for senators, and 100 percent for governors. In Georgia, South Carolina, Arkansas, Florida, and North Carolina GOP House candidates, on average, received at least 30 percent of the vote virtually in every election.

Across the South the percentage of victories that GOP House candidates achieved since 1960 has been comparable to that of Republican gubernatorial and senatorial candidates. Between 1962 and 1978, GOP candidates won nearly a quarter of House elections, compared to 20 percent for the other two offices. By the 1980s, GOP House candidates won about a third overall, comparable to winning percentages for governor and senate. By the 1990s, Republicans had won about 40 percent of House elections, less than for governor and senator.

Again, however, the aggregate figures mask some significant variations within the region. They suggest that there remain areas of individual states where Republicans have difficulty contesting elections and mounting campaigns that are fundamentally local in character. In Louisiana, for example, two-thirds of House seats were not contested by GOP challengers in the 1980s, and still one-third in the 1990s. In Louisiana and Mississippi, GOP House candidates received 30 percent of the vote only in about half the elections, suggesting continuing Republican weakness in some areas. And in spite of the Republican surge in 1994, Republican House candidates won few seats in Mississippi and less than a third in Texas. Louisiana may be the most unique state in terms of Republican fortunes; while GOP candidates fail to contest about a third of elections, they perform well in those they do enter.

Southern Republican Presidential and State and Local Elections Compared, 1962–1992

How have Republican candidates for governor, Senate, and the U.S. House of Representatives in the South fared compared to Republican presidential nominees since 1960? A comparison of data from the previous and current chapters reveals that while there is still a gap in the performance of the two types of candidates, it has closed somewhat from the pre-1960 period.

The comparison is actually difficult to make because of the complexity of presidential politics in the South since 1960. In 1964 and 1976, southern Democratic presidential nominees retained sufficient traditional support that the Democrats were able to capture a majority of votes in the region, although not at the same levels shown prior to 1948. In 1992 a southern

Democrat won the presidency, but with only minimal help from the South. The presence of a Dixiecrat alternative in 1968, George Wallace, undoubtedly undermined the Republican showing. In 1972, 1984, and 1988, the Republican presidential vote in the South was nothing short of awesome. In 1980, Ronald Reagan captured virtually all of the South, defeating an incumbent southern Democrat, Jimmy Carter, by a significant if not overwhelming margin. Likewise, in 1992, George Bush managed a decent effort in the South in a losing cause nationally; it is very likely that Ross Perot hurt him considerably and brought his percentages down from their 1988 levels.

But Republican candidates for statewide office have had difficulty achieving the same level of electoral victory, although a few senatorial candidates have come close: in 1984, candidates John Warner in Virginia (70 percent), Strom Thurmond in South Carolina (67 percent), and Phil Gramm in Texas (59 percent) exceeded Reagan's figures. In 1988 North Carolina gubernatorial candidate Jim Martin (56 percent) approached Bush's 58 percent, while Mississippi senatorial candidate Trent Lott (53 percent) ran somewhat behind Bush's 60 percent. And, as was the case prior to 1960, some GOP House candidates were able to run ahead of the national ticket, even with Democratic opposition.

These, however, are exceptional cases. For the most part successful GOP candidates in the South have run behind the presidential nominee of their party. Presidential coattails have helped elect several GOP senators to office, notably in 1980: Jeremiah Denton in Alabama, Mack Mattingly in Georgia, and Paula Hawkins in Florida. All, interestingly, subsequently lost reelection bids in 1986 while running without benefit of Ronald Reagan at the top of the ballot. In 1992, Paul Coverdell in Georgia and Lauch Faircloth in North Carolina ran ahead of President George Bush in their senatorial campaigns, although by less than 10 percentage points. And of course in any number of U.S. House elections (ignoring those unchallenged by Democrats) Republicans ran well ahead of Bush.

Thus the performance of some GOP candidates in recent elections suggests that the gap between the presidential nominee and state and local candidates may be narrowing. Powerful and popular GOP presidential nominees—incumbents and otherwise—will undoubtedly continue to lead the Republican ticket and in some instances provide at least modest coattails for state and local candidates. But, as Republican incumbents become more common, and more established, it is also true that some will lead the statewide ticket, even during presidential elections, as the previous examples have shown.

Table 5.7

Summary of Southern Republican Penetration, 1990–1994 (percent)

	% No Republican Candidate on Ballot	30% or More of Vote	% Republican Victories
South Total	6	88	48
Deep South			
Alabama	5	89	63
Georgia	17	78	29
Louisiana	10	67	13
Mississippi	2	84	69
South Carolina	6	96	67
Mean	8	83	48
Rim South			
Arkansas	17	78	14
Florida	2	97	36
North Carolina	0	98	48
Tennessee	4	92	63
Texas	4	92	61
Virginia	4	93	63
Mean	5	92	48

Republican Penetration in the South

Just what is the extent of southern Republicanism? How far into the political fabric and culture of the region has the GOP extended? Three separate pieces of evidence can help us answer these questions.

Table 5.7 collapses data from gubernatorial, senatorial, and House of Representative elections in the South between 1990 and 1994. Thus it provides a comprehensive look at the most recent performance of Republican candidates for these offices, and therefore is a handy summary of how well the GOP did in recent years.

The table shows that in the 1990s, Republicans have competed for political office on a regular basis. There are relatively few elections that do not have a Republican candidate on the ballot. Throughout the South, only 6 percent of the elections are uncontested by a Republican. In the deep South 8 percent have had no Republican candidate, while the figure in the border South is 5 percent.

Moreover, if we examine individual states, we see that in some states—notably North Carolina, Virginia, South Carolina, Mississippi, Florida, Texas, and Tennessee—have fewer than 5 percent of elections that are uncontested by Republicans; in North Carolina all were contested. All of the uncontested elections, it will be recalled, were for House of Representative seats. Conversely, while the data are not reported, many seats uncontested by Democrats have actually become safe for GOP candidates.[20]

The table also shows that GOP candidates throughout the region can expect to receive a solid base of electoral support. Nearly 90 percent of GOP candidates get at least 30 percent of the vote; the figure exceeds 90 percent in the border South. In North Carolina and South Carolina GOP candidates receive at least 30 percent of the vote in virtually every election they contest; the same is true in Florida. Only in Arkansas, Georgia, and especially Louisiana do Republican candidates seem to lag behind their counterparts in other states.

Winning elections, of course, is still the most important criterion for judging the success of party strength. The table shows that GOP candidates now win nearly half of the elections. In Mississippi, South Carolina, Alabama, North Carolina, Tennessee, Virginia, and Texas they won more than 60 percent of elections. But in Arkansas, Georgia, and Louisiana Republicans still do not win a substantial percentage of elections.

Care must be taken in interpreting these figures. They report only the 1990s, in which there were few gubernatorial and senatorial elections; a victory or defeat in just one can change the percentages considerably. They are aggregate and do not differentiate among the importance or visibility of offices; the governorship or a Senate seat unquestionably remains a bigger prize for a party than a seat in the U.S. House of Representatives. And data are not reported for other state offices, in which some interesting developments have occurred: in Florida, for example, the GOP has been able to win some state executive offices,[21] whereas in other southern states the GOP has had only limited electoral success in pursuing these other statewide offices.

Yet even given the limitations of the figures in Table 5.7, the conclusion is inescapable that the GOP has made remarkable strides in electoral strength and is now a vital force in electoral politics in almost all of the South. Examination of Tables 5.3–5.7 also shows that much of this mushrooming of Republicanism has occurred during the 1990s; it especially boomed in the 1994 election.[22]

Which states seem to have become the most fertile ground for the Republican Party? This is a difficult question to answer, because it depends on what criteria are applied. Nonetheless, Table 5.7 can provide a modest ranking of sorts.

The least Republican state appears to be Louisiana.[23] It remains a state in which many elections are not contested by Republicans, and only two-thirds of those entering a race receive at least 30 percent of the vote. Only 13 percent of Republican candidates won election during the 1990s in Louisiana.[24]

Following this line of reasoning, Georgia and Arkansas have also seen limited Republican success. Moreover, it is difficult to interpret the results of the 1994 elections in Tennessee, traditionally a strong Democratic state. Whether the complete transformation of the governorship and two senatorial slots from Democratic to Republican lasts remains to be seen; if it does, Tennessee might represent the fastest GOP takeover of a state in the entire South.

In contrast, Alabama and Mississippi have become states of Republican vitality. Republicans regularly contest elections, run strongly, and are victorious at about the regional average. But the southern states where Republicans have become the most powerful are Virginia, South Carolina, and especially North Carolina. The latter two states, in the 1990s, show evidence of Republican domination of major elections. Florida and Virginia are close behind in this regard.[25] Both have sizable Republican memberships in their delegation to the House of Representatives and have frequently captured major state offices. South Carolina, among the deep South states, appears to the most Republican, for the same reasons.

We noted in the last chapter that there was a convergence of the deep and rim South in presidential politics, although in that case the process started in the 1970s. The convergence in state and local politics is really not noticeable until the 1980s. This is not to say that there is no longer any difference in political culture between the states in these two subregions. However, it does suggest that the political upheavals which marked the South during the 1960s and 1970s may be settling down into more discernible and regular electoral patterns. It also means that Republicans can now generally expect to find relatively fertile political soil to till throughout much of the region and not have to write off significant blocs of states where victories are impossible.

Who Holds the Power?

A second piece of evidence regarding the extent of Republican penetration is simply to examine the percentages of important political offices are currently held by Republicans in the South.[26] As of 1996, Republicans hold the following percentages in the region:

Governor: 7 of 11 (65%)[27]
U.S. Senate: 13 of 22 (59%)
U.S. House: 65 of 125 (52%).[28]

These data virtually hit one over the head. Thirty years ago Republicans in public office were hard to find in the South. Now they hold a substantial bloc of offices, in some states a preponderance. Cole Blease must turn over in his grave as each new election cycle approaches in the South.

Republicans in Southern State Legislatures

A final measure of the penetration of Republicans into the political fabric of the South can be seen in the composition of state legislatures. Districts for state legislatures, especially those for the lower house, are generally much smaller than those for the U.S. House of Representatives. They can show fairly precisely how widely dispersed are southern Republicans. More important, they can show how willing southerners have become to vote for Republicans in what are essentially local elections.

Table 5.8 (a and b) shows the percentage of Republicans in southern state legislatures during selected years, or aggregations of years, between 1939 and 1994.[29] The data indicate that prior to the 1960s, very few real Republicans could be found in southern legislatures. Only Tennessee, North Carolina, and Virginia had significant numbers.

By the late 1960s and early 1970s, the percentage of Republicans had increased considerably in southern legislatures, especially in the rim South states. Seventeen percent of the lower house in the border South, and 10 percent of the upper house, were Republican, but the range was considerable. Nearly 40 percent of Tennessee's lower house was Republican, and 26 percent of Florida's. Among the deep South states, Georgia had a significant number of Republicans, owing to the mountainous region in the northern part of the state, as well as Republican suburban rings near Atlanta and Savannah.

What is of interest, however, is that the growth of Republicans in southern legislatures has been fairly slow. By 1989, only 23 percent of the lower house of southern legislatures and 20 percent of the upper houses were Republican. In the 1990s, this figure finally moved over the 30 percent mark. In spite of gains made in the 1994 elections, prior to the elections of 1996 Democrats retained control of all but three southern state legislatures—the Florida Senate and the North Carolina and South Carolina House of Representatives.[30]

There are a number of reasons for the failure of Republicans in southern legislatures to keep up with the progress of their counterparts in other elections. The most important is legislative apportionment. Democratic-controlled legislatures generally sought ways of keeping Republican districts minimized. Also, local tradition and political culture served to stifle rapid switches to the Republican Party: in many areas, it is acceptable to vote for the Republican presidential or gubernatorial candidate but not for

Table 5.8a

Republicans in Southern Legislatures, 1939–1981 (percent)

	1939		1948–51		1966–71		1976–81	
	House	Senate	House	Senate	House	Senate	House	Senate
South Total	3	2	4	3	11	8	14	10
Deep South								
Alabama	0	0	1	0	2	2	2	0
Georgia	0	0	1	1	12	15	13	8
Louisiana	0	0	0	0	2	0	5	2
Mississippi	0	0	0	0	1	1	3	5
South Carolina	0	0	0	0	6	6	12	6
Mean	0	0	<1	<1	5	5	7	4
Rim South								
Arkansas	1	0	2	0	3	1	14	2
Florida	0	0	1	0	26	2	26	27
North Carolina	6	4	11	4	19	13	8	6
Tennessee	17	12	19	13	39	28	36	34
Texas	0	0	0	0	3	3	13	12
Virginia	5	5	7	6	12	11	22	16
Mean	5	4	7	4	17	10	20	16

Table 5.8b

Republicans in Southern Legislatures, 1984–1994 (percent)

	1984		1988–89		1994	
	House	Senate	House	Senate	House	Senate
South Total	23	17	23	20	30	31
Deep South						
Alabama	12	13	15	14	21	22
Georgia	14	16	15	17	28	30
Louisiana	13	3	14	12	15	15
Mississippi	5	6	7	13	20	25
South Carolina	22	22	25	21	40	34
Mean	13	12	15	15	25	25
Rim South						
Arkansas	19	11	9	11	11	14
Florida	36	20	37	37	40	50
North Carolina	32	24	30	25	35	22
Tennessee	37	30	38	30	36	42
Texas	35	19	37	19	38	41
Virginia	34	20	35	25	47	45
Mean	32	21	31	25	35	36

the legislature. Too, the Republican Party is not generally as fully mature at the local level, from which candidates for the state legislature are chosen, as at state levels, thereby impeding the availability of strong Republican contenders for the legislature. We shall return to these points later in the chapter.

The failure of Republicans to constitute a majority in any but three southern legislative chambers does not necessarily mean they are lacking in political power. In some states, such as Florida and Texas, Republicans long ago formed effective coalitions with conservative, boll weevil Democrats, and in some cases became sufficiently strong to determine the outcome of legislation, appointments, and other policy decisions.

Nonetheless, the fact that Republican success in southern legislatures lags significantly behind that for other state offices should give pause to those who argue that the South is now a fully two-party region or that Republican dominance of most of the states is virtually complete and inevitable. There are a number of southern states—Alabama, Louisiana, Mississippi, Arkansas, even Texas—where Republican weakness at the state legislative level suggests that the dispersion and strength of Republicans are not as great as some observers, and even politicians themselves, would have us believe. Reapportionment beginning in 2001 may well give Republicans a boost in state legislatures. Other factors may also contribute, such as improving Republican organization at the local level and weakness of Democratic Party candidates. On the other hand, the extraordinary turnover of seats the Democrats experienced in 1994 appears to have acted as a splash of cold water in the face of state and local party officials. It is not unusual to hear about the 1996 and 1998 elections in the South as "the revenge of the Democrats." Moreover, at least in Florida, Republican success in the Senate was not accompanied by a demonstrable capacity to govern; the party literally floundered, seemingly not knowing what to do. Public disenchantment with the "Republican revolution," palpable at the national level, has filtered down to at least some state capitals as well. Thus it may well be premature to crown the Republicans as the dominant party in the region.

The Growth of Southern Republicanism

Having completed this look at the extent of Republicanism in the political fabric of the modern South, we must now look at how this shift occurred, especially in such a relatively short span of time. What are the major factors that contributed to the sharp rise in the fortunes of the Republican Party at the presidential level and an increasingly noteworthy Republican presence at state and local levels?

One of the most important factors contributing to the growth of Republican success in the South has been in-migration since World War II. One analyst has noted that this was an especially significant force for Republican development in the initial stages of postwar Republican growth.[31] But it has continued to be important well into the 1980s and 1990s.[32]

In-migration to the South since World War II has been heavily white and middle-class. That this group has formed the core of modern Republicanism in the region has been noted for some time.[33] Many brought their Republican attitudes and loyalties with them, along with the furniture, as they came south from the North and Midwest.

Florida provides an illustration of these developments in the South, although in the Sunshine State they may have occurred somewhat earlier, and more rapidly, than in other southern states. In his mid-1970s study of Florida Republicans, Paul Cohen found that newcomers were generally relatively young, educated, somewhat affluent white-collar workers living mainly in the newly developing "suburban horseshoe" of central Florida and the southeastern and southwestern coasts of the state. All of these areas have been among the fastest growing parts of the state and region. Much of this population shift was complicated by another group of in-migrants, some of whom had arrived earlier—the elderly. Only a minority of this group was affluent, and many were deeply concerned about rising taxes, inflation, and other matters important to pensioners. They, too, were heavily Republican. These two major groups did not always have political interests in common, as the subsequent political history of the Republican Party in Florida would show. But there is no question of their partisanship: they were heavily Republican. Indeed, Cohen found that at the time of his study, some 90 percent of the state's Republicans were born outside the state.[34]

The question arises, Why would these in-migrants not become Democrats, like their southern neighbors? There are several answers to this question. As noted, many of the in-migrants were white, middle-class business and professional people. To the extent that they had partisan loyalties, they were more inclined to be Republican (or independents who voted Republican) than Democrats. There were exceptions—in-migrant Jews, for example, who were inclined toward the Democratic Party—but they were comparatively few.

Moreover, while it is true that local culture tends to influence attitudes and beliefs of newcomers so that they can adapt and fit in, in the case of many in-migrants to the South some of the usual process did not seem to work. Where in-migrants settled with large numbers of traditional southerners, there were significant pressures to adapt to southern ways, including loyalty to the Democratic Party. But in-migrants to the South since World War II, especially in states such as Texas, Virginia, Florida, Tennessee, and the Carolinas, often settled in new towns, suburbs, and rapidly developing cities rather than the older, more established and traditional southern cities such as Jacksonville, Birmingham, and New Orleans. As a result, there were fewer pressures to become Democrats. These newcomers did not find a milieu that had the political traditions of Old South cities and communities but rather one in which partisan loyalties were fairly relaxed, even nonexistent. Many newcomers found their neighbors, also recent arrivals, to be political independents, Democrats without loyalty to southern traditions, and even Republicans like themselves. Moreover, many of the recent arrivals were fiscally conservative, heavily mortgaged suburbanites more concerned about taxes, public services, good government, and decent schools than about race. Such individuals would be more likely to be political independents or Republicans than to join the traditional southern Democratic Party.

Finally, particularly after 1960 many in-migrants to the South found the southern Democratic Party in disarray. Even traditional southern Democrats were beginning to question their loyalty to the party, as it seemed no longer to represent southern interests and concerns. Thus in-migrants in many instances saw the local Democratic Party breaking up, even losing elections. The result was to give recent arrivals more flexibility to choose the style and political party (if any) they wished, since old style southern politics appeared to be on the wane.

There were also influxes of blue-collar skilled and semiskilled workers into the South, as well as others with marginal job abilities. Indeed, the number of these immigrants actually increased during the 1980s.[35] There has, however, been no powerful labor union movement in the South with strong ties to the Democratic Party, although there are some exceptions in industrialized urban areas such as Miami, Jacksonville, and Birmingham. In general, southern blue-collar workers have been political floaters, not bound by ties of partisanship and willing to vote for the most appealing candidate. Third-party presidential candidate George Wallace attracted substantial numbers of blue-collar voters in 1968; Republican presidential candidates and some at the state and local level have also been successful in drawing heavy support from these citizens.[36]

A changing southern economy has also contributed to increasing support for the Republican Party in the South. Such factors as the decline in small-farm agriculture and its replacement by agribusiness; the rapid growth of service, commercial, and industrial economic sectors in the region; the decline of ruralism and the mushrooming of southern cities and suburban areas—all are associated with Republican expansion and penetration.[37]

In conjunction with macrolevel economic changes are microlevel developments. Personal income and the percentage of middle-class southerners both rose. Rates of education have climbed, both because of in-migration and indigenous improvements in lower and higher education. Empirical studies have indicated the positive impact these macrolevel and microlevel changes have had on the Republican Party in the South.[38] The result of all of these economic and accompanying social changes has been a new diversity, complexity, and clash of interests that have fostered a breakdown of one-party dominance and aided the rise of the Republican Party.

The politics of race have also contributed to the expansion of Republicanism in a number of ways. Perhaps most fundamentally, growing black demands for civil rights, and the response of the national Democratic Party to those demands, directly assaulted traditional southern mores, attitudes, and ways of life. Many white southerners, especially natives and longtime residents, felt that under these circumstances they could no longer remain Democrats. The modern Republican Party, standing for conservative values and states' rights (the essence of the bargain following the election of 1876) offered white southerners an acceptable, palatable alternative to their traditional party affiliation. A third party, such as the Dixiecrats or Wallace's American Independent Party, might also have served the purpose. But it could not be sustained. Republicans, indeed, were a permanent part of the political landscape and seemed prepared to defend racial and other traditions of the South. As Robert Sherrill has shown, "early" Republicans of the 1960s offered largely unadulterated racism to white southerners precisely when national, and even some southern, Democrats were abandoning it.[39]

Another way in which race played a key role in developing southern white support for Republicans was the so-called southern strategy of the party. While it actually began much earlier in the century, it appeared first in modern form in 1964 and was perfected during the Nixon years. The strategy was a not-very-subtle way of playing on white fears and prejudices, especially among traditional whites and those economically threatened by black demands. What was heralded as the new politics of the South was often little more than old racist appeals dressed up in modern, slick media-oriented campaign rhetoric. Thus, by 1968 and 1972, states' rights and hard-line anticommunism were coupled with racial appeals, often using such code words and phrases as "forced busing," "law and order," and "affirmative action." The message played well in the South, as is shown by the success of Republican presidential candidates in the region.

A third, and related, way in which race provoked Republican support was the presence of a protest vote in the South. It appeared on those occasions when white southerners were angry or dissatisfied because of economic conditions, fears of and hostility toward blacks, threats to states' rights, and patriotic values, international circumstances, or some similar matters. Protest votes did not always aid Republicans (for example, in 1968 when white southerners in the deep South voted for Wallace), but there were other occasions when they did—1964, 1972, 1980, 1988, to some extent 1992.[40] They also appeared in some state and local races as well, and most assuredly in the Republican triumph of 1994.

The protest vote is not always stable, and it can vary in size and intensity. It can include more than just racial issues. Nonetheless, Louis Seagull and Earl and Merle Black demonstrate that where black-white tensions continue to exist, race will serve as the core of the protest vote.[41] The protest vote can be substantial in size: recent estimates suggest that about a third of the white male southern vote can be considered swing or volatile, meaning that it is not fixed to a party, and can erupt as a protest vote when conditions are right.

Developments in the national Democratic Party that affected southerners included race but were by no means limited to this one issue. Many traditional white southerners felt that the national party, by the late 1950s and 1960s and continuing to the present, began to take unacceptable positions on such matters as economic and social welfare issues, federal-state relations, international relations, the military budget, family values, and others. To many southerners, the party became too liberal, as evidenced by such presidential nominees as Hubert Humphrey, George McGovern, Walter Mondale, and Michael Dukakis. Many felt that these northeastern and midwestern Democrats did not represent the interests or concerns of southerners and articulated values and attitudes with which they were fundamentally at odds. Too, many felt that the party had become dominated by shrill, self-interested minority groups, including blacks, Hispanics, women, and gays, who represented positions and directions with which many traditional southerners were out of sympathy.

The result was that many southerners no longer felt compelled or obligated to maintain their traditional loyalty to the Democratic Party. Nor did many even desire to do so. To them, the party had abandoned its traditional interest in the South and willingness to allow southerners to carve out their own political destiny. It was not, as far as they were concerned, that they were leaving the Democratic Party. It was, rather, that the party had abandoned them. Of course all of this occurred as Republicans were launching their modern southern strategy, which enabled many disaffected Democrats to find a new political home.

The type of candidates that Republicans began to put forward also proved far more appealing to many southerners than did those of the Democratic Party. At the presidential level, Barry Goldwater, Richard Nixon,

Ronald Reagan, and George Bush were perceived as closer to mainstream southern values than were Humphrey, McGovern, Mondale, and Dukakis. Even two native southerners, Lyndon Johnson and Jimmy Carter, were seen by significant numbers of southerners as not meeting their expectations of presidential candidates.

Similar changes also occurred at the state and local level. Formerly, as early students of southern Republicanism have noted, Republican candidates were often colorless individuals who represented the country club set and were out of touch with mainstream southern politics. Often they waged desultory, pro forma campaigns scarcely designed to attract notice or gather popular appeal.

But by the 1960s and 1970s much of this began to change. Republican candidates for office, such as Bruce Alger and John Tower in Texas, Howard Baker and Bill Brock in Tennessee, Howard H. "Bo" Callaway in Georgia, Trent Lott and Thad Cochran in Mississippi, Ed Gurney and Louis "Skip" Bafalis in Florida, among a host of others, were often young, attractive, conservative, vigorous campaigners who understood how to use the media to maximize their electoral chances.[42] Even when these types of Republican candidates did not win, they usually waged able, visible campaigns. They presented themselves as desirable alternatives to the tired, familiar faces that until well into the 1970s the Democratic Party continued to put forward. They were especially able to appeal to the new residents of the South, many of whom were Republicans or independents anyway but who in any case had little if any loyalty to the traditional southern Democratic Party and its candidates.

There were also localized pressures and circumstances that gave rise to Republican growth in the South. An important one was public repudiation of the Democratic Party, and corresponding switch to the GOP, by influential southern politicians. Sometimes prominent private citizens did the same. In South Carolina, for example, Strom Thurmond switched to the Republicans in 1964. Immediately the fortunes of the GOP in that state began to rise. In Virginia, the son of Harry Byrd (who took over his father's seat after the latter's death in 1966) became an independent, and twice ran successfully for the U.S. Senate. While the younger Byrd never officially became a Republican, to many observers he appeared to be one and voted like one in the Senate. Also in Virginia, Mills Godwin twice won the governorship—in 1965 as a Democrat, and in 1973 as a Republican. Party switching in Florida began somewhat later, but by the mid- to late 1980s became a growth industry and included the winners of both the 1986 gubernatorial contest, Bob Martinez, and 1988 secretary of state race, Jim Smith, who was a Democrat when he previously served in the state Cabinet as attorney general. The trend continued in 1989 with the switch to the Republican Party of Democratic U.S. Representative Bill Grant (who lost his congressional seat in 1990 to a bona fide Democrat).

In other states, a different set of local conditions promoted the cause of Republicanism. In Tennessee, the final decay of the remnants of the Memphis-based Crump machine lessened the grip of the Democratic Party over state politics. Moreover, the excesses and corruption of some state Democratic figures, notably during the Ray Blanton administration of 1974–78, as well as the emergence of attractive Republicans such as Howard Baker, Bill Brock, and Lamar Alexander, caused many Tennesseans to switch party allegiances.

Disorganization, even collapse, in Democratic Party organizations also aided Republican causes. Key pointed out at midcentury that major consequences of long-term, one-party dominance included a tendency toward complacency and weakness in party organization. With a few notable exceptions (Virginia, for example), most Democratic statewide organizations were so atrophied and splintered that they were unable to cope with a substantial Republican challenge. As a result, party machinery proved ineffective when one appeared, breaking down or fragmenting sufficiently so that the party literally handed the election to the Republicans.

This breakdown has occurred on any number of recent occasions in the South. In 1961, John Tower was elected Republican senator from Texas because of a rift among liberal-conservative, urban-rural, and sectional factions in the Democratic Party. Similar problems aided the election of Republican William Clements to the Texas governorship in 1978 and again in 1986. In Florida, factional disorganization helped contribute to the defeat of Democratic senatorial candidate LeRoy Collins in 1968 and gubernatorial candidates Robert King High in 1966 and Steve Pajcic in 1986. It also was in large measure responsible for the 1989 loss of the U.S. House of Representatives seat held for decades by the late Claude Pepper to Republican Ileana Ros-Lehtinen. In Mississippi Charles Evers's candidacy for the Senate, and his unwillingness to support the nominee of the Democratic Party, virtually gave the election to the Republicans in 1978. And in 1986, a huge fight within the Alabama Democratic Party (so severe that it had to be settled by the Alabama Supreme Court) opened the door to Republican Guy Hunt, who previously had not been expected to win the race.

In the 1990s, congressional and state legislative redistricting have further contributed to the rise of Republicans in the South. Even though southern state legislatures were dominated by Democrats Republicans during the 1991–92 reapportionment cycle,[43] Republicans devised a shrewd strategy designed to improve their congressional and state legislative electoral chances.[44] Republicans in state legislatures throughout the South cut deals with African American Democratic legislatures through which black representation would be enhanced through the creation of primarily, or at least heavily, black congressional and legislative districts;[45] but at the same time, the creation of these districts would "bleed" blacks out of other districts, leaving them mainly white and potentially ripe for Republican victories.[46]

The strategy was a bold one, and its effect was to divide the Democratic Party. White Democrats were fearful of what the Republican strategy meant for the party, for it was clear that any number of districts that had been marginally Democratic because of a significant presence of black voters would likely fall into the Republican column. It has been estimated that anywhere from a dozen to twenty or so congressional districts were thus affected, and while figures on state legislatures are unclear, results of the 1992 state legislative elections assuredly reflected a rise in Republican seats.[47] Black Democrats were faced with a considerable dilemma, insofar as they saw that overall Democratic representation might well fall even as black representation rose; in many instances, the latter value prevailed over the former. And while Republicans were criticized for pushing their divide and conquer strategy on the grounds that it represented a cynical manipulation of blacks, there is little doubt that they benefited from it.

Whether the Republican divide and conquer strategy can be maintained is questionable. In 1995, the U.S. Supreme Court knocked a major prop out from under the creation of black access districts by holding that race could not be a "predominant" factor in the creation of congressional districts.[48] Even as this book is being written, a number of cases are under consideration by the U.S. Supreme Court and lower federal courts that might force changes in congressional and state legislative districts. The effect of some of these changes—especially if they include more black/Democratic voters—might well be to make at least some of the newly Republican districts much more competitive for Democrats.[49] It seems unlikely, however, that a wholesale reversion to earlier Democratic dominance is likely; Republicans are just too entrenched at both congressional and state legislative levels for reversion to occur.

All of these forces contributed, over time, to the rise of the southern Republican Party. In the end, perhaps, it was inevitable. As George Mowry pointed out, there was a "natural" Republican tendency in the South that was suppressed for a long time, largely but not exclusively, by racial issues.[50]

But the modern emergence of the southern Republican Party resulted from more than just the transformation of racial politics in the region. By the 1960s politics in the South had become so complex and had broadened to such an extent that the old, creaky machinery of the Democratic Party literally burst at the seams. New social and economic forces, new demography, and new political rhetoric made the old one-party system obsolete. The evolution of a new set of political structures, institutions, dynamics, and possibilities, created by the rise of a second political party, was inevitable.

The Limits of Southern Republicanism

How Republican is the South likely to become? Are the trends of the past three decades so powerful that eventually the Republican Party will become a majority in the region? Or is there an upper limit beyond which it will have difficulty reaching?

As long as the South continues to develop a service-oriented economy heavily rooted in professional, managerial, and commercial sectors, and as long as white-collar, largely middle-class, suburban, and new-town in-migration persists, economic and demographic pressures fostering growth in the Republican Party should continue.

However, economic dislocations in the mid- and late 1970s, and again in the early 1980s and early 1990s, hit the South very hard. Unemployment rose precipitously—in Louisiana and Alabama it was among the worst in the nation—and severe fiscal crises appeared in most of the southern states, notably Florida and Texas (the latter adversely affected for a long time, along with Louisiana, by a collapse in oil prices).

Much of the 1980s, of course, saw powerful and sustained economic growth that alleviated the fiscal problems in most of the southern states. Opinion among specialists, however, remains divided about the length of this economic vigor, especially in view of the economic difficulties of 1990–91. The recession damaged southern state economies that, while generally more broadly based than they were twenty years ago, may not yet have achieved sufficient breadth to develop the resilience needed to resist rapid dislocation.

More immediately, a decline in economic health could have an adverse impact on the Republican Party. Traditionally, the GOP seems to have been the target of voter uneasiness over the economy. While this connection does not necessarily mean it will happen again, evidence from the 1982 midterm elections, at the height of President Reagan's popularity, suggests that voters continue to blame Republicans for economic problems when they occur. Indeed, in the 1990 midterm elections, Democrats in the South showed remarkable strength, including in Republican growth-states Texas and Florida, both of which suffered economic downturns.[51] This outcome is further support for the contention that the limits of southern Republicanism are indeed tied to the health of state, regional, and national economies.

In addition, there is evidence that both the tide and type of in-migration to the region, so central to Republican growth, have changed in recent years. In Texas economic conditions by the mid-1980s actually produced a net out-migration from those areas most affected by the weakened oil industry. Recent in-migrants into Texas and other states have included increasing numbers of semiskilled and unskilled workers. It is not clear that the regional economy will be able to absorb these people, creating financial pressures on state budgets and demands for greater levels of public services. Neither the type of recent in-migrants nor the social and economic problems they pose for state government are likely to aid the continuing growth of southern Republicanism.

These are significant environmental forces that will affect the continued growth of the southern Republican Party. There are other, more immediately political, factors as well.

Very important has been the counterattack of the southern Democratic Party. While perhaps it was slow to recognize and respond to the Republican threat, by the late 1970s and 1980s and into the 1990s it sought to invigorate itself. Party organization at both state and county levels improved. Recruitment of new members and voter registration drives were introduced, while twenty years ago these were unheard of within the Democratic Party. New leadership emerged whose goal has been to appeal to a broad segment of the community and expand the party's traditional base.

A major emphasis of a resurgent Democratic Party has been to put forward new kinds of candidates, significantly different from those of earlier periods. These candidates are often dynamic, media-conscious, sophisticated individuals who can appeal to a broad range of southern interests, including middle-class whites who have shunned the party in recent years. Examples include Florida's Bob Graham, Tennessee's Albert Gore Jr., and Georgia's Wyche Fowler in the Senate; Mississippi's Ray Mabus, Louisiana's Charles "Buddy" Roemer, Virginia's Douglas Wilder, and Arkansas's Bill Clinton in the governor's office; and Georgia's John Lewis, the late Mickey Leland of Texas, and Florida's Buddy MacKay in the House.[52]

These individuals—and there are many more—have demonstrated that they are capable of building electoral coalitions that cut across racial, class, occupational, and sectional lines to such a degree that they undercut the southern Republican base. Perhaps their major accomplishment is that they have moved the modern southern Democratic Party away from the politics of smoke screens, scapegoatism, and mass entertainment, so characteristic of its candidates in the past, and toward a more serious consideration of issues and problems than the party exhibited previously. These "new Democrats" and the attitudes they convey have proven appealing to the "new southern voter" and frequently have been able to outpoll equally attractive, modern Republican candidates.[53]

Aiding the revitalization of the southern Democratic Party, and also serving as a brake on Republican penetration in the South, has been the entrance of blacks into southern politics in a dramatic and powerful way. As they have moved into the mainstream of the political life of the region, they have registered overwhelmingly—upward of 90 percent in some areas—as Democrats.

The presence of large numbers of black voters has greatly amplified the number of votes Democrats can garner in southern elections. But there is more to it than just sheer numbers, important as they are. In many parts of the South, blacks have entered into coalitions with whites to ensure the election of Democratic candidates; Georgia is an example, with the 1986 election of Senator Wyche Fowler. In some areas, such as Alabama, through the Alabama Democratic Conference, and in some cities, blacks are numerous enough and sufficiently organized to act as relatively independent political forces and thus can deliver substantial blocs of votes to candidates of their choosing.

The emergence of modern winning Democratic coalitions in the South combines elements that a few years ago were thought to be incompatible. Urban-rural and black-white coalitions combined to elect such officials as Buddy Roemer in Louisiana, Ray Mabus in Mississippi, Bob Graham and Lawton Chiles in Florida, Wyche Fowler and Zell Miller in Georgia, and Doug Wilder in Virginia. Precursors of these coalitions can also be found in the elections of Jimmy Carter in Georgia, William Winter in Mississippi, Mark White in Texas, and even George Wallace in Alabama and John Stennis in Mississippi, both in 1982. Black-white coalitions have also successfully been formed at the local level and aided the election of such local officials as Mayors Richard Arrington of Birmingham and Kathy Whitmire of Houston, and City Commissioner Miller Dawkins of Miami.

The emergence of blacks into the political mainstream of the South, whether in coalition with whites or not, creates a real dilemma for southern Republicans. The party has had little to offer southern blacks; indeed, to many it appeared inhospitable to them.[54] It has made little if any effort to recruit black members or candidates. Yet by failing to attract southern black votes, it jeopardizes many of its electoral opportunities.

The extent of the problem that emergent black voters pose for the Republican Party can be seen by the percentage of the southern electorate that is black. It averages about 20 percent in the region, although the range is from about 12 percent in Florida to more than 30 percent in Mississippi. The local variation can be considerable, of course, ranging from counties that have few if any blacks to those in which they constitute a substantial majority.

Any Republican for statewide office who cannot successfully appeal to black voters begins his campaign with a deficit problem roughly approximating the percentage of blacks in the electorate. This problem can be mitigated by a low turnout among black voters, which often occurs. But since even a relatively modest black turnout is likely to go heavily to Democratic candidates, in a close election these votes could spell the difference between victory and defeat for the Republican candidate.[55] It has been estimated that in the deep South there are enough black voters that, with a normal turnout in a statewide race, only about 35–40 percent of whites need vote for the Democrat in order for the Republican candidate to lose.[56]

Moreover, because of the concentration of black voters in some southern counties, blacks have demonstrated that sometimes white votes are irrelevant to the election of a Democratic, especially black, candidate. The 1986 election of Mississippi's Mike Espy to the U.S. House of Representatives is an example of how powerful the black vote can be in black-dominated counties. It is of interest that Espy's 1988 reelection came with considerably more white support than he received two years earlier.

A third major limit on the future of Republicanism in the South concerns organizational problems within the various state Republican Parties. In the past, as Key and others observed, Republican organizations were weak because state leaders did not bother, or even want, to do the routine, tedious, but necessary grass-roots work needed to build a real party.[57] In more recent times, even as Republican candidates began to find success at the polls, party leaders failed to capitalize on these gains by not solidifying local support, recruiting new registrants, attracting local workers, or building statewide coalitions.

Perhaps some Republican leaders assumed that it would not be necessary to build permanent party organizations; their candidates were doing well anyway. But two other problems emerged that, associated with the party's organizational weakness, have created severe constraints on Republicanism: the party seems to have inherited the Democrats' tendency toward fragmentation, factionalism, and in-fighting; and Republicans have not always been able to recruit able, attractive candidates (indeed, some have proven to be unskilled campaigners and/or mediocre officeholders). The result has been that the promise the Republican Party seemed to hold in the late 1960s and early 1970s was not always realized, and in fact in some respects Republicans actually lost ground to Democrats during the 1980s.

Several brief examples will serve to illustrate these conclusions. In the Georgia gubernatorial election of 1966, Democrat Lester Maddox was opposed by Howard H. ("Bo") Callaway. An erstwhile Democrat, Callaway was an able and attractive candidate. He pitched his campaign toward urban centers and a white middle class who found the demagogic Maddox unacceptable. Callaway received a plurality of the vote, but because of the presence of a write-in third candidate (former governor Ellis Arnall), the outcome of the election was determined by the Democratic-controlled legislature. It chose Maddox.[58]

The near victory by Callaway astounded Georgia Republicans, but they failed to consolidate their gains. Indeed, the percentage of the vote that Republican gubernatorial candidates achieved actually declined sharply in the next two elections. Republicans also remained weak in U.S. Senate elections until 1980, when they barely managed to capture the seat held by the disgraced Herman Talmadge. Research on Georgia Republicans has indicated that, overall, the fortunes of the party did not increase very much in the 1980s. In the early 1990s, however, their fortunes again began to rise.[59]

Statewide success for the Republican Party in Florida also began in 1966 with the election of Claude Kirk as governor, largely as a result of a badly fragmented Democratic Party. But it was quickly followed in 1968 when Republican Ed Gurney was elected U.S. senator, defeating former governor LeRoy Collins. GOP fortunes appeared to be on the rise by the early 1970s; for a time the Republicans held nearly a third of the seats in the legislature and roughly the same percentage of the U.S. House of Representatives delegation.

But then there were no further gains, and the party actually regressed. Kirk and Gurney became embroiled in a bitter intraparty dispute with longtime Republican kingpin William Cramer, the effects of which were to split the party for more than a decade. The Democratic Party fought back with attractive candidates, aggressive campaigning, and open recruitment of black voters. Meanwhile, several Republican candidates proved weak campaigners, unable to transcend either Democratic strength or Republican factionalism.

Nowhere is this better seen than in the Florida gubernatorial and senatorial races of 1982. Both Governor Bob Graham and Senator Lawton Chiles were seen as vulnerable, following the overwhelming victory of Ronald Reagan in 1980. The national Republican Party pinpointed Florida for a major campaign effort.

But Republicans seemed unable to exploit the momentum created by their 1980 victory, which included the election of Paula Hawkins to the U.S. Senate. The party could not find candidates of stature to run against Graham and Chiles. When they finally got their campaigns in gear, they discovered that both incumbent Democrats had waged aggressive, strategically sound campaigns. Both Graham and Chiles were easy victors in November 1992.[60]

A survey of the 1986 and 1988 statewide races in the South shows a continuation of many of these same trends. Each of the five Republican senators elected in 1980 (from Alabama, Florida, Georgia, Louisiana, and North Carolina), largely on the strength of Ronald Reagan's coattails, was defeated by a Democratic challenger. While there were varied reasons for the defeats, a common denominator was that Democrats seemed to put forward more vigorous and attractive candidates, ran more aggressive campaigns, and successfully assembled black-white coalitions sufficient to ensure victory. Indeed, one national Republican figure was heard to mutter, after losing all five southern senate seats, that the party should have put forward better candidates in 1980 so that they could resist the Democratic challenge in 1986.

Republicans did win the governorships in Alabama, Florida, South Carolina, and Texas in 1986. They also squeaked to victory in the 1988 Senate race in Florida. In all but South Carolina disorganized Democratic Parties had as much to do with the defeats as Republican strength. But Democrats won the governorships in Tennessee in 1986, as well as those in Mississippi, Louisiana, Virginia, Texas, and Florida later. In Virginia the Democrats also won a Senate seat held formerly by the GOP.[61] Moreover, while Republicans won some congressional seats in Florida previously held by Democrats, the Democratic Party in 1989 successfully held onto the Texas seat previously held by the disgraced Jim Wright and captured a Mississippi seat formerly occupied by the late Republican Larkin Smith. Also in Florida in 1990, the Republican Party threw away the potential to achieve majority control of the Cabinet when its major candidate for commissioner of agriculture, the incumbent lieutenant governor,[62] inexplicably withdrew from the race, thereby handing the office back to the Democrats.

These major Democratic gains in the late 1980s have to be balanced against the Republican surge of 1994. In that year, Democratic incumbents fell all over the South, although there were exceptions. We already noted the reelection of Democratic Governors Chiles in Florida and Miller in Georgia. In Florida, not a single Democratic congressional incumbent was defeated, in spite of the toppling of Democratic congressmen in other southern states. Moreover, there is some reason to think that Democrats will see a resurgence in the late 1990s. While Republicans were widely victorious in 1994, they appear not to have consolidated their gains very well. Their record in governance—as opposed to campaigning—has not been sufficiently stellar to have ensured a continuing power base in the future; the public appears to have become virtually as disenchanted with Republicans as it was with Democrats a few years earlier.

Thus it seems clear that while the Democratic Party in the South may be enfeebled at the presidential level, at the state and local level it is not dead but is likely to reemerge as vigorous and competitive, able to cope with strong Republican challenges and offer attractive alternatives to Republican incumbents.

Moreover, while many observers of southern politics have been looking for significant signs of realignment toward a large Republican plurality, even majority, the prospects for dealignment, even decomposition, seem greater. That is, the number and percentage of independent voters is increasing. True, many of these vote Republican. On the other hand, they do constitute swing voters who can be won over to the Democratic Party by the nomination of attractive candidates and effective campaigns.[63]

These constraints on the modern Republican Party in the South are real; they have appeared at the ballot box on election days in recent years, much to the chagrin of Republican candidates, some of whom were expected to win. On the other hand, it should not be assumed that the GOP cannot cope or even overcome them. Nor should they in any way diminish the extraordinary growth of Republicanism in the South in a relatively short period of time. The GOP has very definitely taken up permanent residence in the South. That does not mean, however, that the Democrats have folded and permanently handed the reins of government over to them.

A Two-Party South?

We can end this chapter and this section of the book by posing two very basic questions: Is the South now a two-party region? Has the one-party system, so long dominant, finally been laid to rest?

The second question is easier to answer than the first. The answer is very clearly yes. While there is considerable variation across the South, as we have seen, in no state does the one-party system continue to exist. Republicans appear on the ballot, are competitive, and frequently win major elections.

Immediately objections to this statement appear. Especially for lesser office, such as U.S. House of Representatives, state legislature, and even some executive positions, there are many instances in which Republican candidates still fail to compete. The response to this point is that there are also significant numbers of Republicans who win such races without Democratic opposition. The remnants of one-party politics can now apply, in limited geographic areas of the South, as much to Republicans as to Democrats.

But even though one-party politics is now a historical relic, whether a true two-party system has developed in the South is much more problematic. There are several reasons for this conclusion.

In the first place, in a truly competitive two-party system, Republicans have a reasonable chance to win elections. In some states, they do: South

Carolina, Virginia, Florida, Mississippi, North Carolina. In other states, however, they do not, as our tables have shown. Indeed, during the 1990s, Republicans have only managed to win about 40 percent of all House seats; in the state legislatures, their record of success is lower than that.

During the 1980s Republicans had trouble retaining statewide seats (they have had more luck with U.S. House of Representatives seats, which quickly become safe). They lost many of the governorships, U.S. senate seats, and other positions even after winning them. It is not clear if they will be able to retain those they won in 1994. If so, this ability will be evidence of increasing Republican vitality. But losing many or most they won will constitute evidence of weak staying power by GOP elected officials.

While Republicans have had success in each of the southern states, there is also considerable variation across the region in terms of the degree and extent of that success. Although there is less difference between rim and deep South states, in terms of Republican penetration, than there was formerly, the GOP is much stronger in some areas than in others. We noted above the states where there has been considerable Republican success, but in Arkansas, Louisiana, and Georgia the GOP record has not been particularly distinguished.

Additionally, there is considerable intrastate variation in some states. In parts of Louisiana, Texas, Arkansas, and Georgia, for example, there remain areas where Republicans can scarcely be found, suggesting continuing weakness. This is not a phenomenon unique to southern states. On the other hand, its persistence raises the question of whether a state is truly competitive and two-party, or not.

Finally, political traditions in the South die hard, especially in those areas of the South least affected by in-migration, urbanization, industrialization, and all the other manifestations of the modern new South. Southerners' roots in the political culture of the past are deep, and their political habits in a conservative, tradition-minded region are not easily changed. People in these areas will vote for a Republican presidential nominee; but many draw the line at the state and local level. A quick visit to a political event (a fish fry, a barbecue, a rally in the courthouse square) in a traditional southern town or rural area, even in the 1990 elections, looked and sounded remarkably like one fifty years ago, except that there were more pickup trucks present than mules. There might be Republicans at these events, but, as in the more distant past, they are hard to spot.

That there are two parties in the South is obvious to all. To Democratic candidates and their staffs, many elections that not so long ago were unlosable are now unwinnable because of Republican strength. In the long run, however, it may be that neither party will dominate the region but rather will compete in statewide and some other major elections by seeking to attract the growing body of independent voters, since neither will have a clear-cut majority sufficient to ensure victory.[64]

Assuming this scenario happens, the South may well resemble other parts of the country in the way political parties seem to be evolving (or, perhaps, devolving). In this sense, the South will be less a two-party region than a multiplicity of Democratic and Republican Parties, with neither organizationally powerful enough reduce the other to a sustained secondary position. Along with these parties will be large numbers of independent voters permanently uncommitted to either. Is this a true two-party system? Hardly. Rather, it is a partial two-party system, where the balance depends on how well both Republicans and Democrats do their homework, organize, and find candidates who have broad appeal and can successfully run campaigns attractive to their own members, marginal members of the other party, and a significant number of voters loyal to neither.[65]

Part III

Civil Rights and
Black Political Participation
in the South

6

"I Have a Dream": Toward the Civil Rights Movement

Nobody expects 10,000 Negroes to get together and march any-where for anything at any time. . . . They are supposed to be just scared and unorganizable. Is this true? I contend it is not.
—A. Philip Randolph, 1941

America was born in a revolution, and as a nation we tend to apply the term loosely to anything from the most trivial fads in fashion and lifestyle to the most fundamental restructuring of basic institutions. The civil rights move-ment in the South was one of the latter. It represented an enormous up-heaval in which southern blacks rose up, confronted the oppression of racial bigotry and second-class citizenship imposed on them, and demanded the rights that the Constitution and the tradition of the nation guarantee to all Americans. That the movement was only partially successful in no way detracts from its importance. It is no exaggeration to say that the civil rights movement ranks near the top of human efforts to throw off tyranny and reassert the dignity of human life.

In this and the following chapters, we shall examine a part of southern life that makes a significant break from the old style politics of the past. The entrance of blacks into southern politics and their transformation from polit-ical victims into independent political participants represents a very sub-stantial step in the development of a new South and new southern politics. In this chapter we shall look at how and why the civil rights movement came about. In the following chapters we shall assess the accomplishments of the movement, as well as how far it has yet to go.

Goals of the Civil Rights Movement

On the most general level, the civil rights movement had as its goal the complete political and social transformation of the South. It was meant to confront, directly, a traditionally Jim Crow society that had relegated blacks to second-class status, to throw off the kinds of discrimination that were the twentieth-century vestiges of slavery, and to gain equality of opportunity and treatment for southern blacks. It was in this sense that the goals of the movement must be seen as fully revolutionary.

But the goals of the movement were not just abstract and societal in scope. They extended down to the sidewalk level, into the lives of individuals as well. Blacks in the South were tired of the humiliations, insults, and indignities they had suffered for so many generations, and they sought to be rid of them. These indignities ranged from the benign paternalism of southern whites who "took care" of their black domestics but never bothered to learn their names or anything about them, to the forced use of second-class waiting rooms, "colored" water fountains and rest rooms, seats at the "back of the bus," and segregated schools unworthy of the name, to repressive forms of economic exploitation and terror, and ultimately to sadistic beatings, lynchings, maimings, and murder. In a sense, the civil rights movement can be seen as a collective cry by southern blacks, not of self-pity but of anger, fatigue, and frustration: ENOUGH!

These goals might seem very general, but in fact we can point to four very specific, concrete objectives that lay at the heart of the civil rights movement.

Equal Access to the Ballot

For most of this century blacks in the South were denied the right to vote through elaborate legal and administrative mechanisms.[1] Even in those instances, particularly in urban areas and border South states, where blacks could vote, they were manipulated and did not act as an independent bloc of voters.[2]

In spite of the hurdles placed in front of them, at least some blacks tried, during the first sixty years of the century, to register to vote. In border states, registering could be a difficult and sometimes humiliating step for blacks. But in the deep South, efforts by blacks to register could have serious consequences for them. It was not unusual for blacks seeking access to the ballot to find their house bombed or shot at, their employment and/or credit terminated, their children dismissed from school, or themselves or their families targets of beatings and murders.[3]

Perhaps because of these difficulties, blacks early on made equal access to the ballot a major goal of the civil rights movement. There were at least two reasons for this. First, the right to vote in America is an indicator of full-fledged citizenship and political legitimacy. Those persons who can vote are entitled to all the rights, privileges, and responsibilities that citizenship conveys. Conversely, denial of access to the ballot means the person is relegated to second-class citizenship. It is an indication that the person or group does not have the same status as those who do. In its more pernicious forms, denial of the right to vote creates a sort of pariah class who can be victimized or discriminated against.

Second, voting is not purely symbolic but has important instrumental purposes. In American political thought, it is regarded as a major method through which citizens select their leaders and representatives and influence what government does. Thus it is an important mechanism of democratic control through which citizens try to create their own political destiny.[4]

Both of these reasons lay at the heart of southern blacks' search for political equality. They formed the foundation of the famous "Give Us the Ballot" address given by Martin Luther King at the 1957 Prayer Pilgrimage to Washington, D.C.

> Give us the ballot and we will no longer have to worry the federal government about our basic rights. . . . Give us the ballot and we will no longer plead to the federal government for passage of an anti-lynching law. Give us the ballot and we will no longer plead—we will write the proper laws on the books. Give us the ballot and we will fill the legislature with men of goodwill. Give us the ballot and we will get the people judges who will "do justly and love mercy." Give us the ballot and we will quietly, lawfully, and nonviolently, without rancor or bitterness, implement the May 17, 1954, decision of the Supreme Court. . . . Give us the ballot and we will transform the salient misdeeds of bloodthirsty mobs into the calculated good deeds of orderly citizens.[5]

Equal Access to Public Facilities

As a result of the doctrine of "separate but equal" announced in *Plessy v. Ferguson,* southern blacks were forced to utilize separate public facilities from whites.[6] The most famous were public schools, but they were by no means the only ones: restaurants, hotels, tourist courts, and theaters routinely excluded southern blacks. Bus and train stations had separate waiting rooms, as did many white doctors and dentists. Many medical facilities, including hospitals, were not even open to blacks. Stores had segregated drinking fountains and bathrooms. Blacks could sit only in the back of buses, in specific railway cars, and usually could hail only black-owned taxis.

The facilities available to blacks were decidedly not equal to those of whites. To take the most famous and important example, on virtually any measure of school quality (per pupil expenditures, professional credentials of teachers, availability of books and other educational facilities, richness and diversity of the curriculum, quality of school services, and adequacy of the physical plant), black schools ranked far behind those of whites.

But it was not equal facilities that blacks sought. The lack of equality rankled badly, but it was the fact that they had to attend separate facilities that was painful and humiliating. Thus it was equal access to the same facilities that whites used, not different ones, that became a major goal of the civil rights movement. It was therefore with great joy that southern blacks greeted the overturning of "separate but equal" on May 17, 1954.[7] As Louis Lomax later wrote, "That was the day we won; the day we took the white man's laws and won our case before an all-white Supreme Court with a Negro lawyer, Thurgood Marshall, as our chief counsel. And we were proud."[8]

To Be Treated with Respect

This goal was less concrete than the others but no less important. The Jim Crow system itself was demeaning and insulting. But blacks faced, on a daily basis, extraordinary levels of rudeness and indecency. Often they were called "Boy" or "Mary" regardless of their name; professional titles or other titles of respect, even "Mister," were seldom used by whites addressing blacks. The famed civility and courtesy of southern life did not extend to relations between whites and blacks. Occasions in which whites and blacks came into contact, as they did daily in spite of the Jim Crow system, were often marked by humiliation, embarrassment, or harassment. Store clerks were often rude, condescending, or inattentive. In the deep South, blacks generally had to step into the gutter when meeting a white person on the sidewalk, regardless of the weather. In many parts of the South, blacks were outlawed from town limits after sundown; to violate the prohibition was an invitation to serious trouble.

Blacks knew that more than legal or structural changes in southern society were needed before they could expect to be treated with decency and respect. Attitude changes were needed, which might take a long time. On the other hand, they felt that part of achieving full citizenship was the right not to be called "Boy" or "nigger" (or its "polite" form, "nigra"). They also felt that full citizenship meant that contact between the races would not have to become occasions for embarrassment and a loss of dignity.[9]

Greater Economic Opportunity and Outcomes

It became obvious to Martin Luther King, as well as some of the more radical leaders of the movement, that achieving political and social goals alone would not fully bring about the levels of equality blacks needed and desired. They needed greater economic clout. Indeed, at the time King was murdered in Memphis in 1968, he was pushing for more black economic opportunity in the form of better jobs, housing, schools and training programs, health care, and so forth.

By the time this goal moved to the forefront of the civil rights movement, it was already badly fragmented, for reasons we shall explore. Even many white allies of the civil rights movement, who were very supportive of blacks' demands for equal opportunity and treatment, had doubts about blacks' calls for more equal economic outcomes, for they might require expensive "redistributive" policies and could involve controversial matters such as "racial quotas" and "affirmative action." Moreover, many blacks, as well as whites, became frightened by radical slogans such as "Black Power," the militant writings of authors such as James Baldwin, and the black separatist ideas of fire breathers such as Malcolm X, Stokely Carmichael, H. Rap Brown, Bobby Seale, and Eldridge Cleaver.

Thus, the goal of greater economic equality for southern blacks never achieved quite the consensus that the other three did. Ultimately, too, it became the most elusive, and probably the least achieved, of all. But it, too, needs to be included as a significant goal of the civil rights movement, for it became one after some of the earlier political goals were achieved.

Preconditions of the Civil Rights Movement

The goals of the civil rights movement were, in some respects, similar to those which blacks had sought since Emancipation. The question is, then, why did it come about when it did? What was the confluence of conditions and events that allowed it to go forward? While there were many, in the rest of this chapter we shall discuss six—the rise of black political consciousness and mobilization; organization; leadership; ideology; the development of strategies and tactics; and changes in the national political environment.

Collective Consciousness and Political Mobilization

Political mobilization refers to the ability of a group to undertake political activity, that is, to get involved in politics in order to accomplish some purpose. For southern blacks during much of this century, significant levels of political mobilization were impossible. Exploitation, manipulation, and oppression by the white community prevented it.

But there was another reason as well. The southern black community was socially fragmented and divided. As many observers have noted, including prominent blacks such as George Washington Carver, W.E.B. DuBois, Marcus Garvey, and Mary Bethune, southern blacks traditionally had difficulty uniting, organizing and working for collective goals, or seeking to create a consensus about the common good. It was precisely this problem that prompted A. Philip Randolph, longtime militant head of the Brotherhood of Sleeping Car Porters, to make the comment with which this chapter began.

Why southern blacks were so fragmented and divided is a matter that takes us beyond the scope of this book. But its effect was to prevent the widespread development of political or collective consciousness among southern blacks. Seldom did they think of themselves as a political community with common interests that could be identified, form the basis of common goals, or be used to design strategies for reaching them.[10] Yet until this kind of collective political consciousness began to develop, it was virtually impossible for the southern black community to become politically mobilized to confront successfully the Jim Crow society in which they lived.

By midcentury, a number of developments had occurred that encouraged the rise of political consciousness among southern blacks and later spawned a growing political mobilization. Some of these, such as organization and leadership, developed internally within the southern black community. We shall touch on them shortly. Others were a result of larger, external forces that affected the southern black community deeply.

Three of the latter that were most important were changes in the southern agricultural economy, especially the beginnings of the demise of the sharecropper-tenant system by the late 1930s, black urbanization, and black migration out of the South to the Midwest and Northeast.[11]

The effect of each of these developments was to diminish somewhat southern blacks' dependence, especially economic dependence, on whites. The sharecropper system was little more than a twentieth-century version of slavery. In cities, blacks found somewhat greater social and economic opportunities, as well as a racial climate somewhat less oppressive than in the rural and small-town South. In southern cities blacks found social institutions, especially the church, where they could gather in substantial numbers; indeed, the "critical mass" of blacks needed to foster political consciousness and political mobilization was easier to achieve in cities than in the rural South. And even though racism pervaded northern and midwestern communities, the limited possibilities open to blacks who had migrated to these regions were still greater than they had had as oppressed dirt farmers in the South.

The impact of each of these forces was gradual. But their effect was magnified by the onset of World War II. Indeed, in retrospect the war was perhaps the biggest single factor contributing to the political consciousness of southern blacks. The reason is that it highlighted, for all Americans to see, the existence of institutionalized racism in the United States.

Blacks who went north looking for work in defense-related industries found that often these workplaces were rigidly segregated. Even if they could find work, they were generally relegated to menial and janitorial jobs; the better paying jobs were reserved for whites, even white women. The armed forces were also segregated. Blacks were usually assigned to all-black units that were often given the most undesirable of tasks, such as latrine duty, garbage collection, trench digging, and maintenance work. Opportunities for promotion were limited. Relatively few blacks were members of the officer corps. Moreover, as President Franklin D. Roosevelt himself noted to visiting blacks, the attitude that enlisted men and officers exhibited to blacks in the service was often of an offensive, Jim Crow nature, even by nonsoutherners.[12]

The bitter irony of World War II was not lost on southern blacks. Part of the rationale for America's war effort was to defeat the racism and bigotry of Adolf Hitler, Benito Mussolini, and the Japanese. In spite of their willingness to join their fellow citizens in this endeavor, blacks found that they were victimized by the very attitudes at home and in the service against which they were fighting abroad. Thus the democratic system that thousands of blacks gave their lives to protect excluded them from equal participation in it.

Protests from American blacks against these practices actually began before the nation entered the war. A. Philip Randolph sought to organize a national protest march by blacks on July 1, 1941, at the Lincoln Memorial in Washington, D.C. He had earlier opposed American participation in World War I as "a mockery, a rape of decency and a travesty on common justice" as long as "lynching, Jim Crow, segregation and discrimination in the armed forces and out . . ." existed.[13]

Randolph was dissuaded from calling the march by other black leaders and by President and Mrs. Roosevelt, herself an outspoken advocate of civil rights. Each of these individuals argued that a show of divisiveness would be a comfort to America's adversaries.[14] In return, Roosevelt issued an executive order (Number 8802) banning discrimination in defense-related industries, and establishing a Fair Employment Practices Committee to monitor discriminatory employment practices in war industries. It did not, however, ban discrimination in federal agencies or the armed forces.

Racial protests against discrimination occurred only rarely during the war, as blacks set aside their dissatisfactions in favor of a united war effort. But two other events occurred during the war years that underscored both black and white concern with segregation and aided the development of blacks' sense of political consciousness.

The first came in the hot summer of 1943, when blacks in the ghetto of Detroit, and later in New York City's Harlem, rioted. Forty people died, hundreds were injured, and property damage was in the millions of dollars as a result of these upheavals. The following year, as a direct result of these riots, saw the publication of *An American Dilemma,* the watershed study of American racial problems by the Swedish social scientist Gunnar Myrdal. [15]

Both these events raised the consciousness of white and black Americans about the extent and depth of racial hostility and problems in the country. It was the first real indication for many Americans that racism was not just a southern problem but a national one. The message for blacks was clear: there was no promised land north of the Mason-Dixon line, and the problem of bigotry and discrimination extended deep into the social fabric of America. The further message was that it would largely be through their own efforts alone that blacks could overcome Jim Crow; northern and midwestern whites were not necessarily any more willing to help them than were their white southern neighbors.

Even with changing economics and black urbanization, the impact of World War II, the urban riots, and Myrdal's massive book, the growth of southern political consciousness took time. An oppressed, poverty-stricken population accustomed to exploitation and victimization could not rapidly coalesce into a community with a clear sense of identity and political purpose. Nor could it rapidly mobilize its growing consciousness, energy, and resources into direct political action. Other developments had to occur, and it is to these that we now turn.

Organization

For the civil rights movement to take place, organizations capable of carrying on the struggle had to develop or be created. Indeed, even with the growth of a collective political consciousness, real political mobilization would have been impossible without organization. It provided a means for combining and multiplying individual energies, allocating resources in a coherent way, defining goals, and creating appropriate strategies and tactics for achieving them. Without organization, coordination was nearly impossible, and waste was inevitable.

But for southern blacks, organization was a serious problem. As we noted earlier, the black "community" in the South for much of this century was highly fragmented and dispersed, unaccustomed to collective action. Overcoming this problem was a critical matter for leaders and architects of the civil rights movement. They did so in two ways. First, existing indigenous black organizations were enlarged and strengthened so that they could effectively carry on civil rights activity. Second, new organizations were created at the national or regional level, but they existed as federations that could extend downwards to local, grass-roots communities. Not all of the organizational problems were solved by these two approaches, but ultimately they proved effective in achieving some of the movement's goals.

Indigenous Organizations

In spite of the fragmentation of the southern black community, three indigenous organizations existed that proved critical to the origins and progress of the civil rights movement: the southern black church, neighborhood associations, and black colleges.

The role played by religion and the church among southern blacks has been well recognized for a long time. In some rural areas, the church was virtually the only institution that existed for black collective activity. It had important spiritual functions and social and economic ones as well. The church provided an opportunity for blacks to communicate with one another, to interact on a variety of levels, and, within the constraints of massive poverty, to offer assistance to those in need.[16]

The rural church, however, generally proved to be less important for the civil rights movement than the urban black church. Rural churches tended to be small and economically weak. Their congregations were generally poorly educated and, because they were heavily made up of sharecroppers, economically dependent on whites. They had little, if any, tradition of social activism. Rather, their religious focus was otherworldly, often aimed at transcendental rewards and salvation in the next life instead of on present problems and concerns.

The ministers of rural churches were also not well equipped to act as secular leaders. Generally they were too poorly educated and trained to do so. Indeed, it was fairly rare for a rural black church in much of the South to be able to afford its own minister. Often numbers of churches would share a minister, who made a circuit, stopping in a given church only occasionally. Thus the leadership potential of the rural clergy was limited.

While urban black churches were denominationally similar to rural ones, in fact they were quite different.[17] In general, they were larger. Their congregations tended to be better educated and somewhat advantaged financially. More important, they tended to be less dependent on whites than were their rural counterparts. Many urban black churches could afford a full-time minister, sometimes several. Black ministers in urban areas tended to be better trained and educated than rural clergy. Thus they could potentially serve as secular as well as religious leaders.

Urban black churches grew at a much faster rate than rural ones. While the number of black churches in the South grew relatively slowly between the 1920s and early 1960s, church membership expanded considerably—93 percent by one estimate. The vast majority of this growth was in urban black churches as blacks moved off the land into southern cities and other urban places.[18]

Even more important was the secular tradition of the black urban church. Besides spiritual guidance, it offered to congregants a concern for local problems. Not infrequently, the urban black church encouraged blacks to vote, to support particular candidates, to become involved in community affairs. Gradually this concern with "involvement" evolved into advocacy of social activism: the origins of the Montgomery bus boycott in 1955 can be directly traced to the city's black churches. Also, the urban black church often served as a critical linkage between the white and black communities, because whites felt safe in dealing with blacks through ministers and churches.[19]

The urban black church also served as a linkage between, on the one hand, citizens and civil rights organizations that existed or were created locally and, on the other, branches of regional and national civil rights organizations that came in from outside. Sometimes it was even difficult to tell where the church left off and a civil rights organization began. Memberships overlapped, the church often provided facilities for civil rights meetings and rallies (which often included prayers, Bible readings, and hymns), and the ministers were often the leaders of civil rights organizations and activity. Linkages between urban black churches also formed a useful communications network for exchanging information and plans and coordinating activity.

A second type of indigenous organization helpful in fostering the civil rights movement were the so-called neighborhood associations. They were almost exclusively urban in character, and sometimes had connections with black churches. They came in a variety of kinds, of which we can mention three.

Improvement associations were often ad hoc, created to address specific problems and concerns of a social or political nature.[20] The black clergy of Montgomery, for example, formed themselves into the Montgomery Improvement Association (MIA) for the purpose of conducting the bus boycott. It had parallels in other communities.[21]

Businessmen's associations were essentially organizations of the small black business and professional middle class. They were almost exclusively urban organizations. Often very moderate and accommodationist in outlook, they frequently had access to the white business and political community and, because of their nonmilitant style, were usually regarded as safe by whites. They nonetheless served as important communication linkages between whites and blacks during the civil rights movement.

The most famous of the neighborhood associations were voter leagues. Frequently they were tied to urban black churches. They provided a vehicle whereby blacks could seek to register and vote as a group, thereby permitting a level of safety not available to the individual. Voter leagues also made demands on local election officials concerning registration hours and procedures and protested the imposition of poll taxes and discriminatory literacy and character tests. Voter leagues, which existed well before the civil rights movement began, became more numerous as efforts to secure the franchise started in earnest.

The last indigenous black institution to be discussed are black colleges, and their students. Black colleges in the South provided a locus for learning, exploration of ideas, and discussion of the meaning of the black experience in America. They were an intellectual haven in which bright young men and women could develop a sense of who they were and what they could become. The academic environment, particularly after World War II, thus provided the opportunity for the development of an intellectual cadre of individuals who understood the position of blacks in the South, were impatient with and angered by it, and could explore ways to transform it.[22]

Black colleges thus provided institutions for the development of ideas and leadership. But they also formed an important network that became crucial for the civil rights movement. Many of its later leaders noted that they met one another in college or in other black colleges they visited. They were influenced, positively and negatively, by influential blacks who visited campuses. The colleges themselves had important roots in the South that provided students with access to the larger black population.

It was by no means clear that southern black colleges would play this role. For decades in this century, many were marginal academic institutions, barely worthy of the name "college." Many were just inferior training schools. But as a result of a 1938 U.S. Supreme Court case,[23] southern legislatures were forced to pump additional resources into black colleges, thereby upgrading them. Moreover, the impact of World War II pushed black faculty and students toward a more assertive stance in overcoming segregation. Thus by the 1950s southern black colleges, populated by young, middle-class, urban blacks no longer willing to wait to gain entry into the promise of American life, became important organizations for civil rights activity.

Outside Organizations

As significant as indigenous organizations were, they probably would not have been sufficient, by themselves, to overcome entrenched southern racism. Other organizations with greater strength and access to national resources were needed. While there were a considerable number of these, including some that existed outside the South and whose memberships were heavily white (the United Auto Workers, headed by Walter Reuther, was an example), four became so important as to eclipse all the others. Known collectively as the Big Four, these were the National Association for the Advancement of Colored People, the Congress of Racial Equality, the Southern Christian Leadership Conference, and the Student Nonviolent Coordinating Committee.[24]

These organizations frequently engaged in disputes and institutional rivalries, although they supposedly agreed to work together through an umbrella organization called the Council of Federated Organizations.[25] Their leaders often bickered publicly. Nonetheless, they proved effective in seeking many of the goals of the movement. They had wide followings, if not memberships, among southern blacks, probably because they were closely allied to existing indigenous organizations such as churches and colleges. They tended to be organized in a federated system, which meant that decisions could be made at the grass-roots level about civil rights activity rather than always being imposed by national headquarters or by leaders brought in from outside. And unlike indigenous organizations, they served as key links to the media, national leaders in Washington, D.C., and sympathetic white citizens and groups outside the South. This link was extremely important, since the movement came to rely heavily on outside publicity, money, and support to go forward.

The National Association for the Advancement of Colored People (NAACP) was the oldest of the civil rights organizations. It had been founded in 1909 as an alternative to Booker T. Washington's "gradualist" philosophy of black improvement. From its earliest days, it was composed primarily of middle-class blacks. Before and during the civil rights movement, it had a reputation as an establishment, even conservative, organization. Part of its reputation also stemmed from its legalistic strategy for promoting social and political change. From its earliest years leaders chose court action as the primary weapon for attacking discrimination, and by the 1930s the NAACP and its activist arm, the Legal Defense and Educational

Fund, began to chip away at *de jure* segregation. The NAACP selected its legalistic strategy because it wanted to attack the "separate but equal" doctrine at its constitutional roots and also because earlier in the century no other political arenas besides federal courts seemed accessible to them.

The NAACP never abandoned its legalistic strategy. Nonetheless, it tended "to speak in whatever idiom was being voiced by the rest of the movement."[26] While it and its famous leader, Roy Wilkins, were frequently criticized by other civil rights activists—especially younger ones—as too slow and passive, it continued to enjoy considerable support at both national and grass-roots levels. It was probably the only one of the Big Four that maintained a high level of support from nonsouthern whites. And it frequently became the major target of bitter legal and political attacks by white southerners: Alabama actually outlawed the NAACP, several other southern states passed repressive laws against it, and many southern politicians enjoyed mocking its acronym, thereby titillating audiences with low-level jokes.[27]

The Congress of Racial Equality (CORE) was officially founded in Chicago in 1942 following the successful desegregation of the Jack Sprat restaurant by a biracial group of community activists and pacifists from the University of Chicago. From its inception it was dedicated to the principles of nonviolence articulated by Mohandas Gandhi and A.J. Muste; in this it anticipated Martin Luther King Jr. by two decades.[28]

The founders of CORE, including James Farmer, Bernice Fisher, Bayard Rustin, and others, were determined to move nonviolence beyond ideology to become a strategy, even a tactic. In fact, in 1942, Rustin undertook a bus ride between Louisville and Nashville in which he refused to sit in the back of the bus. Arrested, he responded with passive nonviolence, and ultimately his confused captors released him. From the start, CORE was primarily a northern and border South organization. Prior to the 1960s, it had scarcely any local affiliates in the South, and it never became a large organization there. Nonetheless, its influence was substantial, because when nonviolent protest became a major strategy of the civil rights movement, CORE provided almost a generation of experienced personnel and leadership to call upon. James Farmer, appointed its national director in 1961, became one of the civil rights movement's most articulate and persuasive leaders. And one of its major civil rights thrusts in the South, the 1961 freedom rides, became extremely important in desegregating bus terminals and other public accommodations.[29]

The Southern Christian Leadership Conference (SCLC) became very well known throughout the nation. It attracted considerable media attention, and may have been regarded by blacks and whites alike as the archetype civil rights organization. In part its reputation was based on its involvement in some of the civil rights movement's most critical and dramatic moments, such as Albany, Georgia, in 1962, Birmingham in 1963, St. Augustine in 1964, and Selma in 1965. But mainly SCLC was regarded as the archetype because it was so closely identified with, and eventually became the personal instrument of, its charismatic founder, Martin Luther King Jr.[30]

SCLC was organized in January 1957, after the Montgomery bus boycott had been successfully concluded. King, who had emerged as the boycott's leader, felt that the civil rights momentum built up by that event should not be wasted. Accordingly, he called a meeting in Atlanta of sixty black leaders from ten states, the majority of whom were clergy. After a considerable search, the name Southern Christian Leadership Conference was chosen.[31]

SCLC tried to combine both Gandhian and Christian doctrines as its guiding philosophy; as one of its earliest pronouncements suggested, southern blacks needed " 'to understand that nonviolence is not a symbol of weakness or cowardice, but as Jesus demonstrated, nonviolent resistance transforms weakness into strength and breeds courage in the face of danger.' "[32] Nonetheless, from its outset SCLC was primarily an action organization. It was closely tied to local churches and clergy and therefore was able to draw upon considerable resources of manpower and energy to engage in civil rights work. Coupled with the immense appeal of King, the close tie between SCLC and local religious groups enabled it to surmount its ongoing financial weakness to become an effective civil rights organization.

SCLC, like the NAACP, was often criticized by both blacks and whites. It was alleged to pick and choose very carefully when and where it would become involved and to undertake projects only when leaders could be assured of maximum exposure and the greatest likelihood of success. King, in particular, was criticized for failing to take the lead in formulating plans but instead would appear on the scene of ongoing civil rights activity and seek to grab the limelight.

Some of these criticisms were valid. On the other hand, SCLC and King, for many individuals, black and white, north and south, became symbols of the civil rights movement. What King said and did, and whenever SCLC undertook a project, became front-page news. Thus the symbolic and emotional role that SCLC and the dynamic King played in the civil rights struggle became every bit as significant as their substantive accomplishments.

The Student Nonviolent Coordinating Committee (SNCC) was created in 1960. Originally an offshoot of SCLC, its purpose was to provide a vehicle for students to become involved in civil rights activity. Some have argued that King wanted SNCC under his control so that he could direct its activity and assure that it adhered to the principles of nonviolence. But neither King nor any other outsider ever controlled SNCC. From the outset it was an impatient, militant organization whose tone was established early by one of its founders, Robert Moses: " 'go where the spirit say go and do what the spirit say do.' "[33] While it ostensibly held to nonviolent principles, in fact it often went beyond them, especially by the mid-1960s as the black nationalist movement took SNCC and its restless militants by storm. In its finest hour, the Freedom Summer of 1964 when it engaged in the dangerous work of registering blacks to vote in black-belt Mississippi, many of its workers carried guns, a practice that King and other civil rights leaders never condoned.

SNCC was the most militant of the Big Four. Its outspokenness and impatience goaded other civil rights organizations into more active, even aggressive, postures. It achieved great popularity among young southern blacks, appealing to college and even high school students.

Eventually, SNCC may have become too shrill for its own good. By the mid-1960s, it virtually abandoned all pretense of nonviolence. Its increasing emphasis on black nationalism forced white supporters out of the organization, even those white students who had spent years as active members. Some of its leaders, such as Stokely Carmichael and H. Rap Brown, became so antiwhite and hostile to King and other moderate black leaders that the credibility of the organization diminished considerably.[34]

Leadership

Leaders were critical to the formation and activity of the civil rights movement; they made the organizations go. They established goals, set priorities, made plans, allocated resources, and coordinated the efforts of people to accomplish the purposes of the civil rights movement.

But civil rights leaders had an importance that transcended even these functions. They became the energizers and motivators that transformed a politically inert southern black population into sympathizers, volunteers, participants, and activists. This inspiration was extremely important because the southern black population had no tradition of social activism on which to draw. Moreover, the inspirational, emotional roles that civil rights leaders played were essential when civil rights progress seemed slow, blacks' hopes too high, and goals too distant to be realistically achieved. These leadership attributes were crucial during those many episodes of the civil rights movement when individuals were called upon to put life and limb in jeopardy as a part of protest activity.

A number of the leaders of the civil rights movement actually became so closely identified with it that they became the embodiment and symbols of its purposes and hopes. The most important of these was King, but there were other figures whose influence may not have been as widespread as his, but who were nonetheless extremely effective. Many had to function in conditions of considerable self-sacrifice, personal danger, and an absence of resources.[35] Some of these leaders were purely local, while others, such as John Lewis, Andrew Young, Bayard Rustin, James Farmer, Julian Bond, Joseph Lowry, Fred Shuttlesworth, Hosea Williams, and Ralph Abernathy, achieved regional and even national attention. A number of these continued to work in political and/or civil rights activity even after Selma in 1965, achieving further prominence.

The modern reader may well ask why such dynamic, forceful black civil rights leadership could, or should, have emerged by the mid-1950s. The answer is complex, involving the growing sense of self-identification by southern blacks as a political community, availability of organizations, appropriate ideology as well as strategies and tactics that could prove effective in carrying out the struggle, and important changes in the national political environment. But a more immediate and significant reason is that the founders and architects of the civil rights movement, as well as many of its field leaders, came from the southern black clergy.[36]

At least four reasons can be identified why the black clergy, especially those from urban churches, should have emerged as the leaders of civil rights activity.[37] First, as a group, the black clergy, especially those in urban churches, were better educated than most of the rest of the black community. The combination of learning and formal education (in urban churches this could include a college degree, possibly even graduate work) gave the black clergy an important social status that fitted them for leadership positions for both spiritual and secular purposes. Moreover, if the clergyman was perceived as divinely inspired or called to the pulpit, his social status and leadership role would be additionally enhanced.

Second, black clergymen in the South were less economically dependent on whites than were most of their congregants. This observation was especially true in those urban areas where churches were large and wealthy enough to hire full-time ministers. In these circumstances, the clergy had considerable freedom to preach, to counsel, and to conduct religious and secular affairs without white interference or immediate fears of reprisals. This relative independence from whites gave black clergymen an advantage over other blacks, including the opportunity to act as spokesmen for, and leaders of, the community.

Third, as Joseph Lowry pointed out (he was himself a clergyman), southern black Christianity provided clergymen with considerable intellectual freedom and the right to discuss from the pulpit issues that were denied to white clergy. For example, because the southern black church viewed Jesus Christ as a liberator, black clergy were both permitted and encouraged by the church to speak out on political and secular topics on a regular basis.

The white clergyman, in contrast, was "pretty much restricted to the responsibilities of his parish."[38] Thus, especially in urban areas, it was possible, although not necessary, for the black minister to serve as both spiritual and secular adviser to his congregation and therefore to emerge as a community leader on secular affairs because of the intellectual, religious, and pastoral freedom he enjoyed.

Fourth, black clergy often had access to the white community and were generally seen as "safe" by whites. Traditionally in the South, black clergy formed the link between whites and blacks when contact between the two communities became necessary. White southerners often perceived the black clergy as the spokesmen for blacks and usually felt comfortable dealing with black clergy because they felt (wrongly, as it eventually turned out) that they would be reasonable—that is, conciliatory and not especially demanding, perhaps even accommodating and passive. Thus the black clergy's acceptability to the white community, as well as the access many black clergymen had to white leaders, underscored their position as leaders in their own communities.

Another important group of black civil rights leaders were faculty and students at black colleges in the South. Some, such as sociologist and minister Edward Edmonds, were primarily involved in local issues.[39] Others, like John Lewis, Andrew Young, and Julian Bond, were active throughout the region.

Faculty and students enjoyed a certain independence from the white community and were somewhat less vulnerable to white pressure than were other southern blacks.[40] Administrators at black colleges, however, as well as public school administrators and teachers were extremely vulnerable. They were heavily dependent for funds and employment on white legislators and local officials, many of whom took a hostile view of "uppity" blacks. Many who may have wished to take more active civil rights leadership roles were constrained from doing so because of these pressures.

Finally, one of the remarkable aspects of the civil rights movement was the way in which circumstances and events created leaders out of ordinary people who had no particular ambition or even background for leadership roles. Many were local businessmen, professional people, or laborers and wage earners who were members of the NAACP, a neighborhood association, or similar group. Most of these individuals took considerable economic and personal risks to involve themselves in civil rights work. A famous example of the latter was E.D. Nixon, a sleeping car porter who was instrumental in establishing the Montgomery bus boycott and in some respects launched the career of Martin Luther King Jr.[41]

A substantial number of the everyday leaders of the civil rights movement were women. Some became symbols of the movement, like Rosa Parks, who essentially started the Montgomery boycott, or Autherine Lucy Foster, the first black admitted to the University of Alabama, which promptly expelled her for "insubordination." Others became active leaders, such as Fannie Lou Hamer, whose account of her beating in Winona, Mississippi, during the summer of 1963 touched the conscience of the nation.[42] Later she was active in Mississippi's Freedom Democratic Party.

Women played an active role as leaders and participants in the civil rights movement. It is of interest, however, that their leadership roles were largely confined to local action. None became regional or national leaders of the Big Four. Indeed, only Coretta Scott King, widow of Martin Luther King, became nationally recognized as a civil rights leader, but not until after his murder. The absence of women from prominent, visible leadership positions is all the more notable in view of the crucial social role of women and the matriarchy in traditional southern black culture.

Ideology of the Civil Rights Movement

Another key element in the rise and flowering of the civil rights movement was the creation of an appropriate ideology. In the sense meant here, "ideology" is less a codified doctrine than a series of principles that could serve as both philosophical underpinning and practical guide for the movement. Without the creation of a convincing ideology, it might have been difficult for advocates, participants, and leaders of the movement to justify their work to themselves, other black southerners, and the rest of the nation.

While Martin Luther King Jr. is often credited as the architect of the movement's ideology, in fact he was not. His contribution came in refining and shaping it in ways that could be readily communicated and easily understood by movement participants and observers. Its roots lay in several sources that King helped combine into a coherent whole: the pacifism of Gandhi and A.J. Muste, whose influence on the founders of CORE we noted earlier,[43] and elements of Christian theology, especially the ideas of the modern thinker Reinhold Niebuhr.

Gandhi had developed the idea of passive resistance and nonviolent protest to help India gain independence from Great Britain. Its basic thrust was that evil (in this case, British imperialism) could be overcome not by violence, which Gandhi abhorred, but through the power and moral suasion of nonviolent resistance to it. The key notion was nonviolence, for Gandhi (and Muste) recognized that if protesters engaged in violence or other behavior destructive of human life or property they would immediately subvert the moral legitimacy and power of their position.

Thus Gandhi, and later King, recognized that although peaceful, nonviolent protest might be perceived as illegitimate, even illegal, in fact it was not, because its purpose was to force those engaged in evil, wrongful behavior and acts to recognize the error of their ways and change. In their view, the moral rectitude, not physical force, of the protesters would carry sufficient power to cause those doing wrong to alter their behavior, rescind laws, or restructure social institutions. Indeed King argued that it was not nonviolent protest that was wrong or illegitimate, but apathy and complacency that allowed evil to continue, since not to confront and overcome it by nonviolent means actually meant an acceptance of evil, which was morally wrong.[44]

A modern cynic might regard this rationale as "the ends justify the means." But King became quite convinced that nonviolent protest was much more than this, because it was based in a higher level of morality and right than evil, or even of violent approaches to overcome evil. Indeed, at least initially King felt that the moral force of peaceful, nonviolent protest against segregation would force southern whites to recognize and change the inherent evil of the system they had created. Later King was to modify his ideas, but he never abandoned his faith in or conviction about the inherent moral and legitimate power of nonviolent protest.

Another source of the movement's ideology were ideas of Christian love and redemption. King's speeches and writings were filled with the notion that regardless of the oppression of blacks by white southerners, they should show only love in return. He took very seriously the Christian doctrine of "love thine enemy." For him, it was not an abstract religious idea but a practical guide for living and acting, particularly since he saw that if civil rights protesters treated whites with the same scorn and hatred shown them, their credibility and legitimacy would be undermined.

Christian redemption was also important. King placed great emphasis on the importance of individual and collective struggle, as Niebuhr had, in spite of the dangers and hardships it meant. Ultimately, he argued, it would pay off, for those who suffered undeservedly would be rewarded.

As the civil rights movement wore on, this idea became ever more important to King and civil rights activists. The reason was that in calling for peaceful protest, King jeopardized the lives and livelihoods of people, including the elderly and children. Thus he needed a way to justify the sacrifices he asked them to make and a persuasive argument to convince people to imperil themselves time and again. An appeal to traditional black Christian notions of suffering and ultimate redemption and salvation proved effective.

There was another aspect of the movement's ideology that had more immediate, and less intellectual or spiritual, roots than pacifism or redemption—direct mass action. King probably derived it from A. Philip Randolph. In adopting this idea, King differed somewhat from traditional pacifist ideas. The latter generally involved relatively passive forms of mass protest. For King, however, protest had to be active and confrontational. It involved immediate and direct contact by civil rights participants against the practices of segregation. Yet it also had to be nonviolent if it was to be effective.

King's ideas about the importance of direct, confrontational mass action developed over time.[45] If, as he initially felt, the moral suasion of nonviolence would create change, aggressive, violent behaviors were not necessary. But King eventually came to realize that only the most active, confrontational nonviolent means would work. Southern racism was too entrenched and the traditional racial ideas of the South were too embedded to be excised by moral suasion alone. Therefore more active steps, albeit still nonviolent ones, needed to be taken. This evolution in King's thinking marked his increasing political sophistication as he changed from idealistic southern preacher to politically savvy, media-conscious mass leader.

Let us make one final observation about the movement's ideology: it was complemented and accompanied by a host of emotional appeals, slogans, and songs. The movement's ideology was not meant as a series of abstract concepts to be debated by scholars. It was designed to be a convincing, energizing guide to individuals who put themselves on the line to overcome segregation. It needed to be vibrant, emotional, motivating, inspirational.

Because the movement was rooted in southern black religion, its ideology could therefore borrow much of the style of black church services to create the emotional intensity needed to carry on civil rights activity. Hymns and old spirituals, with their inspirational texts and melodies, were sung in churches, civil rights meetings, and on the street during protests. The movement anthem, "We Shall Overcome," was often sung, and its melody was even recorded by popular singers of national stature. "Freedom, Now!" became a widely used slogan, chanted in rhythmic cadences at rallies and demonstrations. The effect of this emotional style was not just to motivate civil rights participants but to give southern blacks a feeling of community and personal involvement in a common purpose, even when they were strangers to each other and danger was imminent.

Strategies and Tactics

Strategies and tactics appropriate for civil rights activity in the South had to meet three criteria. They had to be compatible with the theory of nonviolent protest. They had to highlight the evils and discrimination inherent in the Jim Crow South, for if they did not, it would look as if the protests were unjustified. And, to achieve maximum credibility, they had to be rooted in the American tradition of protest.

This last point was important. Civil rights leaders knew that protest would probe and extend beyond legal limits in the South; much of what they would do was illegal, according to laws in southern states, their moral rectitude to the contrary notwithstanding. Thus they had to anchor their activity in the grand tradition of American protest guaranteed by the Bill of Rights (freedom of speech, freedom to assemble, freedom to petition the government). Protest activity that appeared to white southerners and the rest of the nation as a Mau-Mau uprising or a revolution that threatened to rip the entire fabric of American life had therefore to be avoided lest the protesters' credibility and legitimacy be undermined.

Appropriate strategies and tactics that met these criteria were not created all at once. Their development from relatively passive to more active forms reflects the growth of the movement from its first, tentative beginnings to full vigor and self-confidence. We shall look at five of the major strategies and tactics; it should be remembered that they often occurred together.

Passive Protest: Meetings and Court Action

Southern blacks did not suddenly begin to protest segregation on southern streets in the mid-1950s. The struggle against segregation had been going on for quite some time through a variety of means, including meetings, conferences, and court action. We can regard each of these as relatively passive forms of protest.

Meetings and conferences were common in the South, especially in border states and urban areas; rural areas of the deep South were not places where serious white-black meetings could take place. These were occasions for discussing conditions among local blacks and exploring the problems of the local area; they were almost always defined as black problems, not white ones. Whether the meetings took place in comfort of academia or a downtown office, or were held in a neighborhood church, they seldom led to direct action. Even rallies, attended virtually exclusively by blacks, often failed to result in concrete action.

Meetings were, however, one of the few safe means of communication open between whites and blacks. King, for example, frequently alluded to the helpful and informative biracial meetings held during his years at Morehouse College in Atlanta. They served blacks as a way to articulate their concerns in a way that was not threatening to whites.

The problem with meetings and conferences as a political strategy, however, was that blacks had virtually no leverage to force results. Whites could respond, or not, with impunity, for there was no pressure on them to do anything. It was no wonder that young blacks often regarded meetings as useless and black leaders who participated in them as "Uncle Toms."

Also, as E.D. Nixon of Montgomery pointed out, over time, as white officials and businessmen met with black leaders, co-optation was inevitable. A few bones would be thrown, a few favors granted to a select group of blacks, thereby capturing them and rendering them useless as advocates of black concerns.[46]

The NAACP adopted court action as its primary protest strategy early in its history. In fact, no other avenues of peaceful protest were open to the NAACP since legislatures, executives, and bureaucrats were unresponsive to their concerns. The choice also made sense because, in a nation of laws, the legitimacy of legal action is beyond reproach, making it desirable as a respectable form of protest activity.

However, legal action is seldom a good political strategy for getting immediate results; indeed, it is essentially a passive approach to protest. The right set of circumstances and facts have to be found in order to have a real chance of success; it was sometimes difficult to locate these. Courts insisted on specific evidence of deprivation or injury, especially in federal court when a claim was entered that the plaintiff had been denied "equal protection" of the law, or "due process" under the Fourteenth Amendment.

The time frame and cost of a court case can be discouraging; three or four years to fully litigate a case is not unusual, and the cost was often more than an individual could bear. The emotional strain of serving as a plaintiff was also often beyond the capability of many southern blacks. And unless the case represented a class action suit, even a favorable judgment would be inapplicable to persons in similar situations and additional suits would be required.

But the most serious problem with court action as a protest tool concerned enforcement. Even the U.S. Supreme Court has difficulty enforcing its own decisions and decrees, and the situation was made worse by the ingenuity of southern officials in avoiding compliance. As a result, even favorable court decisions for southern blacks were often more symbolic than real: relatively few more blacks were able to vote because of the *Smith v. Allwright* decision declaring the all-white primary unconstitutional; and Oliver Brown's daughter Linda never attended a desegregated public school even though she was only eight years old when the Brown suit was originally filed.[47]

A Moderate Approach: Boycotts

Boycotts as a form of civil rights protest can be considered moderately active because while they are more assertive than meetings, or even lawsuits, they are not quite as confrontational or dramatic as some other activities to be considered in a moment.

Several different kinds of boycotts were organized during the civil rights movement, but they all had a common purpose: by withholding black support from a service (like buses) or business (a store that refused to employ or sell to blacks, for example), the economic pressure thereby applied by blacks would force a change in segregationist practices. Thus the ability of the black community to apply economic sanctions was central to the effectiveness of the boycott, since the idea was that attacking Jim Crow through white pocketbooks would produce desired results. Also important to the boycott's success was the negative publicity that the boycott presumably brought to the service or business.

Boycotts involved risks for blacks. In some states they were illegal, and leaders could be jailed for promoting them, as happened to Martin Luther King Jr. They were often accompanied by harassment and intimidation of blacks. In Montgomery, for example, the police systematically ticketed private cars carrying more than one black during the bus boycott. Beatings and economic sanctions applied against boycotting blacks also occurred.[48]

If they were well organized and supported, boycotts could be an effective strategy. They usually caught the immediate attention of whites, in contrast to meetings and lawsuits. They tended to be dramatic, at least in their early stages. Also, boycotts polarized issues, casting them in fairly simple pro and con terms that could be understood by virtually everyone. Thus they had media appeal, for they could be readily covered by journalists looking for a "story" sure to grab headlines. Finally, boycotts, when successfully done, demonstrated to southern blacks that they were capable of carrying out a concerted, coordinated, collective form of protest.

But boycotts also presented some tactical problems to southern blacks. Perhaps most important, an effective boycott requires massive community organization, effective leadership, and a substantial commitment by a very large segment of the population that it would participate. A halfhearted boycott, or one in which only a minority of blacks participated, could not have worked in the South, because whites would have had little difficulty cracking it.

Boycotts could not be used to illuminate the full range of Jim Crow repression: they might work against a store or service but would be meaningless against police brutality, unresponsive fire departments, or a dual school system. Also, the time frame for an effective boycott could be lengthy, presenting the obvious problem of keeping interest and commitment sustained during the weeks, even months, when little except harassment of boycotters was happening. Finally the media, crucial for publicity, also tended to lose interest once the drama evaporated and the novelty wore off. Thus boycotters engaged in a lengthy siege could find themselves without an audience and very little to show for their efforts.

Direct Action: Demonstrations and Sit-Ins

At the active end of the spectrum of strategies and tactics used in the civil rights movement were demonstrations and sit-ins. While neither was initially a part of the civil rights protest repertoire, they were later so commonly used that they became synonymous with the movement itself. The reason was that civil rights advocates discovered that Jim Crow was so entrenched in the South that only the most active forms of protest could successfully confront it.

Demonstrations took a variety of forms. The most common was a kind of parade, in which blacks marched from one place (often a church, where an earlier rally would have taken place) to another, such as city hall, the county courthouse, a jail, or even a private location such as a store, motel, or theater. Marchers were often neatly dressed and would have been coached in appropriate behavior. Usually this meant orderly demeanor, nonviolence, and passive resistance if attacked, confronted, or arrested. Along the way marchers often sang civil rights songs and hymns, or chanted slogans, but silent marches were also common. When they reached their target, usually demonstrators would insist on meeting with officials or proprietors. Sometimes a petition or grievance would be left. The march would then conclude with more speeches or hymns, after which the demonstrators would disperse or return to their starting point.

Another form of demonstration was the picket line. Usually the target was some visible forum of segregation: a bus station, restaurant, or government agency, for example. Picketers, often singing and chanting, marched back and forth across the entrance to the establishment, usually blocking it in such a way as to deny entry or exit. The emphasis was on nonviolent behavior, even if they were confronted. Picketing continued either until the goal was achieved or an accommodation reached.

The sit-in was a dramatic form of demonstration, its effectiveness underscored by the fact that it was carried out in an immobilized rather than mobile way. The sit-in was not created by the civil rights movement: some labor strikes during the 1930s were early examples of sit-ins, as were the "Hoovervilles" of the early Depression years.[49] Moreover, although conventional wisdom has it that the sit-in began as a protest strategy in 1960 in Greensboro, North Carolina, when students from North Carolina Agricultural and Technical College sat in at a Woolworth's lunch counter,[50] in fact sit-ins were carried out by CORE, in Chicago, in 1942, in Kentucky in the early 1950s, in Oklahoma in 1958, and in Miami in 1959.[51] Ultimately, however, the sit-in became the quintessential civil rights protest technique, virtually synonymous with it.

The sit-in was simplicity itself. Groups of people would enter a segregated facility such as a restaurant or bus station. They were usually refused service, and they simply continued to occupy the counter, tables, and benches until they were arrested, the establishment closed, or some accommodation was reached. It was an excellent strategy, if carried out in a dignified manner, for convincingly and dramatically documenting that southern blacks were truly subjected to a degrading, brutal society. As the old-guard southern conservative editor of the *Richmond News Leader,* James J. Kilpatrick, editorialized after an early sit-in:

> Here were the colored students, in coats, white shirts, ties, and one of them was reading Goethe, and one was taking notes from a biology text. And here, on the sidewalk outside, was a gang of white boys come to heckle, a ragtail rabble, slack-jawed, black-jacketed, grinning fit to kill, and some of them, God save the mark, were waving the proud and honored flag of the Southern states in the last war fought by gentlemen. . . . Eheu! It gives one pause.[52]

Another feature of the sit-in was its adaptability to a range of circumstances. It could be used equally well in restaurants, bus and train stations, hospitals and doctors' offices, rest rooms, or other public facilities. There were "shoe-ins" at shoe-shine parlors, "swim-ins" in swimming pools, "golf-ins" and "wade-ins" in parks and beaches. A very common form was the "jail-in," in which those arrested for some other civil rights protest would refuse bail and simply occupy the jails in as large numbers as possible, thereby disrupting the criminal justice system.

Active forms of protest, whether demonstrations or sit-ins, could be very effective because they were dramatic encounters with considerable media appeal. They polarized issues in a way that could be readily communicated to participants as well as through electronic and print media. Their ability to focus issues, messages, and activity resulted in a foreshortening of time needed to protest, in contrast to less active forms of protest.

There were some serious problems with these active forms of protest as strategies, however. They were effective only to the extent that the protesters maintained peaceful behavior; to engage in violence was to destroy their legitimacy, for then they became no better than any other mob. Yet the discipline and forbearance required for a peaceful, nonviolent demeanor was difficult to achieve and sustain, particularly in the face of taunts, arrests, and attacks from whites. As a result, tremendous time and resources were required for training of protesters, and effective leadership of protest activity was essential. Even so, there were occasions when blacks lashed back at whites who assaulted or attacked them, thereby undermining black effectiveness.

Environmental Changes

Developments outside the South, at the national and even international level, also aided the origins and progress of the civil rights movement. It is fair to say that without these changes in the political environment, the civil rights movement would have had even rougher sledding than it did. We begin with developments in the federal government.

Following the *Plessy* decision in 1896, the federal government did virtually nothing to combat racial discrimination in the South. The bargain created in 1877, under which the South was left alone to deal with racial problems, was honored in Washington. In some ways, the federal government actually made matters worse, first by ignoring the obvious injustices perpetrated by southern states against blacks, and second by its own practices and policies. Illustrative of the latter were such presidential actions as William Howard Taft's refusal to support voting rights for blacks (he felt they were "political children, not having the mental status of manhood"); Woodrow Wilson's resegregation of federal agencies; and Warren G. Harding's comment on the "fundamental, eternal, and inescapable differences" between blacks and whites that made him "stand uncompromisingly against every suggestion of social equality. . . . Racial amalgamation there cannot be."[53]

In the 1930s, the first winds of change began to blow. The Supreme Court in a number of decisions started to expand the constitutional guarantees of the Fourteenth and Fifteenth Amendments. One estimate of Supreme Court decisions on civil rights issues in the 1931–55 period suggested that they were 91 percent favorable toward blacks.[54]

There were other signs of a more favorable federal attitude toward blacks, as well. Beginning in 1936, President Roosevelt openly courted black voters in his re-election campaign, even at the risk of alienating white southerners. We have already noted his establishment, in 1941, of the Fair Employment Practices Committee. President Harry S Truman went even further, much to everyone's surprise since he was thought to be very pro-southern in his racial attitudes. He issued an executive order eliminating segregation in the armed forces; established a forward-looking Commission on Civil Rights; and became the first president, in 1948, to recommend a broad-based civil rights law to Congress that embodied the recommendations of his commission. Moreover, in 1944 and especially in 1948 the platforms of the Democratic National Convention contained significant civil rights planks.[55]

The substantive effect of these developments should not be overstated; obviously they did not end discrimination. But their importance to southern blacks was substantial. They signaled that they could begin to expect some support from the federal government in seeking their civil rights. Perhaps this understanding was best expressed in a January 1951, editorial of *The Crisis,* an old and prestigious black periodical associated with the NAACP: "Some might call these mere straws in the wind, but they do indicate the direction in which the wind is blowing."[56]

The evolutionary movement of the federal government toward a more sympathetic view of southern black conditions was underscored, in the late 1940s and early 1950s, by developments at the international level. We have already noted the impact of World War II on the growth of southern black collective consciousness and political mobilization. The same was also true of the Korean War, which was supposed to "save" Korea from the communist menace in the same way that the earlier war was supposed to rid the world of fascist racism.

Indeed, it was precisely America's hard-line, cold war, anticommunist foreign policy that, beginning in the late 1940s and continuing throughout the 1960s, helped move the federal government into a posture more supportive of southern blacks. International events began to take the form of a gigantic morality play, in which America sought to "contain" the spread of communism while at the same time creating and reinforcing Western-style democracy in both emergent and existing nations, including Western Europe, where communism appeared to be gaining footholds.[57]

But the American case could not be convincingly made, especially in Asia, the Middle East, and Africa, if the United States were seen to be harboring a racist, segregated society. Thus federal efforts from the late 1940s into the 1970s to address and redress the problems of southern blacks became a part of U.S. international propaganda apparatus to convince other nations of America's commitment to democracy and of the dangers of communism.

These efforts actually intensified during the late 1950s and early 1960s, especially once the Kennedy administration began. At least as hard-line as the previous Eisenhower administration, it nonetheless was very anxious to demonstrate understanding of, and support for, newly emergent nations of Africa and Asia. Many of these nations had only recently thrown off the shackles of colonialism, and were joining the so-called nonaligned Third World. Hostile toward anything that looked like imperialism and often suspicious of America's real motives in world politics, leaders of these nations were quick to point out the way in which southern blacks were treated in the supposedly democratic United States. Thus international pressure to secure the support of these new nations forced the administration to turn its attention to the problem of racism in America.

Besides these international factors, a number of purely domestic pressures forced the Kennedy administration to become more closely associated with the growing civil rights movement in the South. Its public relations program was aimed primarily at projecting an image of youthful vigor, of executive activism, and a "can do" attitude. While the administration did not design a coherent civil rights policy until its last few months, it nonetheless recognized that enforcement of existing civil rights laws and Supreme Court decisions provided just the necessary vehicle for projecting this image, placing it in stark contrast to the Eisenhower years. This strategy was especially suitable in view of the rise of massive resistance in the South in the late 1950s and the Kennedy administration's need to confront it as it sought to enforce federal law.[58] In addition, political realities within the Democratic Party forced the Kennedy administration to take an increasingly pro–civil rights stance in order not to jeopardize its 1964 reelection chances.

This latter point needs a comment. Occurring at this time, and in many respects symbolized by the Kennedy administration, was a growing public belief that government could be used to solve, or at least counter, growing social problems in America. Paramount among these was the "discovery" of hunger in America, especially in Appalachia.[59] The public acceptance of governmental activism and increasing concern for poor people spilled over into greater awareness of the problems of minority groups, including southern blacks. This impulse, too, prompted the Kennedy administration into a more forceful pro–civil rights role.

An important extrapolitical change in the environment of civil rights that aided the onset and development of the movement was the growth of television as a news and communications medium. It worked in several ways. By the mid- to late 1950s, television sets had become widespread across the nation, including among blacks in the South, especially the urban South. Their prevalence enabled the transmission of news and information about events within the black community to be quickly spread across the region and nation. Television proved especially helpful to the growth of black political consciousness, for previously there were few effective ways to reach large numbers of blacks quickly.

Moreover, television, through programs and commercials, brought the promise of American life into southern black homes. To watch television is, in many ways, to see the values and lifestyle of what is considered ideal in American life. For the poor, television can serve both as a source of frustration and as an incentive to participate in the good life dangled before them on the screen. For southern blacks, it was another reminder of the way in which a Jim Crow society prevented them from participating in the very kinds of experiences that were open to other Americans.

The onset of the civil rights movement was also aided by the growth, in the mid- to late 1950s, of professional electronic journalism and the rise of television news as a major enterprise. This period saw the creation of important television news programs, both on Sundays and in the early and late evening hours during the week. Previously television news had been more or less an adjunct to entertainment, but producers and executives began to make massive commitments to network, and even local, news as they grasped its value as a source of viewers and, not incidentally, advertising revenues. Coupled with the news programs was the emergence of serious, professional television news journalists such as Edward R. Murrow, Walter Cronkite, Chet Huntley, David Brinkley, John Chancellor, Frank Reynolds, Howard K. Smith, and others. Skilled in the reporting of news on television, they rapidly became television celebrities in their own right, with an enormous influence on what issues Americans saw on the television news, what Americans thought about them, and what Americans discussed.

The civil rights movement provided exactly the kind of dramatic events whose meaning could readily be told by pictures needed by the new television news industry to build acceptance as a regular part of American home life. Thus a kind of symbiotic relationship developed between the nascent civil rights movement and the equally young electronic journalism industry.

This symbiosis was aided by technological advancements in television. By the late 1950s, TV equipment, while still bulky by modern standards, had become much more portable and flexible than it had been. Under the right conditions it could even be brought out of the studio to broadcast events "live." Thus it could actually be on the scene of civil rights activity, bringing events to people all over the nation.

But even when live telecasts were not possible, television news was aided by the availability, in the late 1950s, of coaxial cables, jet aircraft, and high-speed film developing techniques. Thus events that occurred even in remote areas of the rural South were accessible to television journalists, and their reports could be broadcast the same day from regional centers via coaxial cable or their film rushed by jet plane to New York and developed quickly for broadcast the same evening.

Summary

This chapter has sought to examine the preconditions necessary for the civil rights movement to be conceived, grow, and flower. Major social movements do not simply happen, of course, but are the product of numerous forces and events that gel in ways that permit change to occur.

We have seen that within the South at least five major developments occurred that helped pave the way for the civil rights movement. The growth of a collective consciousness and political mobilization were perhaps the most basic, for without them very little activity could have taken place. Black organizations and leaders had to be present to further mobilize people, structure activity, allocate resources, make plans, and inspire the population. A set of guiding principles or ideology was essential for giving both a rationale and a sense of purpose to the movement. Tactics and strategies appropriate to the principles and goals of the movement had to be created.

Beyond these factors, America itself, in the form of the federal government, had to become more sensitive to, and aware of, the problems of southern blacks if they were to have any real chance of successfully attacking segregation. Both international and national forces helped push the federal government into this posture, and the national media helped educate white America about the movement, its dynamics, and its objectives.

But the civil rights movement was more than just the product of forces. It represented the commitment and courage of millions of Americans, black and white, to overturn the old Jim Crow ways of the segregated South. The civil rights movement, perhaps most fundamentally, should be seen at least as much in human terms as in societal ones. Therein lie both its triumphs and tragedies, its successes and failures. It is to an assessment of the impact of the civil rights movement that we now turn.

7

"We Shall Overcome": The Politics of the Civil Rights Movement

We conclude that in the field of public education the doctrine of "separate but equal" has no place. Separate educational facilities are inherently unequal.
—*Brown v. Board of Education,* Topeka, Kansas, May 17, 1954

My feets is tired, but my soul is rested.
—Attributed to an elderly civil rights demonstrator, quoted by Martin Luther King Jr. in his "Letter from Birmingham Jail," 1963

Exactly when the civil rights movement began is uncertain. Perhaps it was the moment when the first black slaves brought to American shores cried out against their condition. Possibly one of the violent slave uprisings that occurred from time to time was the real beginning. Even the Emancipation Proclamation of 1863, the Thirteenth Amendment (1865), the Civil Rights Act of 1866, the Fourteenth Amendment (1868), the Fifteenth Amendment (1870), or the Enforcement Acts of 1870–71 could be regarded as the start, since they were aimed at giving freedom to blacks and offering them the promise of participation in American life.

As we saw in the last chapter, the civil rights movement as a period of social transformation, even revolution, did not start in an active way until the 1950s. But it did not just begin, nor did it happen all at once. Major changes took place in the South, and in America, that created the right mix of events, forces, and circumstances which enabled the civil rights movement to be born, move at first very tentatively, and then evolve into a major political and social movement.

But even if we cannot fix with certainty the exact moment when the civil rights movement began in the South, two events were of such importance that they can serve as convenient places to start: May 17, 1954, when the first *Brown* decision was announced, and December 1, 1955, when Mrs. Rosa Parks was arrested in Montgomery, Alabama, for not giving up her bus seat to white riders. Eldridge Cleaver was to write years later that when Parks refused, somewhere in the universe a gear shifted and things were never quite the same afterward. But the same could also be said of the aftermath of the *Brown* decision. While it was not the first legal victory for the civil rights movement, it was certainly the most important. It was a signal by a branch of the federal government, for the first time in nine decades, that the system of segregation in the South would have to "come tumbling down."[1]

In this chapter we shall examine the entrance of blacks into southern politics as they confronted the oppressive Jim Crow society. It is not meant to be a history, or even a chronology. But we can look at some of the major events in the movement and ask several important questions: What happened? How do these events show the rise of collective consciousness and political mobilization, organization and leadership, and ideology and strategy, discussed in the last chapter? How do these events show the change in southern blacks as they evolved from political victims to political activists? What was the response of southern whites to civil rights activity? And how did the rest of the nation, including the federal government, react to events in the South and influence their outcome?

Let us begin with the two first major shocks of the earthquake that was to follow—Brown and Montgomery.

Brown v. Board of Education of Topeka, Kansas, 1954–1955

The *Brown* case was actually one of five brought before the U.S. Supreme Court to challenge the existence of legally established, segregated school systems in the South and border states.[2] The others came from South Carolina, Virginia, Delaware, and Washington, D.C.[3] While there were factual differences among the cases, the constitutional and legal questions were similar: black plaintiffs argued that dual, racially segregated school systems violated the "equal protection" clause of the Fourteenth Amendment to the U.S. Constitution. In essence, they argued that their "separate" education was not "equal" to that of whites and thus they were denied their constitutional rights.

The questions raised in the cases constituted a direct challenge to the "separate but equal" doctrine established in 1896 by the *Plessy* decision.[4] This case, which actually dealt with railroad coaches, gave southern states the approval, or at least the permission, of the federal government to establish dual school systems and other segregated facilities. *Plessy* was a legitimization of Jim Crowism.

Brown did not suddenly burst from the Supreme Court. It was the culmination of the legalistic strategy adopted by the National Association for the Advancement of Colored People (NAACP) early in its history and designed to attack segregation at its constitutional and legal roots. While it had not brought a broad-based attack on dual school systems previously, by the early 1950s there was reason to believe that, because of a number of decisions in higher education, the federal courts might listen favorably to an argument that segregated schools constituted a denial of equal protection.[5]

In a major victory in 1938 for the NAACP, the Supreme Court ruled that Missouri had to provide equal facilities for black law students instead of paying their tuition at out-of-state schools; it was the first indication that the Supreme Court might take seriously a challenge to the separate but equal doctrine.[6] In 1948 the Court ruled that Oklahoma either had to admit qualified blacks to its law school or provide equal facilities for them in-state.[7] Two years later, in two separate cases the Court expanded this idea, arguing that in graduate and professional education the concept of separate but equal was essentially impossible to achieve and black students had to be admitted to white programs.[8]

The *Brown* decision, announced on May 17, 1954, seemed at the time both forthright and satisfying to the claims of the plaintiffs. Speaking for a unanimous Court, Chief Justice Earl Warren reviewed the importance of education in America: "In these days, it is doubtful that any child may reasonably be expected to succeed in life if he is denied the opportunity of an education. Such an opportunity, where the state has undertaken to provide it, is a right which must be made available to all on equal terms."[9]

Warren next addressed the constitutional issue raised by the case: "Does segregation of children in public schools solely on the basis of race, even though the physical facilities and other 'tangible' factors may be equal, deprive the children of the minority group of equal educational opportunities"? His answer: "We believe that it does." After reviewing both legal precedent and social science evidence concerning the effect of segregation on children, the Court flatly stated, "We conclude that in the field of public education the doctrine of 'separate but equal' has no place. Separate educational facilities are inherently unequal."

Warren ended the brief decision by noting that a legal decree was not possible "because of the great variety of local conditions" and "problems of considerable complexity" that the decision was certain to generate. Instead, the case was to be reheard the following year, during which "further argument" by all the parties involved was invited. Thus, no timetable was established on May 17, 1954, for dismantling the segregated school systems of the South.

The response of southern blacks to *Brown* was euphoric. It was seen as an extraordinary victory, the first substantial indication that Jim Crow could successfully be attacked. It raised great hopes for an end to segregation in other aspects of southern life. In their flush of enthusiasm southern blacks were joined by white allies elsewhere in the nation, parts of the media, and important political figures. Notably lacking from the latter, however, was the president of the United States, Dwight D. Eisenhower.[10]

Eisenhower's failure to endorse the decision was to have very crucial consequences for the civil rights movement, as we shall see. As it happened, there were other problems with the decision as well. Perhaps most important was the lack of a decree, especially of a timetable. The failure of the Court to force southern states to begin an immediate dismantling of segregated schools and to provide a timetable within which progress had to be shown gave a substantial advantage to the states. Instead of putting them on the defensive, the decision actually gave them time to determine ways to avoid compliance. Indeed, when the Court finally announced its timetable for compliance, it did so ambiguously: "with all deliberate speed."[11]

By the time this language appeared in the second *Brown* decision in May 1955, much of the early enthusiasm had worn off. It was very clear to southern blacks that the Court had fallen over backward to accommodate southern states. Some analysts have even argued that both *Brown* decisions represented as much a victory for white southerners as for blacks, since they were given time to retrench and to find ways to avoid compliance.[12]

While it is an overstatement to conclude that *Brown* was a victory for segregation, it is true that the Court, wittingly or not, actually contributed to the rise of that period of the civil rights movement known as "massive resistance." Additionally, the Court made no provision for monitoring the progress of desegregation. Thus the burden continued to fall on black plaintiffs to return to court, again and again, to insist that states and local school districts comply with the law. Moreover, with Eisenhower's failure to endorse either *Brown* decision, the Court found itself isolated, unable to push compliance, until the president's hand was forced by events in Little Rock.

In spite of these difficulties, the *Brown* decisions were significant victories. They sent a signal to blacks that it was possible to attack segregation. They suggested a willingness by the federal court system to side with blacks in their assault on Jim Crow. They were a sign to the South that the

agreement of 1877 was becoming undone. And it was a powerful reaffirmation of the centrality of equality in the American democratic experiment.
Perhaps most important, *Brown* gave southern blacks and their allies hope
that change was possible. This message was to be underscored by events in
Montgomery, Alabama, in 1955–56.

Montgomery, 1955–1956

Montgomery, Alabama, called itself "the Cradle of the Confederacy," and
in the mid-1950s it was still very much an old South city. Nonetheless, by
late 1955 blacks in Montgomery were becoming restive. The year before,
they had convinced city officials to hire four black policemen, and the black
Women's Political Council had been instrumental in persuading businessmen to eliminate separate "white/colored" drinking fountains and to use
titles such as "Mr." and "Mrs." on envelopes when sending bills.[13] However, they were becoming increasingly disillusioned over prospects for
school desegregation and like many other southern blacks were outraged at
the murder of four blacks in Mississippi during 1955, the most prominent of
whom was the teenager Emmett Till.[14]

But the black community in Montgomery was sharply divided and had
never exercised any independent political power.[15] Indeed, as Martin Luther
King Jr. observed shortly after taking his first pulpit there in 1954, there
seemed to be little black leadership and little sense of cohesiveness. Moreover, while respected individuals such as E.D. Nixon—head of the local
NAACP, disciple of A. Philip Randolph, and longtime civil rights activist—
had advocated more concerted political activity and had even suggested
boycotts to accomplish their goals, very little had been done to bring changes
about. In part lack of action was owing to internal divisions. In part it was
because white politicians were adept at co-opting some black leaders,
thereby rendering them ineffective as political spokesmen for, and mo-
bilizers of, black people as a whole. And it was also because the "right"
event or incident had not occurred that could capture the imagination of the
black community, help bring them together, and encourage political action.[16]

But the right moment came on Thursday, December 1, 1955, just as the
evening rush hour traffic was getting under way. The streets and buses were
especially congested because of holiday shoppers. Mrs. Rosa Parks, a black
seamstress at a downtown department store, boarded a bus for the ride home
and was able to find a seat at the front of the Jim Crow section. The bus filled
up rapidly, however, and the driver told her to move to the rear (where there
were no vacant seats) to make way for white passengers. She refused and was
promptly arrested by the bus driver. When asked later why she had not moved,
as city ordinances required her to do, she said, "My feet hurt."[17]

Instantly, the black people of Montgomery seemed to gel. Leaders noted that blacks were already upset with recent events. Moreover, the "victim" this time was a married, religious, eminently respectable working citizen. Accordingly, E.D. Nixon and Jo Ann Robinson, president of the Women's Political Council, decided this was the moment to act. They invited a number of ministers and other important black leaders to an organizational meeting at the Dexter Avenue Baptist Church on Friday evening. The new minister there was Dr. Martin Luther King Jr.

Originally the bus boycott they planned was to last only one day—Monday, December 5, the day of Rosa Parks's trial. However, the boycott was a great success, partially because of the mood of black people in the city and partially because black ministers the preceding day had been able to communicate from their pulpits the importance of the boycott. Thus King and other leaders decided that it should be continued.

After three days King met with the mayor, other city officials, and representatives of the bus company. He found them intransigent, unwilling to listen to black complaints. White Montgomerians were scornful of the boycott. Even though blacks accounted for 75 percent of the bus ridership, whites felt that blacks would be unable to sustain the enthusiasm and cohesiveness needed for the boycott.[18]

But after two months, whites were not quite so certain. The boycott was effective: the bus company lost 65 percent of its revenue, and downtown merchants had lost more than $1 million in sales. Accordingly, white politicians decided to retaliate: a program of police harassment began, and proved threatening, against black drivers of the carpools arranged in the community to substitute for buses. Toward the end of January 1956, blacks in Montgomery were becoming nervous. The boycott threatened to come to an end.[19]

Then the police made a mistake. They arrested King, allegedly for speeding. His jailing rekindled enthusiasm for the boycott, as hundreds of blacks demonstrated at the jail and forced his release on bond. Shortly thereafter, as King addressed a rally, his home was bombed, and although none of his family was hurt, the damage was considerable. It angered the black community once again, and while King urged nonviolence, he helped blacks recommit themselves to the boycott.

But the white community would not give in. The program of police harassment continued. In late February city officials obtained indictments against King and other black leaders for carrying on the boycott. Later it also obtained an indictment against the Montgomery Improvement Association[20] (the organization that "ran" the boycott) for operating a car pool business without a license. At the same time, the state outlawed the NAACP in Alabama and fined it $100,000 for refusing to surrender its membership list.[21]

By the middle of fall King saw that time was beginning to run out. Enthusiasm among blacks was again declining as white intimidation and harassment took a heavy toll. In mid-November he once again had to appear in court, before the same judge who had previously found Montgomery Improvement Association leaders guilty of running an illegal business. As he awaited his sentence, King was handed a note: the U.S. Supreme Court had just announced a decision affirming a lower court ruling that state and local laws in Alabama requiring segregated buses were unconstitutional. The boycotters had won.

The boycott did not actually end until December 21, 1955, as black leaders waited until the Supreme Court ruling reached city officials. It had lasted 381 days, and when the buses began to leave their depot at 5:55 A.M., King and other black leaders sat in the front seats. There were a few acts of retribution: some buses were fired upon, a black girl was beaten, and a shotgun blast hit King's home. Interestingly, however, some white Montgomerians condemned these terrorist acts, and many seemed to accept the desegregated bus system with an air of indifference and inevitability. An incident reported in the *New York Times* seemed to reflect most white opinion: two white men in a bus happened to remark that the coming Christmas would not be a white one, and a black turned to them and said, " 'Yes, sir, that's right.' " At that point, the *Times* reported, "all rancor seemed to evaporate."[22]

The gain of a desegregated bus system was a modest one, seen only in substantive terms. Symbolically, however, it was very important. It demonstrated to blacks that through collective action, organization, and strong leadership they could confront the white power structure. They were not strong enough, by themselves, to succeed: they had needed the support of the U.S. Supreme Court. But blacks were heartened by the fact that they had shown that they could come together and engage collectively in political protest over a long period of time. This collective action had not before happened in the South.

Thus the Montgomery bus boycott was one of the critical first steps of the first active phase of the civil rights movement. But if blacks thought that segregation in Montgomery and elsewhere would collapse as a result of the boycott, they were doomed to disappointment, just as they were following the *Brown* decisions. Indeed, the next few years were a time of white retrenchment and reprisal, one that made the second phase of the civil rights movement beginning in the 1960s even more difficult than the first one.

Massive Resistance

The *Brown* decision was not wholly unexpected in the South. Perceptive journalists, academicians, lawyers, and politicians had assumed for some time that eventually the federal government would begin to attack segregation. Initial reaction to the decision was cautious, as politicians and editorialists sought to test public sentiment. Some moderate voices could even be heard that expressed a wait-and-see attitude or even emphasized respect for the decision, disagreeable as it was, as the law of the land.

However, the initial voices of circumspection and moderation were quickly swept aside by a vast outcry of rage, defiance, and disappointment at what the Court had done. These, in turn, led to a host of political acts designed not only to thwart the decision but indeed to create a "fortress" against further intrusion by the federal government into southern racial affairs. They were also aimed at smashing the growing internal "threat" of a southern black civil rights movement. This period, which lasted into the 1960s and in vestigial form may still exist in some areas today, has been called the time of "massive resistance." It was a period of the "circling of wagons," a manifestation of the southern siege mentality that typified traditional southern attitudes toward the federal government and toward racial issues.[23]

Massive resistance took a number of forms throughout the South. In the deep South states it took on its ugliest aspect, not only in the rhetoric of racial vituperation but in acts of violence and repression. In the border South massive resistance tended to be more moderate and began to disappear sooner than in the black belt. But there were exceptions: Virginia and Arkansas both saw intransigent behaviors that were anything but moderate.

Although the modern reader may find the southern reaction to *Brown* distasteful, it is nonetheless understandable.[24] To many southerners, it was the final sign that the federal government had abrogated the agreement of 1877. To others, it represented an attack on traditional southern culture and ways, and would force a restructuring of southern society. For states' rights advocates, the intellectual heirs of John C. Calhoun's nullification doctrine, the Court had overstepped its appropriate bounds and therefore its decision was invalid and not binding. Finally, many southerners felt that the decision represented the beginning of a second Reconstruction, a period when another "army of occupation" might return, in legalistic and bureaucratic form, if not in military uniform. In some ways, they were right—although, as it turned out, the armies did return as well.[25]

The southern circling of wagons took place quickly and forcefully. Its effect was to eliminate moderate voices and pragmatic political discussion from most areas of the South. The southern political stage seemed to be taken over by extremists who sought to define issues in polarizing terms, the effect of which was to stifle, even quash, discussion and dissent.[26] The voice of Roy Harris, president of the White Citizens Councils of America, was typical of the way in which moderate voices were shut out and political discussion was polarized: "If you're a white man, then it's time to stand up with us, or black your face and get on the other side," he told a Florida audience in 1958. The only real issue in a campaign, he argued further, was, "Who's the strongest for segregation?"[27]

Thus during the period of white resistance it was difficult to find southern voices of moderation or efforts to seek middle ground. Those few who tried discovered they had no legitimacy or audience; some were even subjected to harassment and intimidation by extremists.[28] Even George Wallace learned how rigid and single-minded southern attitudes became, as he remarked after losing the 1958 Alabama gubernatorial primary that he had been "outniggered."[29]

Electoral Politics

Massive resistance could be seen in electoral politics ranging from gubernatorial contests to purely local ones. Southerners, even in border states such as Tennessee, which elected as governor the segregationist Buford Ellington in 1958 following the moderate Frank Clement, seemed to take very seriously Roy Harris's question: Who was strongest on segregation? A brief look at three gubernatorial elections showed how strongly feelings ran.

The 1954 Georgia Democratic primary took place in early fall, but politicking began the day after the *Brown* decision. Nine candidates emerged, of whom three could be considered moderate; one, an Atlanta Sunday school teacher, actually endorsed *Brown*. The favorite was the candidate of the pro-Talmadge faction, Marvin Griffin, a race-baiter and rabid segregationist. He promised to protect Georgia's states' rights "come hell or high water."[30] He essentially saw the South as a victim of a communist plot. But he was by no means the most extreme of the candidates. One promised to abolish the Supreme Court. Another would have required all parents to take an oath-administered poll, asking their position on "mixing" races in schools; those choosing desegregation would be judged "diseased" and placed in state mental hospitals.

Griffin won a plurality of the vote, but under Georgia's county unit system he received nearly 75 percent of the total.[31] One of those defeated was a former governor, Ellis Arnall, a racial moderate who retired from politics and returned to his law practice in Atlanta. The Sunday school teacher finished last.

The Florida Democratic primary in the spring of 1956 was unusual in that it featured an incumbent, LeRoy Collins, who had served two years after winning a special election in 1954. Collins's major opponent was Sumter Lowry of Tampa, a wealthy businessman and vicious racist. Segregation was his only issue, and he denounced "integration as part of a communist conspiracy to destroy the moral fiber of the nation by creating a 'mongrel' race incapable of preventing a red take-over."[32]

All the candidates in the race, including one former and one future governor, announced their support of segregation with varying degrees of enthusiasm. Collins himself agreed to support it, but his major emphasis was on the need to uphold the law of the land. Lowry denounced Collins as the NAACP candidate, but his extremist rhetoric seemed to backlash in favor of Collins, who put together a coalition of moderate urban voters and was personally very popular, having "cleaned up" the state from the corrupt previous administration. Collins's strategy worked: he won the primary outright with 52 percent of the vote, receiving 70 percent in the ten most populous counties. Lowry was second with 21 percent.

Alabama's 1958 gubernatorial primary was similar to the 1954 Georgia contest. Fourteen candidates announced, all of whom were segregationists. John Patterson, state attorney general, was the favorite. He openly courted the Ku Klux Klan and enticed Robert Shelton, one of the Klan leaders, to campaign on his behalf.

Another candidate was a little-known county official named George Wallace. He was not especially racially oriented and preferred to discuss the political agenda of his populist mentor, "Big Jim" Folsom. He finished second in the primary but was defeated in the runoff by Patterson. It was as a result of this election that he vowed never to be "outniggered" again.

Legislative Defiance

But massive resistance went beyond election-year posturing. It was also prominent in legislatures ranging from the U.S. Congress to southern state legislatures. Indeed, in the latter, members actually vied with each other to express ever more outrage and indignation over what the Supreme Court had wrought. Legislative careers were made and lost by the degree of vitriol brought forth and the solutions proposed to maintain segregation.

The most famous legislative act of defiance was the so-called Southern Manifesto, issued in early 1956. The document, whose actual title was "Declaration of Constitutional Principles," was not a formal resolution of Congress but rather a nonbinding statement by southern senators and congressmen condemning the Supreme Court and *Brown*: it declared the rulings "unwarranted" and complained that the Court had substituted "naked power for established law."[33]

Ninety-six legislators signed the original manifesto, and five more were added later. Twenty-seven did not sign, of whom sixteen were from Texas.

Texas's Lyndon Johnson, who was Senate majority leader, was not asked to sign. Tennessee senators Estes Kefauver and Albert Gore, father of the later vice-president, refused. But signers included some of the Senate's most important members, including Harry F. Byrd of Virginia, Strom Thurmond of South Carolina, and Richard Russell of Georgia. Byrd was the key figure, because he was a man of unimpeachable integrity and reputation and his prompt endorsement of the manifesto gave it both visibility and a certain respectability.

At the state level, also, southern legislators sent out the same message, although unlike in the U.S. Congress, formal resolutions were actually passed. While they took a variety of forms, they were essentially of two types. Resolutions of nullification were statements in the John C. Calhoun tradition, in that states had the right to declare federal statutes and court opinions "null and void." Resolutions of interposition sought to place the state between federal law and citizens, thereby "interposing" state sovereignty and protecting citizens from federal excesses. By mid-1957, eight southern states had passed one of these resolutions, and Texas, North Carolina, and Tennessee had voiced some other form of protest.[34]

But southern legislators went beyond these largely symbolic gestures and actively sought ways to thwart efforts by the federal government to force school and other forms of desegregation down their throats. Southern officials and lawyers were truly ingenious in these efforts, and it has been noted many times that if they had put even a fraction of such imagination and effort into compliance as they put into avoidance, desegregation in the South would have been relatively easy.

A variety of techniques were used to keep schools segregated. "Freedom of choice" and "pupil placement" laws looked as if they might help black students to enroll with whites but in fact allowed local officials the actual decision about where they would attend schools. "Gradualist" plans permitted desegregation of one grade a year, a process that, barring administrative and legal delays, would have taken years to implement fully. Virginia passed even more draconian laws, closing the public schools in Prince Edward County and opening "private" schools paid for with public moneys but open only to whites.

The effect of these effects was to minimize the process of desegregation. By February 1959, only four black children attended all-white schools in racially moderate Dade County (Miami), Florida. Throughout the South, virtually every step toward desegregation was legally tested, the litigation creating lengthy delays. Local officials added additional hurdles through increased administrative requirements. And local officials found strong allies among southern state and even federal judges whose rulings and legal orders frequently undermined or curtailed efforts to desegregate schools or other facilities.

The Ku Klux Klan and White Citizens Councils

Another very important source of southern massive resistance were white voluntary organizations, to which everyday citizens could belong. Two of the most important of these were the Ku Klux Klan and White Citizens Councils.

The Klan had its origin late in the nineteenth century, in the Midwest, not the South.[35] It was never a single organization but a series of often competing groups. Membership and activity for much of its history tended to be episodic and sporadic.

The period immediately following *Brown* was another occasion for the emergence of Klan activity. Each of the southern states had Klan organizations, but they were most common in Alabama, Georgia, Florida, both Carolinas, and Tennessee. Klan memberships have always been secret, but reliable estimates suggest that by the late 1950s they may have reached between 10,000 and 100,000.[36] More important than the actual membership, however, were the vast numbers of supporters and fellow-travelers they could attract to their rallies; in the mid- and late 1950s reports of more than a thousand participants, including women and children, were not unusual. Not all were widely attended, however: a much-publicized, four-state rally near Columbus, Georgia, in late 1956 produced only three Klansmen, who nonetheless went ahead with their cross-burning.[37]

The Klan was primarily composed of rural and small-town whites, generally at the lower end of the socioeconomic scale. Some analysts have suggested that Klan membership provided a real psychological need for people who led economically marginal existences, who felt insecure and threatened by blacks, and who may have been fearful of the future.

But the impact of the Klan was more than psychological. It had virtual freedom to engage in violence and terror with no fear of retribution. Beatings, bombings, maimings, cross-burnings, rallies, and parades by Klansmen were common in the years following *Brown*. These activities had a chilling effect on blacks (and even whites appalled by Klan violence), because the criminal justice system would not intervene against them. Sometimes law enforcement officers were even members or sympathizers of the Klan. And the reverberations of even a single act of Klan violence echoed across the entire South.

The White Citizens Councils were the "respectable" analogue of the Klan. They were not related, and memberships usually did not overlap. Their goals were the same—preservation of a segregated society—but their methods differed. Where the Klan engaged in violence and terror, the councils sought political conformity through seemingly peaceful, but repressive, means.

Membership in the councils was never large, even though chapters grew up in each southern state following *Brown*. Their importance resulted from the kind of persons who belonged—white businessmen, professional people, and politicians. They were respectable, establishment members of the community who could not, or would not, associate with the Klan but who nonetheless stood for the same goals and objectives.

The councils used a variety of respectable means to further their goals, but their most common, and infamous, technique was the use of the "questionnaire." In fact, it was a propaganda tool. Candidates for office (including those nominated by the council) would be given questions designed to show their commitment to maintaining segregation. The results would then be widely publicized. Those not measuring up would be denounced, even smeared, by councils and their candidates. Few whites dared to risk the consequences of advancing alternative views on racial or states' rights questions. The effect was to force a political conformity onto candidates, as the council sought to project a solid South image throughout the region and nation.

Little Rock, 1957

A major demonstration of the doctrine of massive resistance took place in fall 1957, at Central High School in Little Rock, Arkansas. That it should have happened there was something of a surprise. Little Rock was a moderate-sized southern city with a business and political community that tried to project a progressive, modern image.[38] It had a history of moderate racial policies, and its school board had adopted a desegregation plan at the relatively early date of spring 1955. It was a gradualist plan, designed to go into effect in 1957 and to be completed over an eight-year period. It had evoked little comment in the white community and seemingly was opposed only by the NAACP, which regarded it as tokenism.[39]

Preparations for the desegregation of Central High School, where initially nine black students were to join two thousand whites, went forward smoothly. The new, all-white high school in the wealthy, exclusive fifth ward of the city was not to be desegregated. No trouble was expected, or planned for, as the opening of school on September 3 approached.

But Governor Orval Faubus had other ideas. He was searching for an issue that could improve his chances for a third two-year term, something that no Arkansas governor had achieved in more than fifty years. Accordingly, on September 2, the night before school was to open, he suddenly went on television to announce that he had received information that trouble was expected because of the "forced integration" that was to occur the next day. He then ordered the Arkansas National Guard to Central High, allegedly to protect the children and ensure peace. Instead, when the black children appeared in the morning, the guard turned them away, as the governor had apparently ordered them to do. The children had no choice but to turn back, and indeed they did not appear later that day, or on Tuesday.

Events deteriorated rapidly. Blacks sought another court order to force desegregation, and it arrived in time to accompany the children on Wednesday. They were again met by the guard and turned away. But this time an angry mob also appeared in front of the school, shouting "nigger" and other nasty epithets.

In the meantime, the national media focused attention on Little Rock and on President Eisenhower. Clearly his was the next move, since Faubus through an act of physical interposition had successfully juxtaposed state and federal power. The president, however, declined to act. He had never supported *Brown,* showed no interest in civil rights, and seemingly felt as strongly about not expanding federal authority at the expense of states' rights as the most ardent southerner. Indeed, during the week of the crisis Eisenhower made oblique comments during a press conference that implied that he was not especially on the side of the black children.

In the meantime, white southern public opinion rallied behind Faubus. He rapidly emerged as a hero of massive resistance. On September 14, national pressures forced a meeting between the president and the governor. It was, however, inconclusive.

Finally, on Friday, September 20, blacks obtained another court order forcing the governor not to interfere with desegregation. Faubus's response was to withdraw the guard. On Monday morning, a screaming, hysterical mob was in front of Central High School, and it became even more unruly when it learned that the nine students had been ushered into the building through a side door. White students began a walkout, precipitating still more rage from the crowd. Violence threatened to erupt. The mayor had the black children removed.

That Monday evening President Eisenhower appeared on television ordering the obstructionists to leave. The next morning an even larger, more disruptive mob appeared. The president had no choice but to send a thousand paratroopers and to nationalize the Arkansas Guard. On Wednesday morning troops escorted the black students to class. They stayed at the school for two months, and even after they left, the federalized guard remained for the rest of the school year. The fears of many white southerners had been realized: federal troops had returned to the South.

The episode was a victory for Faubus: he had no trouble winning reelection. It was also a victory for massive resistance. Little Rock provided an outpouring of southern feeling against *Brown* and the Supreme Court. Southerners succeeded in forcing President Eisenhower's hand, and discovered that the commitments and priorities of the chief executive did not extend to black civil rights. Thus, even though northern armies had returned, they did so only in a limited way. Finally, southern extremists felt vindicated: hard-line, massive resistance was worthwhile, because the federal government chose to respond only meekly.

It was a long time before Little Rock's progressive business community recovered from its shock, and sought to reestablish its pre-eminence in the city.[40] The message of Little Rock was not lost on whites elsewhere in the South. Nor was it lost on blacks, who saw that the victories of *Brown* and Montgomery were small, indeed.

The Apogee of Massive Resistance

Massive resistance in the South did not die for a long time. Nonetheless, even as George Wallace was being "outniggered" in Alabama, there was reason to think that some of its steam was beginning to dissipate.

In particular, the first signs of a moderate white voice opposed to extremism started to appear, especially in the border South states and urban areas. School closings and strife over desegregation plans took their toll, and businessmen and other professionals started to realize the negative impact these conflicts had on the economic and social life of their communities. Towns and cities were literally ripped apart by conflict, and many felt that continuing the course of massive resistance carried too high a price.

Public school professionals also came to the defense of the educational system. In a number of border South states, they were able to argue successfully that children were suffering, and the educational enterprise failing, by making the schools a battleground over social policy. Even in Virginia, intellectual birthplace of massive resistance, public school personnel and their allies rejected continuing efforts to close schools and insisted that ways be found to prevent further disruptions.

Even some conservative politicians and journalists began to shift ground slightly. In Virginia, Governor J. Lindsay Almond, no desegregationist, nonetheless began to steer a course different from that of his mentor, Harry F. Byrd, and showed somewhat more flexibility than other state leaders on massive resistance. Florida Governor LeRoy Collins fought hard to find a moderate racial course that would prevent his state from following the path taken by its deep South neighbors. Even the dean of conservative southern journalists, James J. Kilpatrick, urged a rethinking of the massive resistance strategy.[41]

Too much should not be made of these developments. They did not signify a sudden willingness by southerners to accept *Brown* or other aspects of desegregation. Nor were they the harbingers of any new political order. At most they represented cracks in the facade of southern solidarity on massive resistance. Much work had to be done, and blood shed, before desegregation was anything but a pipe dream. Moreover, episodes such as Little Rock, including the behavior of the president of the United States, made blacks wonder whether they would ever succeed.

The Civil Rights Movement: Second Phase, the 1960s

It would not be correct to say that there was no civil rights activity in the South in the latter part of the 1950s. Indeed, a great deal happened. Martin Luther King Jr. made upward of two hundred speeches a year, traveling extensively throughout the nation, meeting with important political figures and other opinion leaders, and attempting to gain support for the movement. A march on Washington, D.C., in support of voting rights was held in 1957, and Congress passed civil rights laws designed to secure them for southern blacks in 1957 and 1960. Bus boycotts were held in Tallahassee and other southern cities. Other local forms of protest were also common in communities throughout the region. Numerous court battles were fought at local, state, and national levels designed to force southern schools to desegregate.

But progress was slow. In spite of King's growing reputation and the prominence he and other leaders, as well as their organizations, achieved, massive resistance was still a reality. Racism and bigotry were so firmly entrenched in the South that the moral suasion of nonviolent protest simply did not work. States' rights attitudes were so deeply embedded in the political fabric of the South that there was virtually no communication between southern officials and Washington on reaching accommodations or solutions for desegregation problems.

King and others began to realize that methods of nonviolent protest more direct than conferences, petitions, meetings, lawsuits, speeches, and prayer marches were needed to confront segregation successfully. They also saw that the solution to segregation would have to come from inside the South, not outside. In this they were joined by southern black college students, who were rapidly becoming impatient with the pace of desegregation. Four, in Greensboro, North Carolina, became so incensed that they decided to act on their own. Their actions became another crucial moment in the civil rights struggle.

Greensboro, North Carolina, 1960

Like Little Rock, Greensboro was a medium-sized city that prided itself on its progressive outlook.[42] It tried to embody the political tradition of North Carolina: cosmopolitanism, moderation, sophistication. It had a substantial economic base and a good deal of wealth. Several colleges were in the area, including black North Carolina Agricultural and Technical College. "Race" had never been much of a "problem" in Greensboro.

But the students at A&T were losing patience. For several years they had complained about racial policies in the city. The slow pace of desegregation and the treatment blacks received at the hands of local businesses rankled them. Some campus protest activity had occurred, and one of the faculty, sociologist and minister Edward Edmonds, was an outspoken activist. Students were also in close contact with those on other campuses, and their mutual impatience was reinforcing.

Late in January, one of the A&T students, Joseph McNeil, returned from a trip to New York and had been refused service at the bus station in Greensboro.[43] While he had been refused service before, this time the incident especially bothered him. He talked about it with three friends who also had been involved in civil rights activity. By the evening of January 31, they decided they had talked enough and it was time to act.

The next afternoon they met at the downtown Woolworth's. An associate meanwhile notified a sympathetic journalist of what would happen. The four young men picked out some school supplies and paid for them. They then moved to the lunch counter, sat down, and ordered coffee and donuts. When they were refused service, one of the students, Ezell Blair, asked why they could not also be served at the counter, since they had just bought supplies in the store.[44]

Other customers saw what was happening. One white woman came by, patted their backs, and remarked that they should have done this years ago. Others made nasty comments. A black dishwasher appeared and called them troublemakers and rabble-rousers. The manager came over, tried to be friendly, and asked them to leave. But they continued to sit until the store closed.

News of the sit-in preceded the students' return to campus. Within a very short time it reached the highest levels of state government in Raleigh. A&T became a beehive of activity. Further sit-ins were planned. The next day twenty-three A&T students returned to Woolworth's, along with several from another black college. By Wednesday there were enough students sitting-in so that virtually the entire lunch counter was occupied all day. On Thursday they were joined by several white students from nearby colleges.

By Saturday night students agreed to stop the sit-ins while an agreement was hammered out. It was not, and on April 1 they resumed. By the end of April white leaders began having the sit-in participants arrested. Blacks then began a boycott of white-owned stores, which proved successful. Finally, on July 25, six months after the first sit-in, a black was served a meal at Woolworth's.[45]

As William Chafe points out, the sit-ins in Greensboro were only a limited success. True, the initial target, Woolworth's lunch counter, was desegregated, but only after a protracted struggle. But hamburgers were not the real issue: desegregation of public facilities and the right to be treated as equals were the goals. "Progressive" Greensboro proved to be bitterly divided, race relations deteriorated badly, and for years afterward Greensboro was an unhappy place where whites and blacks regarded each other suspiciously.

But in a larger sense, Greensboro was a success. The sit-in was instantly seen to be a powerful tool for attacking segregation, and its use spread rapidly. Within a week sit-ins could be found elsewhere in North Carolina and in Tennessee and Virginia. Within six weeks they had spread to every southern state except Louisiana and Mississippi. According to the Southern Regional Council, by September 1, 1960, more than twenty states and one hundred cities reported some form of sit-in; more than 70,000 persons participated in them, and more than 3,600 were arrested.[46]

The significance of Greensboro went beyond the discovery of the sit-in. It was exactly the dramatic moment that served to reenergize the civil rights movement. It proved, from a media standpoint, an ideal strategy, since sit-ins were easily covered and the issues sharply drawn and contrasted. And it provided the opportunity for an enthusiastic army of civil rights activists—black college students—to find a role in the struggle. It was no accident that the Student Nonviolent Coordinating Committee (SNCC) was founded just after Greensboro concluded.

Presidential Politics, 1960

On October 19, 1960, Martin Luther King Jr. and a group of students attempted a sit-in at the lunch counter of Rich's Department Store in downtown Atlanta. He and a number of others were arrested, but they declined bail, opting instead to hold a "jail-in." Nonetheless, the mayor intervened, and the charges were dropped. Shortly afterward, an obscure Georgia judge ruled that King's participation in the illegal sit-in had violated his probation from an earlier traffic conviction and sentenced him to four months of hard labor.

Immediately appeals were made to the White House to intervene on King's behalf. There was genuine concern not just about the legal issues but about King's life, since Georgia prisons were infamous for their treatment of black prisoners. The Justice Department prepared a statement for President Eisenhower, but he declined to issue it or act in any way except to order the attorney general to cooperate with King's lawyers.

The presidential election was only eight days away when King was jailed. Richard Nixon, the Republican nominee, made no comment. But John Kennedy personally called Mrs. Coretta King and assured her of his concern and assistance. The next morning Robert Kennedy interceded with the Georgia judge and succeeded in arranging bail for King.

The whole episode was widely reported in the national media. Some analysts have felt that it persuaded many black voters to support Kennedy, perhaps helping to assure his razor-thin margin of victory. Indeed, the Sunday prior to the election a grateful Martin Luther King Sr., who previously had endorsed Richard Nixon, announced from his pulpit that he had a "suitcase" full of votes that he would now deliver to Kennedy.[47]

The Freedom Rides, 1961

Early in 1961, the Congress of Racial Equality (CORE) appointed a new president, James Farmer. He was a longtime civil rights activist whose involvement had begun in Chicago. His job was to energize the organization and give it a prominent role in the civil rights movement.

Farmer quickly decided that CORE would not engage primarily in sit-ins. Students and SCLC had undertaken that strategy, and he saw that whatever CORE did along those lines would be "anticlimactic."[48] Rather, his organization had to adopt its own course and strategy. He settled on freedom rides throughout the South modeled after the one attempted in 1947 by the old Fellowship of Reconciliation, a precursor of CORE.

Farmer was committed to the principles of nonviolence, but he was equally firm about the need for direct action and confrontation to overcome segregation. The freedom rides would prove an excellent technique for combining both. In 1947 the Supreme Court had ruled unconstitutional segregated seating on interstate buses and in 1960 had expanded the ruling to include bus terminals serving interstate vehicles and passengers.[49] Southern states ignored both rulings.

The freedom rides, in Farmer's view, would test these decisions. Moreover, Farmer was anxious to quash a piece of conventional wisdom: that civil rights activity, to be successful, had to be initiated and carried out by local citizens; "outsiders" simply made matters worse. Farmer wanted to establish the point that blacks could move freely throughout the region, demanding their civil rights regardless of where they came from.

In spring 1961, Farmer recruited an interracial group of thirteen people and brought them to Washington, D.C., for training in nonviolent protest. At the same time, he wrote to the president, the Justice Department, the Federal Bureau of Investigation (FBI), and the Greyhound and Trailways bus companies outlining what the freedom riders planned to do: leave Washington on May 4, bound for New Orleans. During their journey, Farmer wrote, they would deliberately test segregated facilities at bus stations and restaurants in a nonviolent way. Farmer never received a reply to any of his letters.

On May 4, the group was split in two interracial parts, one to leave on Greyhound, the other on Trailways, and headed south. There were no problems in Virginia or North Carolina. There was some evidence that signs indicating segregated facilities in the terminals had recently been taken down. Farmer took their absence to mean that his letters had done some good. But there was later evidence that some of the signs were replaced once the freedom riders reboarded the buses and left town.

Rock Hill, South Carolina, was the scene of the first violence. Future Georgia Congressman John Lewis was beaten when he tried to enter a white waiting room, and two other freedom riders, including a white woman, were also attacked. No arrests were made, and they left. In Winnsboro two freedom riders were arrested at a lunch counter. But the ride through Georgia was uneventful, and on May 13 the freedom riders arrived in Atlanta, preparing for the trip into Alabama and Mississippi.[50]

The next day, May 14, was Mother's Day. It turned into a nightmare. One of the buses stopped at Anniston, Alabama, about sixty miles from Birmingham, the day's destination. Anniston was a known enclave of Klan activity. The bus, upon arrival, was immediately surrounded by a yelling mob of men carrying iron bars. They attacked the bus, smashing as much as possible. The police finally arrived and allowed the bus to leave.

However, the mob followed in cars, like a vigilante posse. Six miles out of town the bus broke down; there was later reason to think that its tires had been shot out. The mob again attacked the bus, only this time an incendiary or smoke device was thrown inside. All exit doors on the bus except one were locked; as the terrified freedom riders tried to leave, they were beaten. Meanwhile, the bus exploded, burned, and turned into a charred mass. The riders were cut by flying metal and glass or were sickened from the acrid smoke. They were taken to a hospital in Anniston, but the medical staff refused to treat them. Fortunately, a caravan headed by the Reverend Fred Shuttlesworth arrived from Birmingham and took the freedom riders there.

One rider noted that each car contained weapons, in spite of Shuttlesworth's public commitment to nonviolence.[51]

Meanwhile, the second bus managed to reach Birmingham after a stop in Anniston; during the respite the freedom riders were beaten on the bus, one of whom was left permanently brain-damaged. At the depot in Birmingham about forty whites were waiting. They beat the departing passengers for about fifteen minutes before police arrived, in spite of the fact that the police had previously been notified. Later it was learned that Public Safety Commissioner Eugene "Bull" Connor had ordered his policemen not to intervene for at least fifteen minutes after the beatings began. Connor, when asked why no police had met the bus when it arrived, said that because it was Mother's Day most of the police were with their families.[52]

Bruised and beaten, the freedom riders left Birmingham for New Orleans on a special flight arranged by the Justice Department. They were replaced by a contingent of students from Nashville, led by John Lewis. These students were immediately taken into "protective custody" by Connor, driven 150 miles to the Tennessee border, and simply left there. Finally arriving back in Birmingham, they waited at the Greyhound station for a bus. But no driver would take them. At last Attorney General Robert Kennedy intervened with the company and a driver appeared; Kennedy unsuccessfully sought also to reach Governor John Patterson to persuade him to ensure the safety of the riders.

The trip to Montgomery, the next stop, on May 20 was uneventful. There was a police escort for the bus, and occasionally helicopters appeared. But upon their arrival in Montgomery the escort disappeared. The bus terminal itself was quiet, until the passengers disembarked. Suddenly another mob appeared, and a brutal scene followed. More than a thousand whites beat anyone they could find, including several federal officials and Justice Department observers. One person was set on fire. While John Lewis was lying unconscious in a pool of blood, he was handed an injunction forbidding interracial travel in Alabama. No ambulances appeared; when asked about this later, the police chief said they had all been reported out of order.[53]

By this time, the freedom riders and their reception were receiving national and international attention. Events were reported extensively in the world press and became a major source of propaganda in communist and Third World nations. The Kennedy administration had repeatedly sought to secure the cooperation of Alabama's Governor Patterson, but had failed. Now, embarrassed, it had to act. President Kennedy declared the situation to be one of the "deepest concern." More than six hundred federal marshals were sent to Montgomery; Governor Patterson complained to Attorney General Kennedy that the state was being "invaded."

Meanwhile, King arrived in Montgomery to urge on the freedom riders. He joined Ralph Abernathy in a huge rally at the First Baptist Church the evening of May 21. A large mob of whites gathered outside, but no police were in evidence. The whites began to attack the church, first heaving rocks and smashing windows, then throwing smoke bombs, and finally threatening to break in. Panic began in the seriously overcrowded church. Suddenly, however, federal marshals appeared and managed to get the mob away. Blacks had to remain in the church all night, however.[54]

This violence was the last straw for the Kennedy administration. It insisted that Patterson declare martial law, which he reluctantly did. It also demanded that he provide protection for the freedom riders as they left for Mississippi.

At the same time, however, the administration urged freedom riders to pause for a cooling-off period. It was concerned about its international image and the upcoming meeting with Soviet Premier Nikita Khrushchev. King, the civil rights leader most sensitive to the pressures facing Kennedy, seemed willing to agree. But the request was flatly refused by the fiery Farmer, who remarked that "We had been cooling off for a hundred years. If we got any cooler, we'd be in a deep freeze."[55] Freedom riders left for Jackson, Mississippi, on May 24. Mississippi Senator James Eastland gave his assurance that freedom riders would be protected. There were arrests, but they were peaceful, and no more mobs appeared.

By the end of the summer, more than a thousand people participated in other freedom rides. The technique spread to airports and train stations. More than 350 arrests were made. On September 22, the Interstate Commerce Commission, at the request of the administration, issued new rules prohibiting racial discrimination in interstate travel.[56]

The freedom rides were important for a number of reasons, not the least of which was that they forced the federal government to intervene on behalf of the rights of southern blacks. The initial response of the Kennedy administration was, to be sure, hesitant. Many blacks were disappointed and felt that more forthright action would have prevented violence. They also resented Kennedy's attempt to mollify southern politicians. However, it is also true that once the Kennedy administration decided to act, it irrevocably put the federal government on the side of southern blacks. This stance represented a great change from the Eisenhower years.

Oxford, 1962, and Tuscaloosa, 1963

The tentative, ambiguous response of the federal government toward civil rights activity can be seen in efforts to desegregate two major universities in the deep South—those in Mississippi and Alabama. Both became battle-grounds demonstrating the confrontation between federal and state power that the civil rights movement evoked.[57]

Oxford, Mississippi, in 1962 was a sleepy college town. The campus exemplified what a southern university should look like, with stately columned buildings and tree-lined quadrangles. Its institutional culture overtly sought to maintain the glories of the southern past: its athletic teams were called the "Rebels," and "Dixie" was the school fight song. Its all-white student body represented the cream of Mississippi society.

On May 31, 1961, a black former Air Force sergeant, James Meredith, sued the university for admission. He argued that his prior rejection had been based solely on race. On September 20, 1962, armed with a court order, Meredith attempted to register at the university. His way was blocked, personally, by Governor Ross Barnett. Four times Meredith sought to register, but each time state officials denied him. Although he had a federal court order, no federal marshals tried to enforce it.

Behind the scenes the Kennedy administration tried to reach an accommodation with Barnett. Essentially it sought guarantees that the governor would ensure Meredith's peaceful enrollment in order that the federal government would not have to present a show of force. Several plans were considered, including one in which Meredith would be registered in Jackson (the state capital), and not on campus. Another called for a "capitulation" of Mississippi guardsmen before federal marshals. None of these plans came to fruition, however, and after federal officials withdrew on September 27, Barnett was cited for contempt.

On September 29, President Kennedy nationalized the Mississippi National Guard to provide protection for Meredith. On September 30, he was assured by the governor's office that state troopers would assist federal marshals in maintaining order. Instead, Barnett ordered the troopers out of Oxford. That night a mob of more than 2,500 people gathered on the campus. When violence erupted, it quickly escalated into a full-scale riot. Rock throwing and yelling gave way to gunfire. Two persons, including a French journalist, were killed, and hundreds injured. More than 160 marshals were hurt, of whom twenty-nine received gunshot wounds.[58]

The next morning, when Meredith appeared for class, he was escorted by 5,000 troops. More were added later, and then withdrawn. But some troops remained until June 1963. Meredith received his bachelor's degree in August of that year. Contempt charges against Barnett were eventually dropped, ostensibly because of October's Cuban Missile Crisis, which preoccupied the administration.

Oxford illustrates Kennedy's on-again, off-again approach to civil rights.

The administration did not wish to do more than was minimally necessary to bring about desegregation. Its tentative, circumspect approach turned a difficult situation into a tragedy.

To its credit, the Kennedy administration seemed to learn from its mistakes at Oxford. It did not repeat them at Tuscaloosa. The federal government had a dismal record in efforts to desegregate the University of Alabama. As early as 1956 the university had lost a three-year court battle to remain segregated and was forced to admit black Autherine Lucy. She did not stay long. When she appeared on campus, turmoil ensued involving both students and "outside agitators." University officials first removed, then permanently suspended, Lucy for "insubordination." No federal marshals came to her assistance.[59]

By spring 1963, things had changed a good deal. The university was again under court order to admit another black student, Vivian Malone. But George Wallace had only a few months earlier been inaugurated as governor of Alabama. This time he had been "right" on race, and in his inaugural address he made his famous pledge: "I draw the line in the dust and toss the gauntlet before the feet of tyranny, and I say, Segregation now! Segregation tomorrow! Segregation forever!"[60] When the federal government in June 1963 sought to force the entrance of Malone, Wallace reminded Alabamans of his pledge and promised not to let them down.

Wallace tried not to. He made his famous "stand in the schoolhouse door" on June 11, trying to prevent the entrance of black students. In a carefully staged encounter, Wallace was confronted by the U.S. Attorney General Nicholas Katzenbach, who had been sent by President Kennedy to ensure that peace was maintained as students were enrolled. Katzenbach was backed by an array of federal officials as television cameras recorded the entire event, including Wallace's dramatic capitulation. That evening President Kennedy made perhaps his strongest statement to date on behalf of civil rights, arguing before a national audience that it was a "moral issue." He also pledged immediately afterward to work for a strong civil rights bill, which he intended to submit to Congress. Kennedy linked the racial violence in Birmingham that spring with the show of force in Tuscaloosa and made clear that his administration would no longer tolerate southern efforts to put off desegregation of public facilities.[61]

On the other hand, the administration allowed Wallace a graceful face-saving in agreeing to participate in the schoolhouse door drama. And the administration also adopted a largely hands-off attitude toward the gigantic August 1963 March on Washington, held by blacks in support of the civil rights legislation proposed by Kennedy; it was at this rally, attended by more than 200,000 people, that Martin Luther King made his passionate "I Have a Dream" speech.[62]

Thus, even though the administration avoided the mistakes of Oxford at Tuscaloosa, there remained some doubt in the minds of many civil rights leaders as to how far the administration was prepared to go to help them. Its efforts at conciliation on campus, its seeming indifference to the March on Washington, and even its initial response to the violence in Birmingham did little to reassure southern blacks or to relieve the ambiguity of its position.

Birmingham, 1963

As spring came to the South in 1963, Martin Luther King Jr., and perhaps the entire civil rights movement, needed a victory. King had spent much of his time from late 1961 through the end of 1962 in Albany, Georgia. But his campaign there was not a success. His efforts to desegregate this Old South city proved futile because his campaign suffered from a lack of focus, insufficient media attention, black violence, and the shrewdness of Police Chief Laurie Pritchett, who completely buffaloed King.[63]

As a result, King's reputation as titular leader of the civil rights movement was in jeopardy. Southern resistance to desegregation efforts elsewhere proved intractable. King and other civil rights leaders badly wanted a campaign that would be a success for the movement, rejuvenate and reenergize it, and reassert King's leadership role. They found what they were looking for in Birmingham.

Birmingham had always had a reputation as a "tough" town. Highly industrialized, its economy based heavily on steelmaking, its working-class, blue-collar image was well-deserved. It was also one of the most rigidly segregated cities in America. Residents went to great lengths to maintain Jim Crow practices. The local baseball team at one point during the 1950s was disbanded rather than desegregated. Efforts were even made to keep "black" music off "white" radio stations. Even elevators were segregated. For white Birmingham residents, racial segregation was not merely a way of life; it was an article of faith.

This reputation alone made Birmingham a likely target for a major SCLC campaign. But there was more. Birmingham's police commissioner and mayoral candidate in 1963, Eugene "Bull" Connor, was the perfect foil for King. Heavy, foul-mouthed, and quick tempered, Connor made no secret of his contempt for blacks. He could be expected to respond to civil rights authority in a violent, provocative manner, unlike the cautious, circumspect Laurie Pritchett in Albany. Moreover, Birmingham had already been the site of considerable civil rights action. The Reverend Fred

Shuttlesworth, head of the local SCLC affiliate, was well known for his personal bravery and willingness to engage white Birmingham on behalf of blacks. Accordingly, late in 1962 when Shuttlesworth "invited" King to campaign in Birmingham, King quickly accepted.[64]

The campaign did not begin until April 3, the day after Birmingham held its mayoral election. As demonstrations began, SCLC issued a four-part list of demands: desegregation of public facilities in the city, hiring of blacks for white-collar sales and clerical positions by local businessmen, establishment of a biracial civic committee to deal with local problems, and release of jailed demonstrators.

The first several days of activity were relatively low key. Sit-ins and small demonstrations were held downtown, and arrests followed. But Connor responded with restraint, and dramatic confrontations did not occur. Still, King did succeed in galvanizing Birmingham blacks, and national media attention began to focus on the city.

The pace of events began to quicken during the following weekend. Connor arrested participants in marches on City Hall, including one on Palm Sunday. The demonstrations and arrests had full media coverage. On April 10, the city obtained a court injunction forbidding racial demonstrations. Injunctions became a common tactic in the South, designed to force civil rights activity outside the law and permitting mass arrests to be made.

King argued with his aides that the injunction had to be ignored, because it was itself illegal, and that to obey it meant that they would have to end the campaign and leave town. Accordingly, on April 12, Good Friday, he led a march of about fifty people toward City Hall. More than a thousand blacks lined the streets in a show of support. Connor, accompanied by a group of vicious police dogs, had the demonstrators arrested.

This arrest became a critical moment in the civil rights movement. It was the manifestation of a turning point in King's thinking. He finally came to recognize that the moral suasion of nonviolence was not itself powerful enough to undermine segregation. Rather, nonviolence had to be used in a direct, confrontational way to provoke, deliberately, a violent response, even if this provocation meant endangering the lives of protesters. Only in this way would the moral suasion and justification of civil rights demands become apparent.[65]

Thus the manner of the April 12 arrests became as important as the arrests themselves. Connor had hoped to show the world how Birmingham treated those violating court injunctions. But what it actually saw were police dogs attacking peaceful marchers on a holy day. It was an omen of things to come.

Perhaps as a result of the dramatic arrests, and the ensuing "Letter from Birmingham Jail," which King wrote while incarcerated, blacks in the city continued to demonstrate. Connor responded with more violent arrests. They also pursued a boycott of downtown businesses, which had an immediate economic impact. But city officials and businessmen were equally resolute, and as April wore on a stalemate seemed inevitable.

The murder of William Moore on April 23 near Gadsden, Alabama, began to push events forward. Moore was an eccentric white mailman from Baltimore who was determined to march from Chattanooga to Jackson in a one-man campaign for black equality. His body was found on a desolate stretch of Alabama highway. Members of Birmingham's black community then rushed to Gadsden to complete Moore's walk. They were arrested. Another, biracial, group, which took their place on May 1, was set upon at the Alabama-Tennessee border by an angry mob, severely beaten, and attacked by highway patrolmen with electric cattle prods.

Taking advantage of the anger of the moment, King on May 2 began his most provocative act, one for which he was severely criticized even by supporters. It was a dangerous strategy that might have backfired badly. But it did illustrate the extent to which he came to believe that to be effective, nonviolent protest had to evoke a violent response.

King organized more than a thousand children, ranging in age from six to late teens, to demonstrate for civil rights on the streets of Birmingham. They were promptly arrested in front of cameras and journalists. The next day, another thousand children met in the Sixteenth Street Baptist Church to receive marching orders. Connor had the exits barred and severely beat those managing to escape. He also used dogs, maiming several children. He then turned his forces on a group of blacks watching from a park across from the church. Besides the usual clubs, dogs, and cattle prods, he employed high-pressure fire hoses on the crowd. This attack had a devastating effect on the crowd, and some blacks began to fight back with bottles and rocks.

Within a few days more than 1,300 children had been arrested, plus hundreds of adults. Pictures of the violence, including of women and children being beaten, attacked by dogs, and fire-hosed, were broadcast throughout the world. President Kennedy announced that they "sickened" him, although as of early May the federal government had not moved to assist civil rights activists. Indeed, the administration had criticized King for being deliberately (and in its view, unnecessarily) provocative.

Demonstrations peaked on May 6 and 7. Thousands poured into the streets, only to be beaten and arrested. Connor added an armored water cannon to his arsenal and used it indiscriminately. Injuries were extensive, including to Shuttlesworth, who was flung against a brick wall by water and was hospitalized. Connor even had journalists and cameramen attacked; newsmen were present from all over the world.

At this point the federal government began efforts to mediate the crisis. Burke Marshall and John Doar from the Justice Department were sent by the president to reach a compromise. Moreover, the business community in Birmingham had had enough. The boycott had hurt them, and the continued violence threatened to destroy whatever business climate remained in the city. Accordingly, the Chamber of Commerce and other business leaders began negotiations with King, using federal representatives as intermediaries. As Sid Smyser, president of the chamber, was later reported to have said, "I'm a segregationist from bottom to top, but gentlemen, you see what's happening. I'm not a damn fool. Now, we can't win. We can't win. We gon' have to stop to talk to these folks."[66]

King was ready to accept a compromise whereby demonstrations would cease as negotiations on the four demands went forward. But just as he was to announce the agreement, along with the president in Washington, Shuttlesworth, who only moments earlier had left the hospital, refused to go along. He reminded King that they had agreed that the demonstrations would continue until all four demands were met. Accordingly, nonstop negotiations continued for three more days, until finally on May 10 an agreement was reached. King promptly left for Atlanta.[67]

The agreement did not end the hostility. Connor and other public officials immediately denounced it. That night a giant Ku Klux Klan rally was held nearby. After it ended, two bombs exploded in the black community. One nearly destroyed the home of King's brother (also a minister), and the other severely damaged the Gaston Motel, King's "headquarters" during the Birmingham campaign. Blacks, infuriated, went on a rampage. They battled police and destroyed property. White citizens and businesses were attacked. More than fifty persons were injured. King raced back from Atlanta the next day, working furiously to ensure that the agreement stayed intact.

But bitterness on both sides remained. It climaxed on September 15, when a bomb was set off under the Sixteenth Street Baptist Church, scene of the earlier "children's crusade." Four black girls were killed by the explosion, which took place on Sunday morning, and dozens were hurt. Later the same day a white policeman killed a black youth with a shotgun blast in the back, and several white toughs murdered a thirteen-year-old black riding his bicycle.

Birmingham did not have a happy ending. On the other hand, it was in many ways a successful campaign for King. It was a dramatic, media-centered civil rights protest. It reestablished his position as titular leader of the civil rights movement; he emerged with his reputation enhanced as a result of his leadership in Birmingham (even if President Kennedy reportedly told him, not wholly in jest, that Bull Connor did more for civil rights in Birmingham than King did). Indeed, in 1964 King received the Nobel Peace Prize in recognition for his commitment to nonviolent means to promote civil rights in the South.

Birmingham was also a crucial moment in the political education of King and other civil rights leaders. They understood the need for sharply focused objectives that could be communicated readily to the public. They saw the importance of dramatic confrontations between nonviolent protesters and white segregationists. And they saw how crucial were organization and discipline within the black community, for if black violence flared, it undercut the credibility of the protest.

Birmingham was also another important step in positioning the federal government on the side of civil rights. While the government did not act until national and international abhorrence of white violence demanded that "something" be done, the administration then worked both publicly and behind the scenes to forge an agreement in Birmingham. As a result of what happened in the city, the University of Alabama that same spring, and in other parts of the South, the Kennedy administration submitted an important civil rights bill to the Congress. Thus Birmingham and the spring of 1963 proved to be a major turning point, not just for King and the whole civil rights movement, but for the entire nation.

Freedom Summer, 1964

Martin Luther King Jr. and Alabama seemed to grab most of the civil rights headlines during 1963. But a great deal of civil rights activity occurred elsewhere, some of it quiet, some of it provocative, all of it intense. As Thomas Brooks noted, it was a time when southern blacks were very much "in motion."[68] Perhaps nowhere were their efforts more difficult, and dangerous, than in Mississippi.

Mississippi had a reputation as the most violently racist state in the South. The "closed society," as the eminent historian James Silver called it, Mississippi was an inhospitable place for blacks to live and for civil rights activity to take place.[69] During the first half of the twentieth century lynchings and murders of blacks were fairly common, even when there was little provocation. Violence against blacks continued well into the 1950s. The murder of fourteen-year-old Emmett Till was but one example; also in 1955 the Reverend George Lee and Lamar Smith, both active in voter registration in the state, were shot down in broad daylight. In 1961 Herbert Lee and Lewis Allen were murdered, allegedly by a state legislator, on the pretext of being friendly with civil rights workers. No one was convicted of these crimes, and rarely were blacks' assailants even prosecuted. On June 12,

1963, Medgar Evers was killed as he returned home in Jackson following a civil rights meeting; it was the day after President Kennedy had insisted on national television that civil rights was a "moral issue."

Because Mississippi was so rural, the urban-oriented SCLC never made much headway there. Besides, from the early 1960s the Student Nonviolent Coordinating Committee (SNCC) decided that Mississippi was "its" state. It did not welcome King's participation. By 1962 SNCC had largely broken with King over goals and priorities. Desegregation of public facilities, it decided, was largely a black middle-class, urban concern, essentially irrelevant to poverty-stricken, rural Mississippi blacks. Under the leadership of its dynamic leader, Robert Moses, SNCC determined that voting rights had to form the basis of its civil rights activity. It felt that only through the ballot box, and not the right to sit at a lunch counter, could Mississippi blacks expect a better future.

Blacks in Mississippi had the lowest rates of voter registration in the South. In a number of delta counties, blacks actually constituted a majority of the population but not a single black was registered. In other counties officials claimed that some blacks were registered, but no one could find them, and no one remembered seeing any try to vote.

SNCC began its voter registration campaign in 1962. Ostensibly it did so to assist the Voter Education Project, an Atlanta organization founded to increase the level of black registration and voting in the South. By fall 1963, however, the project had left the state, discouraged over the lack of response by Mississippi blacks and harassed by whites. SNCC remained, however, and continued its efforts in hard-core delta counties to register black voters.[70]

In fact, progress was slow. Relatively few blacks agreed to register. Many were fearful of white reprisals, but Moses and his colleagues also found that large numbers of ill-educated blacks failed to understand the importance of the franchise. Accordingly, he determined that a massive voter education campaign was needed, culminating in a mock election.

Working with black and white volunteers, many of whom were college students, SNCC established voter education centers in churches, storefronts, homes—wherever space was available—to acquaint Mississippi blacks with the importance of voting and to teach them how to register. But, as the distinguished southern writer Robert Penn Warren observed, the effort was actually much more. It became a gigantic educational enterprise that ranged from the teaching of elementary reading to sophisticated discussions of American constitutional and political history.[71]

As a result of this activity, some blacks were registered to vote. The numbers were not great, amounting to a couple of hundred. But the symbolism was important. And in the August primary, some blacks actually voted. As Stokely Carmichael later observed, "Two years ago we would have been shot for a stunt like this."[72]

Even more impressive was the response of Mississippi blacks to the "mock" election held by SNCC on the same day as the "real" governor's contest in November. Aaron Henry, a Clarksville druggist and state NAACP president, was the black gubernatorial nominee. The lieutenant governor was Ed King, the white chaplain at nearly all-black Tougaloo College. Close to 90,000 blacks across the state turned out at the "polls," representing about a quarter of eligible blacks and more than three times the number actually registered.

Moses and other SNCC leaders then had to face the next step. They decided to build on the success of the mock election and would spend the summer of 1964 in a massive voter registration project. It became known as "Freedom Summer."

White Mississippians were not caught off guard. On April 24, before the influx of black and white volunteers began, many of them college students, crosses were burned in sixty-four of Mississippi's eighty-two counties. Once the volunteers started to arrive, violence escalated at a dizzying rate. Between January and August 1964, thirty Mississippi blacks were murdered. By the end of the summer, the Council of Federated Organizations reported three more killings, eighty beatings, thirty-five shootings, thirty-five churches burned, and thirty homes and other buildings bombed.[73]

Of this violence, the most infamous was in Neshoba County, near Philadelphia. It came early in Freedom Summer and cast a pall over the next months. Three volunteers—Andrew Goodman, Michael Schwerner, and James Chaney—passed through Philadelphia on the way to their base in Meridian. They never arrived, nor was any trace of them found except for their burned-out car. President Lyndon Johnson ordered an investigation by the FBI, and a massive search took place that included the use of sailors. After six weeks, their bodies were found under an earthen dam. Chaney, black, had been badly beaten and shot; the two whites were killed by bullets in the head. Late in December the FBI arrested twenty-one persons in conjunction with the killings, including the sheriff and deputy sheriff of Neshoba County. All had connections to the Ku Klux Klan. Their indictments were eventually thrown out by a Kennedy-appointed Mississippi judge.[74]

Mississippi's Freedom Summer was marked by extreme fear and tension. Many SNCC workers began to carry guns. After the death of Schwerner, Goodman, and Chaney, SNCC largely abandoned its commitment to nonviolence. It formed its own vigilante group, the Deacons for Defense and Justice, for protection. The federal government offered no help. J.

Edgar Hoover, head of the FBI, made disparaging remarks about the Freedom Summer effort. Lyndon Johnson, who signed the 1964 Civil Rights Act into law on July 2, apparently felt that it should be given a chance to work before any additional federal assistance was forthcoming.

Freedom Summer also caused an irrevocable split in SNCC between blacks and whites. Many became resentful of white participation. Blacks bitterly complained that the FBI and sailors were used to look for the murdered volunteers in Philadelphia because two were white.[75] They pointed out that the federal government had made no similar effort to find blacks who had disappeared.[76] By the end of the summer, few whites remained in SNCC. As an organization it became so radicalized that it openly criticized King and began to embrace the growing black nationalist-separatist movement espoused by Malcolm X and other black fire breathers.

In spite of the massive voter registration efforts during Freedom Summer, only about 1,200 additional blacks were added to the rolls. The violence and anxiety of the summer took an enormous toll in human life, feelings, and property.

In some respects, Freedom Summer was a success. More than fifty voter education schools were established and maintained afterward. Another fifty community centers were created, which formed the basis for later political action. Enough political mobilization occurred among Mississippi blacks that the Freedom Democratic Party was created, which challenged the regular Mississippi Democratic Party at the 1964 Convention.[77]

Freedom Summer did not, however, result in broad gains in voting rights for blacks, either in Mississippi or in other states. Rather, these had to wait until further steps were taken in Selma, Alabama, the following spring.

Selma, 1965

After the 1964 Civil Rights Act took effect, the focus of civil rights activity in the South sharpened and narrowed. The reason, as we will see in more detail in the next chapter, is that the act paved the way for achieving one of the major goals of the movement—desegregation of public facilities. Accordingly, civil rights strategists moved to put their energies toward another critical goal—voting rights.

While many federal officials, including President Johnson, were hopeful that the Civil Rights Act would prove effective in promoting voting rights, it became apparent that it did not significantly increase the ability of the federal government to prompt local voting registrars to enroll more black voters.[78] Martin Luther King Jr. felt that continued pressure was needed to force the federal government to attack voting rights specifically. This idea became increasingly clear to him as Johnson unveiled his legislative program following his landslide victory and a new Congress elected with overwhelming Democratic majorities: Johnson had made no provision for a voting rights bill.

In the fall of 1964, King and his aides began to plan "Operation Alabama," designed to pursue voting rights. They found a suitable location in Selma.[79] It was a fairly mild place, by deep South standards. The mayor was descended from an old, aristocratic family. The police chief was thoroughly professional and seemed not to be motivated by racial considerations. King and his aides experienced no difficulty in checking into Selma's major, previously all-white, hotel when they arrived in town.

Voting rights, however, were in the hands of county, not city, officials. The most important officer in Dallas County was the sheriff, Jim Clark. He was a man in the same mold as Birmingham's Bull Connor—irascible, apoplectic, and a vicious racist. He had continually harassed SNCC workers who had been in the area since 1962. King thought he would be an ideal foil for civil rights activity aimed at voting rights.

The campaign did not go well at first. There was open conflict between SCLC and SNCC. The increasingly militant and angry students were hostile to King's calls for nonviolent protest. They resented King's "invasion" of Selma, territory they had staked out and worked (even with indifferent success) for two years. It was but another instance, they felt, of King's building on the groundwork laid by others but grabbing the headlines for himself.

Another problem for King was Sheriff Clark. King began demonstrating in January 1965. Almost daily he led marches to the county courthouse, demanding that blacks be added to the voting rolls. By the end of the month, about two thousand blacks had been arrested. But Clark's behavior was remarkably restrained, reminiscent of Laurie Pritchett's in Albany, Georgia. This situation proved to be frustrating for King, since media from all over the nation and world were present but there was remarkably little to report.

King stepped up the pace in February, and within the first three days Clark arrested another two thousand demonstrators. He was becoming edgy. Then the inevitable happened, raising the level of anger and tension on both sides. The Reverend James Bevel, one of King's aides, was beaten by Clark's deputies on February 10 and was hospitalized with severe head injuries. In Marion, a few miles from Selma, Jimmy Lee Jackson was murdered by law enforcement officers during a voting rights demonstration there.[80]

These events galvanized Selma blacks. SNCC and community leaders demanded militant action. King urged a more cautious approach, for there had been no national cry of outrage at the violence and he did not wish to pressure President Johnson, whose support he knew was critical. However, he did agree to a march on Sunday, March 7, from Selma to Montgomery, where a petition demanding voting rights would be given to Governor Wallace. The march was to be led by one of King's principal aides, the Reverend Hosea Williams, as King claimed he had to return to Atlanta.[81]

On the morning of March 7, about five hundred blacks assembled at Brown's Chapel preparatory to the march toward Montgomery. Leading were Hosea Williams and John Lewis of SNCC, who had been beaten on the freedom rides and was later a U.S. representative from Alabama. They moved toward the main highway accompanied by an array of journalists and camera crews. As they reached the Edmund Pettus Bridge, they found about one hundred of Clark's men lining both sides of the highway and bridge. On the other side were about fifty state troopers, including fifteen on horses. Williams sought word with the troopers' commanding officer, Major John Cloud. He, however, ordered the marchers to turn around, giving them two minutes to retreat.

All was orderly until suddenly Cloud commanded his deputies and troopers to attack. It was a massacre. The marchers were unprepared and unprotected, and the violence of the attacking law enforcement officers overwhelming. Clubs, tear gas, horses, fists—all were used indiscriminately against men, women, and children. Journalists covering the event were attacked, and television and photographic cameras were smashed. There was total panic as some marchers ran back to town, some jumped off the bridge, and some simply lay where they had been beaten down. Sixteen marchers were hospitalized with severe injuries, including Lewis, whose skull was fractured. Fifty others received emergency medical treatment. The Selma police chief, Wilson Baker, prevented additional carnage by encouraging retreating blacks to seek refuge in Brown's Chapel and then demanding the Clark's deputies and the troopers leave his jurisdiction.

That night, and the next day, millions of Americans saw on television and read in the papers what had happened. The national outcry was enormous. The White House and Congress were besieged by demands for action, and throughout the nation thousands of people marched in "Selma sympathy" marches. Even in the White House a brief sit-in was held by a group of students. Numerous clergy and other persons made plans to go to Selma to participate in future marches, while others organized protest trips to Washington to demand that "something" be done. Subsequent events in Selma did, in fact, involve large numbers of white volunteers.

King, meanwhile, returned to Selma. He organized another march for Tuesday, March 9. But he was again in an awkward situation. President Johnson was opposed to another march. The march was actually enjoined by a federal court, although King was under tremendous pressure by Selma blacks to ignore the injunction. Under a compromise worked out by LeRoy Collins, a former governor of Florida, racial moderate, and head of the new federal Community Relations Service, established by the 1964 Civil Rights Act to assist communities with desegregation efforts, King was to lead marchers over the bridge, be halted by troopers, pray, and then return to Selma. They were guaranteed safe passage throughout. But when King and 1,500 marchers (about a third of whom were white) reached Major Cloud, he suddenly ordered his men off the highway, leaving the way clear to Montgomery. King hesitated, and then returned with his forces to Selma.

It was another low point for King; he promptly was denounced by militants in SNCC and other blacks in Selma. But a tragedy again strengthened his position. The Reverend James Deeb, a white minister who had come to Selma, was severely beaten by white toughs as he left a restaurant. He died on March 11. His two white religious colleagues were also badly beaten. Again national outcries that Washington act were loud and clear. The president could no longer sit idly by.

On March 15, eight days after "Bloody Sunday," President Johnson addressed a joint session of Congress and by television the entire nation. It was a historic moment. Johnson linked the events at Selma with critical points in the nation's history: "At times history and fate meet at a single time in a single place to shape a turning point in man's unending search for freedom. So it was at Lexington and Concord. So it was a century ago at Appomattox. So it was last week in Selma, Alabama." He then pledged his support for a voting rights bill, arguing that "Every American citizen must have an equal right to vote. There is no reason which can excuse the denial of that right. There is no duty which weighs more heavily on us that the duty to insure that right." He then inextricably linked the federal government with the civil rights movement by invoking its anthem, "We Shall Overcome."[82]

It was a dramatic moment, one that had been a long time in coming. In some respects it was the climax of the civil rights movement. Never before had a president—a southern president, no less—spoken so fervently on behalf of civil rights. The legislation that Johnson immediately submitted to Congress and signed into law only a few months later, on August 6, 1965, was the Voting Rights Act.

The Selma campaign did not end, however, with Johnson's speech and proposal. On March 21, three hundred marchers set out from Selma to Montgomery. They were protected by federalized troops of the Alabama National Guard. Six days later they reached "the Cradle of the Confederacy." On the steps of the Capitol, more than 25,000 people gathered to watch and listen as a petition on voting rights was presented to Wallace. He declined to be present, although some said he could be seen peeking through the blinds in his office. Nonetheless, a national television audience heard King and other civil rights luminaries demand the right to vote.

But tragedy was again to strike Selma. Mrs. Viola Liuzzo was white, the wife of a Detroit labor union official, and the mother of five children. She had gone to Alabama because she felt the need to participate in the civil rights movement and because, as she had told her husband, "It was everybody's business." After the Montgomery rally she taxied marchers back to Selma. During her return trip to Montgomery for another group, she was shot dead by four Ku Klux Klan members. A few hours later President Johnson again appeared on television to denounce the "horrible crime," to announce the arrest of the Klansmen, and to recommit himself to the pursuit of voting rights for southern blacks.

After Selma: The Civil Rights Movement in Decline

The civil rights movement continued after Selma and after the passage of the Voting Rights Act. It continues to this day. But after 1965, it was never quite the same again, for a number of reasons.

In the first place, it was a victim of its own success. Desegregation of public accommodations and access to the franchise had been achieved. While much work needed to be done to ensure that the promises of the 1964 Civil Rights Act and 1965 Voting Rights Act were realized, most activity shifted from the streets to legislative chambers, courtrooms, and administrative offices to ensure that it did. But these are essentially nondramatic political arenas, where progress is incremental, even subtle. Once the main goals were achieved, the locus and pace of civil rights activity changed so significantly that media interest, and even the interest and commitment of civil rights activists, began to wane.

Next, the focus of the civil rights movement shifted. After 1965 and until his death, King began to attack economic discrimination as well as social and political discrimination. But economic equality proved even more difficult to obtain than political and social equality. Many Americans sympathetic to the political demands of blacks were not willing to support the movement's new calls for substantial redistribution of resources in the nation.

This reluctance was especially true as the civil rights movement began to move north and west. Not that all the battles in the South had been won. But it became clear to King and others that discrimination against blacks was far more of a problem in the North and West than many white citizens in those areas were willing to admit. Especially was this true since discrimination and segregation there were based not on legal principles (*de jure*) as was the case in the South, but occurred rather as a function of historical trends and circumstances in migration, housing patterns, employment practices, and the like (*de facto*). Thus it was not easy to create the kind of targets in the North and West that civil rights leaders had found in the South. While there were analogues of Bull Connor and Jim Clark in those regions, it was by no means certain that a sense of moral outrage in the general population could be created because of the very different tradition in which northern and western discrimination against blacks had developed.

Also, in the years immediately following 1965, Vietnam and its accompanying turmoil began to take over the nation's headlines. In a sense, black civil rights in the South had had its day in the sun, and the nation's attention was increasingly directed elsewhere. Economic difficulties, rapid inflation, budget deficits, higher taxes—all of these accompanied the Vietnam era, and they did not provide the kind of political milieu in which increasing demands for civil rights (especially those that looked expensive in economic and social terms) would be favorably heard.

Related to these concerns was the growing white backlash which could be felt, almost palpably, in the nation after 1965. It was not limited to the South, by any means. Many white Americans felt that blacks had been given enough, and it was time to stop. Indeed, it was only a few short years from Selma to 1968, when George Wallace brought his campaign of massive resistance to the national political stage and forced both the Republican and Democratic Parties in that year to become more circumspect on civil rights. While the Democrats were in total disarray over Vietnam, Richard Nixon won both the nomination and the presidency by including an overtly southern strategy, which promised a slowdown in federal support for black civil rights, in his campaign message.[83]

Finally, the civil rights movement itself became irrevocably split. King was seen as too moderate by many northern and western blacks. Black nationalism had permeated the country, captivating many younger, urban blacks, and frightening many whites. Spokespersons such as the late Malcolm X, Stokely Carmichael, H. Rap Brown, Bobby Seale, Eldridge Cleaver, and Angela Davis rivaled the more moderate King, Roy Wilkins, Whitney Young, and James Farmer for the attention of the nation. It was difficult to reconcile a militant black separatist movement with calls for greater black equality and participation in American life.

As a result, the direction of the civil rights movement became confused, diffuse, uncertain. This lack of focus was further compounded by King's assassination in early 1968 and that of Bobby Kennedy later that spring. King's death left the civil rights movement without a center of gravity and without the one individual who could serve a nationally visible and credible leader. Kennedy, of course, served as a link to the hopefulness of his brother's administration and also as a powerful political force that could continue to secure white support for black civil rights.

Some former white allies of the movement joined the increasingly shrill black militants, while others became disenchanted and felt that the movement neither wanted nor deserved white support. By the late 1960s and early 1970s, it was almost impossible to tell what civil rights leaders, and the black community—southern and otherwise—really wanted. Indeed, in some ways the southern situation proved easier for Washington to deal with than elsewhere, since it continued to fight the remnants of southern segregation. But the time had passed when a purely regional civil rights policy could be supported by a president or enacted by Congress.

This is not to say that nothing further happened. Indeed, politics in the South as a result of the civil rights movement was never the same again. Let us now turn, then, to an examination of the success and shortcomings of the civil rights movement in the South and its short- and long-term effects on the political life of the region.

8

"Free at Last"?:
The Civil Rights Movement
in Retrospect

We're not what we oughta be. We're not what we're gonna be.
But thank God, we're not what we was.
—Attributed to a black preacher during the civil rights movement

Free at last! Free at last! Thank God Almighty, I'm free at last!
—Old black spiritual, epitaph on the memorial to
Martin Luther King Jr., Atlanta

How successful was the civil rights movement in the South? Did blacks achieve the goals they wanted? Have they achieved political and social equality in the region? What accounts for the degree of success and the shortcomings of the movement?

In this chapter we shall look at this last question first. We need to examine the reasons why the movement proved successful in achieving some of its goals as well as where it fell short. The major portion of the chapter will be devoted to an examination of the actual effects and outcomes of the movement. While there are many possible areas to look at, we shall deal with four—federal legislation; black voting; black elected officials; and public service delivery patterns for blacks. We shall conclude the chapter with a short discussion of continuing racial problems in the South.

Determinants of Civil Rights Success

When we began our discussion of the civil rights movement in the South, we noted that there were a number of preconditions needed for it to take place: growth of political consciousness and political mobilization; organization; leadership; movement ideology; appropriate strategies and tactics; and changes in the national political environment.

Without these preconditions, there would have been no civil rights movement. But more was required for the civil rights movement to produce positive outcomes. Jim Crow racism was firmly entrenched in the region, and, as we saw, white resistance to the movement was often intransigent. For the movement to produce desired results required additional factors above and beyond those needed just to get it started and keep it going. Let us briefly examine each of these in turn.

Individual Courage

In their search for explanations of social phenomena, political scientists often look beyond individual acts and behaviors. But it must be remembered that no civil rights movement would have taken place without the willingness of individual southern blacks to confront a repressive Jim Crow society. The risks taken were substantial. They may have been greatest in the deep South states, where terror and violence were coupled with psychological intimidation. But the difference between the subregions is more one of degree than of kind. Wherever they lived, southern blacks put life and limb in jeopardy and demonstrated great physical and emotional courage to pursue their civil rights.

Why were so many people willing to do this? The reasons seem to vary as much as the participants themselves. Religious conviction motivated some, while rage and impatience over centuries of second-class status was crucial for others. Many wanted to improve their lives and those of their children. The civil rights movement was a way for southern blacks to participate fully in the promise of American life, something that had been denied them for centuries. And for others, peer pressure and a desire to be involved in a cause in which their neighbors, friends, and family also participated was a motivating force. Whatever the reasons, the result was a veritable army of blacks willing to participate in civil rights causes.

Political Participation: Blacks as Political Actors

On one level, the civil rights movement can be viewed as a test of wills, individual and collective, between white southerners desperately seeking to hold onto their traditional society and blacks wanting to transform it to the extent that they could claim their rightful place and full equality. But on another level, the civil rights movement marked the emergence of new political actors in the South. Indeed, it is the rise of black political participation through the civil rights movement that contributed greatly to its successes and served to transform the politics of the region.

What is especially important, and notable, about the rise of black political participation in the South is that both qualitatively and quantitatively it marked an abrupt change from the past. Through civil rights activity, southern blacks became independent participants in the political process, constituting a political force that they themselves largely controlled. Blacks had been involved in southern politics before, but never as autonomous actors. They were involved to the extent that whites allowed them, playing on a "white" field using "white" rules. Moreover, black political participation in the South prior to the civil rights movement was generally defensive and reactive in nature. It was often limited to accommodationist, consensus-oriented tactics, and militancy and confrontation on the part of southern blacks were virtually unheard of prior to the civil rights movement.

The emergence of blacks as autonomous, independent, even aggressive political actors in the South became a crucial factor in the success of the civil rights movement. Where blacks remained passive, intimidated, and controlled by whites such as in rural areas of the deep South, civil rights goals were difficult to achieve. But where blacks organized themselves in sufficient numbers and acted in a coherent way to confront whites directly and nonviolently, as in many urbanized areas of the South, then greater possibilities of achieving goals existed.

As the preceding chapter showed, the emergence of blacks as independent political actors occurred neither quickly nor easily. It was a long way, politically and temporally, from the Montgomery Improvement Association at Martin Luther King Jr.'s Dexter Avenue Baptist Church in December 1955, to the Edmund Pettus Bridge in Selma ten years later. The process of moving from dependent to independent political action occurred fitfully and inconsistently throughout the region. The modern reader must remember that southern blacks had no history or tradition of independent political action.[1] They had to learn the hows, whens, and wheres of effective political activity. Even leaders such as King, John Lewis, and James Farmer needed to evolve from rather naive political reformers into hardheaded political strategists who knew how to make effective use of limited resources. Rank-and-file participants needed to learn to channel their energies and frustrations into disciplined demonstrations and other nonviolent forms of protest and to avoid random, uncoordinated, or violent activity in order to achieve concrete results.

Independent political activity by southern blacks took a variety of forms, ranging from the most passive to extremely active. What is most interesting, and important, about this participation was its extent. We do not know, exactly, how many southern blacks actually became politically active during this period. Part of the problem in estimating is that so frequently participation means active forms of involvement. But for a previously politically inert population, even a discussion of civil rights with family, schoolmates, neighbors, or the barber was a big step forward, and attendance at a civil rights prayer meeting and rally an even greater one. Judged by these criteria, hundreds of thousands, perhaps millions, of southern blacks became political participants.

If we examine only membership in formal organizations, we seriously underestimate the extent of political involvement. Actual dues-paying membership in the Big Four civil rights organizations by southern blacks was relatively small, and many of their resources actually came from outside the South. But clearly the organizations had great appeal among southern blacks and created large numbers of sympathizers and fellow-travelers. The close connection between these organizations and local churches, improvement associations, and college campuses accounts for their ability to marshal substantial participation at the local level for their civil rights campaigns.

Some figures for the events mentioned in the last chapter can suggest an order of magnitude for the most active forms of black political participation. The Montgomery bus boycott was estimated to be 90 percent effective among its black population.[2] Sit-ins became popularized by three students in Greensboro, but within a few weeks they had spread throughout the South. By September 1, 1960, more than 70,000 people had participated in sit-ins in twenty states, of whom 3,600 were arrested; the vast majority of those sitting-in at this early date were black. More than 1,000 people participated in freedom rides during 1961, of whom 350 were arrested; the initial group was biracial, but later became predominantly black. More than 2,000 persons spent time in Albany, Georgia, jails, although many were repeaters; but not everyone who demonstrated was arrested. In Birmingham, thousands of blacks took to the streets; 1,300 children alone were arrested. The 1963 March on Washington was attended by more than 200,000 people, many of whom were southern blacks. Later that year, nearly 90,000 previously disenfranchised Mississippi blacks participated in a mock gubernatorial election conducted by SNCC. More than 25,000 people saw Martin Luther King Jr. on the steps of the Capitol in Montgomery present a petition to Governor George Wallace on behalf of voting rights.[3]

But these figures are ultimately deceptive, because they do not reflect the large numbers of blacks who were involved in some form of civil rights activity throughout the South. Often these were just small groups of people, such as the fifty civil rights workers in Danville, Virginia, who were severely beaten by police and firemen in June 1963; or the seven Mississippi blacks, including Fannie Lou Hamer, whose arrest and beating became infamous as the Winona incident;[4] or the group of Texas Southern University students who helped to desegregate restaurants and theaters in Houston.

The civil rights movement did not always involve large numbers of people massed together in one place for a joint enterprise. It did involve large numbers of people throughout the South, often working in relative isolation but always with a common purpose and toward common goals. Regardless of location or numbers, the crucial point is that they participated as independent political actors, no longer manipulated by southern whites.

Clarity of Objectives and Goals

A third important determinant of the relative success and failure of the civil rights movement was the clarity of its expressed objectives and goals. To the extent they were clear and focused, so were the possibilities for achieving them greater. Lack of clarity seemed to undermine the likelihood of success. Thus goals and objectives had to move beyond vague statements such as "elimination of Jim Crow" or "better treatment by whites." The more concrete were the goals, and the less diffuse and abstract, the better.

Clarity of goals was important for several reasons. For civil rights participants, it was easier to make a commitment to act if they knew exactly what they were striving toward and for what purpose their energies and resources were being used. Making demands on white officials and businesses could be done more effectively if they were communicated in a sharp, focused manner. And for explaining the goals of the movement to the media, whites outside the South, and national leaders, clarity and precision were essential.

A brief look at several of the campaigns indicates how much help clarity of goals and objectives was to civil rights advocates. In Montgomery, the goals were sharp and relatively modest; boycotting of buses to force an end to Jim Crow seating. In Birmingham and later in St. Augustine,[5] King reduced the list of demands to four that could be simply stated, and communicated readily to the media, participants, and their target. During Freedom Summer and in Selma, the list of demands was reduced still further, to an elemental simplicity—the right to register and vote.

In contrast was Albany, Georgia, where leaders of the movement never articulated sharply their priorities and objectives. King himself seemed to change direction on several occasions, and local civil rights leaders found themselves uncertain how to proceed. As a result, as the campaign wore on, it lost a good deal of momentum merely because local citizens—black and white—seemed unsure of what it was really all about.

Highlighting Jim Crow

To shape public opinion, capture the support of moderates inside and outside the South, and dramatize the extent of the pernicious, discriminatory social system in the region, blacks had to demonstrate that racism went beyond a bland, condescending paternalism to an outright hatred and violence. This side of racism was readily shown in Birmingham, Selma, and elsewhere. But because black behavior in Albany did not provoke a violent white response, due in part to the political sophistication of Sheriff Laurie Pritchett, the city did not look to outsiders like a repressive, Jim Crow—dominated community.

In a sense, the legitimacy of blacks' claims for greater levels of political equality was enhanced by efforts of white southerners to prevent them from achieving it. The contrast between the claims of blacks to secure their constitutionally sanctioned civil rights and the repressive, violent white response was essential, for it tended to polarize the issue into a for-us-or-against-us mode, left little room for ambiguity, and was deliberately aimed at building white sympathy for the blacks' cause.

Thus both the use of nonviolent behavior on the part of black protesters and a violent white response were critical for highlighting Jim Crow. So, too, was the political education of Martin Luther King Jr. and other civil rights leaders. It was one thing to preach about the moral suasion of nonviolent protest from the pulpit in church or dais at a rally but something else again to find that it did not work against tough, traditional southern segregationists. Rather, these leaders learned that nonviolent protest had to be used to provoke white violence. Only in this way could Jim Crow be shown in deep relief. Only in this way could the way the goals and objectives of the movement be dramatically highlighted and contrasted with white behavior through the electronic and print media and thus communicated effectively throughout the nation and world.

Black Violence

In some instances of civil rights activity, blacks did not maintain nonviolent behavior but engaged in acts of violence. This action tended to undermine the legitimacy of black claims and make achievement of civil rights goals more difficult. The contrast between nonviolent, legitimate demand of constitutional rights and the repressive, violent response was lost. To those whose support blacks needed, inside and outside the South, violence on both sides was simply hooliganism repugnant to everyone.

It did little good, as some of King's aides claimed at Albany and Birmingham, that those blacks who threw rocks at police or went on a rampage through the community were not part of the real demonstrators. When whites—southern and otherwise—saw blacks engaged in violent behavior, they did not concern themselves with a distinction between demonstrators and street thugs. While blacks in peaceful protest could favorably impress even crusty traditionalists such as James J. Kilpatrick, those who became violent—even if their behavior was provoked—cost the movement support and allies.

One of the remarkable things about the civil rights movement in the South, however, was how relatively infrequently blacks engaged in violent behavior in spite of the provocations they often faced. Why they refrained is a matter of some speculation. In part it rests on the traditional failures of southern black violence to succeed: slave revolts were usually brutally suppressed, leaving little incentive for further violent acts. In the twentieth century, southern blacks understood that because of traditional racial attitudes, violence—or even engaging in "uppity" behavior—on their part was likely to result in white reprisals and further repression, not less. And it is also true that the relatively small amount of black violence in the civil rights movement resulted from the effectiveness of its leaders and a real commitment to nonviolent protest as a means of achieving civil rights goals.

Involvement of White America

It is no put-down or insult to civil rights activists, and southern blacks generally, to say that their struggle was a necessary but not sufficient condition to bring about desired results. Without white involvement, there probably would have been fewer positive outcomes for civil rights leaders than ultimately occurred. Indeed, part of the strategy of Martin Luther King Jr. and other movement leaders, from the late 1950s on, was aimed at whites outside the South, not just for money but for political and moral support as well. They saw that southern blacks could not "go it alone" to secure their goals.[6]

The need for involvement of whites outside the South became obvious to King and other leaders because they needed allies who could bring pressure to bear that would force change in the South. The moral suasion of nonviolent protest could not do so by itself, and indeed as southern repression of black civil rights activists escalated, leaders began to realize that even white violence against southern blacks would not do so. White America, in the form of public opinion, national leaders, the president, and even leaders of the private sector, could bring about the necessary pressure for change.

To what extent were the efforts by King and other civil rights leaders to secure the support of nonsouthern whites successful? While this matter is complex to investigate, we can make some inferences based on public opinion data on civil rights issues collected during the movement.

Initial support for *Brown* was favorable: 54 percent of all Americans endorsed the decision in a July 1954 Gallup Poll, while 71 percent of southerners opposed it.[7] By June 1961, 62 percent of Americans approved of *Brown,* while 69 percent of southerners were opposed.[8]

On the other hand, polls taken in 1961 on civil rights issues other than school desegregation indicate a more mixed attitude. Sixty-six percent of Americans polled in June 1961 expressed approval of the *Boynton* decision, which required desegregation of bus terminals serving interstate traffic. However, only 24 percent of Americans approved of the freedom rides, under way that summer, designed to test *Boynton.*[9] In a related poll taken a week later, when Americans were asked if they felt that sit-ins, freedom rides, and other forms of protest helped or hurt the civil rights cause, only 27 percent felt they helped, while 57 percent thought they hurt. In the South, 70 percent thought they hurt.[10]

On the basis of these polls, it appears that Americans outside the South made a distinction between legal requirements and political activism for achieving civil rights goals. While the former were acceptable, the latter may well have been too confrontational and disruptive for many Americans outside the South to accept, at least at that relatively early date.

Over time, nonsouthern whites proved to be more sympathetic to the plight of southern blacks. As white violence began to intensify in places such as Oxford and Birmingham, nonsouthern white support rose. By February 1964, when the Civil Rights Act was before Congress, 71 percent of whites outside the South approved of it, particularly the public accommodations section.[11] By late May, as the St. Augustine civil rights campaign was winding down and President Lyndon Johnson was about to sign the Civil Rights Act into law, 59 percent of whites outside the South approved of the president's approach to civil rights. Interestingly, by that time 36 percent of southern whites approved, and only 39 percent disapproved. Further, in public opinion polls conducted in April 1965, following the Selma campaign, 60 percent of whites outside the South felt Johnson was pushing integration either "about right" or "not fast enough." Seventy-six percent of all Americans reported themselves in favor of the Voting Rights Act, which the president had submitted to Congress at that time; 49 percent of southern whites approved of the bill.[12]

Too much should not be read into these figures; they do not, for example, reflect the intensity of white feelings, that is, how much whites really cared about these issues. On the other hand, the evidence seems clear that during the civil rights movement, whites outside the South, and even increasing number of southern whites, became sympathetic to the concerns of southern blacks. The evolutionary process of this development, however, was not smooth or linear and undoubtedly took longer than civil rights leaders hoped it would.

What brought about the increasing sympathy of nonsouthern whites toward southern civil rights issues? Undoubtedly the massive public relations campaign conducted by King and other leaders outside the South from the mid-1950s on began to pay off. So, too, did the clear articulation of civil rights goals and substantial civil rights activity by southern blacks, as they were able to show nonsoutherners the extent of the repressive Jim Crow milieu in which they lived.

But three other factors also need to be briefly mentioned. One was the increasing role of the media, especially television. As the civil rights movement progressed, the national and international media extensively covered it. Television and photographic cameras were actually on the scene at a number of crucial moments, including Wallace's stand in the schoolhouse door in 1963, and at the Edmund Pettus Bridge in 1965. Thus dramatic occurrences were brought live into the homes of nonsoutherners, or were shown shortly thereafter on film. It seems likely that the role of television, as well as extensive, on-site print coverage, in shaping the perceptions of white America about civil rights in the South was similar to that of only a few years later in bringing the horrors of Vietnam battlefields into American living rooms.

A second force that may well have helped shape the feelings of nonsouthern whites was the emergence of a moderate, white southern voice. For a considerable period at the beginning of the movement, it appeared to those outside the South that massive resistance was the region's monolithic response to civil rights activity and that southern spokesmen were un-Reconstructed, sometimes violent, extremists.

But over time a more moderate, business-oriented white voice emerged in the South.[13] These individuals were not necessarily prodesegregation, but neither did they want to continue the violence and repression that marked much of the response to civil rights demands. They sought accommodation, or at least took a pragmatic approach toward solving what they perceived as a real southern social, economic, and political problem. These voices were seen as legitimate, reasonable, and respectable by nonsouthern whites. The fact that they came out opposed to white extremism (even if not always in support of southern blacks) actually increased the legitimacy of black civil rights demands in nonsouthern white eyes. The result seems to have been an increased willingness on their part to listen sympathetically to the problems of southern blacks engaged in the civil rights struggle.

Finally, the creation of white martyrs of the civil rights movement served to crystallize white public opinion in support of southern blacks. Specifically, the murder of such whites as William L. Moore, Andrew Goodman, Michael Schwerner, the Reverend James Reeb, and Viola Liuzzo, all of whom gave their lives on behalf of civil rights for southern blacks, had an impact on the attitudes of white America toward conditions in the South. As a result of these murders, civil rights was no longer seen as just a southern or black problem, but one that concerned all Americans.

There is a certain bitter irony in this final factor. Blacks had been molested, maimed, lynched, and murdered in the South throughout the twentieth century, and of course earlier as well. While there was an occasional outcry of protest, even the most senseless, brutal murders of southern blacks, such as that of the teenager Emmett Till in 1955, the spring 1963 shooting of Medgar Evers in Jackson, and the September Sunday school bombing that year of four young black girls in a Birmingham church, failed to crystallize white support on behalf of blacks. Yet the killing of a relatively few whites touched the nerves, and conscience, of white America as none of these black deaths did, and not a few southern blacks were angered as a result. The difference was painfully obvious to them when President Johnson gave a national television address decrying the death of Liuzzo but had not done so in conjunction with the assassination of Jimmy Lee Jackson in Marion, near Selma, only a few days earlier.

The Federal Government

Another critical determinant of the success of civil rights movement was the changing role played by the federal government. It may well be that, in terms of the part played by the president and Congress on behalf of civil rights, the federal government followed, rather than led, public opinion. Ultimately, however, the power of the federal government proved to be a crucial asset to southern blacks seeking their civil rights.

From the onset of the civil rights movement, the federal judiciary, especially the Supreme Court, was the most consistent supporter of southern blacks. There were exceptions, as some southern federal district judges joined in the massive resistance effort. But for the most part, the Supreme Court, alone of the three branches of the federal government, was out in front of public opinion. It sought, from the 1940s well into the 1970s and early 1980s, to further blacks' civil rights.[14] *Brown* was the most significant, but by no means the only, decision of the court in this regard.

In a sense, the Court moved faster than the country as a whole, and the president and Congress in particular. It was so far ahead that it did not have the support of the other branches of government on which it had to rely in order to enforce its decisions. Thus, following *Brown,* and probably even *Boynton* in 1960, the Court had to wait for the rest of the federal government to catch up to it to enforce the law. On the other hand, the Supreme Court has the luxury of not having to watch public opinion polls or stand for election.[15]

An evolutionary process can be seen in the case of presidential leadership on civil rights. Over a ten-year period, presidential priorities and commitments moved from low levels to very high. They may have followed, rather than led, public opinion, but there seems little question that presidential commitments were crucial to the achievement of civil rights goals.

President Dwight D. Eisenhower's performance on civil rights can only be described as dismal. His failure to endorse *Brown* and to line up the power of his office behind the Supreme Court undoubtedly contributed to the entrenchment of southern massive resistance. The message that his behavior sent to the South was essentially a license for arch-segregationists in the region to pursue whatever policies of massive resistance (including violence) they chose.

Whether Eisenhower harbored racial prejudices himself is not at issue. Eisenhower's professed concerns were with states' rights; he was very hesitant to use federal authority to intervene in state affairs on behalf of civil rights. But the cost of his position was to give a free hand to state and local officials to handle civil rights however they wished. True, he did accept the 1957 and 1960 Civil Rights Acts. But these were essentially forced on him by Congress, including members of his own party. Whatever were the other accomplishments of the Eisenhower administration, support for black civil rights was not one of them.

The Kennedy administration presents a more ambiguous, mixed record on civil rights. It perhaps represents a transitional phase between the indifference and insensitivity of the Eisenhower years and the substantial commitment of the early Johnson administration.

It seems fair to state that prior to the Birmingham campaign in spring 1963, the Kennedy administration had no coherent civil rights policy. It sought instead to operate on an ad hoc, crisis management basis. The administration assumed that it could deal with civil rights matters on a case-by-case basis, negotiating with relevant parties to find a compromise or steer a midcourse that would somehow end the crisis.

This strategy did not work. For the most part, it did not head off violence, as events during the freedom rides and at Oxford, among other
places, showed. Nor did the seat-of-the-pants approach necessarily produce
desirable outcomes for southern blacks, as the experience of Albany, Georgia, demonstrated.

Moreover, the Kennedy strategy sent very mixed signals to both blacks
and whites in the South. Before Birmingham, civil rights leaders were uncertain of John Kennedy's real commitment. He talked as if he were behind
them, but his actions were often different. Likewise, southern whites were
uncertain as to how far the administration was prepared to go to force civil
rights on them: Governor Ross Barnett was held in contempt for blocking
James Meredith's enrollment at Oxford, but later the administration let him
off the hook by quashing the legal proceedings.

Although Kennedy himself seemed sympathetic to civil rights issues,
there were several reasons why his administration seemed to take a go-slow
approach. His 1960 electoral victory was razor-thin, and his first year was
very rocky, including the disastrous Bay of Pigs episode. The administration needed to take a cautious approach to a variety of public issues, including civil rights, to shore up its strength as it looked to the 1962 midterm
elections and the 1964 presidential contest. Also, Kennedy did not wish to
offend the many powerful southern representatives and senators whose support he needed for his New Frontier programs. Finally, the administration
sought to minimize civil rights conflict and violence in order to project a
harmonious image to emerging Third World nations and the Soviet Union.

Whether any of these purposes were well served by the Kennedy strategy
is a matter of debate. Birmingham, however, represented a watershed in
presidential attitudes toward civil rights. The president himself seemed personally offended by events there. But his willingness to take a firm, decisive
stand behind civil rights issues was also prompted by a groundswell of
public horror based on media coverage of white violence. For Kennedy not
to have acted firmly on behalf of civil rights, at that point, would have been
a grave political error.

Kennedy's assassination created an image of a president who cared
deeply about civil rights. Indeed, in death he may have become more of a
champion of civil rights than he was for all but the last few months in
office. President Johnson, in committing himself firmly behind the civil
rights bill that Kennedy had submitted, stated that he wanted it passed as a
memorial to the dead president.

Johnson's own administration represented the high point of any presidential involvement in civil rights; only Presidents Jimmy Carter and Bill Clinton, also southerners, could later approach him in commitment and support.

As Senate majority leader, Johnson was instrumental in the passage of the 1957 and 1960 Civil Rights Acts. He pushed the 1964 Civil Rights Act from his earliest days in the White House. And his prompt action following events at Selma contributed greatly to passage of the 1965 Voting Rights Act.

Not every aspect of the Johnson presidency was supportive of civil rights. Johnson had difficulty working with King and reportedly was jealous of him. He regarded Freedom Summer as too militant and deliberately confrontational. He initially did not want to push for a voting rights act until violence in Selma forced his hand. A certain paternalism seemed to mark his interest in civil rights (as in other areas): he wanted gratitude for the work he did on its behalf, and when it was not forthcoming, he became resentful.

These reservations should not disguise the fact, however, that the Johnson administration was the focus of the most important civil rights legislation passed in this century. As a southerner who endorsed the black struggle for equality, Johnson signaled to the South that the time for resistance was over. He provided presidential legitimacy to the growing view that a new, multiracial, multicultural South was developing.

Civil Rights: A Conservative Revolution

A final important determinant of the success of the civil rights movement was the kind of revolution it embodied. It was a very conservative one, deeply embedded in traditional, mainstream American values. This is not to say that it did not produce fundamental change. But it did so in a way that reinforced the great promise of American life and did not seek to undercut or destroy it.

Three of the major goals of the civil rights movement, it will be recalled, were the rights to vote, to use the same public facilities as whites, and to be treated with dignity and respect. In brief, southern blacks sought equal opportunity and treatment in American life. These were not new or radical notions. They represent precisely the goals that white Americans sought for themselves prior to the Declaration of Independence and were included both in that document and in the Constitution. They are among the fundamental principles on which the whole political structure of this nation rests.

· Thus southern blacks did not seek a departure from mainstream American life and values. Rather, they sought to enter them. It was the Jim Crow South that was out of step with the rest of America and its political tradition, not black demands for civil rights. It took a good deal of time before whites throughout the country realized what the essence of the civil rights movement really was. Even today, some arch-traditionalists in the South refuse to recognize the extraordinary dissonance between Jim Crowism and American democracy.[16]

Had the civil rights movement began as it eventually became—shrill and demanding of racial separation—its course would surely have been different. That message and posture were not rooted in mainstream American values and traditions but were a deliberate departure from them. Ultimately, however, civil rights advocates were able to underscore the mainstream nature of their demands. The fact that they were able to do so increased the legitimacy of their claims and helped pave the way for southern blacks to enter as full partners into the American democratic experiment.

The Success of the Civil Rights Movement

What did the civil rights movement accomplish? How close did southern blacks come to achieving their major goals? Let us now turn our attention to these important questions by examining results and outcomes of civil rights activity in four key areas.

Legislation

As a direct result of civil rights protest in the South, Congress passed, and President Lyndon Johnson signed, two very significant pieces of legislation. Their effect has been to bring fundamental changes to the South and to irrevocably alter its social and political makeup.

1964 Civil Rights Act

The original 1964 Civil Rights Act, subsequently amended, contained eleven titles. Titles II, III and VI were perhaps of the most immediate help to southern blacks. Title II forbade discrimination in such public accommodations (even if they were privately owned) as hotels and motels, restaurants, lunch counters, movie theaters, sports arenas, and so forth. While there were a number of exemptions (for example, for stores not serving food), the effect of the title was to end segregationist practices in public facilities throughout the region.

Under Title III, the U.S. attorney general, upon receiving written complaints of discrimination, could undertake civil suits to force desegregation. This title, then, became the stick to force compliance with the provisions of Title II. Title III was especially important because it shifted the traditional burden of responsibility for bringing suits. Previously the onus was on individual blacks to file complaints and bear the cost of litigation. While they could continue to do so if they chose, the Civil Rights Act provided that they could also insist that the legal power of the federal government be used in their behalf, thus shifting some of the burden away from them.[17]

Title IV of the act forbade racial discrimination in any public agency or service receiving federal funds. Thus, for example, hospitals built even partially with federal dollars could not discriminate on the basis of race. Public schools receiving federal moneys (for example, for school lunch programs), and institutions of higher education that received federal grants (for example, for construction or research) could no longer use race as a criterion for admission. State programs that were even partially funded by federal dollars had to operate in a racially nondiscriminatory way. Even contractors getting funds under federal public works programs had to hire employees in a nondiscriminatory way.[18]

Under the provisions of the legislation, if the federal government found that any of these rules were abrogated, it had the right to cut off funds from the public agency or program following a hearing and appropriate appeals procedures. In the case of public schools, colleges and universities, and other institutions heavily dependent on federal dollars, this provision was very important. Thus the federal government gained a powerful stick that it could wield over state and local governments to force desegregation. The message sent to southern blacks was that the federal government had the tools needed to force compliance with desegregation requirements. Blacks still had to be willing to file complaints with the federal government, but at long last federal machinery existed that could work on their behalf as they sought to desegregate the South.

Other titles of the act also were important. Title IV authorized the U.S. Office of Education (precursor of the Department of Education) to conduct the first national survey of equal educational opportunity in this country. The report that it eventually produced proved to be a remarkable and shattering picture of both equal educational opportunity and the general quality and effectiveness of American public education.[19]

Title V of the Civil Rights Act extended the life of the U.S. Commission on Civil Rights, originally established in the Truman administration. Title VII established the Equal Employment Opportunities Commission (EEOC). Initially this office was charged with overseeing the right to equal opportunity in employment. Later it was responsible for administering federal affirmative action programs. Title X created a federal Community Relations Service, designed to help local communities proceed with desegregation plans.

Title I of the 1964 Civil Rights Act contained voting provisions. It was aimed at enrolling large numbers of southern blacks onto lists of registered voters in southern states and counties. It proved, however, too weak to accomplish this purpose, as we shall see in the next section, and was super-seded by the Voting Rights Act.

The 1964 Civil Rights Act was a wide-ranging and powerful tool through which the federal government was able to bring about substantial levels of desegregation in the South. Progress was not always smooth or rapid, and substantial litigation and administrative pressure were needed to accomplish the purposes of the legislation.

However, it is also true that in many parts of the South voluntary compli-ance with the provisions occurred, including those on school desegregation. Undoubtedly part of the reason for voluntary compliance was that officials and other state and local leaders did not wish to engage any longer in costly, lengthy legal and administrative battles or to risk losing needed federal funds. The burden of proof was on them to show that they were not discrim-inating against blacks, and many realized that they could not make such claims in court. Part of the reason, also, was that many southerners, by 1964, realized the inevitable, that the time for resistance was over and a new era in southern life had to begin.[20]

1965 Voting Rights Act

Numerous ways, some ingenious, had been designed by southern whites during the twentieth century to keep blacks from voting.[21] Some of these techniques also kept poor whites from the polls as well. The all-white primary was one such technique aimed at blacks, but after it was declared unconstitutional in 1944,[22] an array of other mechanisms continued to keep blacks from voting. The poll tax was an economic barrier to poor people, black and white. Literacy tests were common and differentially applied. Often they required prospective voters to read and explicate complex parts of the U.S. or state constitutions. Even educated blacks would not be passed, while semiliterate, ill-educated whites frequently managed to give the right answers. In some areas, character references were needed, in which a prospective voter had to be endorsed by already enrolled voters (usually whites); only rarely were these endorsements given to blacks.

The Civil Rights Acts passed in 1957, 1960, and 1964 were aimed at remedying these practices and enrolling more black voters. The initial legis-lation permitted blacks to go to court seeking injunctions against practices that prevented their voting. The second act permitted federal judges or special referees to enroll qualified blacks who had been refused by local officials. By 1964, a sixth-grade education was made a presumption of literacy, and special panels of federal district courts could be established to hear voting rights suits.[23]

None of this legislation worked very well. The major problem was that these laws relied upon a case-by-case approach to seeking remedies, an arrangement that placed an enormous burden on individual black plaintiffs to bear the expense and burden of court action. Moreover, because of the length of time litigation can take, the election in question might have long been over before the complaint was resolved.

Nor did the acts allow the federal government to intervene, independently, on behalf of aggrieved blacks. Because of the nature of the American federal system, in which authority over registering voters and conducting elections is reserved to state and local officials, local voting registrars maintained control over procedures and records. Thus very little progress in voting rights was made under this legislation. Between 1957 and 1962, black registration across the South increased by only 4 percent.[24]

The 1965 Voting Rights Act attacked low levels of black voting through four major provisions. First, specific target areas were selected where federal pressure could be brought to bear to enroll black voters. The trigger mechanism was activated when the following conditions were met: a literacy or similar test had been required for voting as of November 1, 1964,[25] and fewer than 50 percent of the eligible voters were either registered or had actually voted in the 1964 presidential election. Under the formula, the states of Alabama, Alaska, Georgia, Louisiana, Mississippi, South Carolina, Virginia, twenty-six counties in North Carolina, and one county in Arizona were covered by the act and were therefore subject to federal intervention.

This provision proved to be both important and controversial. It permitted the federal government to focus its energies in precisely those areas where the greatest levels of discrimination took place. Opponents of the provision, who included not only southerners but even some supporters of voting rights, argued that it was not acceptable or constitutional, since federal policy must apply equally throughout the nation: this was nothing less than a new Reconstructionist policy aimed exclusively at the South. We shall return to this point shortly.

Federal intervention under the terms of the legislation meant more than lawsuits. The attorney general was empowered to send voting examiners into areas covered by legislation to sign up eligible blacks. While the examiners could not actually put the names on the rolls (local voting officials still did that), they could gather lists and then present them to local officials, who were required to add them to the voter records. This meant that federal examiners could seek out voters by traveling about to find them, rather than by waiting for them to come to a central (and, for many southern blacks, inconvenient and/or intimidating) location. Moreover, the attorney general was also empowered to send observers to watch over the conduct of elections in covered areas, to make certain that blacks were actually permitted to vote and that their ballots would be counted.

The Voting Rights Act further eliminated the use of literacy tests and similar devices as a prerequisite for voting. Completion of the sixth grade was assumed to constitute literacy, even if the school language was not English.

A fourth major provision of the act was perhaps its most controversial. It was called preclearance. Under its provisions, states or local governments covered by the trigger were required to submit any proposed changes in voting laws or practices to the Justice Department or the Federal District Court of Washington, D.C. The purpose of this preclearance was to prevent southern states and counties from finding new ways to keep blacks from the polls. Any contemplated changes would have to be reviewed by one of these agencies to assure that they did not perpetuate discrimination.

The Voting Rights Act represented a substantial extension of federal power and authority into areas of public life from which it had previously been excluded. The power of these new weapons, which could force the enrollment of blacks as voters, oversee their participation, and ensure the integrity of their ballots, was not lost on southerners. South Carolina promptly sued to test the legality and constitutionality of the law. But in a case that found its way very quickly to the Supreme Court, Chief Justice Earl Warren, speaking for a unanimous court, upheld each of the law's provisions. Recognizing that this was "an uncommon extension of federal power," the Court felt that the "array of potent weapons" was needed because "exceptional conditions can justify legislative measures not otherwise appropriate."[26]

Thus the Supreme Court, in unequivocal language, endorsed the role of the federal government in demanding and securing voting rights for blacks. The new law, as well as Warren's opinion, were significant because they fully shifted the burden of seeking those rights from blacks to the federal government. Indeed, the legal principles behind the law actually went further: local voting registrars in covered areas had the burden of proof to show that they had not discriminated against blacks, for the nature of the triggering mechanism was *prima facie* evidence that they had done so.

The role of the federal government in demanding voting rights also changed dramatically as a result of the law and court decision. It moved from a passive to very active one. This new, activist, field-centered approach to civil rights (as opposed to the slower, courtroom-centered approach) can best be seen by the speed at which enforcement of the law began. President Johnson signed it on August 6, 1965; the next day the Justice Department began to carry out its provisions, and within three days voting examiners were on their way to targeted areas. It was a remarkable demonstration of the way in which the federal government finally helped southern blacks achieve one of their major goals, the right to vote.

Problems arose in conjunction with implementation and enforcement of the legislation.[27] Relatively few examiners were actually used; instead, the Justice Department relied heavily on voluntary compliance. But the threat of a possible visit by federal examiners did serve as an inducement to many communities to change their practices and allow blacks to vote.

Voting observers did not always understand their roles and sometimes protected local officials, not blacks. Preclearance requirements found the Justice Department seriously understaffed. More than 35,000 submissions were made by 1980, and very few (just over 2 percent) were rejected outright; many were voluntarily withdrawn, however. In many cases, the Justice Department preferred to negotiate with local officials over changes rather than haul them into court as the law permitted. The result was that in some cases local officials could create voting changes with relative impunity.

Finally, in 1970, 1975, and 1982, the Voting Rights Act was renewed. Each time its focus was expanded considerably. These changes included extending the franchise to eighteen-year-olds, which potentially added millions of young voters to the voting rolls, and bilingual provisions in 1975, which required that all voting information and ballots be printed in English and other languages appropriate for local citizens. The 1982 changes may have been the most significant since the original act was passed in 1965. Amendments to Section 2 in 1982 sought to foster minority representation in Congress and state and local legislatures, in part through the creation of minority access and influence districts; these have proven effective but highly controversial.[28]

As a result of these changes, the Voting Rights Act now covers the entire nation, not just the South. Some analysts have argued that the breadth of coverage seriously handicaps the power of the law, since it cannot be enforced as effectively on a nationwide basis as it could be in focused, targeted areas where discrimination continues. On the other hand, the continuing power and controversy of the Voting Rights Act can be seen in some of the recent major Supreme Court decisions, as voting rights in the South continue to occupy a prominent role in the nation's legal and political agenda.[29]

Presidents have differed sharply in their commitment to enforcement of the legislation. Presidents Johnson and Carter were vigorous in their demands for compliance. President Clinton has continued in the same vein. Presidents Gerald Ford and Richard Nixon wanted to gut key parts of the legislation, especially the triggering and preclearance provisions. President

Ronald Reagan actively opposed renewal of the legislation in 1982 but bowed to the wishes of Congress, including members of his own party. President George Bush showed no particular interest in voting rights issues.

In spite of these difficulties, the Voting Rights Act and its subsequent modifications have proven to be enormously important. They have literally changed the face of southern politics, as we shall see shortly when we examine the impact of black voting in the region. Indeed, some observers have termed the Voting Rights Act the most effective piece of civil rights legislation ever passed in America.[30]

Black Voting in the South: After the Voting Rights Act

Increasing the participation of blacks in southern politics was a major goal of the civil rights movement. If we examine one form of participation, voting, we can readily see that the effect of the movement, especially the Voting Rights Act, was profound. Whether we look on a regional or state-by-state basis, the increase in black registration and voter turnout was substantial.

Between 1957 and 1962, it will be recalled, black voter registration increased by only 4 percent, in spite of the two civil rights bills passed by Congress designed to increase it. In absolute numbers, by 1960 only about 1.4 million southern blacks were actually registered to vote, or about 28 percent of those eligible; the majority of these were in the border and/or urban South. By 1964, another 10 percent of southern blacks were registered, increasing the total to about 38 percent. But in the three years immediately following passage of the Voting Rights Act, black voter registration increased dramatically; by 1968, it had risen from just under 2 million to about 3.3 million.[31]

It is possible to be more specific about changes in southern black voter registration. Examination of data indicate that the greatest changes in black registration occurred in precisely those states targeted by the Voting Rights Act. Mississippi represents the most extreme case: in 1965, only about 7 percent of eligible blacks were registered to vote, compared to 70 percent of whites (a 63-point gap). But two years later, 60 percent of eligible blacks were registered, compared to over 90 percent of eligible whites. Thus, the black-white voting gap was virtually halved in a short period of time.

If we look at the average of the states covered by the Voting Rights Act between 1965 and 1967, estimated black registration rates rose from 30 percent to 55 percent in just two years. After 1967, the changes are not quite as dramatic, but the gap between white and black registration in covered states fell fairly steadily from 44 percent in 1965 to just under 10 percent by 1984. It should also be noted that the falloff in registration rates beginning in 1972 reflects, among other things, the inclusion of eighteen- to twenty-year-olds in the eligible voter pool; this population cohort is notorious for low rates of political participation, including voting.

In the original noncovered states, which included most of the border South, similar if less dramatic patterns can be seen. In these states it was never quite as difficult for blacks to vote as in the hard-core, deep South. Arkansas and Florida, both of which have some old South areas in them, had the greatest percent change over time. Indeed, by 1972 Arkansas actually had a greater percentage of blacks registered than whites, although in absolute numbers whites far outnumbered blacks. The average black-white registration gap in noncovered southern states fell from 17 percent in 1965 to 8 percent in 1984."[32]

A significant, if unintended, consequence of the Voting Rights Act was on white registration. Many voting practices designed to keep blacks from the polls also discriminated against poor whites. Once they were gone, whites were able to register as well as blacks. An additional incentive to white registration was the realization by many white southerners of what would happen as blacks registered to vote in large numbers and decided to exercise their franchise on election day: they might actually take over, or at least substantially influence, the outcome of elections. Self-interest by many southern whites undoubtedly played a significant role in their decision to register to vote.

Rates of voter registration, in spite of their importance, really only demonstrate political potential. Actual turnout rates indicate how that potential is turned into political activity and strength. Examination of data between 1964 and 1984 indicates that southern whites averaged about 59 percent turnout in presidential elections.[33] Estimates are that blacks averaged about 49 percent, leaving a gap of about 10 percent. Data from the 1990s suggest a continuing gap between black and white turnout in elections, presidential and otherwise.[34]

Although these data are estimates only, and should be treated as such, they do represent a potential problem for southern blacks in terms of their impact on politics in the region. Their registration rates continue to lag behind whites, but their turnout rates are even lower than whites. The effect is to diminish some of their potential political strength in the region and thus essentially hand over additional voting clout to the majority white community. Interestingly, in some elections during the late 1980s and early 1990s, black turnout in parts of the urban South, especially among young people, actually exceeded that of whites. If this occurrence portends a trend, it could add to black political strength. It does, however, represent an exception to the normal pattern in which southern whites have voted in greater percentages than blacks.

Why this differential is true deserves some attention. There are a number of significant influences on black turnout in the South, but three appear to be especially important.[35] First, the presence, or absence, of a black candidate on the ballot has a major effect on blacks' willingness to vote. While blacks do not always turn out to vote when a black runs against a white, nor do they always vote for a black over a white, the likelihood is greater that they will.[36] In general, the presence of a black candidate on the ballot serves as an incentive for blacks to register and actually vote.

The particular salience, or perceived importance, of the election for blacks influences turnout. If the contest is seen as largely "white man's business," with few perceived stakes for blacks (for example, the candidates seem indifferent or hostile to their concerns), black turnout is likely to be lower.

Finally, analysts have noted that in some black-belt counties of the deep South, where blacks constitute a substantial proportion of the voting population, perhaps even a majority, turnout is frequently low. In these cases, blacks have trouble electing one of their own, or a white ally, to office. The reason appears to be lingering fear of political involvement based not only on white attitudes but on blacks' economic vulnerability. In other words, in mostly rural areas where blacks remain poor and are still economically dependent on whites, they remain fearful of exercising their political muscle. Fear of white reprisals, perhaps not in physical but in economic and social terms, prevents them from voting.[37] To the extent that economic vulnerability continues among southern blacks, it may well serve to depress voter turnout.

In spite of these difficulties, the impact of a greatly enlarged black electorate in the South had an electric effect on the politics of the region. In the next two sections we will examine two major effects of the rise of black voting. But a brief look at a few major elections will illustrate just how dramatic, and fundamental, the changes were.

In 1964, Haydon Burns, mayor of Jacksonville, was elected governor of Florida in a contest following hard on the heels of the bitter St. Augustine civil rights campaign. Burns made it clear that he was no friend of blacks or of civil rights. But in 1966, when he was forced to run again in a special election, he had a sudden change of heart and overtly appealed to blacks to support him and his troubled administration. They were not fooled, however, and at least partially as a result of blacks' support of his Democratic opponent, Robert King High (mayor of Miami), Burns failed to win the renomination of his own party.[38]

In 1971, John Lewis and Julian Bond, two major leaders of the civil rights movement, held a civil rights meeting at a small church in Belzoni, Mississippi. It had been the site of several murders of NAACP workers in the 1950s and had been considered one of the places in rural Mississippi most hostile to civil rights work. But on this occasion, the white mayor came into the meeting, welcomed Lewis and Bond warmly, and openly solicited black support in his upcoming reelection campaign.[39]

In one of the most ironic occasions of the post-1965 South, black voters in Alabama helped George Wallace win his final gubernatorial term in 1982. It was one of Wallace's closest races, and there is substantial evidence that black voters, especially rural black voters, gave him the margin of victory. In his campaign, Wallace openly courted black support against his law-and-order, tough-talking opponent. He readily admitted past mistakes on civil rights. While many urban blacks and some black political organizations remained skeptical, apparently many rural black voters felt he had changed, repented, and deserved another chance. Thus the man who had been "out-niggered" in 1958 came full circle as his political career entered its last hurrah. Also in 1982, Mississippi blacks helped reelect the state's senior U.S. senator, John Stennis. He, too, had belonged to the South's old guard but sought and welcomed black support in his campaign.[40]

Our last examples come from 1986, when Mississippi voters elected a black lawyer from Yazoo City, Mike Espy, to the U.S. House of Representatives; Espy later became secretary of agriculture in the Clinton administration. Local residents regarded the victory as a miracle: one older black resident was quoted as saying, "This is Mississippi. There was a time when I didn't think a black man would ever get elected anything in Mississippi."[41]

On the same election day in 1986, John Lewis, the civil rights warrior, was also elected to the U.S. House of Representatives from a heavily black Atlanta district that had previously been held by a white man, Wyche Fowler. Fowler, in turn, defeated the Republican incumbent U.S. senator, Mack Mattingly, in large part because of heavy black support across the state.[42] Ironically, to receive the Democratic nomination for Congress, Lewis had to defeat his old civil rights ally, Julian Bond, in a primary. Yet the fact that these two prominent public figures contested for the nomination illustrates the richness and complexity of black electoral politics that developed in the South in just a twenty-year period.

These brief vignettes illustrate the changes that have occurred because of the rise of black voting in the South since 1965. White politicians quickly realized, especially if they were Democrats, that in many instances they could not win primaries, and sometimes general elections, without black support. Indeed, because of the tendency of blacks to register as Democrats (figures of upward of 80 percent are not unusual), both office seekers and blacks themselves discovered that they could hold the balance of power in elections if they went to the polls.

But the emergence of black voters did not just mean support for white politicians. Increasingly, as we shall see, blacks have been able to elect members of their own race to public office. Nor are blacks anymore the handmaidens of white Democrats. In some areas, notably in Alabama, where the Alabama Democratic Conference has held a substantial voice in state politics, and in Atlanta, where blacks have been politically organized for some years, blacks have been able to mobilize themselves as independent political forces that white (and black) candidates must woo in order to secure support. Of course, throughout much of the South the relatively low rates of black turnout, compared to whites, means that any politician seeking or relying on black support must redouble his efforts to ensure that they actually vote on election day.

Not all black voting results in victories for black candidates or favored white candidate. Occasionally in the South office seekers still campaign by making it clear that they do not want black support and do not favor black interests.[43] Lower rates of black registration and turnout may prevent blacks from maximizing their electoral strength.

On balance, however, as a result of the civil rights movement, and especially the Voting Rights Act, blacks have emerged as a powerful, independent force in southern politics. Whether they have achieved full equity and representation is a matter we shall address later. But gone are the days when blacks across the region were politically inert, intimidated, or manipulated. Through voting, and through other forms of participation, they have made themselves a political force to be reckoned with across the South.

Electing Blacks to Office

Another indicator of the success of the civil rights movement is the extent to which blacks have been elected to public office.[44] This matter is complex, often controversial, with both substantive and symbolic dimensions.[45] Some might argue that color or race is irrelevant to the nature of representation: whites can potentially represent blacks as well as blacks can. Yet others feel that race is germane to representation and removing it from this context is artificial, because race is so pervasive in the South and America generally. Moreover, these advocates continue, the presence of black elected officials is an indication of political legitimacy that transcends voting. By having blacks elected to office, they move past the electoral door and into the actual arenas and processes where political decision making takes place.[46]

While the merits of these positions can be debated, the historical fact remains that blacks have long sought to elect members of their race to public office. During Reconstruction, for example, blacks were commonly found in state legislatures and in local offices, and some even in Congress. While none were governors of southern states, a few blacks occupied state executive positions.[47]

After the institution of Jim Crow laws late in the nineteenth century and the disenfranchisement of southern blacks, the possibility of electing blacks to public office in the South fell to virtually zero for much of this century. Thus, with the onset of the civil rights movement and especially the rise of black voting, it once again emerged as a key objective of southern blacks as they sought participation in the political life of the region.

The impact of the Voting Rights Act, and increased black voting, on the election of blacks to office in the South can readily be seen. Prior to 1968, virtually no elected black officials were present in the region. Between 1968 and 1982, the number of southern blacks elected to office rose tenfold, from 248 to 2,601; by 1987, the figure reached 3,685; and by 1993, 4,924.[48] Clearly, then, the movement of blacks into the mainstream of southern electoral politics has had a dramatic impact on the numbers of blacks elected to public office.

The numbers tell only part of the story, however. What is most significant about the figures is that they mask the nature of political offices held by southern blacks. They have been, and continue to be, the lowest level positions. In 1968, 31 percent of black elected officials held city council or commission slots, and 21 percent held school board positions. By 1982, the figures were 42 percent and 22 percent, respectively; by 1986, they were 44 percent and 21 percent. In 1993, 65 percent of all elected black officials in the South were in city or county positions; only 5 percent were in state offices, including legislative and administrative positions.[49] Thus, while the absolute numbers of blacks elected to public office have increased, black officeholders remain at the lowest rung of the political ladder. Some blacks have succeeded to higher office: lieutenant governor and later governor of Virginia,[50] U.S. House of Representatives, and state legislatures. But the fact remains that blacks continue to face difficulties as they seek to enter politically higher, perhaps more sensitive, offices.[51]

The point is underscored by looking at figures for mayors and state legislators. In 1968, only 4 blacks of 248 elected to office were mayors (less than 2 percent). In 1982, 131 of 2,601 black elected officials were mayors, only 5 percent. While the raw figures were higher in 1987, the percentage remained at 5 percent.[52] Similarly, in 1968, 9 percent of state legislators in the region were black, but by 1982, only 5 percent were; in 1987, the figure was still about 5 percent. In 1981, the U.S. Civil Rights Commission estimated that only about 5 percent of all elected officials in the South were black. Thus in terms of the kind of political offices that blacks have had a reasonable chance of winning, as well as the relative equity of their proportion in elective office, they still have a long way to go.[53]

In addition to being relegated to low-level political offices, elected blacks are found most commonly in very small cities and towns, in spite of the fact that some of the South's largest cities have elected black mayors. One study found that about two-thirds of black city council members were found in places of less than 5,000 people, about half of whom were in towns of 1,000 or less. Only about 10 percent were in the largest cities, those with populations over 100,000. For mayors, the figures are also sharply focused: 87 percent were in towns less than 5,000, and 54 percent of the total held office in communities of under 1,000. Not surprisingly, black elected officials can be found most frequently where blacks constitute a majority of the population. Interestingly, however, they are more likely to be found in communities where blacks occupy a fairly low proportion of the population (0–39 percent) than where they occupy a midrange, but minority, percentage (40–49 percent);[54] we shall return to this point shortly.

What seems most to influence the election of blacks to office? Available research indicates that many factors are important, including purely environmental conditions (such as the relative wealth and educational levels of black and white populations), the sophistication of blacks as political actors, the impact of the media, and the role of parties, interest groups, and other organizational features of the election.

But two factors also seem to stand out as critical—the size of the black electorate and the nature of the electoral system.[55] The first point seems self-evident: where blacks constitute a substantial proportion of the population (although not necessarily a majority), the likelihood of electoral success is enhanced. Matters are not always so straightforward, however. Sheer numbers alone will not elect blacks to public office. Blacks have to be sufficiently registered and motivated—that is, politically mobilized and organized—to go to the polls, cast a vote, and make a difference. For reasons already noted, this motivation is not always present. Moreover, the existence of midrange black populations does not always result in black representation, for whites sometimes feel threatened by this level of black population and will organize to keep blacks from winning office.

Scholars have also found that the kind of election system helps influence the electability of blacks. Single-member districts seem to offer the greatest possibility for blacks, depending, of course, on how district lines are drawn. Single-member districts can concentrate the voting power of minority groups in relatively small areas, thereby increasing both their strength and the possibility of electing a member to office. Multimember districts, and at large elections, tend to dilute the vote of minority groups, lessening the chance for victory.

Moreover, since 1960 the Supreme Court has insisted that as voting lines are drawn, minority groups not be gerrymandered out of existence.[56] Rather, attention has to be paid, whenever possible, to respecting their geographic and demographic compactness.[57] Thus, as reapportionment and redistricting occur, legislatures must pay attention to these factors, since increasingly courts have required that single-member districts be created to promote the likelihood of minority representation, and as the lines are drawn they must ensure that no further discrimination of minority groups takes place.[58]

Blacks assuredly can win elections under other circumstances. For some offices, such as the mayorship, or statewide offices, district or multimember elections are irrelevant. On the other hand, in these cases a certain dual legitimacy must be created by black candidates so that they can appeal to both black and white constituents, placing a further burden on them beyond what they already bear as a result of race and creating a political tightrope on which it is difficult to balance.[59]

What impact, if any, have black elected officials in the South had? To paraphrase both Peter Eisinger and the late Peter Sellers, are they able to "do something" and not simply just "be there"?[60] Available research suggests they have been helpful in both substantive and symbolic ways.[61]

Elected black officials have a modest but noticeable effect on increasing certain types of social welfare expenditures and improving the quality of public services for blacks. They may also have served to stimulate public employment of blacks and to assist in attracting state and federal grants (many of the federal dollars disappeared during the Reagan, Bush, and Clinton administrations, however).

On a more symbolic level, elected black officials seem to have helped improve race relations and break down racial stereotypes. Whites, for example, have sometimes felt that a town or city would "go to the dogs," or worse, if blacks were elected to office; but they found that blacks can govern as effectively as whites. Thus whites' perception of blacks as legitimate political figures tends to increase with blacks in office.

The presence of black officials may also serve to increase interest in public affairs in the black community and improve its affect toward political life. It has also constituted a psychological boost for many blacks, whose feelings of political legitimacy and efficacy increased with the presence of black elected officials. No longer were politics just "white men's business"; as one black official noted, his presence on the city council helped it from becoming another white country club.[62] As blacks are elected to office, government and politics in the South may well become more accountable and responsive to populations that were previously ignored.

Southern elected black officials also have some handicaps that limit their effectiveness in office.[63] They often enter office with enormous expectations held by other blacks. Failure to produce instant success or miracles has led to disillusionment and cynicism. Whites, too, tend to be suspicious, at least at first, until blacks prove that they are "safe." But some whites have proven hostile from the outset and have sought to isolate or outright oppose blacks elected to office. Given their greater experience in, and sometimes knowledge of, political affairs, this hostility has in some instances limited blacks' effectiveness.

Many black elected officials also face severe economic circumstances that hinder their ability to solve problems. Many elected black officials, it will be recalled, hold office in small, often rural, communities, many of which are in severe economic distress. When state and federal grants are available, some of the economic constraints they face can be ameliorated. But where they are missing, these impoverished communities have few options open to them.

Moreover, in some instances companies and other forms of private capital are unwilling to invest in these areas, not simply because they are poor and offer low levels of public service but because some of the governing officials are black. Sometimes the election of blacks to public office has caused the white population, capital, and therefore jobs, to flee the area. White officials must also worry about the demographic and economic bases of their communities, but when race also becomes an issue, there is a whole other set of problems that must be addressed before real solutions can be developed. Short of massive tax incentives that make investment in these areas attractive, as well as the availability of state and federal grants, it is difficult to see how many of these smaller communities where blacks are elected to office can begin to resolve many of the economic and social problems facing them.

Electing blacks to public office has been, and continues to be, a major goal of civil rights activists. The reality, however, is that as important as elected black officials have been, their presence and performance have not matched the hopes of blacks. They continue to be elected overwhelmingly to low-level positions in small, often impoverished, communities. They continue to be significantly underrepresented, relative to their share of the population, in office. Yet the visibility and achievements of those black officials elected to significant city and state offices throughout the South act as an important incentive for continuing efforts to elect more blacks to office.

Distribution of Public Services

Another of the major goals of the civil rights movement, it will be recalled, was for blacks to achieve greater levels of equality, not only in terms of opportunity but treatment as well. The 1964 Civil Rights Act was designed to ensure that they had equal access to and treatment in public accommodations. The 1965 Voting Rights Act attempted both to secure equal access to the ballot for blacks and to assure that their votes would be counted in the same way whites' were.

But another dimension of the quest for equality was in the provision of public services. There was evidence that in the past southern state and local governments did not treat blacks in the same way they treated whites. Schools were the most obvious example. But even in such other areas as police and fire protection, availability of paved roads and sewers, and access to parks and other recreational facilities, blacks frequently got short shrift. Often local governments, usually financially strapped in the South anyway, and state governments operating in a traditional political culture of low taxes and low levels of service, neglected the black community entirely as the distribution of these and other public services was made. In other words, for southern blacks "separate" was never "equal."

The question arises, then, did the civil rights movement have any effect on the allocation of public resources and services? Were greater levels of equality achieved so that blacks could have access to services comparable to those of whites?

Although these are hard questions to answer, in part because it is not always self-evident what constitutes equal levels of service, research suggests that some changes in the allocation of public services did occur at the local level as a result of civil rights activity.[64] The changes made, however, were usually modest and often limited by particular circumstances and conditions.

Summarizing what we know about these changes suggests that they occurred more readily in new South or border areas than in old South or deep South communities. Frequently these areas were somewhat more economically advantaged than old South places and thus had a little more budgetary flexibility. Also, many of these areas lacked the long tradition of virulent racism and bigotry that marked many old South communities and thus there was a somewhat greater willingness to heed black demands as allocations for services were made.

Also, the size of the black population in the community appeared to be important in bringing about greater equality of services. Where blacks constituted a majority (especially a voting majority), change was possible. In communities where blacks constituted a relatively small percentage of the population (less than 30 percent), change was also feasible, especially in border South areas; perhaps these rather small populations did not represent a threat to whites and thus accommodations could be made. But where blacks constituted a large minority of the population (30–50 percent), whites appeared to be threatened. Racial conflict over the allocation of services was not unusual in those areas, and changes were hard to secure. Interestingly also, in those communities where blacks made up a majority of the population and "took over the town," there is some evidence that they began to discriminate against whites as services were allocated, much as whites had done against them.[65]

Capital intensive services may also have been somewhat easier to make more equitable than human services. The former only involve spending money in different ways. Paving streets or putting in sewer lines are examples; they do not involve fundamental changes in public attitudes about race but only in some decisions about which side of town is to receive an improved street or perhaps new basketball courts.

But human services do involve fundamental values and attitudes. Public employment is an example; often changes in attitudes were required to hire a black instead of a white, especially if the job was other than a janitorial or low-level one. In the case of fire department, an additional problem existed insofar as blacks and whites not only worked together but lived and ate with one another on shift. Thus these human services, imbued as they are with feelings, prejudices, and traditional attitudes, have often proven difficult to change.

What accounts for the changes that did take place? Which civil rights strategies seemed to be the most efficacious, and which less so?

Available research is not fully conclusive, but some interesting findings can be noted. Conventional political strategies, especially blacks' attending public meetings and electing blacks to office, seem to have been the most important, perhaps because they permit blacks to have an immediate and direct say as local officials allocate resources and public service. Relatively unconventional strategies, such as demonstrations and protest marches, appeared to have only a slight positive effect on public service allocation (they may have been more useful for other problems), as whites reacted negatively to them. Rioting appears to have been dysfunctional, in the short run, to more equitable distribution of public service, although there is some evidence that in the long run it may have forced some public service changes.[66]

In contrast to much American folklore, and even American democratic theory, voting has had only a modest positive impact on reallocating public services. This is not to argue that voting, or the right to vote, is unimportant. It may be highly significant for other matters. But those who thought that fundamental change would occur in the South as a direct result of blacks' securing of the franchise have proved to be incorrect.[67]

Have blacks achieved parity with whites in terms of the allocation of public services by southern local governments? While an answer cannot be given conclusively, available data suggest they have not. Some improvements have been made, most notably in hardware and capital services. In the more sensitive areas, such as police protection and government jobs, allegations of discrimination continue to occur rather frequently. Southern local governments may be somewhat more responsive now to demands by blacks for better levels of public services. But continued political pressure, both through the ballot box and by other, more direct means, seems essential if blacks are to approach more closely their goal of equal treatment with whites.

Symbolic Achievements

Thus far in our discussion we have concentrated mainly on tangible, substantive changes that have occurred in the South following the entry of blacks into the region's politics. But there have also been changes that are more difficult to quantify, perhaps to discuss and understand. They refer to changes in atmosphere or ambiance in the South; perhaps we can call them symbolic changes. Systematic evidence of them might be difficult to obtain, but they seem clear enough in the daily lives of citizens.

Perhaps the most apparent of these symbolic changes is the way in which blacks and whites now interact and work together, often in the closest proximity, with little or no apparent racial discord. Blacks and whites ride buses together, go to school and college with one another, eat at the same restaurants and lunch counters, use the same (public) recreational facilities, shop in the same stores and malls, and so forth. This is not to say that there is no racial antagonism, or that white and blacks may not feel uncomfortable with or suspicious of one another, even today. Incidents continue to occur. And lacking from the previous list are references to living, housing, and churchgoing; these continue to be segregated on racial, as well as social class, lines.

Yet walking the streets of the South, from Jacksonville to Little Rock, from New Orleans to Richmond, leaves the distinct impression of blacks and whites existing in close proximity, often with an air of indifference. The same impression can be gained in many urban high schools and on the region's college campuses (even some of the more traditionally southern ones). While whites and blacks may not regularly be fully involved with one another through close friendships, it is also true that the atmosphere of indifference or unconcern with one another is occasionally punctured by the adulation of black athletic heroes (professional and on campus), the presence of black cheerleaders and homecoming queens, and even some interracial organizational activity, academic endeavors, and casual social interaction, including dating.

Too much should not be made of these relationships.[68] In very few places can it be said that complete racial acceptance has occurred; continued segregation in housing, religion, and private organizations are testament. Moreover, the late 1980s and 1990s witnessed a disturbing rise in racial incidents on southern college campuses (as well as in virtually all regions of the country), suggesting that earlier tranquillity simply masked deep-seated feelings and resentments. Perhaps the essence of modern race relations in the South can at best be described as unsettled, incorporating a restrained tolerance and indifference, only occasionally reaching a grudging acceptance, and not infrequently marked by hostility and animosity.

These observations seem most true of the South's urban places. In rural, small-town, and less cosmopolitan areas remnants of past, discriminatory practices can still be found with disturbing frequency. Bus stations and lunch counters may no longer be segregated, but one does not have to search long before hearing references to "niggers." Indeed, when the journalist Chet Fuller left Atlanta to find the new South outside of that sophisticated, glamorous city, he quickly discovered that the roads led him to areas that looked, and felt, remarkably like the old South. When early in 1987 the Ku Klux Klan and its sympathizers attacked a "freedom march" held in an all-white north Georgia county, it reminded participants of the worst days of the pre–civil rights movement South.[69] And in the middle 1990s a white state senator in Alabama was still convinced that there was biblical justification for slavery,[70] suggesting that not all southerners are yet reconstructed.

And yet, whether one examines the modern black-white southern experience from the standpoint of hard data or everyday life, the conclusion is inescapable that things are much different in the post–civil rights movement South from the way they were twenty and more years ago. Most important, blacks, especially in urban places, need no longer fear that interactions with whites, whether in a bus station, doctor's office, restaurant, department store, principal's office, or college classroom, will be occasions for humiliation, harassment, and embarrassment. Yet the search for self-dignity and for the right to be treated with respect and decency is an ongoing one that must be renewed daily. While southern blacks have not fully won this battle—there are too many contrary instances to say they have—it is also true that since the civil rights movement they can insist on being treated in a decent, not humiliating, way. To this extent, then, it is reasonable to argue that progress has been made.[71]

Have southern whites changed their minds? Have the traditional attitudes of bigotry and racism disappeared, and stereotypes abandoned? It is difficult to say. Public opinion surveys on these issues are of dubious value: people may lie, hide their true feelings, or respond in a way which they think is respectable. And such surveys cannot uncover how people think, talk, and behave in private circumstances. Even psychological profiles are not immune to these deficiencies.

Thus we actually know very little about how white southerners really regard blacks. In the old days it was easy: it was both respectable and even necessary in many parts of the South to castigate blacks, and even worse, on a regular basis. It is no longer respectable or legitimate to do so, at least in most areas and under most circumstances. This fact in itself represents a significant positive change from the past. Moreover, while it would be both naive and dangerous to assume that racial prejudices and stereotypes will eventually disappear, perhaps as young southern children, black and white, grow up in a region no longer obsessed with race some of these traditional views may ease, and indifference and restrained tolerance might move toward greater levels of acceptance.

Unfinished Business

It would be pleasant to end this chapter, and this section of the book, on a sanguine note. But it is not possible to do so, because too many problems remain and there is too much unfinished business from the civil rights movement.

We can do little more than list the extent of this business here; other books need to explore it in depth. An examination of southern residential patterns would undoubtedly reveal extensive, and growing, segregation not unlike that in northern and western metropolitan areas. Schools may be more desegregated in the South than elsewhere, but second-level segregation has occurred in which blacks and whites are frequently separated in the school building by ability groups and academic tracks. Questions continue to be raised about law enforcement and the criminal justice system in the South, particularly in such areas as the application of the death penalty and the quality of police protection.[72] The difficulties southern blacks face in public and private employment opportunities continue to abound, and to be well documented, in spite of affirmative action programs, greater levels of black education and skills, and general economic improvement.[73]

In politics, too, problems remain. Blacks continue to be underrepresented in decision-making arenas, and while improvements have occurred, blacks continue to occupy the lowest level of official positions. In spite of the provisions of the Voting Rights Act, federal enforcement has often been lax.[74] The result is that at least in some areas southern voting registrars are again finding ways, through changes in election practices, to keep blacks from voting.[75] Blacks have failed to maximize their potential electoral strength because of registering, and turning out, to vote in proportions considerably less than those of whites. Indeed, continuing economic vulnerability, as well as fear, often prevents blacks from taking a more active political role.

This discussion raises another serious problem for southern blacks—that is, the extent to which the civil rights movement may have been of economic help to them as well as providing political and social benefits. Has the civil rights movement's emphasis on political involvement, and greater social legitimacy, been translated into economic improvement for southern blacks?

Even a brief perusal of some fundamental facts suggest that the civil rights movement has had only a marginal impact on the economic life of southern blacks. Census data from 1960 show that black median income in the South at that time was only 41 percent that of whites.[76] Data from the 1980 census reveal improvement, but substantial disparities between whites and blacks on key economic indicators continues. In 1980, black median income in the region was still only 59 percent that of whites; by 1990 it had not improved in any meaningful way.

The mean income of black males in the South in 1979 was only 57 percent that of white males. The mean agricultural income of black males was only 52 percent that of white males, and the percentage was the same in the professional service sector. While in some other economic sectors the percentage was somewhat higher, only in one sector (transportation, communications, and utilities) did average black male income exceed 70 percent that of white males. While average black female income was nearly 90 percent that of white female income, the ratio of mean female to male income in the South was less than 50 percent, suggesting that gender-related income disparities in the region are as egregious as race-related ones.[77]

Similarly, in 1979, the ratio of southern blacks below the poverty line to whites in the same category was nearly 3:1. The ratio of blacks whose income was less than 75 percent of the poverty figure to whites (in other words, a measure of the poorest of the poor) was slightly more than 3:1. Unemployment rates among southern blacks (male and female) were each more than double that of southern whites. As late as 1979, the percentage of blacks completing four years of high school still lagged behind whites by about 5 percent.[78] By the 1990s, there was little change in all of these figures.

These figures, dramatic though they may be, obscure the fact that they represent human beings caught in an economic dilemma from which they may not be able to escape. In spite of the many significant accomplishments of the civil rights movement, the transformation of traditional southern society and the entry of blacks into political life in a massive way, little improvement in the relative economic condition between whites and blacks has taken place. That blacks are better off, economically speaking, now than they were twenty and more years ago is beyond dispute; so are southern whites. But this change may have occurred more as a result of a changing, and expanding, southern economy, and state and federal programs, than the increased political involvement of blacks. Very important, the economic gap between southern blacks and whites continues to remain wide.[79] Efforts to close it will probably require massive public programs in the region, many of them purely redistributive in nature, aimed at redressing this imbalance. Whether the political will, commitment, and resources are all present to implement these programs remains to be seen.

Was, then, the civil rights movement a success? In many ways, the answer is assuredly yes. The position of blacks in the South is far different in the late twentieth century from the way it was at the beginning or middle. But important inequities remain—in social life, political life, economic conditions. As long as these inequalities remain, the civil rights movement as a major force in bringing about the full transformation of the South will remain incomplete.

Part IV

Political Leadership:
Southern Governors

9

Steering the Ship of State:
The Southern Governorship

*Come to my house, where you will find the door open. Take a
chair, put your feet on the mantelpiece, and spit on the floor.*
—Joseph Johnston, governor of Alabama, 1900

*A governor has stacks of written material, full of all kinds of
valuable information, but it is like trying to take a drink of
water out of a fire hydrant. And about the time you begin to
understand some of the things—you are out of office.*
—Ernest Hollings, governor of South Carolina, 1967

*It is really a damned foolishness for you taxpayers to train a
man like me four years for something, and then, poof.*
—Winthrop Rockefeller, governor of Arkansas, on failing
to win a third two-year term, 1970

We move now in our discussion of southern politics to a consideration of
political leadership in the region, focusing specifically on southern governors. We need to include this topic in the text because of the importance of
leaders in the U.S. political system. Leaders make decisions, run the machinery of government, and "make things happen." They reflect acceptable
or legitimate political beliefs and attitudes. Thus studying leaders provides a
window through which to see political life in very vivid terms.

There are more types of leaders in states than governors, but we shall
limit our discussion to them. They are among the most visible political
leaders in the state. While not necessarily the only state executive elected by

269

the entire population, governors are viewed as central. Indeed, in any survey of political leaders, governors would undoubtedly be considered the most prominent and influential in the state and region.

In this chapter we shall first look at the traditional problem of political leadership in the South. We shall examine those cultural and institutional factors that seem to account for the traditionally weak leadership of southern governors. In the following chapter we shall look at the styles and range of southern gubernatorial leadership, seek to assess the quality of their leadership, and examine the emergence of the modern southern governor.

The Problem of Southern Political Leadership

Political leadership in the South, according to V.O. Key, was one of the region's most pressing and chronic problems.[1] It was most notable for its absence, at least if leadership is understood to involve more than a mere reflection of elite interests and styles but rather concerns itself with agenda setting, problem solving, and policy formation.[2] Political leaders in the South were often mere mouthpieces or fronts for sometimes scarcely visible but usually powerful segments of business and commercial interests or were closely tied to important "courthouse gangs" and political factions existing at both county and state levels. Rarely independent forces for political change, southern political leaders frequently were little more than malleable men whose task was to protect the political and economic status quo. Thus any measure of success of southern political leaders based on the articulation of diverse interests, protection of minority rights, assemblage of broad-based coalitions, successful management of public affairs, or problem solving or policy innovation would find very few successful southern leaders.

It should not be surprising to the modern reader that this situation existed. Southern politics for much of this century was not for the many but the few. The dominant regional political culture demanded passivity from much of the population and created sometimes repressive means to ensure that it remained politically inert. Similarly, political institutions were notable for their lack of vigor, energy, and strength. Government was to remain as minimal as possible; politics ensured that the scope of governmental activity remained modest and constrained. The one-party, factionalized political system discouraged political opposition and conflict.

All these factors militated against the rise of strong political leadership in the region. Leaders, insofar as they exerted influence, had as their primary goal the maintenance of southern ways. To the extent that they were active politically, for the most part leaders sought to perpetuate past practices, not create new ones. Thus political campaigns were often empty disputes over personality and style or over which candidate was more "right" on race; a serious discussion of public problems and possible solutions was seldom heard. Leaders' political rhetoric and behavior often involved little more than flag waving, appeals to a mythical, glorious past, and occasional vague promises left cynically unfulfilled.

The great majority of southern leaders, whether in Congress, the statehouse or legislature, or county seat, were for most of this century men lacking vision or the desire to move their polities forward. Most looked backward, or at the best sideward to other states and communities. Some, especially governors, faced severe institutional constraints that prevented them from acting more vigorously even if they wished to do so. Most did not. Most had a limited view of what they could or should do and acted accordingly.

Perhaps inevitably, the southern leaders who attracted the most regional and national attention, particularly the demagogues, were the most damaging to the region. Not only did they perpetuate traditional stereotypes about the region's politics, but they diverted attention away from the South's real problems of poverty, racism, ignorance, and underdeveloped human and natural resources, toward political sideshows. With few exceptions, southern leaders, whether of the timid or demagogic type, failed to speak to the needs of the region and its people during much of this century. As a result, the concept of leader and leadership, as they were often understood throughout much of the nation and as they are recognized in the South today, were almost completely unknown.

The Southern Governor in Historical Perspective

In this century, it has become common in America to think of governors as the center of gravity of state politics. In the South, this idea is of fairly recent origin. Early in the South's political history, gubernatorial powers were significantly circumscribed by other actors in state politics and by limitations on the office itself.[3] When the first state constitutions were written following the colonial period, they reflected the mistrust that Americans developed about executive powers. The vast, centralized powers that many colonial governors had and that they used in arbitrary, even capricious, ways, were not compatible with the new nation's view of limited government and balanced political powers. Thus as executive branches were established by these early state constitutions, the governors' powers were especially curtailed. As one delegate to the North Carolina constitutional convention noted, the governor was given "just enough [power] to sign the receipt for his salary."[4]

Later in the nineteenth century, some expansion of gubernatorial powers occurred, especially in the South following the Civil War, as Reconstruction governors were given considerable authority by Republicans and carpetbaggers. The Florida Constitution of 1868, for example, provided for a powerful chief executive. But at the end of Reconstruction, a reaction set in. Governorships throughout the region were weakened considerably. Other factors, especially those stemming from the progressive movement late in the nineteenth century, also served to curtail gubernatorial authority, such as the proliferation of (presumably nonpolitical) boards and agencies separate from the governor that were supposed to administer some state functions, and the long ballot, which removed important gubernatorial appointment powers and replaced them with popular elections.

The Depression, with its severe economic distress, dealt the governorship a major blow because many states found themselves in such precarious financial positions that they could do little to help themselves and their populations and had to look to Washington for relief. The situation in the South was especially acute, on the one hand because of the severity of the Depression in the region, and on the other because many southern governors and other state politicians feared relying too heavily on Washington, since doing so might permit an opening of doors leading eventually to efforts by the federal government to force an alteration of traditional southern racial policies. Many southern governors were essentially paralyzed in terms of what they might do to relieve conditions stemming from the Depression. Thus the nadir of southern gubernatorial authority and powers probably occurred, at least in this century, in the years prior to World War II.

Southern Governors: Constraints on Leadership

Let us now examine the constraints that most southern governors faced as they assumed office and sought to carry out their responsibilities. It should be emphasized that the constraints and problems traditionally facing southern governors did not necessarily constitute a straitjacket that condemned incumbents to failure before they even began their administrations. Most governors, since they were socialized from early in their political careers into a limited view of the office, simply accepted the limitations, and worked within them without seeking change. But some governors saw the office as an opportunity, not a series of constraints or dead-ends. These were rare individuals who sought to move their states forward, and while they may have felt frustrated at the constraints of the office, they tried to find ways of overcoming or changing them.

Low Expectations

Perhaps the most basic problem with the traditional southern governorship, in terms of its leadership potential, was that it existed in a milieu or environment of low public expectations. The office was not seen as designed to provide active, dynamic leadership. It was not an institution whose major function was problem solving, agenda setting, opinion leadership, or policy development. In other states, such as New York, New Jersey, Pennsylvania, Illinois, Ohio, and California, the governorship by the end of the nineteenth century was seen as a powerful office for shaping the future of the state. The governor himself was expected to be a vigorous leader, actively involved in and serving as the focal point of state politics.

The South was slow to develop a political tradition in which the office of governor, or its incumbent, was seen in this light. State constitutions established at the conclusion of Reconstruction severely limited the nature of the office, deliberately curtailing its powers so that its capabilities were modest. White conservatives and representatives of business interests who became dominant political elites strove mightily to protect their positions. They established political institutions that would not rock the boat but rather would respond to these elites, thus creating weak, often highly decentralized, governorships.

Similarly, they made certain, by controlling entry and access to the office, that its occupant would not be viewed as a popular hero, one who would take up the cause of everyday people. The southern governor, then, by the beginning of the twentieth century, was not expected to be a vigorous problem solver or policymaker but rather a largely ceremonial figure who reflected dominant political ideas and values. The public expectations of the office and incumbent did not match those held by citizens in other states, elsewhere in the nation.[5]

None of this discussion is meant to imply that the office of the southern governor was trivial. The appointments he could make and the patronage he could dispense were critical to the winning faction of state politics. Even ceremonial and ambassadorial duties were important for the southern governor because of the rewards (symbolic and tangible) that they could provide for the governor and his winning faction. The vigorous Democratic primary contests for the office that usually occurred are testament to how much of a prize the southern governorship was.

But the southern governorship was not popular in the sense that the public (most of which was politically disenfranchised or inert anyway) viewed it as a positive force for improving their lives. Nor did southerners view it as a source of solutions to the problems confronting their existence.

For all but the small stratum of politically active white southerners, who occupied the governor's office was a matter of indifference; neither he nor the office had anything to offer them.

If we look at governors' campaign speeches, inaugural addresses, messages to the legislatures, and other public utterances, we see that they seldom responded to any sort of public mandate, charge, or set of expectations. Indeed, the themes that consistently dominate the public remarks of most southern governors in the first half, and more, of this century scarcely reflect any attention to public need, pressure, or desire—low taxes, low levels of state services, conservative fiscal policies (often billed as "pay as you go"), and a businesslike approach to running state government. Indeed, it was not unusual for a southern governor to characterize himself and his approach to the job, not as a spokesman for popular concerns or issues, but as a businessman or corporation head and to be concerned less with the public welfare than with the financial health and integrity of the state.

Recommendations for services rarely extended beyond education, roads and highways (major sources of patronage), occasionally old-age pensions, and (during the Depression) unemployment compensation. Few were the southern governors who supported substantial redistributive, regulatory, or extractive programs and policies in the first six decades or so of this century. Moreover, the levels of support for these services advocated by governors were barely minimal. To demand more would have opened them to the criticism of "creeping government" and fiscal profligacy.[6]

It might be objected that other states also demonstrated this same narrow range of policy concern and limited spectrum of gubernatorial activity. This observation is true. But the southern states show an extraordinarily long-term attachment to this approach to state government and gubernatorial leadership: governors' messages opening southern legislative sessions in the 1950s, and in some cases into the 1960s, show remarkably similar tone and content to those of thirty and forty years earlier. By midcentury, when governors in other states had awakened to the need for more active, policy-oriented state leadership, the South had not yet done so.

The effect of this ingrained political culture was to frustrate those occasional southern governors who hoped to use their office to do more than just continue past practices but rather to strike out in new directions. Florida's LeRoy Collins is one such example: his pursuit of moderate racial policies, constitutional reform, and legislative reapportionment in the 1950s found little support in the state. A thoughtful man, he later recognized that he may have tried to move too fast and exceeded the boundaries of public expectations and acceptance by his far-reaching agenda.[7]

More typical, perhaps, of southern governors is the example of one of

Collins's not-too-distant predecessors, Fred Cone. Cone was hesitant in his campaign to lay out any set of executive priorities. Once in office, he provided only vague generalities about the need for economy in government and failed to push the legislature for any policy development. Nor did he seek to mold public opinion on behalf of any far-reaching agenda. He suffered a lengthy and incapacitating illness while in office, but given his gubernatorial style and the low level of expectations held by the public toward the office anyway, he was scarcely missed.[8]

North Carolina: A Major Exception

LeRoy Collins was not the only southern governor who tried to throw off the anchor of low public expectations and citizen apathy and leave a substantial mark on his state. Each of the other states also saw exceptions to the general pattern of timid, undistinguished southern governors.

But in one state—North Carolina—the exceptions were actually the most common. Of the more than twenty governors holding office in North Carolina during this century, at least thirteen can be identified as active, vigorous leaders who challenged the state and sought to use their office to solve problems and direct the state toward a well-defined vision of the future. In this case, public expectations were higher than they were elsewhere in the region, and governors felt it was their obligation and responsibility to assume an activist posture in office.

Why North Carolina is different in this regard is a complex matter whose full resolution is beyond the scope of this text. In part it stems from the early history of the state, when its tradition of state provision of public services began. The progressive movement in the period before and after World War I found fertile ground in the state, and dominant business interests accepted the idea (unheard of elsewhere in the region) that the state could "spend its way into prosperity."[9] Also, while not wealthy, it has been somewhat financially advantaged, compared to other states in the region, a position that gave governors more flexibility to advocate state investment in education and other social services. The rapid growth during this century of industry, business, and commerce in North Carolina also served to increase the visibility and activity of governors and therefore the set of public expectations surrounding the office. The reason is that they were needed to recruit new enterprise and capital for the state and because governors could advocate and establish the right mix of business climate and support services (such as education) that made North Carolina attractive for business investment.

The result of these and other factors was that throughout this century North Carolina had a succession of governors who were actively engaged in leading their state. In further contrast to other states in which governors largely ignored the record of their predecessors (this was the norm in Florida, for example), North Carolina governors seemed to take pride in continuing and expanding the paths laid out by those holding office before them. North Carolina governors have also been notably "weak" in terms of formal powers, and yet many were able to transcend limitations on the office through a variety of means, including personal conviction and political skill, to leave lasting marks.

Public education was the major policy area in which North Carolina governors were especially active. The pattern in this century was established early by the southern progressive Charles Aycock (1900–1904). He was later known as the "education governor" because of the way in which he intensively sought to upgrade the state's educational system. An ardent segregationist and white supremacist, Aycock nonetheless advocated the cause of black education. He even threatened to resign when the legislature considered an education bill appropriating school funds on the basis of the tax contribution of each race.[10]

Other governors with similar ideas followed: William Kitchin, Thomas Bickett, and Cameron Morrison all held office in the first quarter of this century and strongly advocated and fought for improved schools even while maintaining traditional southern racial values. None, however, engaged in the wild demagoguery of Mississippi's James Kimble Vardaman, Theodore Bilbo, and their counterparts in other states. Nor were they similar to the populism of the eccentric Jeff Davis of Arkansas or the colorful Napoleon Broward of Florida. These North Carolina governors, in fact, were a fairly bland, colorless, business-oriented lot. But they, and their successors, such as J.C.B. Ehringhaus, Kerr Scott, Luther Hodges, Terry Sanford, Robert Scott, and Jim Hunt, were all strong governors and vigorous advocates of public education.

Their efforts ranged beyond education as well. The early North Carolina governors were strong proponents of southern progressivism, which involved expansion of state services such as roads, provision of social services such as child labor laws, and regulation of railroads, utilities, and banks. William Kitchin, in fact, was actually opposed by some business interests and was called a "socialist" by his more traditional, business-oriented opponents. Gregg Cherry, Kerr Scott, and Luther Hodges, while essentially business-oriented conservatives, also sought to steer moderate racial courses in the 1940s and 1950s, just when southern governors in other states were becoming increasingly shrill, even demagogic, on racial issues. Terry Sanford, Robert Scott, and James Hunt, while not liberals as the term has become known in American politics, nonetheless advocated increasing levels of equal opportunity and treatment for blacks and other minority groups. They continually pressed for improved social services, environmental and consumer protection, and upgraded schools and universities.

Not all of the North Carolina governors fit this mold. Some, such as A.W. McLean (1924–1928), advocated the same kind of economy and efficiency in government rhetoric and "pay-as-you-go" approach to public finance that could commonly be found in statehouses from Virginia to Florida to Arkansas. Also, it should not be assumed that the activist, progressivist posture of many North Carolina governors carried over into all aspects of political life in the state. The close tie between big business and politics in North Carolina has been well known for a long time, especially textiles, tobacco, banking, and insurance. The result was that little, if any, gubernatorial leadership was ever evidenced on behalf of blue-collar industrial workers. Quite the contrary, in fact: North Carolina governors often fought labor unions and other efforts to improve conditions for workers, such as minimum wage laws, workers' compensation, and unemployment insurance.

Nor did governors actively seek to upgrade the state's industrial profile from the low-level, low-wage, low-technology base on which it rested. The result was that by the late 1970s North Carolina began to find itself challenged by other states, including its southern neighbors, in the competition for modern, smokeless, high-tech industry; it was not until the two administrations of James Hunt in the 1980s that this situation began to turn around.[11]

Still, most North Carolina governors, even while conservative, fought hard to move the state forward. They took seriously the tradition, developed early in this century in the state, that the governor was the "point guard" of state politics. He was expected by the citizens to be their leader. But the North Carolina example stands in stark contrast to the other southern states, where this tradition, set of expectations, and challenges for the governor scarcely existed at all.

Structural Problems

The low set of expectations that many southerners had for their governor was only one of the major factors that served to prevent strong gubernatorial leadership from developing in the region. Throughout the eleven southern states the office of governor during much of this century was structurally very weak. There were inherent constraints—some constitutional, some statutory—on the way in which the office was established. These served to diffuse gubernatorial powers to force the governor to deal with an array of political competitors who were often nearly as powerful as he, and in some cases more so.

While gubernatorial powers in many other states elsewhere in the nation were also undercut by structural weaknesses in the office, in the southern states the limitations imposed on the governor's office by state constitutions and laws were raised almost to an art form. Moreover, southern states were much slower than those elsewhere to begin to increase gubernatorial powers and to permit greater centralization of authority. It was not until after mid-century, and in some cases the late 1960s, that southern states began constitutional and statutory reform that redressed some of the structural weaknesses in the office.[12]

The Southern Governorship: A Measure of Weakness

Just how weak was the southern governorship? What exactly were its structural problems? The range is considerable and in some cases idiosyncratic to individual states. Fortunately, Joseph Schlesinger some years ago created an "index" of the formal powers of the governor, which we can use for measuring and demonstrating the weakness of the southern governorship.[13] Schlesinger constructed his index just at the time when many southern states were about to begin restructuring the office. Thus it serves as a useful guide for examining its features for much of this century and assessing subsequent changes.

The Schlesinger index uses four major categories of gubernatorial activity for assessing the strengths and weaknesses of the office—appointive powers, tenure potential, budget powers, and veto powers. This list of variables to measure is manageable, and there is no doubt that they represent major formal gubernatorial powers. However, it is possible to criticize the list: appointing a person says little about how the person will behave in office; removal powers are not included; and there is some question whether each variable used is of comparable importance to the others.

Of the forty-eight states examined (Alaska and Hawaii were omitted), the New York governor ranked at the top. Of the eleven southern states, only Virginia ranked in the top ten (tied for fourth with Pennsylvania, Washington, and California). Alabama was in fourteenth place; Tennessee, seventeenth place; Louisiana, twenty-fourth; Georgia, twenty-sixth; Arkansas, thirty-second; North Carolina, thirty-seventh; Florida, forty-third; and Mississippi, South Carolina, and Texas, tied for last.

The meaning of this index is clear. Of the states in the South, only Virginia made the top ten. Only four states were in the upper half. Seven were in the lower half, and four of these were near or at the very bottom. In spite of the deficiencies of the index, and in spite of the fact that the South did produce some notable governors in the first six decades of this century, the conclusion is inescapable that southern governors have been saddled with weak offices. Indeed, given a political culture in which the public held low expectations for the governor, combined with its structural limitations, perhaps it is amazing that the region produced any governors of note.

A Fragmented Executive

Let us now look more specifically at the major problems causing structural weaknesses in the southern governorship. The first is the fragmentation and divided control of the executive branch. Schlesinger refers to this matter as largely one of the governor's appointment powers. Indeed, appointments are of critical importance to the governor, as a number of scholars have pointed out, because through loyal, capable appointments, the governor establishes his priorities and seeks control of major state offices.[14]

But for the southern governor, administrative problems have been much greater than just appointments. Southern governors have had great difficulty controlling their own executive branch of government because their appointment powers were so constrained. In fact, most of them have been faced with a host of political executives, usually elected separately from the governor, who may or may not have reflected his priorities and ideas and who usually owed him little or no political obligation.

The result was that the governor had to spend a great deal of time bargaining with his own executive branch to induce cooperation in priority setting and program implementation. Even significant, wide-ranging patronage powers, which governors elsewhere have often used to help create an environment of mutual obligation in the executive branch, have often been denied the southern governor. Frequently the separately elected state executives had their own sources of patronage which they could use for the benefit of themselves and their own departments, not necessarily on behalf of the governor.

Even in cases in which the governor did have appointment powers, he often had to share them with the legislature (generally the senate) or sometimes another state agency or board. He could usually appoint individuals he wanted, but he had to negotiate with legislators to ensure that his appointments would be approved. This necessity served to use up some of his political currency with the legislature, which he might hope to use on other matters. It also created a sense of gubernatorial obligation to the senate (or individual senators, whom he lobbied for support) that he might have to honor for issues such as the budget or legislative pet projects. Involvement in the appointment process by legislators or other state officials additionally forced the appointee to keep at least one eye partially on them as he conducted the affairs of his department, thus undermining, if only slightly, his usefulness to the governor.

What are these other state executive positions which the governor could not always fill and whose occupants sometimes served as competitors? The Council of State Governments, in its 1960–61 survey of gubernatorial appointment powers, listed sixteen major executives frequently found in states. While not all of them existed in each state, and there are some omissions (superintendents of prisons, for example, and banking commissioners), they nonetheless constitute the key executive offices responsible for running the major departments of state government at that time—secretary of state, treasurer, auditor, attorney general, tax commissioner, director of budget and finance, budget officer, comptroller, commissioners of education, agriculture, labor, health, welfare, insurance, highways, and conservation.[15]

Calculations were made of the percentage of these officials who were appointed either by governors alone or in conjunction with the legislature (usually, but not always, the senate). Offices that did not exist in the state were omitted. The figures derived range from a low of 20 percent (South Carolina) to 73 percent (Tennessee and Virginia). The mean for the eleven southern states was 40 percent; for all fifty states, the mean was 53 percent. Only Virginia and Tennessee compared favorably on this measure of appointments and gubernatorial control with other states considered to have powerful governors—New Jersey and Pennsylvania (81 percent); New York (71 percent); Illinois and Ohio (67 percent); California (50 percent).

The reader might object, at this point, that too much is being made of the importance of appointments by the southern governor. After all, gubernatorial influence over appointees often fades once the individual takes office because of lack of gubernatorial attention, few real sanctions available to the governor, complex pressures on the appointee, and so on. Even if the executives are elected, they were almost always members of the governor's own party, and although listed separately on the ballot they could form tickets to cue voters that a vote for one candidate should be accompanied by a vote for other members of the ticket. Even if there were no tickets, state executives could form functional alliances with the governor based on other factors, such as common ideology, sectional or interest group support, business or professional association, service in the legislature together, or just membership in the "good old boy" network.

The answer to these objections is that they were either inapplicable to, or true only to a limited extent in, the South. True, prior to 1960, virtually all state executives were Democrats. On the other hand, as we have seen, one-party politics is really no-party politics. No party ties existed to bring executives together; as Schlesinger observes, "While governors may come and go, a party organization has a memory which enables future governors to reward administrators for past services,"[16] but this continuity did not develop in the South. Moreover, the formation of tickets, in which several candidates create an alliance for the purpose of the campaign, seldom occurred, except occasionally in bifactional states when pro- and anti–Huey Long or Gene Talmadge slates might form.

More commonly, candidates for state executive positions ran separately from the governor. They often tried to distance themselves as much as possible from the leading gubernatorial contenders in order to avoid becoming embroiled in factional disputes for the governor's chair. Also, many state executives had no limitation on reelection, while southern governors did. These executives very well might have already been in office for some time prior to the governor, and they certainly could expect to stay in office essentially as long as they wished; incumbents seldom were defeated and often ran unopposed. Needless to say, the governor could scarcely expect to receive, automatically, the support and help of these other officials. Instead he had to try to win it. But the cost of doing so, in terms of political obligations incurred, could be very steep.

There were mitigating circumstances. An extremely popular governor, one who could demonstrate considerable electoral strength and public opinion support, could insist on cooperation from other state officials, especially at the start of his administration. Also, many state officials were willing to work with and support the governor, since they could be rewarded or punished at budget time. Also, the recruitment process for the governorship and other state offices meant that many of the aspirants and occupants knew each other (even if as opponents) and had gone through a similar socialization process as they rose through political office. They understood one another's attitudes and values. Sometimes, in fact, shared background experiences could bridge wide political differences. But if hardball politics was needed, the governor could attempt to force administrative reorganization bills through the legislature or use his budget powers and line-item veto against administrative agencies in punitive ways.

Thus the situation was not always as bad as it might seem for southern governors. They and state executives could fashion ways to work together. But always the problem remained that the executive branch of southern states resembled feudal baronies. The executive branch was fragmented, the southern governor had trouble making it respond to him, and he was chief executive in name only.

Most of the southern states have undergone some form of administrative reorganization within the past two decades, and the effect has been to improve the position of the governor with respect to appointments, as well as his administrative agencies. Calculations were made of the appointment capabilities of southern governors for forty-six major state administrators in 1988.[17] The mean for the eleven states was 45 percent. Virtually every state except South Carolina (18 percent) and Texas (27 percent) improved considerably.

Governmental reorganization has also increased the likelihood that the governor can have a greater effect than earlier on the affairs of important agencies. The Florida experience is illustrative in this regard. In 1969, reorganization reduced the number of state agencies from more than two hundred to twenty-two. While this streamlining did not eliminate the problem of executive fragmentation, it created the possibility for "more centralization and consolidation of executive responsibility and authority in the office of the governor at the expense of the elected department heads' powers."[18]

Thus, it is fair to say that the modern southern governor is in a much more advantaged position with regard to appointments and executive fragmentation than his predecessors. A major structural problem inhibiting strong gubernatorial leadership has been somewhat alleviated in recent years. This change alone does not account for the rise of the modern, more vigorous southern governor, but it certainly has helped expedite his appearance.

The Florida Cabinet

Let us look briefly at the Florida Cabinet as a case study illustrating the themes developed in the preceding section. The Cabinet is a unique political institution, unlike any other in the South or the nation. On the other hand, the problems it has created for the Florida governor dramatically illustrate those which other southern governors have had to face.

The Florida Cabinet system is a mechanism exquisitely designed to prevent consolidation of political power in the hands of the governor.[19] It was created by the Florida Constitution of 1885, largely as a response to the powerful chief executive established by the Reconstruction Constitution of 1868. Since 1885 numerous attempts have been made to abolish or modify it, and governors, both while in office and afterward, have criticized it severely. Yet none of these efforts or tirades have altered the basic shape of the Cabinet, although some changes occurred as a result of the Constitution of 1968. It appears that the Cabinet is a fully ingrained part of Florida's political life, and serious attempts to abolish or modify it further are not likely to be found in the foreseeable future.[20]

The Cabinet consists of six separately elected executives: the attorney general, secretary of state, treasurer (also state insurance commissioner), comptroller (also state banking commissioner), commissioner of agriculture, and commissioner of education (previously called the superintendent of public instruction). The governor sits and votes with the Cabinet, although he is not officially a member of it; he, along with Cabinet members, are known as the "Cabinet system." Cabinet members serve four-year terms, all concurrent with the governor.

While cabinetlike structures can be found in other southern states, the Florida Cabinet is unique in that these seven individuals serve, through constitutional mandate, as a collective decision-making body that deals with a broad range of state issues.

Originally the Cabinet served as twenty-two boards and commissions. By the 1940s, the number had grown to thirty. The major ones were the Budget Commission, State Board of Education, Board of Commissioners of State Institutions, Trustees of the Internal Improvement Fund, Board of Administration, State Pardon Board, Board of Pensions, State Board of Conservation, Board of Drainage Commissions, Labor Business Agents Licensing Board, and the Agricultural Marketing Board.[21] During meetings, the Cabinet would "switch hats" to reconstitute itself as one or more of these boards in order to transact state business. To complicate things further, not every Cabinet member (including the governor) sat on each board. In the 1940s, the governor sat on nineteen of the thirty boards and commissions; secretary of state on ten; comptroller on thirteen; treasurer on seventeen; superintendent of public instruction on seven; commissioner of agriculture on ten; and attorney general on seventeen.

The fact that the governor was not a member of every board meant that he could not directly influence, or control, all aspects of state administration. But matters extended even further. The governor has always been seen as but one member of a collegial body. True, he was "first among equals." Nonetheless, he had to "clear" matters of broad policy with members of the Cabinet. These individuals had important allies in the legislature and among powerful interest groups, who could sabotage the governor's agenda if they were not consulted or did not approve. Thus in many respects what governors hoped to accomplish depended on the cooperation of other state executives, even if the topic extended beyond the scope or purview of individual members.

In truth, the Cabinet did not always oppose the governor, and in fact on matters of little concern or indifference members would not block him. Also, they generally understood that governors were expected to focus on a broad range of issues, and their immediate concerns were much more limited.

On the other hand, gubernatorial initiatives in areas of direct importance to one or more members of the Cabinet would be given the greatest scrutiny, and governors would often find it very difficult to move forward in those areas if Cabinet members resisted. Also, if one Cabinet member felt the governor was "intruding," other Cabinet members would come to the

Cabinet member's aid. Thus, a sort of "territorial imperative" developed in which Cabinet members would protect themselves and each other. This cohesiveness served to limit gubernatorial effectiveness, both on administrative matters and on legislative initiatives that might have involved Cabinet members.

Lengthy terms of service by Cabinet members also created difficulties for governors. Unlike the governor, there was no limit on the length of service of other members. Between 1900 and 1970, they served an average of twelve years, and some much longer: one secretary of state was in office thirty years, and a commissioner of agriculture, thirty-seven.

Because of this longevity, Cabinet members developed close working relationships and mutual sets of understandings with one another. They also created similar relationships with members of the legislature, their own departments, interest and clientele groups, and local officials. They were used to seeing governors come and go; to some, in fact, the governor's seat in the Cabinet Room was just a game of musical chairs. The mobilization of conservative bias that this arrangement created was very hard for governors to dislodge. The Cabinet developed "its" way of doing things, including ways of nondeciding or resisting policies or proposals that members saw as unacceptable.[22]

On occasion, the Cabinet has been an asset to the governor. It took the political heat during a period of great racial tension in the post-*Brown* years when Governor LeRoy Collins commuted the death sentence of a black man accused of raping a white woman. In the early 1980s, Bob Graham enlisted the aid of Cabinet members in promoting several important policy initiatives, including upgrading the state's public schools. The Cabinet was of some help to Lawton Chiles during a severe state fiscal crisis in the early 1990s.

Thus the Cabinet has not always been an albatross for governors. Nonetheless, on balance it has served to diffuse executive authority and to limit his policy-making capabilities. Even though he still had his so-called little cabinet—a host of agencies and boards whose members he could directly appoint—the Cabinet acted as a real brake on the ability of Florida governors to control their own administrations.

Gubernatorial Tenure

A fragmented executive was not the only structural problem facing southern governors. A second issue to which the Schlesinger index calls our attention was his tenure. Florida was not the only state where the governor's office was something of a revolving door. Indeed, a frequent criticism of the southern governor was that his term of office was so limited that it constrained, even inhibited, the leadership capabilities of all but the most powerful executives.

For at least part of this century, six southern states (Alabama, Arkansas, Georgia, South Carolina, Tennessee, and Texas) have limited the governor to a two-year term. Alabama moved to a four-year term in 1902; South Carolina in 1926; Georgia in 1942; Tennessee in 1954; Texas in 1974; Arkansas in 1986. No southern state currently retains a two-year gubernatorial term.

The two-year governor's term was an example of the long-held southern fear of excessive gubernatorial power and a desire to keep the legislature supreme in state politics. Defenders have argued that it forces governors to be accessible and responsive to voters because elections make it necessary that governors stay in touch with them. Others have argued that the short term (even if consecutive elections were permissible, as was true in all six states) reduced the likelihood of corruption.

Critics have claimed that the two-year term made the governor a slave to reelection. Long-range planning became impossible. And the likelihood of governors' making politically difficult but necessary decisions (such as item vetoes of legislative pet projects) was thereby reduced as well.

A brief examination of the two-year term suggests that it was not quite the revolving door many critics alleged it would be. Relatively few governors served only two years. Seventy percent of all governors in states with two-year terms won at least one consecutive reelection. A few served even more: in Arkansas, populist Jeff Davis served three consecutive terms between 1900 and 1906; later in that state demagogic Orval Faubus won election six consecutive times in the 1950s and 1960s. Another demagogue, Eugene Talmadge in Georgia, served four terms, although only the first two were consecutive. In Tennessee, the shrewd Austin Peay (1922–28) and wartime governor Prentice Cooper (1938–44) each served three consecutive terms. The moderate Frank Clement, also in Tennessee, served one two-year term followed immediately by the state's first four-year term (1952–58); he later served still another four-year term. In Texas, business-oriented conservatives Allan Shivers, Price Daniel, and John Connally each served three consecutive two-year terms in the 1950s and 1960s.

But these were the only southern governors in office for two consecutive two-year terms who successfully campaigned for a third. Six who made the attempt failed: four in primaries and two (Alfred Taylor in Tennessee in 1922, and Winthrop Rockefeller in Arkansas in 1970, both Republicans) lost in the general election.[23] All of the other governors retired after two two-year terms.

An important question arises: If incumbency carries an electoral advantage, why did so few governors seek, and succeed to, a third consecutive two-year term?[24] Answers are necessarily speculative. Many undoubtedly tired of, or felt frustrated by, the office. Some—especially the Texas governors—went on to lucrative business or legal careers. Malcolm Patterson in Tennessee and Jim "Pa" Ferguson in Texas managed to alienate so many citizens by their antics that another reelection was not possible.

Probably the major reason, however, was the traditional public attitude that four years was enough for a governor. More than that could only be gained by an unusual person or under unusual circumstances. Support for this cultural-historical explanation can be found by examining the four states that early discarded the two-year term in favor of a four-year one. In each case no consecutive reelection was possible, essentially limiting the governor to four years in office. Texas and Arkansas, the last states to throw off the two-year terms, did permit two consecutive four-year terms, but by the time they took this action other southern states had already adopted the practice.

On balance, the two-year term was probably not the millstone for southern governors that some critics would have us believe. Most could be reasonably assured of one reelection. The list of those succeeding to a third term contains some distinguished southern governors. Whether the two-year term made governors more accountable to the public or reduced the likelihood of corruption is a matter for another study. But an important question remains: Did the four-year term solve the tenure problem for southern governors?

Florida, Louisiana, Mississippi, North Carolina, and Virginia are the only southern states that provided governors with a four-year term throughout this century. Without exception, the four-year term did not provide for consecutive reelection for the governor even though, as we saw, other state executives were not subject to this stricture. What were the consequences of this four-year term for southern governors?

It did provide some advantages to the governor that the two-year term did not. At least some measure of planning and agenda setting was possible. Perhaps, too, the governor was seen in a somewhat more serious light, if only because citizens could be certain that he would be around longer than his two-year colleague.

The major potential benefit, however, may well have been that he did not have to face reelection. He was spared both the hurry-up pressures facing the two-year governor, and he did not have to concern himself with positioning himself for a reelection effort. Whether this assurance also gave him more political freedom, especially to make statesmanlike (rather than narrowly political) decisions is a matter for dispute. More likely this ability depended more on the individual in office and his character and willingness to make these kind of decisions than on the structural feature of a four-year term.

But the four-year term still had one very major drawback for gubernatorial leadership. It did not solve the problem of the revolving door governor. Indeed, it assured that as soon as the governor was elected, he was an instant lame duck.

Nowhere was this consequence more evident or important than in the governor's relations with the legislature. Essentially he had only one chance to lay out his programs and push them through the legislature. The reason is that for much of this century, southern legislatures met only every other year, and for a limited number of days (sixty was common). Special sessions were possible, but they were politically costly, to be used only as a matter of last resort. By the time of the second regular legislative session (which normally came in the governor's third year), politicking for the next gubernatorial election was already under way. Given that a very common source of candidates was the legislature, especially the state senate, it was not unusual for legislators and reporters to pay more attention to colleagues running for the governorship than to the lame duck incumbent.

Politically, then, southern governors holding office for a four-year term began to vanish in their last two years. This practice was certainly a source of frustration for governors, as many commented, but, more important, it was a source of structural weakness in the office. As noted, this longer term might have given the governor a chance to make statesmanlike, courageous decisions. More commonly, the southern governor simply retired from public view. On occasion, the governor used his invisibility to engage in venal activity, rewarding himself and his friends with state contracts and other forms of patronage. But usually the last eighteen to twenty-four months of an administration were marked by a lack of activity and initiative, and in many respects the state was rudderless, pending the outcome of the next gubernatorial election, after which the cycle would begin again.

Southern governors with a four-year term could hold office again if they waited for a subsequent election. However, while a number of former governors sought the office again, it was very rare that they were successful. In general, state politics seemed to move past them while they were out of office, and the public seemed to want new faces, not old.

There were some interesting exceptions. Earl Long, brother of Huey, won in 1948 and 1956. While not the political strongman his brother was, he was equally colorful and managed to resurrect something of the populist coalition of rural whites that had propelled Huey to power.[25] Also in Louisiana the equally flamboyant Edwin Edwards (who won successive elections in 1972 and 1975) set himself up as governor-in-exile during the

1979–83 tenure of Republican David Treen. Edwards even held news conferences, issued policy and position papers, and generally comported himself as a governor would. Edwards regained the governorship in 1983, lost in 1987, and won again in 1991 against a former member of the Ku Klux Klan, David Duke.

Frank Clement in Tennessee was not as colorful as either of his Louisiana colleagues, but he was the first beneficiary of Tennessee's four-year term, in 1954, after first winning a two-year term in 1952. While he could not succeed himself, he did win another term in 1962, largely on the strength of solid, progressive leadership in his first six years in office, particularly in education, reapportionment, and civil rights. He was also the beneficiary of factional fights within the Buford Ellington wing of the Democratic Party.

George Wallace in Alabama provided the most interesting way in which a four-year governor sought to overcome the problem of a prohibition against consecutive terms. Wallace ran successfully for the governorship in 1962 and spent the next four years defending segregation against Yankees and the federal government. In 1966, unable to run again, he copied the Ferguson model from Texas and had his wife Lurleen run instead. Just as Jim Ferguson had promised Texans "two governors for the price of one," George set up his own office right next to his wife's. It was very clear to Alabamans who was the "real" governor from 1966 to 1970. At the conclusion of his wife's term, Wallace successfully ran again, in spite of the near fatal gunshot wound he received in 1968 while running for president. Beginning in 1968, Alabama permitted governors to succeed themselves, and thus Wallace was able to run again, successfully, in 1974. He again was reelected in 1982, after sitting out the 1978–82 period, and finally retired in 1986.[26]

There were a few other instances in which southern governors served more than one term. In South Carolina, Olin Johnson won in 1934 and 1942. In Virginia, Mills Godwin won in 1965 and 1973 (in the latter election he switched parties and ran successfully as a Republican). In Tennessee, Buford Ellington succeeded Frank Clement in 1958 and 1966. Prior to Jim Hunt, no North Carolina governor served more than one term during this century, although Kerr Scott's son Robert won the office twenty years after his father did.

Most southern governors serving four years did not even try to win another term. For those who did, success was rare. Fuller Warren in Florida provides a typical example. A personally popular man, he had served with little distinction from 1949 to 1953.[27] But when he ran again in 1956, he seemed almost lost by the rapid changes in Florida and was unable to recapture either his personal popularity or the moderately populist constituency that had elected him the first time. He finished last in a field of six in the Democratic primary.[28]

By the late 1960s and early 1970s, most southern states had moved through constitutional reform, and statutes allowed four-year governors to succeed themselves. Only Virginia currently retains the four-year limitation. In some states, such as Alabama, governors (in this case, Wallace) sought the reform so they could succeed themselves. In most cases the changes resulted from efforts by state reformers to modernize state constitutions, such as occurred in Florida. It had become apparent in the southern states that a single four-year term did not solve the revolving door problem of the governorship. Complex issues of the late twentieth century required the possibility of stronger executive leadership, and thus changes were made to allow governors to stay in office longer.

In fact, southern governors did so. In those states in which one reelection became possible, every eligible incumbent has sought reelection except George Wallace, who retired in 1986 after four terms (not counting the "surrogate" tenure of wife Lurleen). In not every case was reelection assured. Claude Kirk lost in Florida in 1970 after a flamboyant, demagogic first term. Both Bill Clements and Mark White lost reelection chances in Texas; conservative Republican Clements lost to populist White in 1982, while the colorless White gave the office back to Clements in 1986. Ann Richards was defeated after one term in Texas (1994). Edwin Edwards finally lost a Louisiana election in 1987. In Florida, Republican Bob Martinez lost a reelection bid in 1990.

But other governors have been more successful and have turned their tenures into eight years in office. Their tenure has made a difference in public expectations surrounding the office and in gubernatorial performance. The revolving door and instant lame duck problems of the four-year governor have all but disappeared. Legislators, interest groups, other executives, the media, and public at large have been forced to pay more attention to the governor. He, in turn, has the time to push through some major programs, attend to some long-standing problems, and make a lasting impact on the state. His increased longevity has made the southern governor a far more powerful player in state politics than was the case for most of this century.

Budgeting

Public budgeting is another key element of gubernatorial responsibility that demonstrates traditional weaknesses of the southern chief executive. The budget, after all, is not simply a fiscal document. It must also be viewed as a policy and management tool, for through it the state lays out its priorities and programs, decides how to spend its moneys and in what amounts, and even determines the administrative procedures to be followed.

In a real sense, the budget is the governor's ultimate political instrument. It represents his vision of what the state's future ought to be. Thus to the extent that the governor can control the budget process, he can shape the politics of the state, dominate policy making, and control his own executive branch. To the extent these powers are limited, the governor will find that his impact on the state is also curtailed.[29]

For much of this century, the southern governor was in a weak budgetary position. In virtually all of the states the governor found his budget powers constrained, including the eight southern states using the so-called executive budget, in which the governor or his representative prepares the budget and submits it to the legislature. In three states—Arkansas, Florida, and South Carolina—the governor had very few budget powers.

Structural peculiarities of a variety of kinds in five southern states (the above three plus North Carolina and Texas) also served to undermine gubernatorial control of the budget. Without detailing each of the idiosyncrasies, in these states the governor was forced to share important budget-making or administrative authority with other members of the state executive or even with the legislature. The latter was most notable in Arkansas and Texas and involved the actual participation of legislative officials in preparing the budget. In Texas, for example, both the Speaker of the House and lieutenant governor had budget authority that rivaled, and at times exceeded, that of the governor.[30] Moreover, even when legislators were involved in constructing the budget, they still had an additional opportunity to consider and vote on it once it was submitted to them by the governor.[31]

There are a number of reasons for this fundamental weakness in the office of southern governor. The first and most obvious was a result of his limited tenure in office. He simply did not have the time in office to use the budget as a means of controlling his executive branch, establishing his priorities firmly on the public agenda, and moving the state toward his view of the future. The problem became even more acute because both the budget and legislative sessions were biennial. Thus the governor with a two-year term might have only one chance, and governors with a four-year term at most two opportunities, to use the budget as a policy and/or management tool.

But this problem was compounded by the fact that no southern governor entered office with a clean budget slate. In spite of campaign pronouncements, every governor found upon entering office and beginning his first budget process that commitments of the previous governor could seldom be ignored. Thus the new governor was saddled with the legacy of previous years. While he quickly realized that this arrangement would also apply to his successor, it was small consolation to the new governor who had probably made budgetary promises but who found he could not always deliver them.

An even greater problem for many southern governors during this century was the actual budget structure, including the executive budget. In virtually all the southern states, much of the budget was actually beyond the governor's immediate control because of heavy reliance on specialized, earmarked funds. These were moneys collected from particular sources and taxes that by law had to be spent in particular ways or on particular items. Education and roads were especially susceptible to this pattern, but in fact matters extended further. Ransone found that in Alabama (to take but one example of a state using the executive budget), there were seven special funds in 1900, fifty-four in 1936, and one hundred in 1942. In the latter year, 88 percent of the state's tax yield came from special funds. Moreover, only a little over 9 percent of the state's expenditures were from the state's general fund; the other 91 percent were from special, earmarked funds.[32]

The Alabama experience was fairly typical of the kind of problems governors throughout the South had in controlling the budget. The state's general fund was essentially the only fiscal area in which the governor had substantial discretion, but it often constituted a small part of the total budget. Moreover, because other state officials, especially legislators, could have a significant impact on the budget process, it is fair to conclude that the southern governor's fiscal powers were decidedly limited. The situation began to change after World War II as new techniques of public finance were slowly introduced into the region. Nonetheless, recent studies suggest that southern governors have immediate control over as little as one-quarter of the state's total expenditures.[33] By the 1990s, owing to state fiscal pressures in such areas as welfare and Medicaid resulting in part from reduced federal dollars, the governor's discretionary budget had dipped into percentages, in some cases, in the low teens.

Yet another problem that limited the southern governor's budget powers was the size of his personal staff. For much of this century, in fact, southern governors have had very little professional help in their offices. Even clerical and secretarial personnel were scarce. In the late 1940s, most southern governors had only one or two members of their staffs who could be regarded as "professional" in any real sense of the term. By the late 1960s, it was still less than seven.[34]

There have been specialized agencies of state government devoted to preparing the state budget. Frequently, however, the professionals staffing these offices did not work directly for the governor. Thus they did not necessarily assist him in gaining greater control over the budget. If he wished to do so, he needed people in his own office who were skilled in the highly complex tasks of public budgeting. Members of the southern governor's traditionally tiny staff were necessarily generalists; neither by training nor job specification could they compete with state budget specialists whose loyalty was not always to the governor.

In recent years, this situation has changed completely. The personal staffs of southern governors have been significantly enlarged and professionalized. Every southern governor now has professional budget personnel working directly in his office. Thus he has the expertise on his staff to deal adequately with the budget. Indeed, it is fair to say that few aspects of the southern governorship have been strengthened as much as his staff and budgeting capabilities. But until this happened, the use of the term "governor's budget" was a serious misnomer.

Several other recent developments have also served to improve the modern southern governor's budgetary powers. Economic forecasting, while not an exact science, has become far more sophisticated than it was earlier in the century, when it was little more than crystal ball gazing and guesswork. Thus southern governors have much better information about future tax receipts, and fiscal requirements, than their predecessors. This information allows for better planning and a more realistic approach to agenda setting and program planning.

Also, the improved economic status of southern states has increased the southern governor's budget powers. The basic poverty, poor tax base, and low tax revenue of most southern states during this century was a severe constraint on those few but active governors who wished to use the budget as a policy tool; the low-tax, low-service political culture of southern states was a further brake.

Not all of this political culture has disappeared, of course. But as the next chapter will show, many modern southern governors have demonstrated a willingness to become budget and policy activists in search of solutions to contemporary public problems. Political constraints may still hamper their willingness or ability to raise additional revenues through new or greater taxes and fees. But the crushing burden of poverty and do-nothing political culture no longer offer an excuse, or refuge, for failing to act.

During the 1990s the do-nothing view turned into do-little. In part this change was a function of a continuing southern political culture, one that has died hard and, in fact, is not dead at all. But both partisan and ideological elements have contributed to a go-slow attitude on the part of many southern governors. As we saw earlier in the book, by the mid-1990s a majority of southern governors were Republicans who bought heavily into the fiscal conservative ideology remarkably similar to their Democratic colleagues from earlier in the century. Also, during the 1990s, the conventional political wisdom, in the South and elsewhere, became one of "mistrust government" and "get government off our backs."[35] Given this set of views, it was no wonder that even moderate Democrats, such as Lawton Chiles in Florida, became as fiscally tightfisted as the most ardent Republican governors. The early and mid-1990s, with few exceptions in the South,[36] became a time of fiscal retrenchment, not expansion.

Finally, the introduction of more sophisticated budgeting techniques than existed under the old, purely line-item system, has improved the budget powers of the southern governor. While the line-item budget has not been abandoned, it has been supplemented with variations of program, zero-based, and performance budgeting mechanisms. These enable governors to focus on whole programs and results, thereby approximating a thorough "root-and-branch" approach to budgeting and permitting much greater executive control of the budget process than existed previously under the largely incremental, highly politicized earlier approaches.[37]

Thus recent trends have greatly increased the southern governor's budget-making capabilities. But for most of this century, rather than being an asset to the southern governor, the budget process was largely a source of discontent, frustration, and political weakness for them.

Executive Vetoes

Southern governors have had an array of vetoes at their disposal, including line-item and pocket vetoes besides the more standard kind in which the executive refuses to approve a legislative act. The one major exception in the South has been North Carolina. Its governor has not had a veto.

Use of the veto has often been associated with the growth and exercise of executive powers.[38] The standard view is that the veto represents a major weapon through which the governor deals with the legislature. If he cannot accept its action, he repudiates what it has done. The legislature, in turn, either overrides the veto or capitulates. Even the threat of a veto can be as potent as its actual use, since the threat defines the boundaries of what governors will accept.

In the South, the veto has not necessarily been the source of strength for governors that observers have found elsewhere. Perhaps the lesson of North Carolina is instructive in this regard. It is doubtful that governors in the other southern states have necessarily had an easier time than Tarheel governors did in shaping policy or influencing legislative deliberation solely because they had a veto and their North Carolina colleague did not. Nor have North Carolina governors necessarily been at a disadvantage in shaping state agendas solely because they lacked a veto power.

While the veto is not an irrelevant gubernatorial power, at least in the South the ability of the governor to direct the legislature has depended on more than just this one capability. His personal and political stature, his skills and capability, the tradition and culture of the state, public expectations of the governor's office, economic circumstances, and national and even international events are at least as important in this regard.

Perhaps the line-item veto has been the most helpful to southern governors. Given their problems in budgeting, the line-item veto has permitted them to attack individual expenditures that they have felt are not in line with their priorities. Seen in this way, the line-item veto could be used, as Frank Prescott suggests, as the "gun behind the door."[39] However, shrewd governors could also employ it as a bargaining chip in negotiations over what items remained in the budget, or as a scalpel, used with care and finesse as offending parts of appropriations bills were removed.

But even the line-item veto could be of questionable value to the southern governor. While it did allow him a last say on appropriations, it also attacked legislators at one of their most sensitive points—"pork barrel" projects. These have been, and probably remain, extremely important to members of southern legislatures. "Pork" is a primary mechanism through which legislators bring state "bacon" to their home districts.[40]

Thus, pork served to aid the people whom legislators are supposed to represent. Particularly in the poor, rural, heavily agricultural South, these pork projects have been of tremendous importance, whether they were roads, buildings, bridges, or something else, because counties and towns were usually too poor to afford them by themselves. Moreover, bringing home pork was a sure way for legislators to establish themselves firmly with their constituencies, thus increasing their chances for lengthy legislative service. For governors to knock out pork, then, was to undermine both the projects and the political standing of individual legislators. While for the most part governors did not have to worry about reelection chances, antagonizing individual legislators, county courthouse gangs, and perhaps whole regions could nevertheless come back to haunt them while they remained in office.[41]

These considerations, in fact, point to the major problems which vetoes posed for southern governors. The veto is an "ultimate weapon," a sort of political thermonuclear device. As such, it is fundamentally a negative force, destroying much and leaving few survivors. Governors concerned with policy formation and problem-solving have found that vetoes left voids, for much effort is always involved in passing legislation. Most would rather accept half, or part, of a loaf than be left with nothing to show for the investment in time, commitment, and energy.

It is true, of course, that vetoes have political uses and can be employed to foist blame onto the legislature. But for the southern governor this tactic did not work. Most never tried to defeat legislative opponents of their programs in elections; those who tried rarely succeeded. And since relatively few southern governors, until recently, could succeed themselves, the use of vetoes as a reelection offensive weapon was limited.

On the other hand, some governors have used vetoes as a means of making a full-blown political statement. For example, in 1994 the Florida legislature passed a products liability law aimed at forcing the tobacco industry to pay for Medicare and Medicaid costs resulting from health problems associated with tobacco use. In 1995, under business pressure, the legislature repealed the law, but the repeal was vetoed by Governor Chiles. Tobacco interests, some parts of the business community, and some Republicans vowed revenge in 1996. However, Chiles placed sustaining his veto at the center of his legislative program for the 1996 session, and he was successful. Thus while in one sense the veto was a destructive force and assuredly colored the whole 1996 session, in the end it became a major test of political wills and power between the governor and legislature, one that Chiles won after being beaten several times in 1995.

In each of the southern states, except North Carolina, legislatures can override gubernatorial vetoes if they are especially unhappy with executive action. In reality, overrides seldom happened.[42] Southern legislatures have been generally so institutionally weak that it was difficult enough for leaders to organize them sufficiently to pass legislation with a simple majority. It was even harder to obtain the extraordinary majorities needed to override.[43] Time constraints, especially toward the end of legislative sessions, often prevented serious reconsideration of legislative vetoes and served to prevent the formation of coalitions needed to do so. Also, as a number of studies have found, legislative overrides are more frequently found in states that have "divided control"—that is, the governor is of one party and at least one branch of the legislature is held by another.[44] But in the one-party South, divided control did not exist prior to 1960 and has only occurred a limited number of times in the 1980s and 1990s.[45]

Is the veto power more significant for the modern southern governor than for his earlier colleagues? Answers must be speculative, for available research on this issue in recent years is sketchy. The increased tenure potential of the southern governor could make the veto a more attractive weapon, since it could provide a way for him to impose his priorities on the legislature; previously it could just "wait him out." The veto's political advantages for reelection campaigns might make it more useful as well.

On the other hand, vetoes continue to represent a breakdown in communications between the executive and legislative branches. Governors interested in policy formation quickly recognize that they have to keep these lines open if they are to be successful. Thus negotiating, bargaining, and compromise, rather than vetoes, are likely to serve the governor in better stead than the repeated use or threat of a veto.

Conclusion

There have been other sources of gubernatorial weakness besides those of the office itself—lack of party organization, a weak legislature, powerful interest groups, poverty, and race. But just as the office of southern governor has been modernized, so developments outside of it have increased the possibility of strong leadership by the contemporary southern governor.

Stronger party organization provides additional sources of strength and a relatively ongoing base of support for the modern southern governor, in contrast to the old factional system. Southern legislatures in the past two decades have been reapportioned and professionalized. While ongoing legislative-executive tensions will continue to exist, it is also true that increased legislative willingness to deal with serious problems and issues will prove beneficial to governors anxious to solve problems and move the state forward. Powerful interest and clientele groups remain a potential hazard for southern governors and will continue to do so if party structures do not become strong enough to act as buffers against them. But shrewd governors, such as Bob Graham of Florida, Jim Hunt of North Carolina, Lamar Alexander of Tennessee, and Richard Riley of South Carolina, among others, learned to use the power of interest groups to aid gubernatorial powers and plans, and it is likely that other governors will follow their example. The decline of massive poverty and racial issues have also freed the southern governor's agenda and allowed him more room to maneuver in policy making.

Thus the office of southern governor and the milieu in which it exists have overcome some of its traditional weaknesses. The potential for more vigorous leadership by southern governors is less hampered by structural problems than previously. Whether the potential of the office is realized, however, goes beyond structural and formal matters, and it is to this issue that we now turn.

10

Red Galluses No More: The Leadership of Southern Governors

If you rednecks or hillbillies ever come to Little Rock, be sure to come see me—come to my house . . . make it your home while you are in the capital city. If I am not at home, tell my wife who you are, tell her you are my friend, and that you belong to the sunburnt sons of toil. She may be out in the backyard making soap, but that will be all right; you will be properly cared for, and it will save you a hotel bill.
—Governor Jeff Davis, Arkansas, 1900

We played the fiddle, were fond of dogs, and loved our fellow man.
—Governor Alfred Taylor, Tennessee, 1927

When I took the oath as governor, I didn't take any vow of poverty.
—Governor Richard Leche, Louisiana, 1938

The judgment evidenced by the [governor's] opportunities will determine whether the state will enjoy four years of politics or four years of capable government.
—Governor Millard Caldwell, Florida, 1947

The epigraphs that introduce this chapter suggest something of the range of styles and the quality of leadership shown by southern governors during this century—the populism of Jeff Davis; the "Goodtime Charley" administration of Alfred Taylor; the venality of Richard Leche; the dour sobriety of the conservative Millard Caldwell. This is not to say that these four examples constitute the universe of gubernatorial leadership in the South during this century. Indeed, it was, and is, richly varied.

In the previous chapter we investigated the institutional milieu in which southern governors operated and discussed the constraints facing them as they sought to carry out their tasks. We also looked at some of the major changes in the office, which presumably give contemporary southern governors more flexibility and greater opportunities to lead their states than existed earlier.

But we have not specifically looked at what southern governors actually did while in office or how they acted. Nor have we examined their impact on the political life of their states and region. In short, we have not yet assessed the quality of political leadership demonstrated by southern governors during this century.

Leadership is not a fixed political phenomenon; rather, it has an organic quality to it. It changes over time, in style, in its importance to the state, and in its impact on politics. Types of leadership common in one era may diminish in importance subsequently or even disappear completely, as they are supplanted by new ones. This ebb and flow of gubernatorial leadership is worth investigating, especially to try to understand why some types disappear, while others, unknown or uncommon earlier, come to the fore.

Assessing gubernatorial leadership allows us to address squarely the human element of southern politics. In their search for political understanding, students and observers of politics, and participants as well, should not forget that individuals and their behavior can play major roles in determining political outcomes. This insight is especially true in the South, because the region has seen more than its share of political characters among its governors, many of whom are worth studying in detail. Space obviously prevents our doing so; nonetheless, to omit the impact of individuals on gubernatorial politics, and state politics generally, would represent a serious gap in our examination of southern politics.[1]

A Model of Leadership for Southern Governors

If we are to fully understand and assess the nature of political leadership by the southern governor, it is essential that we develop sound criteria for determining what aspects of the governorship to look at and making judgments about them. To these ends, we shall briefly put forward a model of leadership for southern governors.

The model, based on available literatures as well as previous work done by the author,[2] encompasses environmental, structural, personal, and political dimensions of the leadership of southern governors. It differs from other models in that it is more broadly based and deliberately includes a range and variety of influences on leadership. Also, while recognizing the importance of psychological variables of political leadership, it includes relatively few of them in the model. The reason has less to do with controversies surrounding the proper role of these phenomena in leadership than with difficulty in gathering appropriate data for their inclusion; psychological data for recent governors are extremely difficult to obtain and, for those in the past, virtually impossible.[3]

There are four major parts to the model; a drawing to help the reader visualize it is shown in Figure 10.1. These parts are Environment; Structure of Office; Personal Attributes; and Political Tasks. The model is designed to show the types of influences on the leadership of the southern governor, account for the particular type of leadership he provides, indicate something of the impact his leadership has on the state, and provide a basis for sound judgment about the adequacy of his leadership.

While fundamentally qualitative in nature, the model nonetheless provides guidelines for a rigorous examination of governors and their leadership. But the goal, in this case, is not just to understand how individual southern governors have behaved. Later in the chapter we shall use the model to construct a typology of gubernatorial leadership in the South and show how it has changed during the first nine decades of this century.

The Environment of Leadership

Leadership does not take place in a vacuum but rather in a particular milieu of present circumstances and the historical forces that helped create them. Two dimensions of this environment are important for understanding the leadership of southern governors.

The first is socioeconomic conditions. Students of leadership have long noted that particular kinds of social and economic circumstances influence what leaders do.[4] These can be both opportunities and constraints, depending on the nature of the conditions (an unexpected windfall in the state treasury, a sudden rise in unemployment, or a fall in the price of farm products), and how the southern governor chooses to deal with them. For the southern governor, the most important socioeconomic conditions he has had to face (although with which he may not have chosen to deal) have been the crushing burden of poverty, the presence of a large black underclass, and hostile attitudes toward blacks in the white community.

The second dimension is historical-cultural forces. Governors enter of-

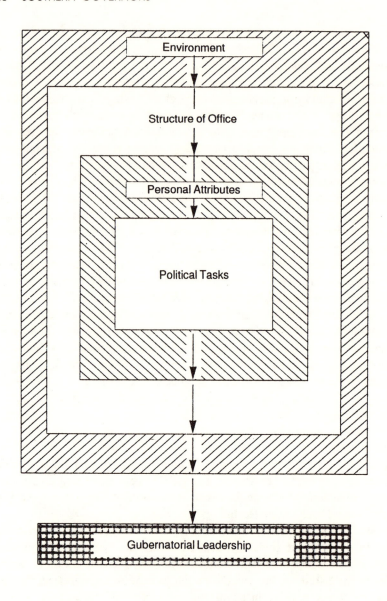

Figure 10.1. **A Model of Southern Gubernatorial Leadership**

fice with a set of public expectations about what they are to do, where they "fit" in state politics, and what the public thinks about the governorship (aside from what people think of him personally). These are not straitjackets but rather are pressures on the governor, built up as a product of history, culture, and tradition, about what he should, can, and may not do. As we saw, in the South public expectations for the governor for much of this century have been low. Many governors acted accordingly; others saw governorships as an opportunity to enlarge and improve the office for the benefit of the state, themselves, and their successors in office.[5]

It is important to realize that these environmental forces, as well as the structural features of the office, are not determinative. Rather, they provide a set of constraints and opportunities facing individual southern governors. Likewise, it is not always possible to tell in advance how these factors will influence gubernatorial behavior; different governors, facing similar circumstances, might react very differently. For example, a rapid decline in the state's economy might frustrate, even paralyze, some governors, and they will do little or nothing except ride things out. Others might be energized to begin to revamp the economic base of the state, seek tax reform as an economic stimulus, or do something else. In spite of the range of possibilities, however, any effort to understand and assess the quality of southern gubernatorial leadership must take account of how governors coped with the environmental conditions they faced.

The Structure of the Governor's Office

The second major part of the model concerns the nature of the governor's office. As we saw in the last chapter, the structure of the southern governor's office has been very influential in the kind of leadership possible by the incumbent. A sharply divided executive, for example, or a two-year term limited what governors could reasonably be expected to do.

Because the last chapter detailed the structural problems of the southern governor's office, there is no need to repeat them here. Two points about them are worth emphasizing, however. First, the constitutional-legal provisions of the office are not the only structural features significant in influencing leadership. Also important is its relationship—formal and informal—to other actors in the state political system. In a sense, then, the governor's office is more than the "sum" of its constitutional-legal base. How it is seen by citizens, by other actors in the political system (for example, legislators, interest groups, party leaders, local officials), and how it was used by his predecessors in the office help determine what the office really is.

Second, as the last chapter has shown, the southern governorship has, in recent decades, seen a good deal of structural change. Many previous constraints have been reduced or eliminated, so the modern southern governor has more opportunities and possibilities than his predecessors. But the expectations and responsibilities for governors are also increased, something that must be considered in studying and assessing their leadership.

Personal Attributes

Personal attributes, the third part of our model, have caused great difficulty in studies of leadership. While it seems intuitively obvious that particular personal attributes will influence what a governor does, and how others react to him, efforts to specify these qualities (psychological and otherwise) often break down. Intelligence, health, and personality type, for example, would seem to make a difference in leadership, but exactly how is not clear.

The present model seeks to overcome these difficulties by specifying four personal attributes whose importance to the quality of southern gubernatorial leadership can be readily understood and demonstrated. These are—attitudes toward the office, response to events, style, and ideology.

Attitudes Toward the Office

Attitudes toward the office are connected to the governor's own conception of the office—what it has been in the past, what he can and should do while occupying it, what its limitations and possibilities are. Some governors have had a very passive view of the office;[6] others see themselves as managers, conciliators, and referees of political struggles going on around them; still others are vigorous and active, seeking out problems to tackle and new areas for gubernatorial involvement.

How a governor viewed the office did not always determine his actions. Nonetheless, if we are to grasp, and assess, the leadership of the southern governor, we must begin with his own view of what he thought of the office and how he should use it.

Response to Events

Every southern governor entered office with at least a vague idea of what he hoped to do (or not do). But none, in this century, has had the luxury of finding a tabula rasa after his inauguration; all have had to cope with conditions left them by their predecessors. Moreover, to make an obvious point, time passes and things happen, many of which are unforeseen and not a part of a governor's original plan for his administration.

The relevant issue for this book is, How well did the southern governor deal with unexpected, unanticipated, sometimes crisis events? Was he the master of them? Or was he overwhelmed by them? The extent to which the southern governor was able to adapt to and cope with changing circumstances, manage crises, and possibly turn a serious setback into an opportunity to move the state forward gives an excellent indication into the quality of his leadership.

Style

Gubernatorial style is often referred to in a colloquial sense: "easygoing," "hard-nosed," "aggressive," "autocratic," "consensus-oriented," "aloof," "friendly," "low-key." The list is endless, and the terms are not always used analytically.

But gubernatorial style is important in understanding leadership for two reasons. First, style is actually an expression of the governor's political persona or identity. It is a definition of who he is and how he intends to behave in office. Second, style helps determine how other political actors relate and respond to him. Thus his style positions or orients him in political arenas and milieus, affects other members of the political system, and influences the nature of his interaction with other actors and participants.

This concept may strike the reader as very abstract. But ultimately style greatly influences the ability of a southern governor to persuade others to follow his lead, adopt his priorities and agenda, and carry out his wishes. As many students of political executives have noted, understood this way, style is the essence of leadership.[7]

Ideology

Often "ideology" refers, in American politics, to an individual's placement on the "liberal-conservative" spectrum of political beliefs and attitudes. But in the South, "liberal" and "conservative" have had meanings different from those they have had elsewhere in the nation. Liberal ideologies have scarcely existed at all, and much of political ideology has been variants on a fundamentally conservative view of the role of government in human affairs.

"Ideology" in the South for much of this century has really referred to positions on race and poverty.[8] Thus, as we refer to ideology in the model, we are talking about the position which southern governors have taken on the traditional problems relating to the existence of a large black population in the region, and the crushing burden of southern poverty.

Political Tasks

The final portion of our model of leadership for the southern governor concerns the tasks that confront any occupant of the office and the way he carries them out. While opinion may vary on the specifics of each activity, there are five that represent an irreducible minimum of gubernatorial activity—symbolic leadership, administration, legislative leadership, agenda setting, and public ethics.

Before discussing these different tasks, we must make explicit a major assumption of the whole model. It is that governors—southern and otherwise—must be fundamentally problem solvers. Gubernatorial leadership is not simply an abstraction but rather is purposive in the sense that it is an activity involved in identifying and defining problems and proposing, creating, and implementing ways to deal with them. The model assumes further that governors have a responsibility to do something to enhance the public good and not simply to protect the status quo or the interests of privileged elites. There is no ideological assumption here; the governor can be liberal or conservative, Republican or Democrat. The main point is that he has a responsibility to act on behalf of the people of the state; political conflict occurs over what goals are sought and what means chosen to reach them.[9] To the extent that governors carry out these tasks, or at least seek to do so, we can regard their leadership as effective. To the extent that they shy away from them, fail to propose solutions to real (not simply imaginary or chimaeric) problems, or deal solely with tertiary problems and side issues, we can say that they are less effective.

Symbolic Leadership

Symbolic leadership is the first task to be considered. In many ways is similar to Clinton Rossiter's view of the president as "chief of state."[10] It does involve ceremonial tasks, and those in which the governor represents the citizens of the state in public functions and occasions.

But for the southern governor, symbolic leadership extends well beyond ceremony. Because of structural and contextual constraints on the office, some southern governors have found that symbolic leadership has important, substantive consequences. One of the most crucial examples of symbolic leadership in this sense has been his ambassadorial duties, in which he represents the state to other states, Washington, and foreign lands. Even more important has been his ambassadorship to the private sector, in seeking outside capital investment.[11]

Another important kind of symbolic leadership concerns how the southern governor defines his real political constituency. Which groups will he recognize? Which are important? What rewards will he provide? What about minority groups? Through his definition, he helps create, expand, or contract the state's active political community.

Symbolic forms of leadership, then, can involve very hard political decisions and choices. For example, just to pursue one possible avenue of symbolic leadership, What kind of outside investment should be sought? Where? What terms should be offered? What about the environmental effects of so-called smokestack versus high-tech industry? What infrastructure and support services will have to be provided to attract this industry? Who will pay? The way in which the governor considers such questions and carries out his ambassadorial duties can have immediate consequences for himself and long-range consequences for the state. Symbolic leadership, then, while often ignored by students of political executives, is in fact central to their leadership.

Administration

Southern governors seldom get political points for being good administrators, since effective executive behavior often means that the public scarcely notices the smooth operation of government. But when administration breaks down or there is a scandal, the governor is the first to be criticized. Even if he is not at fault, the public tends to hold him accountable and responsible. This connection was a special problem for the southern governor, for, as we saw in the preceding chapter, much of his own branch lay beyond his control and any impact he had on it was indirect.

How do we understand and assess the governor's administrative leadership? We can examine those areas of greatest responsibility and ask how he carried them out—patronage and appointments, budgeting, administrative control and reorganization. Following this line of argument suggests that the southern governor's leadership lay on a continuum whose boundaries are defined, at one end, by a spoils system approach to administration, and at the other, by a merit system.[12]

Spoils system governors felt that succession to the office was a license to reward friends and supporters of the winning faction. The system embodied the old notion of "to the victors belong the spoils." Patronage, appointments, budgeting, and control of agencies were to be carried out with less attention to merit, ability, or need than to the simple matter of rewards and punishments. In its most extreme form it allowed, even encouraged, venality and corruption in the administration.

The merit system implies consideration of good government criteria.

While rewarding friends and supporters was important, administrative decisions also had to be made on the basis of merit, need, experience, and the public interest. Governors at this end of the spectrum often advocated merit systems for appointments and competitive bidding for state contracts. This system tended to diminish the importance of whims or personal desires of governors and their friends.

Two points should be made about the question of spoils systems versus merit systems approaches to administrative tasks. First, both are intensely political, but their means differ considerably. Spoils system politics makes no pretense of anything but rewarding friends of the winning faction and punishing its opponents. Merit system politics may have a higher tone and have the effect of improving the quality of appointive personnel and the manner of letting contracts. But even the most fervent believer in the merit system approach still sought to reward his supporters and members of his winning faction; it was just done in ways different from the ways of his spoils system colleague, and through different rationales. To do otherwise would undermine a major purpose of seeking the governorship.

Second, care must be taken in trying to assess whether one or another of these styles is better. The moralistic, good government approach to politics emphasizes the desirability of the merit approach. It makes politics and administration more palatable to citizens. And it is true that corruption and venality cannot be condoned but in fact are injurious to a democratic form of government.

But it also seems true that a spoils system approach to administration is not necessarily incompatible with effective approaches to problem solving. Huey Long in Louisiana and his brother Earl are examples of this point. Likewise, a strict, almost puritanical, merit system approach, such as that embodied by many Virginia and Florida governors, was not necessarily associated with adequate provision of public services or even strong, forward-looking leadership. Rare was the governor, such as Millard Caldwell of Florida, who could combine both a firm insistence on merit system approaches to administration with a strong commitment to problem solving.[13]

Legislative Leadership

Probably no other area of activity for the southern governor has quite the public visibility and importance that executive-legislative relations have had. From the initial campaign promises until the dying days of an administration, the southern governor has been examined by editorialists, other political figures, and citizens for his ability to get the legislature to cooperate and pass his programs. It may be that, at least in the popular mind, the reputation of the southern governor depended more on his legislative record than any other single aspect of his leadership.

The legislative success of the southern governor has often been based on his batting average—that is, the ratio between what the governor proposed to the legislature and what it gave him. This approach is potentially misleading. Many southern governors sought little from the legislature and their proposals were timid, thus assuring success and inflating their batting averages. Others may have put forward elaborate, ambitious plans, and while their batting averages might have been relatively low, the programs enacted may have been significant.

Thus in seeking to understand and assess the southern governor's legislative leadership, we can legitimately inquire into the content of his proposals. Were the issues he defined and proposals he made serious and congruent with the state's real problems? Or was the governor content to limit his proposals to modest ones and popular causes, sure to be enacted? The former represents governors interested in problem solving. The latter place a lower priority on problem solving than on raising their batting averages and maintaining high approval ratings in opinion surveys.

But in looking into executive-legislative relations, we must also look at the interaction between the southern governor and the legislature. He may often have regarded it as a thorn in his side. But he also had to recognize that it was a legitimate part of lawmaking and policy making in the state and that it had interests of its own in problem solving. Obviously the checks-and-balances system of institutional separation and power sharing in state government deliberately ensure tension between the two.[14] But our investigation of the southern governor's legislative leadership would be incomplete unless we observe how the governor dealt with these tensions and sought to accommodate the interests and needs of the legislature in policy making even at the same time as he tried to lead and convince it to follow his direction.

Agenda Setting

Although commonly used by politicians, journalists, and students of politics, the term "agenda setting" in this model has a very specific meaning. It refers to the ability of the southern governor to convey his vision of the state's future to the citizens. It is a recognition that his specific, substantive accomplishments and contributions might be limited, owing to constraints on time in office, resources, political problems, and so forth. But the impact of the governor can last long after he has gone because of the priorities and plans he laid out and the guidelines he established for utilizing state resources in attacking state problems. It may be, then, that the ability of the southern governor to establish and dominate the state agenda represents the longest-lasting aspect of his political leadership, since his successors and other political actors will continue on the paths he laid out.

Agenda setting consists of two dimensions. On the one hand, the southern governor serves as a public educator. In this sense, he has to direct public attention to state problems and convince people of the need, eventual if not at present, to dedicate state resources toward their resolution. Part of this activity involves molding public opinion. But if he is truly to influence the state's long-term agenda, it must extend beyond public opinion to citizens' fundamental attitudes about the nature of their state and the responsibilities of government. He must, therefore, have some impact on the State's dominant political culture, not simply reflect it but shape it.

The second dimension of agenda setting is moral leadership. In this sense (the "bully pulpit" of Teddy Roosevelt), the governor defines state standards of right and wrong, of what is appropriate, responsible behavior by citizens and what is not. Thus to the extent that the governor articulates for the state those high moral and ethical values fundamental to Western culture, so can he be said to set a political agenda noteworthy for its high standards of public morality and to define for citizens their appropriate responsibilities. This agenda, too, can live long after the end of his administration—particularly if the southern governor emphasizes the responsibility of the state to disadvantaged, disenfranchised, and/or minority groups.

Public Ethics

The last part of the southern governor's political tasks concerns his public ethics, which are actually of a highly personal nature. Just above we considered the demands the governor makes on the public's conscience concerning what is right and wrong as the state plots its future course. Here we refer to demands the governor makes on himself, his family, his staff, and his administration in terms of how their behavior embodies moral and ethical issues. Is he honest? Is his character worthy of the public trust? Does he use the office to pursue his private gain or the public good?

Like the public agenda, the public behavior of the southern governor is not morally neutral. He, too, can demonstrate what kind of behavioral standards are acceptable in the state, not only for public officials but presumably for private citizens as well. Clearly the quality of leadership of a southern governor whose own character, integrity, and behavior are above board can be viewed more favorably than one whose are not.

A Typology of Southern Gubernatorial Leadership

This model has sought to provide a way of understanding and assessing the political leadership provided by southern governors during this century. The office of southern governor exists in a particular political-cultural milieu and socioeconomic environment that shapes what the public expects the office to be and what problems and issues face the incumbent. The office itself, because of the way it is structured and positioned in the state's formal and informal structure of power, provides certain opportunities to, and constraints on, the governor. Several personal factors influence what the individual governor does with the office and how he acts while its incumbent. And the major tasks of the governor can be examined, and his performance in each evaluated, on the basis of how he actually carries them out.

Our task now is to examine the quality of leadership that governors have provided, using the model as the basis for our investigation and evaluation. It is not realistically possible to examine each of the more than two hundred southern governors holding office during this century. Nor is it fundamentally sound to take just a sample of individuals for close study, for it may be that one incorrectly drawn will give an erroneous or misleading view of what southern governors have actually been like.

Fortunately, social science provides a suitable technique for the discussion to go forward. A typology can be constructed that illustrates the major categories or types of leadership which southern governors have demonstrated during this century. Like any typology, this one presents relatively pure types. Specific governors may not always fit neatly into the categories, and of course hybrids are always possible. Still, an examination of southern governors during this century reveals that the typology does represent the major types of southern governors holding office and does provide a convenient way to examine, compare, and contrast them.

The Businessman

In their book on Florida politics, William Havard and Loren Beth commented on the number of so-called Chamber of Commerce governors who have occupied the state's executive office.[15] They meant by this term governors who were relatively conservative, business-oriented individuals whose major preoccupation was in keeping state government out of the way of the business community or, where this aim was not possible, making state government work for it. Not an exciting or flashy group, certainly not given to political crusading and not generally very policy oriented, the

Chamber of Commerce governors were notable for their emphasis on stability and continuity in government.

While Havard and Beth limited their discussion to Florida, in fact their categorization of the state's governors would fit many southern chief executives. The "Businessman" could well be considered the archetypal southern governor, even as another type could be considered the stereotype. There were more Businessmen governors than any other type; Businessmen and their variants probably constitute 60 percent and more of all southern governors in this century.[16] But this preponderance is to be expected in a region in which conservative, business-oriented values were the hallmark of the elites that dominated southern politics for much of this century.

In a moment we shall identify several different variants of Businessmen governors. Let us first, however, briefly examine some of the common characteristics of all of them. As a group, they were conservative and consensus oriented. Most actually came from the ranks of business elites in their states. In those cases where they did not, their political recruitment and socialization patterns usually ensured that by the time they attained the governorship they looked and sounded like business executives. In some states, such as Virginia, North Carolina, Florida, Arkansas, and Texas, it was rare to find a governor not of the Businessman type; but even in the remaining states they were quite common.

As a group, Businessmen tended to have a very limited view of the governor's office. They were there to protect the status quo and the interests of business, not to move the state boldly forward in new directions. Reacting to new or changing situations is, of course, a highly personal trait. But in looking at how Businessmen governors met the challenge of a severe crisis, such as the Depression or a natural calamity like a flood or hurricane, there is little cause for admiration. Most were paralyzed into inaction, whether through lack of imagination, programmatic rigidity, unwillingness to mobilize public resources, or something else.

Dave Sholtz of Florida, for example, actually compounded the impact of the Depression in his state by refusing to use state agencies and resources to keep public services operating. He argued that moneys to pay for them should be collected locally, although he never indicated how collection was to be managed by near bankrupt local governments. The result of his inaction was that Florida schools closed for lengthy periods and thousands of schoolteachers were forced to go on relief.[17]

Stylistically, Businessmen governors tended to be quiet and low key. Not infrequently, they were stolid, even phlegmatic, in their public demeanor. Some, especially of a more pragmatic bent, were consensus-oriented managers. But others were distant, almost abstracted from the day-to-day affairs of state. Ideologically the Businessman was almost always conservative and not interested in upsetting traditional racial policies and practices. Nor was he an advocate of redistributive policies, or even substantial distributive ones, that might alleviate some of the state's poverty. It was precisely the Businessman governor who advocated a limited, "pay-as-you-go" approach to state government. This governor would likely advocate economy and efficiency in government as part of his campaign promises and inaugural speech. He would almost always seek to run government like a business, in terms of the policies and practices he sought. Often these platitudes were mere excuses for doing little or nothing.

These same attitudes and values framed the manner in which the Businessman carried out the tasks of the governorship. Because of their business orientation, they could prove able (if not dynamic) administrators. Many, but by no means all, advocated and practiced a merit system approach to administration. But their demands on the legislature were usually small. Nor, as a group, were the Businessmen governors notable for their impact on the later state agenda; most Florida and Virginia governors, for example, simply reflected what had gone on before and would pass the same agenda along, largely unchanged, to their successors. North Carolina's governors were the only significant group of Businessmen chief executives who actually tried to have a major impact on the state's agenda.

Interestingly, however, one area in which the Businessmen governors had a significant impact was in ambassadorial-symbolic roles. Their conservative attitudes and demeanor often meant that they could appeal successfully to business interests elsewhere in the nation to attract outside capital. In this regard, they had an advantage over some of the other, noisier, gubernatorial types. And the fact that they represented stability and continuity in state government meant that outside investors might well take them seriously; they might not if, on the other hand, the governor was perceived as a rabble-rouser or a crank. A number of North Carolina governors, for example, provide instances in which the business orientation, attitude, and demeanor underscored their legitimacy and appeal as they sought to advance business interests in the state and improve the overall climate for business investment.

Because there were so many Businessmen governors in the South, the range of behaviors and styles was actually quite broad. While most examples fit the general mold fairly well, there are three variants, or subgroups, that deserve special mention.

The first is the classic "Goodtime Charley."[18] This type was the extroverted, sometimes jolly, governor who especially relished the ceremonial parts of his job, such as opening new bridges or crowning homecoming queens. Not infrequently he carried out these tasks with a good deal of panache and publicity. But he was hopelessly lost when he had to face the serious policy, administrative, and legislative tasks the office entailed. He was there to entertain friends, and perhaps reward them with appointments or contracts; the Goodtime Charley not infrequently practiced spoils system administrative politics.

On occasion, this attitude could lead to serious breaches of public ethics or violations of public trust. This was certainly the case with Charley Johns in Florida, whose two years in office were notable for the access that his friends had to the state treasury, and later with Ray Blanton of Tennessee, who had to leave office before his term ended because he was caught selling pardons to prisoners. Not all Goodtime Charleys conducted corrupt administrations, however. Some were merely inept, such as W. Lee "Pappy" O'Daniel in Texas.

A second variant of Businessman governor could best be called the "Ghost." This governor was so reticent about using the force of his office or advocating particular policies that he was scarcely noticeable. This governor could merely be incompetent, such as Fred Cone of Florida, who declined to offer either administrative or legislative leadership while in office. More commonly, however, the Ghost was simply invisible. He might emerge, at times, to offer some commentary on public issues (although it rarely extended beyond platitudes), and he would carry out his obligation to open the legislature by sending a bland message to it. After that, he seemed to disappear. State decisions were made, rather, by important legislators, other state administrators, and representatives of powerful interest groups. Rarely pernicious, rarely beneficial, when a Ghost was in office citizens could wonder whether they even had a governor. And when he left office, they would be hard pressed to identify his legacy or impact on the state's agenda. Quite a number of Arkansas governors fit the Ghost category. Cary Hardee in Florida, elegant figure though he was, was a good example of a Ghost governor; so was Texan Preston Smith.

The last variant of Businessman governor is the "Pragmatist." This governor is the most interesting of the Businessman type. It is also fair to say that while some of the other types of Businessmen governors have largely disappeared in recent decades, the Pragmatist is common now. He may well be a precursor of a wholly different type of southern governor that has been emerging.

Like his Businessmen colleagues, the Pragmatist was essentially a conservative, business-oriented executive. But unlike them, he had a much more active view of the office. For the Pragmatist, the office of governor was more than just ceremony or an excuse to reward friends and supporters.

It presented an opportunity to address public issues and, in some respects, to deal seriously with them. Education is a good example. Other Businessmen governors—Goodtime Charleys and Ghosts—paid little more than lip service to public schools and colleges. But the Pragmatist realized that the future of the state, its economic health, and even his own political standing and reputation depended on substantive accomplishments. Thus the Pragmatist was not adverse to using the force of his office to put forward his own agenda or to accomplish certain policy objectives. Unlike his other Businessmen colleagues, he was neither put off nor frightened by confronting public issues and questions.

This point should not be overstated. Pragmatists were still governors whose approach to public issues was essentially slow and incremental. They were not interested, as a group, in creating new social orders or dramatic change. But, as their name suggests, they had a sense for the future and a sense that government had a role, if only a limited one, in shaping it.

In one state, North Carolina, the Pragmatist governor actually became the most common type for much of this century. As we saw in the last chapter, many Tarheel governors combined hardheaded business sense and conservatism with a willingness to attack public problems. Pragmatists may well have been more prevalent in North Carolina than in other southern states, but they were not unknown elsewhere. George Donaghey in Arkansas, William Sherman Jennings in Florida, Carl Sanders in Georgia, Henry Whitfield in Mississippi, James Byrnes in South Carolina, Gordon Browning and Prentice Cooper in Tennessee, and Mills Godwin and Linwood Holton in Virginia are other examples of this essentially conservative, cautious Businessman governor who cast rather long shadows across their states. In more recent times, Lawton Chiles of Florida is an example of a Pragmatist governor.

The Populist

A second major type of southern governor commonly found in the South during this century was the "Populist." Populists constituted approximately 10–15 percent of southern governors, although it should be remembered that this figure represents an order of magnitude, not an absolute percentage.

As the name suggests, these governors had their roots in Southern populism, a political movement that developed in the United States in the last quarter of the nineteenth century, mainly in the Midwest, and which came to the South in the years following the end of Reconstruction. Although it took a somewhat different form from its midwestern counterpart, southern populism shared with it agrarian values—that is, those rooted in small-town and rural life. Southern populism was fundamentally hostile to the values of urban, industrial life and was especially opposed to the disruption and repression of rural life brought on by banks, railroads, and other large commercial or industrial aggregations of capital. In this attitude, of course, there was considerable justification. Railroads and banks were notorious, late in the nineteenth century, for the way in which their business practices ravaged the countryside and ruined the lives of human beings.

Southern populism was essentially an agrarian movement whose base rested on the rural poor. While it involved small-town residents, it included farmers, even tenants and sharecroppers, as well. For a time it actually included blacks as part of the political coalition; as such it was essentially a social class movement rather than a racial one. After the 1890s, however, blacks were eliminated from the coalition and even became its scapegoats through the imposition of Jim Crow laws.[19] It was, nonetheless, very much a movement of the common man, aimed not only at undermining the excesses of the industrial-capitalist system that was "crucifying" him (to paraphrase William Jennings Bryan) but in some respects to glorify him as the custodian of traditional American values and verities.

The southern Populist governor reflected this political tradition. As V.O. Key noted, on occasion a populist candidate would emerge in one or another of the states, often but not always from the hill country—the part of the region where small farmers and towns predominated—and opposed to the Bourbons and "big mules" of the plantation, business, industrial, and commercial South.[20] Not infrequently, they were noisy individuals, promising much to aid the common man by changing, even revolutionizing, the system that oppressed him through greater state regulation of banks and utilities (including the railroads), introduction of workers' compensation and other forms of social insurance, more equitable tax structures, provision of better roads, bridges, and schools, and so forth.

Populists as diverse as Jeff Davis and Sid McMath in Arkansas; "Pa" and "Ma" Ferguson in Texas, and perhaps "Pappy" O'Daniel as well; Huey Long, his brother Earl, and songwriter Jimmy Davis in Louisiana; "Big Jim" Folsom and the early (and late) George Wallace in Alabama;[21] and Napoleon Broward and Fuller Warren in Florida, among others—all reflected these ideas, in varying degrees, as they sought the governorship and once they were in office. Few, however, were successful in implementing their plans. Some were so politically inept or so much alienated parts of the political system through their antics that their base of support was eroded, like the Fergusons. Some were co-opted by powerful interests or essentially sold out to them. Others fought the system that they railed against, such as McMath, but it proved too intransigent to move; some gave up in frustration, and at least one, Jim Folsom, tried to find solace in alcohol.[22]

As a group, the Populist governors had an active view of their office. They recognized that other institutions of state government were firmly in the hands of powerful economic and political interests that were not necessarily reflective of the needs of common people. Thus the Populist governor recognized that he had the responsibility to act in a vigorous way to rein in the excesses of an exploitive capitalist system. Most attempted to do so; whether they acted skillfully or wisely is another matter.

The style of these Populist governors could be overbearing and abrasive: Huey and Earl Long were not known for their tact, and "Pa" Ferguson seemed out of control to many Texans. "Big Jim" Folsom, who referred to himself as the friend of the little man, employed a cacophonous hillbilly band to accompany his campaign, and it seemed to exemplify his political style. He himself had an enormous personality and outgoing manner. Even early in his career George Wallace projected some of the insolence and anger he later used to great political advantage.

Yet the Populists were not always loud, ornery, or colorful. Fuller Warren was noted for his smooth, articulate, mannerly style, and Jimmy Carter, while maintaining a veneer of "country," was sophisticated and cosmopolitan, as at home in the corporate boardrooms and country clubs of Atlanta as on the peanut farms of Plains.

It is in their ideology that Populist governors were the most interesting. Most of them championed the cause of the South's poor, rural population. A number of them seemed genuinely interested in creating some government mechanisms to check the power of large corporations and to find ways of relieving the plight caused by southern poverty. Certainly this was true of the early Huey Long, his brother Earl, Folsom, Davis and McMath of Arkansas, and a few others.

But the concern of the Populists was, almost universally, with the white population exclusively. In contrast to the first southern populists, they did not seek to build biracial coalitions. They espoused and advocated the racial attitudes characteristic of other southern politicians. Until recent years, no Populist tried to undo Jim Crow laws and practices. Many, in fact, were virulent racists. It is well to remember that populism comes in many forms, some of it nativist, xenophobic, bigoted, and extremely right wing; other forms of populism can be more moderate, even leftist; the thread that ties the various forms together is the emphasis on everyday people as opposed to privileged elites and the way in which the populist appeals to and embodies the politics of anger, rage, and protest.[23]

The exclusive concern for whites, and not blacks, is a matter of some speculation. It no doubt reflected the racial destiny of southern populism. Disillusioned southern populists, including the movement's leader, Tom

Watson of Georgia, eventually bitterly denounced blacks as the root of southern and populist failings. Having heard this time and again from fathers and grandfathers, many of the twentieth-century Populist governors reflected the same views. Moreover, even though many grew up in the hill country, racism was still a way of life, and thus their racial attitudes were a product of early socialization. Also, these governors were politicians as well as Populists, and they understood that to be considered legitimate in a racist political system and to have a chance at being elected, they had to espouse normal southern racial attitudes.

But there were enough prominent exceptions to suggest that there was a gossamerlike thread running through southern populism linking race and poverty as they had been at the movement's origin. Some Populist governors recognized that an attack on regional poverty had to include blacks as well as whites if the ongoing waste of southern human resources was to stop. They could not articulate the issue in quite this way, for to do so would have meant defeat at the polls. But their emphasis on economic issues and their refusal to engage in the usual southern race-baiting suggest that they had a view of the crucial link between race and poverty. This insight was characteristic of both Longs. "Big Jim" Folsom thought most of the segregationist saber-rattling in the Alabama legislature was a waste of time and misleading to citizens. Fuller Warren was the first Florida governor to welcome black visitors to the Governor's Mansion and personally endorsed an "unmasking" law making Ku Klux Klan activity more difficult. And Jimmy Carter surprised everyone in Georgia by articulating a new racial and economic opportunity vision for the state in his inaugural address.

Few of the Populist governors had distinguished records in either administrative or legislative tasks. Most were more notable for their failures and shortcomings than for their successes. The reason is that most came into office with limited political experience. Also, they were often perceived as outsiders, not a part of the "good old boy" network (unless, like Huey Long and George Wallace, they became powerful enough to redefine it, with themselves at the center). They did not have the political power base among state and county officials to make themselves effective administrators and legislators. Often, in fact, they seemed to be more at odds with other politicians than to be their allies, largely because of their opposition to traditional power blocs.

However, Populist governors were able to make their mark on southern politics through their symbolic and agenda-setting gubernatorial tasks. They were not always good ambassadors, since both politicians and commercial interests elsewhere in the nation were often nervous about the message of populism. On the other hand, Populists did represent the cause of the poor, or at least the white poor. Without the occasional appearance of a Populist governor, it is not clear that this part of the southern population would ever have had spokesmen in state capitals.

This is not to suggest that the eventual adoption by southern states of many populist ideas was exclusively a result of Populist administrations. Regulation of corporations and railroads, workers' compensation, improved schools and roads, and other parts of the populist agenda, also came about because of action by the federal government, the influence of other states, and even incremental changes in the South itself. Nonetheless, Populist governors laid out a set of issues that southern states eventually had to face, unwilling though many powerful interests may have been to do so. In this sense, the impact and effect of their administrations were strong.

As was the case with Businessmen governors, not all Populists were the same. We can distinguish between two main groups, which, for convenience, we can call "Classic" and "Modern" Populists.

Classic Populist governors articulated the concerns of everyday citizens of the state against the power of corporations and wealthy, private interests. But they were virtually always supporters of the traditional, segregated, southern society. Not infrequently they were vicious racists. And, as George Wallace discovered after his first unsuccessful run for the governorship, it was often necessary to place race at the forefront of a populist agenda just to get elected.[24]

Jimmy Carter of Georgia is perhaps the best example of the Modern Populist governor.[25] While his campaign themes expressed a populist message, the true mark of his modern populism came in his inaugural address. He boldly announced that the time of racial discrimination was over. Georgia, he felt, was obliged to overcome its past and create a state of equal opportunity for both blacks and whites. In his administration he sought, through appointments, policy statements, and legislative proposals, to act on his inaugural blueprint. The effect of his actions was to forge a black-white political coalition in the state that has strongly influenced its politics ever since.

Carter, in a sense, created a modern form of populism which included people of both races. He was echoed in this by a number of other Modern Populists, including Reubin Askew and later "Walkin' Lawton" Chiles of Florida, the unsuccessful gubernatorial candidates Brailey Odham of Florida and Henry Howell in Virginia, William Winter in Mississippi (who was elected to office), and even George Wallace who, in his last administration (1983–87), appeared to return to his early populist leanings, and who advocated a far more racially equitable society than might have been expected of him.

Modern Populist governors have been concerned with more than race, however. They are less hostile to corporations and other aggregations of wealth than were their earlier colleagues; some, such as Carter, had business experience and even secured corporate support for their candidacies, as did Edwin Edwards in Louisiana. But they still tend to favor government regulation of banks, insurance companies, and utilities. Also, like Reubin Askew, they have supported consumer and environmental protection as an additional check on the excesses of industry and commerce.

Thus in some ways the Modern Populists have expanded the state's political agenda well beyond that of the Classic Populists. While their political style may seem rather conventional compared to that of their predecessors, they may also seem less like political outsiders to other politicians. In the long run, this position will prove helpful to the programs they espouse, especially if they continue to speak for the "little people" who often seem forgotten in state capitals.

The Demagogue

The "Demagogue" may represent, to the popular mind, the stereotypical southern politician. Portly, sweating, wearing red galluses and a broad-brimmed Panama, the Demagogue was noted for his oratorical skills and his ability to mesmerize his audience as he spoke, whether from a stump in a hot, dusty courthouse square or in a more formal setting. Here could be found the "essence" of southern gothic politics—fire and brimstone oratory, rabble-rousing, fighting words, an emotionally charged message. It was grand theater to southerners and nonsoutherners alike, operatic in every respect. It is no surprise that Hollywood and New York found Demagogues a rich source of material for movies and, later, television.[26]

Like many stereotypes, there is some truth in this popular image. But it is not the case that they represented the major type of southern governor. Indeed, probably only about 10 percent of all southern governors in this century were true Demagogues, although it is also true that significant numbers of others engaged, at times, in demagogic behavior. But the smoke and fire they created, and the visibility they had, made them seem more numerous than they were. Their influence extended far beyond their limited numbers, for they actually defined the substance and boundaries of southern political rhetoric and behavior for about two-thirds of this century.

Who were the major southern Demagogue governors? The list is one of famous (or infamous and notorious) characters: James Vardaman and Theodore "The Man" Bilbo in Mississippi (and a few others in this state who did not quite reach their level, such as Fielding Wright, Ross Barnett and John Bell Williams), Orval Faubus in Arkansas, John Patterson and the 1963–82 George Wallace in Alabama, Strom Thurmond in South Carolina, the Talmadges and Marvin Griffin in Georgia (some might include Lester Maddox as well, but as Marshall Frady shows, he was more of an inept Populist than Demagogue once he succeeded to the governorship), perhaps Buford Ellington and Ray Blanton in Tennessee, and Sidney Catts and Claude Kirk in Florida.[27]

Some have referred to Huey Long as a Demagogue, although as Harry Williams and others suggest, this characterization is not accurate, for he was far more complex than most of these other figures; so was his brother Earl.[28] Robert Kennon and Jimmy Davis in Louisiana each engaged in demagogic behavior at times, as occasionally did Edwin Edwards, but Kennon was probably essentially a Businessman variant, and both Davis and Edwards fundamentally Populists. Virginia, North Carolina, and Texas never really had full-blown Demagogues as governors, although Jim "Pa" Ferguson may have come close.[29]

Were Demagogues found throughout the South? While most of the states had at least one "classic" Demagogue, in fact Demagogues were more likely to be found in the deep South states. The reason is that in the deep South traditional patterns of racial prejudice, which Demagogues sought to exploit, were most ingrained. Also, in general for much of this century the deep South states had the most poverty, the smallest middle class, and the lowest levels of industrialization and urbanization. It is significant that Demagogues almost always came from rural areas and that the appeals they made found a greater response there than in southern cities.

There were other governors, including in border states, who engaged in demagoguery as the political situation and their preferences warranted. Malcolm Patterson in Tennessee, and Farris Bryant and Haydon Burns in Florida are examples, although each was essentially a type of Businessman governor. Also, there was no shortage of demagogic candidates for the southern governorship, but who failed to win the office. Thus, in contrast to the conventional wisdom about southern politics, it was not the case that a Demagogue automatically won the election.

There is a gray area between Classic Populist and Demagogue southern governors: Lester Maddox is perhaps the best recent example of this blurring of the boundaries. In many ways the classic southern Demagogues shared Populist concerns about the plight of the "little man." But it is precisely at this point that the two types begin to diverge.

Unlike the Classic Populists, some of whom had a complex, sophisticated vision of society, Demagogues were essentially unidimensional and had a fundamentally simplistic notion of social cause and effect. Demagogues laid the blame for the southern condition on blacks (and, to a lesser extent, Yankees). For the Demagogue, the causes of southern misery, poverty, economic exploitation, and illiteracy were easily understood. Blacks caused them, because of biological inferiority (and accompanying moral baseness) and because they exerted a terrible drain on the life, spirit, and resources of the white South. They dragged whites down to their level, imprisoning them in their degradation, or so the message went. Were southern whites to be freed from the burden of black southerners, so might their chances improve for a better life.

There was, of course, a bitter irony here. Demagogues argued that it was whites who were the victims of oppression, not blacks. Demagogues and demagogic rhetoric held that blacks actually "enslaved" whites and caused them misery, the historical record of slavery to the contrary notwithstanding.

This point was crucial for southern Demagogues, for it allowed them to make a convincing argument in favor of ever-greater measures of discrimination against blacks. These steps were essential to "southern" progress. Only through more exploitation and greater repression against blacks could white southerners hope to secure a better life. Blacks had to remain targets of hatred, bigotry, and discrimination and to be held continually in check, for if they were not, then they would seek to break out of their "place" and become an even greater burden for southern whites.

The question may arise, especially to the modern reader, as to why this message was effective. Did anyone actually believe this stuff? The answer is that Demagogues understood that rural, ill-educated, poverty-stricken white southerners, socialized into a culture of racial prejudice and a mythology of a "glorious past" destroyed by the presence of blacks and Yankee intruders, wanted and needed to hear it. These people sought escape, explanations, and causes of their historical downfall and present misery. Targets for their frustration and victims of their anger were essential. Demagogues showed these targets, and more, to them: they justified acts of discrimination, repression, even violence, against a weak, defenseless, vulnerable population.

The essence of the classic demagogic message, then, may strike modern readers as morally bankrupt and reprehensible. But politically it proved effective, for it played on the fears and instincts of a white population that knew no better and that found release and escape from its condition in the rowdiness and excitement of the Demagogues' message.

In the end, Demagogues were most notorious for their cynical willingness to suspend the rules and norms of democratic government. They denied the basic tenets on which democratic government is based—equality, legitimacy, and accountability. Indeed, they denied the basic dignity of human beings, both blacks and whites, for their manipulation of prejudice and hatred is a clear indication of their basic contempt for human life.

In somewhat less abstract terms, Demagogues were also notable for the extent of authoritarianism in their administrations, which also forced a suspension of democratic principles. Private views of their role as governor superseded conceptions of the public good or adherence to democratic rules. It is on this point that Huey Long has been accused of being a Demagogue. While in no way condoning the strong-arm tactics of Huey Long's administration, it is also true that he had a vision of the future, a justification for his heavy-handed use of power in terms of his fervent desire to modernize his state, and a record of substantive accomplishment. Most southern Demagogues had none of these. Rather, they looked backward to an imaginary past and tried to recreate it through smoke screens, mirrors, and bigotry rather than by making serious efforts to deal with the problems of their state and region.

While Demagogues often built considerable personal followings, they were precisely that—personal, not institutional. Most had no real interest in building bridges to other political actors or creating coalitions that would have improved the process of governmental activity. As a group, the Demagogue governors, while often dynamic and exciting to watch, had few substantive outcomes beyond finding additional ways to discriminate against blacks. Indeed their words spoke much louder than their deeds.

As administrators, many Demagogue governors tended toward the spoils system approach to governing. Often they used the office solely to reward their families, friends, and supporters through patronage. Sidney Catts's excesses in this regard are legendary. Some were merely inept administrators. Mississippi's Theodore Bilbo managed to bankrupt the state treasury while he was in office, and there were numerous complaints from legislators, other state executives, and even his own staff that George Wallace was unable, or unwilling, to attend to the administrative tasks of his job.

What distinguished the Demagogues most from other southern governors was their style and ideology. After all, there were other southern chief executives who had few legislative accomplishments and whose administrative performance was abysmal or worse.

The boisterous, cacophonous, often entertaining style Demagogues affected was designed to excite fundamentally apathetic people. The gallus-snapping, wild rhetoric of a Gene Talmadge and the dark angry intensity of a George Wallace and Orval Faubus were designed to have their listeners react emotionally, and to focus on form rather than substance. There seemed to be no end to the rhetorical bigotry, meanness, or anger which Demagogues used. Bilbo, for example, referred to blacks as "apes" on more than one occasion, and other Demagogues used similar words. In the late 1950s and 1960s, when such excesses of vocabulary were still to be heard in the unregenerate, unreconstructed deep South, demagogic governors had "fun" with acronyms such as NAACP and SCLC, as they sought to play upon the racial fears and prejudices of their listeners.

Just as they often maintained an energetic, perpetual-motion style, so too did Demagogues possess a rigid ideology. For them, social cause and effect were easy to comprehend. Issues were, quite literally, black and white. They offered and tolerated no middle ground, no alternative explanations for understanding social phenomena. But it was precisely because they held deeply to this unidimensional view of the southern world that they could reduce political discussion to terms that appealed to downtrodden, poverty-stricken white farmers.

Not all southerners were convinced, however. Some, especially the more genteel middle and upper classes, were merely appalled at the vulgarities and incivilities of the Demagogue. But for others, he represented a real political danger.[30] The personal followings Demagogues created were often viewed as unruly mobs that could threaten the economic and social position of southern elites. Some even worried that the excesses of the Demagogues and their followers, particularly lynchings and other acts of terror, would not be tolerated by Washington or the rest of the country. If that occurred, they feared, the federal government might begin to intervene into southern affairs in ways that it had not done since the end of Reconstruction. There was even the danger that the army of occupation might return.

Thus it was not unusual for middle- and upper-class southerners to oppose Demagogues or at least to try to isolate or co-opt them. These southerners preferred the quieter, more malleable politics of the Businessman governor. In a sense, they were lucky. Many Demagogues proved inept politicians, at least in terms of their ability to function with other actors to carry out their goals. Others simply sold out to dominant interests and even if they continued their noisy rhetoric they did little to oppose them. Vardaman, Bilbo, and Thurmond, for example, actually became spokesmen for powerful economic interests after they became members of the U.S. Senate.

Did the Demagogues affect the future agenda of southern politics? Most assuredly. The reason is that demagogic governors established and maintained race as the principal currency of southern politics. By focusing on the mythical southern past and its present social burden, Demagogues helped define the substance and limits of political discussion for much of this century. They defined what was right and legitimate in politics. To be "soft" on race was to be unsouthern, even communistic, both of which violated the test of acceptability in the South. It took the upheaval of the civil rights movement and the power of the federal government to begin to undo the southern agenda that Demagogues established.

Has the southern Demagogue become an extinct species? There are few, if any, to be found in the 1970s, 1980s, and 1990s, at least in the classic sense described here. Increasing education and sophistication of the population, increasing urbanization and industrialization, a more affluent economy—all these things militate against the appearance of another Gene Talmadge. More important, the presence of a large black vote in the South also discourages classic demagoguery: overt racial appeals cost black votes and alienate important segments of the white community, especially business and commercial interests, who do not wish to turn back the clock. Moreover, the coolness and detachment of television, as a political medium, discourage the flamboyant style of the older Demagogues: long-winded, histrionic rabble-rousing does not work on a fifteen- or thirty-second campaign "spot."

On the other hand, modern demagoguery can be more than just racial appeals. It now can refer to simpleminded, emotional, irresponsible approaches to serious but controversial public questions—for example, abortion reform, gun control, death penalties, nuclear power, and environment protection. These are still in evidence in southern gubernatorial politics. Appeals to racial prejudice are still a part of the southern political scene as well; they may involve using code phrases ("forced busing," "welfare cheats," "crack queens," for example), and the style might be more subdued than Bilbo's or Wallace's, but the effect can still be insidious and hurtful. Thus, even if the classic Demagogue has disappeared from the southern political stage, demagoguery has not. Perhaps the modern figure who comes closest to this traditional style is David Duke in Louisiana. It may be that its practitioners have traded their galluses and broad-brimmed Panamas for dark suits and wing-tip shoes, but the possibility continues to exist that demagogic political figures, including governors, will reappear in the South.

The Policymaker

The last type of southern governor to be discussed is called the "Policymaker." While only about 10 percent of southern governors fall into this category, they have had an important impact on the South. Like their demagogic colleagues, they sometimes attracted national attention. But their reputation was less a result of colorful antics or vicious racism than of vigorous, sometimes courageous, leadership.

The Policymaker saw the governor's office in terms of its impact on public questions and issues. His goal was to address public needs, to define problems requiring solutions, and to propose appropriate steps for them. For the most part, Policymakers had a very active, bold view of their office. Many were restless individuals who sought out new areas of gubernatorial activity and tried to expand the power and prestige of the office which they held.

There is a gray area between the Pragmatist variant of Businessman governor and the Policymaker. The former, it will be recalled, also concerned himself with policy issues, albeit in a fairly limited way. The Policymaker has to be regarded primarily as a problem solver and architect of public policy. The difference between the two, however, is more than just one of degree. The Policymaker is much more willing to take chances, to make bold political choices, and to set his sites on more distant, even lofty, goals than the Pragmatist. One result of this vision was that while the Pragmatist often enjoyed a substantial reputation during his own administration, sometimes the Policymaker did not. The reason is that he tested and pushed the limits of political acceptability and sometimes got too far out in front of what citizens felt appropriate.

Also notable about the Policymaker is his sense that the office represents a tremendous sense of public responsibility. While Pragmatists and other Businessmen may also have felt this way, their view tended to be much more limited about how far this responsibility extended. Populists and Demagogues, of course, had an extremely narrow, even personal, view of the office. "Older" Policymakers such as Charles Aycock and J.C.B. Ehringhaus of North Carolina, Austin Peay of Tennessee, Millard Caldwell of Florida, Ross Sterling of Texas, as well as more recent Policymakers, were willing to mobilize the resources of the governorship to bear on the issues they felt important. While all suffered defeats, sometimes substantial ones, they were notable for the clarity and power of their vision and their desire to realize it.

Stylistically, Policymakers generally shared the public demeanor of Businessmen governors. But even relatively quiet behavior could not mask their intensity of feeling or leadership. Often enormous storms of controversy accompanied their speeches and actions, not because of the way they did things but because of what they proposed. Whether it was the moral disapproval of Aycock, LeRoy Collins, or Frank Clement at the racial posturing struck by their fellow politicians, the boldness of the educational reforms proposed by Caldwell or Lamar Alexander, the environmental protection measures of Reubin Askew, Jim Hunt, or Richard Riley, the innovative tax measures of Buddy Roemer, or something else, the conflict and divisiveness of proposals were in stark contrast to their often mild gubernatorial style.

The concept of ideology, as used in this book, also developed greater breadth with Policymakers. Caldwell, for example, was one of the most politically conservative governors of Florida during this century. Yet it was precisely this conservatism that enabled him to propose bold new programs and sell them to the state; he was always seen as a member of Florida's political establishment, not some sort of nut. This was also true of governors such as Ellis Arnall in Georgia, and several North Carolina governors such as Terry Sanford. Winthrop Rockefeller, Lamar Alexander, William Winter, Charles Robb, Jim Hunt, Richard Riley, Reubin Askew,[31] Bob Graham, Joe Frank Harris, Zell Miller, Buddy Roemer, Ray Mabus, and Ann Richards, among others, while not liberal by national standards, nonetheless advocated substantial development in policies such as education and social services that represented a larger state investment than had existed previously.

It may be that the Policymakers, as a group, represent a unique kind of southern political ideology that we might call "moderate progressivism."[32] It refers to a set of ideas and values in which these governors were willing to use the force of their office to the benefit of citizens who needed help. They also saw that investment in matters such as education, conservation, environmental protection, and public health were not drains on state resources but rather represented appropriate investments for the future. Even older moderate progressives, such as Aycock, Peay, and Caldwell, who shared many traditional southern attitudes on race and poverty, refused to engage in race-baiting. Thus moderate progressivism, even as an ideology found occasionally earlier in this century, included the idea that blacks as well as whites could benefit from public policy. Later many Policymaker governors actually made poor whites and blacks the center of their policy initiatives.

On the other hand, moderate progressivism and many Policymaker southern governors were financially very conservative. Most were fiscal hard-liners even as they sought to improve governmental services. Most also retained conservative, traditionally southern views on family matters and morality and an attachment to time and place.[33] But the difference between Policymakers and other governors with these attitudes was that for Policymakers, these conservative attitudes did not serve as an excuse for doing nothing. Rather, they could find ways of preserving what was good and valuable about southern traditions even while they sought to shape the future.

Moreover, it should be emphasized that Policymaker governors and other southern moderate progressives were truly politicians, and none wished to be a political martyr. They recognized the necessity of functioning in a political environment and achieving their goals through political means. Thus William Winter's desire to rebuild the Mississippi Democratic Party by building a coalition with blacks may well have been based in his long-standing commitment to racial equality. But it was also good politics, because it was the only way for him and other Democrats in the state to have a chance at winning in a state with rapidly developing Republicanism.

While some Policymaker governors were effective administrators, it was not because of their administrative abilities or interests that most achieved prominence. More important were legislative proposals and accomplishments. As problem solvers and architects of public policy, they spent a good deal of time shaping legislative proposals and negotiating with legislators, other state officials interest and clientele groups, and local officials to seek their ends. Often, too, Policymakers tried to reach out to the public to shape public opinion and expand the limits of public acceptability, as they shaped their proposals.

However, the legislative record and batting average of the Policymakers are, at best, mixed. Even the most effective in dealing with legislators met with defeat, while some, such as LeRoy Collins, saw few major proposals on race relations, constitutional reform, and reapportionment accepted.

Why there is a disparity and why even the best Policymakers met with resounding defeat deserve comment. In some respects the disparity resulted from varying legislative skills. Bob Graham, for example, while experienced as a state legislator, seemed unable to communicate effectively with his former colleagues in his first two years in office; later, after modifying his approach, he became very successful. Lamar Alexander entered office as a consensus candidate after the excesses of Ray Blanton and worked from the outset to include legislators in shaping his educational reforms. Some, like Caldwell, were good at "hardball politics": he locked legislators in sweltering chambers during a special session held in a Tallahassee summer to get them to "agree" on a reapportionment bill.

Partisanship and factionalism may also have influenced the Policymaker's legislative success, or lack of it. Rockefeller, for example, was a Republican (and a Yankee), in a predominantly rural Democratic state, and was often frustrated. Alexander, also a Republican, had no such problems because of his willingness to forge legislative coalitions. Collins, while marrying into an old, establishment, political family, eventually became alienated from some of his own coalition because of his position on race and other issues.

The circumstances of election and the ensuing mandate received by the governor, as well as personal factors, also influenced his legislative success. Both Alexander and Askew entered office following eccentric, erratic predecessors; the public seemed to want them to clean things up and move ahead with state business. Both had considerable legislative success. The southern backlash to the civil rights movement seemed to sour the atmosphere in which Collins tried to steer a moderate course, limiting his effectiveness. Events in the form of a collapsing oil economy also seemed to overwhelm Republican Bill Clements and Democrat Mark White in Texas, to the extent that neither quite achieved Policymaker status, although their personal styles (Clements overbearing and abrasive, White reticent) contributed to their difficulties. Indeed, economic factors seem important in fostering the emergence of Policymakers; during periods of economic boom, last seen in the South during the late 1970s and through the 1980s, it was relatively easy for a governor to position himself as a Policymaker, while during the fiscal retrenchment of the 1990s, fewer Policymakers have actually emerged in the South.

Perhaps most important in determining the Policymakers' legislative batting average was the nature of the proposals they made. By design they were often bold and controversial. To the extent that the governor was an effective salesman to the state and could negotiate and deal with other actors, including the media, interest groups, and public, so did his chances of success improve. Some governors, such as Alexander and Graham, proved adept at linking their proposals to traditional conservative interests and agendas. But other governors, such as Collins, Roemer, and Mabus, found themselves too far in front of what was acceptable and suffered defeats as a result.

As important as were their concrete policy accomplishments, it may be that the most significant, long-lasting contribution that Policymakers made to their states was in the area of agenda setting. As a group, they spent considerable time and energy creating a future vision of the state and seeking to begin to achieve it.

Not infrequently, this vision was painted in highly moralistic terms. Policymakers often talked in terms of choices states had to make, about their state's need to commit resources to do what was right and not simply easy or expedient. LeRoy Collins provides a good example, especially when he went on radio to discuss with Floridians his feeling that it was morally wrong to discriminate against blacks.[34]

But Policymakers, because they were politicians, could not limit themselves to the power of moral suasion. Rather, as a group they had a long-term impact on the state's agenda because they could recognize what issues were truly important in the state and whose resolution could only be delayed so long before a crisis was reached. Public education was perhaps the most notable issue on this list, but it also included other services, economic development, tax reform, conservation and environmental protection, ethics and accountability in government, and aid to local governments.

Thus, there was a certain inevitability about the agenda-setting impact of

Policymakers. This is not to say that what they wanted would have eventually happened anyway. Rather, Policymakers had the ability to understand the political realities and problems of their states and had the conviction, even courage, to articulate what could be done about them. Sometimes this conviction involved talking about issues and solutions in ways that were unpopular. Nonetheless, the passing of time and subsequent events continued to prove that Policymakers' insights were correct.

The Quality of Leadership: An Assessment

Having examined the major types of southern governors, can we legitimately ask if one is better than the others? This is a very difficult matter, even if we limit the criteria to the central concern of this book—the changing ability of southern political institutions (in this case, the governorship) to deal with traditional problems of race and poverty. Because this text does not deal specifically with outcomes, it is hard to know what the real impact of governors has been on these problems. Nonetheless, if we ask which governors have been willing to address these problems and mobilize the resources of the state on their behalf, then it is possible to rank-order the different types of governors.

Policymakers have undoubtedly done the most in this regard. This primacy is not necessarily only a result of substantive policy accomplishments, which, as we noted, were not always great. The Policymaker is also in first position as a result of his ability to establish a state agenda of concern for real issues, including those of race and poverty.

The Pragmatist form of Businessman governor would probably rank next. While not especially policy oriented, neither was this governor indifferent to public questions and issues or to the problems of his state. Some of the more perspicacious Pragmatists could recognize the inevitability of the need to seek new solutions to state problems and the necessity to move the state forward to prevent later crises. Governors such as Henry Whitfield of Mississippi, James Byrnes of South Carolina, Gordon Browning and Prentice Cooper of Tennessee, Carl Sanders and George Busbee of Georgia, William Sherman Jennings and Lawton Chiles of Florida, Price Daniel and John Connally of Texas, and Linwood Holton and Ted Dalton in Virginia, among others, fit this mold.

The Businessman governor could play an important role as a consolidating force after a period of reform or modernization. While not innovators in their own right, they could nonetheless help situate new programs into the regular business of the state and make them more acceptable and legitimate to citizens. Thus even though they did not break new ground in attacking problems of race and poverty, among other issues, at least some Business-men governors did not necessarily turn their attention away from them or try to undo previous state efforts to cope with them. Governors William Kitchin and Luther Hodges in North Carolina are good examples of the legitimizing role Businessmen governors could play.

Not all Businessmen governors were like this, however. Some did little or nothing to alleviate the problems of race and poverty in their states, or even made matters worse, such as Governors Farris Bryant and Haydon Burns in Florida, and Robert Kennon in Louisiana. Some of the Modern Populists, such as Jimmy Carter in Georgia, Mark White in Texas, Earl Long and Edwin Edwards in Louisiana, and Sid McMath in Arkansas, actually rank significantly higher than these Businessmen governors in their concern for, and attention to, problems of race and poverty.

But the older, Classic Populists do not rank as high as their modern counterparts, and actually rank with or below many Businessmen governors. The reason is that many, if not most, were overt racists. Their concern with the poor was limited to the white population. Also, a number of Populist governors, such as Fuller Warren in Florida and "Ma" Ferguson in Texas, were such poor politicians that they were isolated and ineffective in office. They had little substantive or agenda-setting impact on the state. While many Businessmen governors also had little of this impact, most could carry out their ambassadorial roles more effectively than Classic Populists.

From the standpoint of the criteria used here, Demagogues demonstrated the poorest-quality leadership in the South. It must be emphasized that they were not always ineffective. Obviously governors such as Gene Talmadge and George Wallace were effective in terms of acquiring substantial mass followings. But Demagogues did not mobilize resources on behalf of the poor and oppressed of the state; they exploited them. Some Demagogues, such as Sidney Catts and Theodore Bilbo, were merely incompetent. But the result was that while the occasional Demagogue may have raised the hopes and expectations of penurious white farmers, he seldom delivered. Each disappointment contributed to the apathy, frustration, alienation, and cynicism that lay at the core of southern attitudes about politics, especially in the deep South. Indeed, Demagogues did not offer solutions; they were very much a part of the southern political problem.

New Leadership: The Rise of the Modern Southern Governor

Has there been any change, in recent years, in the types of southern gover-nors who have emerged? The answer is that if we use 1960 as a rough break point between old and new style southern politics, there is a considerable difference between the two. Indeed, the break with the past is so significant that it is possible to conclude with an optimistic view of the future of gubernatorial leadership in the region.

In the first sixty years of this century, most of the governors in the South were Businessmen types, including Goodtime Charleys and Ghosts. Relatively few were Pragmatists. Occasionally a Populist appeared, and while Demagogues were actually few in number, most appeared early in this period, and their noise and impact made them seem more numerous than they were. Only a handful of southern governors prior to 1960—probably less than a dozen—could be called Policymakers.

As the discussion in this chapter has suggested, Pragmatists and Policymakers in more recent times have become fairly common. Indeed, they may now constitute the major type of southern governor in the last part of this century. The more traditional Businessman governor is also still found, such as Bob Martinez of Florida, Bill Clements of Texas, Kirk Fordice of Mississippi, Guy Hunt of Alabama, and Carroll Campbell of South Carolina. But even these governors have become more policy oriented than their predecessors, even if they have not bought into the ideology of moderate progressivism as much as their Pragmatist and Policymaker colleagues. Goodtime Charleys and Ghosts have all but disappeared.[35] The old variety of racist Populist is also gone (Lester Maddox was probably the last one), to be replaced by the modern variety of Populist represented by Jimmy Carter, Edwin Edwards, and Mark White. And while demagoguery is still possible, the classic southern Demagogue is strictly a museum piece, as V.O. Key might say.[36]

Why should this development have happened? Our search for explanations begins with World War II and its aftermath. The war years were important to the southern governorship. Demands were placed on governors for devising civil defense plans, providing military facilities, and in other ways mobilizing the population behind the war effort. The effect was to raise the level of visibility and public expectations of the office. This enhancement was in stark contrast to the Depression years, when southern governors seemed to go into an eclipse.

Demands on and public expectations of the southern governorship continued in post–World War II years. They took two forms. In the deep South, governors were pushed to find ways to protect traditional southern ways, as Jim Crow laws and longtime southern racial practices started to come under attack from Washington. In the border South, these were somewhat less important than the demands placed on the governor by the rapid demographic changes occurring from massive migration into the region after the war. Governors were expected to plan for and help states cope with these developments.

Thus the southern governorship by 1960 emerged as a far more central, visible, politically sensitive office than it had been prior to the War. In each southern state, governors were forced to deal, either reactively or proactively, with race and growth. The effect was to strengthen the southern governorship.

But, as Earl Black has demonstrated, it was the decline, not the rise, of racial issues that really created the greatest impetus for the rise of the modern southern governorship.[37] Because of the 1964 Civil Rights Act and 1965 Voting Rights Act, southern politics changed forever. Racial issues no longer constituted the currency of southern gubernatorial politics. Rather than castigate blacks, governors had to court them to win. Demagogic appeals no longer were appropriate or effective.

The effect of these achievements of the civil rights movement was to free southern governors and gubernatorial candidates from the shackles of the past. They no longer were chained to the old rhetoric and posturing needed to win elections or succeed in office. Instead, perhaps for the first time in the twentieth century, governors could focus on real problems of their states and regions— poverty, health, education, environmental protection, economic development, crime, governmental accountability, responsiveness, and ethics, and so forth.

The change was immediate and noticeable. Even governors caught on the cusp of the changes had to alter their political style and message. But others, such as Winthrop Rockefeller, Dale Bumpers, David Pryor, and Bill Clinton in Arkansas, Reubin Askew and Bob Graham in Florida, Jimmy Carter, George Busbee, and Zell Miller in Georgia, Edwin Edwards and Buddy Roemer in Louisiana, William Winter and Ray Mabus in Mississippi, Robert Scott and Jim Hunt in North Carolina, John West and Richard Riley in South Carolina, Lamar Alexander and Ned McWherter in Tennessee, Ann Richards in Texas, and Ted Dalton and Charles Robb in Virginia, among others, seized the opportunity presented to move their states forward with elaborate agendas that had nothing to do with old racial ways but in fact often promised ever greater levels of racial equality and economic improvement. Even George Wallace, who dominated Alabama for more than twenty years, abandoned his racial demagoguery and at the end of his career returned to the populist agenda that marked his initial foray into state politics in 1958.

There were other forces that also helped propel the southern governorship forward into a modern political institution and facilitated the emergence of active, vigorous governors. Increasing federal programs in the 1960s and 1970s, for example, aided the governorship. Once race declined as an issue, southern governors could welcome federal dollars into their states since they no longer had to worry about federal prohibitions against racial discrimination. Governors had at least some say about how these moneys were distributed and spent, since states had to pass enabling legislation to receive them. Moreover, the additional federal funds enabled governors to hire more professional staff to oversee administration of programs and gave them additional budget powers as well.[38]

Even the retrenchment of federal programs and the decline of federal funds in the late 1980s and 1990s served further to enhance the southern governorship. The resurgence of federalism placed additional expectations on the governor to take up the slack. Governors found themselves in key positions to find ways, both in programs and in sources of revenue, to replace those no longer coming from Washington.

Finally, as the previous chapter demonstrated, the governor's office in the South also changed. By the late 1960s or early 1970s creaky constitutions were overhauled to streamline and modernize southern state governments. For the governor, the benefits were immense. Successive elections were now permissible in all the states but Virginia. No two-year terms remained. Internal modifications took place also, strengthening the governor's budget and appointment powers and affecting administrative reorganization to the extent that it became somewhat easier for governors to control their own executive branches. By the late 1970s, the southern governorship had become a much stronger office than it was only twenty years earlier.

Gubernatorial Leadership in the Future

It seems clear that the South will continue to have active governors in the future. The likelihood is that Pragmatists and Policymakers will predominate, with an occasional modern Populist emerging as well. Even conservative, more traditional Businessmen governors with a limited view of the office will not be able to avoid a concern with real policy issues.

While a number of reasons could be put forward to justify this prognosis, one seems paramount: public expectations of the governorship and the governor in the South have changed profoundly. The days are gone when the governor could be a figurehead, a Goodtime Charley, or some similarly inept politician. The demands on the job are too great, and the needs of the states and region too pressing to permit backsliding to patterns of the past. Moreover, the politics of the region have become so energized and complex, compared to the past, that the governor, as central figure in the state, will play a great role in the shape and direction those politics take.

Thus it seems certain that more, not less, will be expected of the southern governor in the future. Because the stakes involved are so high, competition for the office is likely to become ever greater. Competition, too, will help make the office more vigorous and serve as an incentive for more capable, visible, dynamic leadership from those occupying it.

Part V

Conclusion

11

The New South

The South is tradition oriented. We cherish ideals of loyalty, gallantry, and honesty. While we frequently fall short of achieving those ideals, we do pursue them.
—James Neal, Nashville attorney

The South has not been as quick as the rest of the country to discard its tradition of courtesy on the grounds that politeness has gone out of fashion.
—Judith Martin, "Miss Manners" columnist

The thing that I love most about the South is the white man. As racist as he is, he is more honest than the northern white man and can be trusted.
—Hosea Williams, Atlanta City councilman and aide to Martin Luther King Jr.

What I like about Dixie are the hot, sultry nights, when the humidity is such that it embraces you, and you can feel the warmth of the air. . . . I love the hot. I love the heat. I love a hot summer day.
—Cornelia Wallace, former first lady of Alabama

Southerners take a while to make up their minds about things. They have their comfortable traditions. They don't take to change as fast. They're slow to accept the new. Their lifestyle is so genteel, so comfortable. Hopefully, they'll keep the rituals.
—Fay Gold, Atlanta art dealer

*My father was from Alabama. My mother was from Virginia. I
was raised on southern cooking. I love black-eyed peas, corn
bread, okra, gumbo, and especially grits.*
—Ben Crenshaw, professional golfer

*When you die, whether you're goin' to Heaven or Hell, you still
have to change in Atlanta.*
—Frequent comment of air travelers through the South

Southerners worry about their region. As the epigraphs suggest, there is pride among southerners about the beauty and virtue of traditional southern ways, but anxiety as well. There is, after all, the danger that what is best about the South, and southerners, might disappear as it, and they, become more like the rest of the country.

There is nothing new in these concerns. For more than a century southerners have been troubled that they might somehow lose their distinctiveness as they were either overwhelmed by the North and Midwest or helplessly caught up in a great homogenization of American life. But the fact that southerners continue to be vexed about these matters suggests that their cultural distinctiveness persists and that it matters to them that it does. As the epigraphs observe, many traditional southern ways have endured.

Only a moron would argue, however, that the South has not seen extraordinary change during the nine decades of this century. Virtually no aspect of southern life has escaped the remarkable, at times violent, upheavals that the region has witnessed. These range from the most profound, as in the vigorous entry of blacks into southern political life, to the trivial: instant grits and microwaveable sausage biscuits are readily available in the grocery store.

It is this juxtaposition of continuity and change that fascinates and baffles southerners as well as students of the South. Now that we have come to the end of our examination of twentieth-century politics in the region, it is time for us to reflect on what exactly has happened to southern politics during the past decades. What changes have occurred? What continuities persist? What place and meaning do politics have in the modern South, and to what extent are they the same as, or different from, old style southern politics? Finally, can we now truly speak of a new South and a new southern politics?

Race and Poverty: Classic Southern Burdens

We began this study by noting that the most distinctive problems of the South and its most classic burdens have been race and poverty. They have not been the only serious matters facing the region, but they have been basic. The first questions that we must squarely address in this conclusion are these: To what extent do race and poverty remain the fundamental problems and burdens of the region, and what role has political and governmental activity played in bringing about any change that may have occurred?

On the basis of the previous chapters, we can point to four major findings which suggest that the problem of race in the South has significantly declined and that politics and government have played an important role in bringing about this change.

The first set of data that support this conclusion rests on the key roles blacks now actively play in southern politics. Two aspects can be highlighted. Perhaps the most obvious is the sizable southern black electorate. For most of this century, the southern black population could not have been called an electorate at all, for it generally lacked the right to participate in electoral politics. When it did, it was not as a legitimate, independent political force but as one that was dependent and manipulated.

This change in vocabulary alone signifies a substantial change in racial politics. Beyond this, the black vote in the South is now frequently the difference between winning and losing for candidates. It is not unusual to hear even conservative, rural white politicians openly courting black support, especially in the various southern Democratic Parties, which for most of this century were especially hostile to blacks.

In not every place in the South have blacks fully utilized their potential political power at the ballot box. Turnouts and participation, as we have seen, continue to be erratic. But the potential for participation now exists as it did not for most of this century. And in some areas, especially in Mississippi, Alabama, and Georgia, blacks have become sufficiently organized to constitute a major source of political energy in the state. These developments represent very real change in southern politics and in southern life.

Another key aspect of the participation of blacks in southern political life is the fact that they now occupy key electoral and appointed positions. They have thus become public officials who occupy formal, legitimate decision-making positions in the political system. True, most of these positions are at the lowest levels of government. But in November 1989, a black politician, Doug Wilder, was elected governor of Virginia; in 1990 Andrew Young, the black former mayor of Atlanta, ran a serious, biracial campaign for governor of Georgia; and in 1995 Cleo Fields did the same in Louisiana. The fact that the last two were defeated in no way detracts from the significance of their candidacy. Perhaps these men represent the vanguard of other black politicians who can successfully compete for high posts in state government.

Moreover, in some respects the point is not that blacks still are underrepresented in electoral politics or that many occupy fairly low-level posts. The point is that merely twenty years ago there were virtually no black elected officials at all. While the number of blacks in appointive positions is still small relative to the population, two decades ago there were essentially no southern black judges, city managers, or school administrators (other than principals of rigidly segregated schools). There is no question that more southern blacks need to occupy elected or appointed public office. The process of increasing their numbers will not necessarily be easy or linear. But the change from the recent past has been nothing short of astonishing.

Another real reduction in the role of race in the South, largely as a function of politics and governmental activity, has been in the everyday desegregation of the region. First noted a decade ago by Neal Peirce as "quiet" desegregation, its effect has been profound.[1] Previously southerners exerted considerable effort and spent substantial resources to find ways of keeping whites and blacks separate, even as they necessarily had to interact in the course of daily life.

Most segregation has disappeared, in part because of attitudinal changes and a slow but growing acceptance of the idea that mutual contact is not necessarily harmful. But there has also been political change, including the civil rights movement, court decisions, and federal legislation, especially those concerning desegregation of public schools and public accommodations.

Initially, the result of these political changes was to force mutual racial contact. It was uncomfortable for everyone at first. But as Peirce noted after a time, fewer and fewer southerners thought anything of it. The result was that not only could blacks and whites stand on lines together,[2] they could sit down as well. In the modern South, while black-white contact still is not always harmonious, neither is it necessarily an occasion for public displays of bigotry by whites or for embarrassment for blacks. Mostly, no one notices. This lack of recognition, in itself, is a major change from the past.[3]

A third indicator of the decline in southern racial politics is shown by party politics, especially in the Democratic Party. Since 1965, and especially since the early 1970s, southern Democratic Parties have openly and actively recruited black members and voters. This recruitment represents a very substantial change from the past, when the Democratic Party was one of the primary perpetrators of racial discrimination.

There is, however, a marked difference between the modern southern Democratic Party's response to blacks and that of the modern southern Republican Party. With the exception of the 1991–92 congressional and state legislative redistricting cycles, when Republicans cut deals with African American legislators to enhance both black and Republican representation, it is hard to find evidence that Republicans in the South have made much of an effort to recruit blacks or attract black voters. In fact, the Republican Party has virtually ignored blacks and black concerns, although individual Republican leaders, such as Winthrop Rockefeller of Arkansas and Lamar Alexander of Tennessee, have not. This is not to say that the modern southern Republican Party has taken over the traditional role of the Democrats as beaters of the racial horse; no overt forms of discrimination exist to keep southern blacks out of the region's Republican Parties. But it is also true that blacks are not made to feel especially welcome. Until they are, it is unlikely that Republican candidates in the region will enjoy much black support, perhaps to the detriment of their campaigns.

A final indicator of real change in the area of race, as a result of political activity, is the way blacks are treated by political leaders, governors in particular. In the past some demagogic governors and other leaders proved so adept at using race as their major political currency that they built entire careers around it. Others, less inclined toward noisy exploitation of racial attitudes, nonetheless found that their political careers were blocked unless they, too, publicly accepted, and in many cases underscored, traditional racial attitudes and practices.

This connection between racial attitudes and success in politics is now gone. David Duke's appeal to racism in Louisiana politics has not put him in office. Largely as a result of the civil rights movement and the entry of blacks into the mainstream of southern politics, exploiting racism is not politically acceptable any longer. When it does appear, many whites feel free to condemn it, whereas earlier they could no more do so than could blacks.[4] Interesting indeed is the fact that many southern whites join blacks in opposing public outbreaks of racism; even if they are not always sympathetic to black demands, neither do they wish to turn back the clock to earlier, unhappy times. Indeed, the norms of political discussion by contemporary southern politicians on racial issues seem to range from benign neglect of black concerns to open solicitation of black support for their candidacies and programs. This range, too, represents major change from the past.

On the other hand, racism in the South persists. Hosea Williams might be right in that southerners are more honest about their racism than people elsewhere. But honesty may not matter much to blacks faced with poor housing and job opportunities, bad schools, and discrimination that continues to manifest itself in a variety of ways.

The civil rights movement and accompanying federal legislation helped reduce racism on matters that are essentially public in character. But on fundamentally private matters, such as jobs, home mortgages, promotions, and club and church membership, as well as purely attitudinal ones, political and governmental activity may have limited capacity to root out racism. It may well turn out that the overt, loud, even violent forms of southern racism were easier to terminate than the more subtle, hidden, private forms that seem to lie beyond the pale of governmental action.

Another problem concerning the persistence of race in the South is the resegregation of the region. Two aspects are especially noticeable—housing and education. Segregated housing patterns in the South seem to follow all too closely those of intensely segregated metropolitan areas elsewhere.[5] These patterns relate to social class and wealth, of course. But there is also evidence that they result from real estate marketing and bank-lending policies.

In schools and colleges, secondary resegregation has also occurred. That is, within schools themselves racial segregation of students occurs on the basis of ability grouping, behavior problems, and curricular and degree patterns. Thus, although government and political action forced open the school portals and ensured that blacks and whites could enter through the same door, they have been less effective in making certain that the students within the same educational institution receive a comparable, equal education.

The effect of resegregation is potentially pernicious. A resegregated South can undo much of what the civil rights movement and governmental action helped accomplish. Of course resegregation may result from large social forces, such as social class divisions, that lie beyond the current will or ability of government to influence. Attitudinal factors also play a crucial part in the maintenance and reinstitutionalization of racism, and government may have little capacity to influence them.

Thus, a troubling problem exists at present: Can public policy undermine the recurrence of southern racism? Southerners could, for example, demand fully desegregated housing patterns and schools, but it is not clear that southerners or their elected leaders and representatives in government are prepared to make such demands. Yet to do nothing ensures that racism persists, and segregation will increase.

There is another crucial dimension to this problem: Even if the will exists among southerners to stop the resegregation of the region, are political and governmental institutions adequate to the task? V.O. Key, it will be recalled, demonstrated that southern political institutions were part of the southern problem: not only did they not alleviate racism, they exacerbated it. Has this situation changed? Do southern political institutions have the capability to successfully attack lingering racism and segregation? We shall return to this crucial question after examining the impact of politics and government on another persistent southern problem—poverty.

The continuation of poverty, and its correlates illiteracy and poor public health, raise even more questions about the reality of a new South than does the persistence of racism, especially when the role of government and politics in alleviating poverty is included in the discussion. There is no question, as we saw earlier in the book, that southern income, wealth, rates of illiteracy, and public health have improved greatly. It is by no means clear that if a national council, such as the one appointed by President Franklin Roosevelt in 1935, were to study economic conditions in the country, it would conclude that the South is still the nation's number one economic problem.[6]

But the South continues to lag behind the rest of the nation on virtually all measures of economic health. In 1986 per capita income in the Southeast was 87 percent of the U.S. figure. But only in Virginia and Florida did it exceed it, while five southern states ranked in the bottom nine of all states. In Mississippi, per capita income in 1986 was still only two-thirds that of the entire nation. As we saw in chapter 2, by the 1990s these figures had not improved, and in some southern states there had been a regression to lower positions compared to national norms.[7]

The South still contains the nation's highest overall rates of poverty and, with them, problems of bad housing, poor job opportunities, inferior education, and inadequate public health. While there continue to be more poor southern whites than blacks, the rate of black poverty remains three times that of whites. Wage scales, particularly for unskilled and agricultural workers, continue to be significantly lower in most southern states than elsewhere in the nation. On virtually any measure of educational quality and public health, the South as a whole continues to rank at or near the bottom of the nation. Indeed, individual states such as Florida, Texas, and Virginia tend to skew the southern figures upward; the rest of the region ranks substantially below them on these measures.

These facts are not purely descriptive. They represent continued human suffering and continued waste in human resources. They constitute an ongoing drag on southern productivity and progress. They suggest that while things have improved in the region, it may be difficult for the region as a whole to catch up to the rest of the country, although in a few border South states they may well do so.

Perhaps most fundamentally, they raise questions about the ability of political activity and government action to solve the long-standing problem of persistent regional poverty. This is not to say that government action has not helped or is not necessary. At the federal level, an array of educational and social service programs have improved the education, health, and welfare conditions of southerners. Even during the Reagan years, and on into the Bush and Clinton administrations, in spite of cutbacks of domestic spending programs, many federal efforts to attack poverty continued.

At the state level, governors have sought to increase the levels of business development and capital investment in states. Efforts have been made to create more jobs of a skilled nature, with correspondingly higher salaries. Worker benefits have increased. Southern states have improved the quality and quantity of health, social, and educational services available to citizens, all of which are designed to attack poverty and improve the lives of even the poorest of the poor.

But the problem is that all these efforts have not really alleviated the traditional widespread poverty of the region. At least three reasons can be suggested why political activity and governmental action have not been as successful as many hoped in reducing the level of southern poverty. In the first place, some government programs may be the wrong ones. They may actually perpetuate poverty and suffering instead of reducing them.[8] Welfare programs, in particular, have been scrutinized with this view in mind.[9] And even some programs that do not actually make things worse may not really address basic problems but in fact treat symptoms instead. Farm subsidy programs, for instance, and some educational programs, have been attacked on this basis.[10]

Second, southern states, for the most part, continue to lack the resources that an all-out effort to combat poverty requires. Most are still among the poorest in the nation yet have large populations requiring substantial levels of services. Even the relatively advantaged states—Texas, Florida, and Virginia—continue to demonstrate relatively low-tax, low-service attitudes that prevent them from fully utilizing their resources to attack poverty.

Third, there is a real question of whether state governmental and political institutions are sufficient, by themselves, to affect the economic lives of citizens sufficiently so that poverty can be fully uprooted. Regional and state economies are influenced by national and international forces over which state government and politicians have little or no control. Business cycles, international trade and investment, new divisions of labor, changing market and investment patterns, the U.S. budget deficit and imbalance of trade payments, wars or other forms of international disruption, energy crises, federal fiscal, tax, and monetary policies—all of these, and more, may affect the economy of the South and its individual states more than what all the governors and all of the legislatures, singly or in combination, are able to do.

Thus, in spite of the willingness of southern states to face economic problems more squarely than they did earlier in the century, it is by no means certain that they are fully in charge of their own economic destinies. The ability of their political and governmental institutions to deal adequately with regional poverty may, in fact, be severely constrained.

The Adequacy of Southern Political Institutions, I

We come, then, squarely to a fundamental question with which we started this book: Have southern political institutions matured and strengthened sufficiently so that they are capable of dealing with the region's problems? Are they more adequate than they once were, to the extent that they no longer underscore or contribute to regional problems but in fact are among the various social institutions available to address, even solve, them? Can they be expected to solve the continuing existence of racism and poverty?

These questions can be addressed on two levels. The first, largely empirically based, rests on the changes that have occurred in southern politics during this century, especially in the last twenty years or so. We have seen the rise of the Republican Party as a significant challenge to the traditional hegemony of the Democratic Party. If the region is not yet fully two party, it is much closer to a competitive two-party model than it was two decades ago.[11] The postwar years also saw the rise of black political participation in the South. After 1965, it occurred in avalanche proportions.

Finally, weak political leadership in the South, which especially concerned Key, has been dramatically transformed. Whereas governors, in particular, were formerly often political followers of limited vision and not infrequently racist tendencies, they have in the South become policy architects and shrewd political stewards capable of using political institutions and resources to achieve desirable public goals.

The question is, What do these changes truly indicate about the adequacy of political institutions? Does change, in itself, necessarily mean better or stronger or more adequate for dealing with regional problems?

A partial answer can come from empirical theories and models of democracy that political science constructs and utilizes as a way of understanding the evolution and capability of political institutions. While there are many such models, some of those from mainstream political science writings suggest that indeed, these changes do represent a real strengthening of southern political institutions and a greater ability on their part to address seriously, if not fully solve, the problems of the South.

Key himself, for example, laid out a model of two-party politics and its relationship to a healthy democracy that has been widely adopted by political scientists.[12] According to this model, a two-party system is best for American democracy because of its ability to provide accommodationist politics, minimize fragmentation, and organize a very disparate electorate into permanent, recognizable political groupings. The efficacy of the model was not based on policy outcomes or outputs so much as its ability to provide for necessary political dynamism, even as it fostered continuity and stability.

The South has not yet achieved this model. Yet it has approached it and continues to do so. Similarly, the entrance of blacks into mainstream southern politics reinforces empirical models in which heightened levels of political participation and the inclusion of groups previously shut out of the democratic process are viewed as healthy for democratic politics. The fact is that political participation among white southerners has also increased in the last twenty years, further underscoring empirical theory which holds that greater involvement by citizens is healthy for democracy.[13]

Finally, the rise of new leadership in the South underscores its importance in democratic politics. Leaders are essential for articulating goals and mobilizing resources to reach them. Strong leaders act as stewards of the public, doing for them what they cannot do for themselves. There are a number of models of political leadership which suggest that as leaders become more dynamic, visionary, and politically capable, even as they operate within democratic norms, they serve to strengthen democratic political institutions.[14]

In sum, based on models of modern empirical democratic theory, southern political institutions have improved and have become more capable of dealing with regional problems. We have shown that this achievement may be more true in the case of racism than of poverty, but this outcome may be more a matter of what lies within the purview of political institutions themselves to handle than a fault of the institutions themselves.

At a minimum, these changes in southern political institutions have greatly increased the richness, the texture, the scope, and the language of southern politics. They have made politics more meaningful for the people of the region. They represent hard evidence that politics is no longer part of the southern problem but an integral part of southern solutions to its problems. On these bases alone, it would have to be said that southern political institutions are more adequate than they were just a generation ago and certainly more than they were for most of this century.

The Adequacy of Southern Political Institutions, II

There is another level at which we can assess the adequacy of modern southern political institutions—that of normative democratic theory. While still empirically rooted, normative models of democratic theory move toward higher levels of abstraction. They force us to think about the basic elements of democratic government and serve as criteria for measuring the performance of political and governmental institutions.[15]

Examined normatively, it is still possible to view modern southern politics as essentially manipulative, dominated by elites, and devoid of substance; in many ways these same comments can by applied to American politics generally.[16] But it is crucial, when viewing southern politics normatively, to take a longitudinal view. Compared to what southern politics was like for the first sixty years or so of this century, it is now unquestionably more open and democratic, less authoritarian and closed, than they were earlier.

True, rates of political participation, as measured by voter registration and turnout, do not always match those of other parts of the country. But the gap has significantly decreased, and in some elections (especially presidential) there is little regional difference. And gone are the days when an average of less than 11 percent of the eligible voters turned out for primary elections, as occurred in Virginia under the Byrd regime. Indeed, gone are the days when the primary election was everything, and the general election nothing. While the former often remain significant, competitive contests (including challenges to incumbents), the latter have achieved a prominence and visibility unheard of just a quarter century ago, especially for major state offices.

Can we be more systematic in our assessment of the adequacy of southern political institutions based on normative democratic theory? To do so, let us briefly examine these institutions based on three fundamental principles of democratic government—equality, accountability, and legitimacy.

Equality

Equality is a major tenet of American democratic theory. It is an elusive, abstract concept involving opportunity, treatment, and results.[17] These are not always compatible. Nonetheless, Americans and theorists of American democracy have held dear the notion that in our nation all citizens are somehow equal, and are to be treated as equal.

Perhaps the greatest evidence on behalf of the view that levels of equality have improved in the South is that which relates to the position of blacks. Previously deliberate victims of discrimination and forced by political and social institutions into positions of inequality, southern blacks have made great strides toward equality with whites.

The areas of equality of opportunity and equality of treatment show the greatest progress for southern blacks and, as far as that goes, poor southern whites relative to middle- and upper-middle class whites. More equal opportunities can be seen in access to educational facilities and programs, which a generation ago were denied them.[18] Improved opportunities also provide black and white southerners with a greater chance of escaping the burden of poverty than existed just two decades ago.

In terms of equal treatment, southern blacks generally now have the same access as whites to public facilities and accommodations such as theaters, hotels, and airports. Their votes count the same. In more private areas, such as jobs and housing, churches and clubs, equal treatment remains elusive. But most important, black-white interaction need no longer be an occasion for embarrassment or humiliation for blacks, as it was for so long in the South. Blacks can expect to be treated with dignity and respect, whereas previously they could not.

Perhaps the greatest continuing problems in southern black equality are in the area of results. While this study has dealt only minimally with outcomes, we saw that at least in the area of southern municipal public service deliveries, blacks, especially in old South communities, still do not receive an equal share. On economic indicators, too, southern blacks lag behind whites. Overcoming these inequities may well require massive distributive and redistributive policies on the part of national and state governments, policies that at the present time do not seem to be a part of national or regional political agendas.

Nonetheless, in spite of these difficulties, it would be wrong to assume that little or no changes in black-white (or white-white) equality has occurred in the South. In fact, this is precisely the point. To suggest that blacks have not achieved greater levels of equality with whites, at least in the areas of opportunity and treatment, is to deny reality. To paraphrase the black preacher, equality for blacks in the South isn't what it might be, or should be, but it certainly isn't what it was. The same is true in many areas of white-white relations, where the inequities of the past have significantly declined.

We saw earlier in the chapter that political activity and governmental action were crucial in promoting black-white equality in the South. Other factors were important, too, such as changing attitudes and migration patterns that brought in new people and new ideas to the South. Yet because of the role of southern political and governmental institutions in reducing inequalities and improving equality among the races in the South, we have to conclude that they are therefore more adequate than they once were in terms of dealing with key regional problems.

There still is a long way to go in the South, as in the nation, in eliminating social, economic, and political inequalities. Some solutions may lie outside of the capacity of government's ability to affect them significantly. But neither of these facts diminishes the supreme responsibility and obligation of government to work toward these goals or gives government an excuse for not addressing them squarely and fully. This conclusion, too, represents a major change in the South from a generation ago.

Accountability

Accountability refers to the relationship between government officials and the public, specifically to the way they must answer to the public for their actions. It also refers to the capacity of governmental officials and institutions to respond to public needs. Government is truly accountable when officials take responsibility for their actions and decisions, when they are sensitive to public issues and problems, and when they deal with serious public questions in serious way.

For most of this century, accountability in southern politics has been minimal. Government was for the few. Much political activity was aimed at keeping people out of politics or manipulating them and ignoring public needs in favor of private interests. The public record suggests that once many southern officials were inaugurated, their attitude became "the public be damned."

Has this attitude changed? Evidence suggests that government and politics in the South are more accountable to the public than they once were. Certainly politics is more open and subject to public scrutiny than it was. Part of this change results from an aggressive media, but it also results from public demand that government do business openly, responsively, and responsibly.

"Sunshine laws" in most southern states, in which politicians must conduct business openly, are examples of new levels of accountability that previously had been lacking. More generally, southern politicians cannot deliberately seek ways of avoiding public scrutiny or of answering for their actions. To give another example, the Voting Rights Act requires local voting officials to make registration procedures open and accessible to the public. This requirement is certainly a far cry from what traditionally occurred in the South.

There is also evidence that southern political institutions are somewhat more responsive to public needs than previously. The Democratic Party, in particular, has sought to expand its membership and its agenda to include blacks and their concerns, which it previously shunned. Southern governors, both as candidates and officeholders, openly address policy issues and public concerns in ways that seldom happened before 1965.

None of this evidence proves that governmental institutions are more accountable to the public than they once were, it strongly suggests that they are. Moreover, the fact that governmental institutions have become more accountable indicates not only that they are more democratic than they once were but also that they are more adequate to deal with public needs. Whereas once they hid from public scrutiny and found ways to avoid responding to public needs, now their close linkage to citizens makes them more effective institutions for coping with public problems in responsible, responsive ways.

Legitimacy

Legitimacy in democratic theory refers to both acceptability and standing. It refers first to a set of norms that determine what is possible or feasible within the political arena in terms of ideas, behaviors, and rhetoric. Legitimacy also refers to the individuals and groups who are allowed to be involved in political and governmental institutions—that is, the right to be considered full-fledged participants in public affairs. Individuals and groups who are legitimate become players in the political process; those who are not are kept out. Likewise, ideas and proposals considered legitimate (that is, within the bounds of acceptability) become part of the political agenda and may even become actual policies; those that are not legitimate are seldom considered seriously, if at all.

On the basis of evidence presented in this book, a considerable broadening of political legitimacy has occurred in southern politics during this century, particularly in the last twenty-five years. Both blacks and poor southern whites have achieved a legitimate political standing that had been denied them previously. Perhaps the most crucial dimension of this development is that both groups have succeeded to first-class political citizenship and can insist on treatment as first-class citizens, whereas earlier they were not considered at that level.

Party politics has demonstrated this broadening of legitimacy. The Democratic Party, especially, has opened its doors to blacks. Republicans have been less active in this regard, but they have embraced southern whites, especially lower-middle-class white males, in ways which they did not do before.[19]

The agenda and rhetoric of southern politics have also been expanded. As Earl Black has shown, following 1965 southern governors have been able to discuss social, economic, and racial issues in open ways not possible previously.[20] True, there continue to be limits on the legitimacy of political ideas in the South. They are still somewhat narrower than elsewhere: political candidates such as Steve Pajcic and Buddy MacKay in Florida who get saddled with a "liberal" label have difficulty winning elections. On the other hand, political rhetoric and discussion in the South are no longer limited to race-baiting, attacks on Yankees and "the feds," or appeals to a mythical, glorious past. While it does not always happen, southern political discussion can now rival that of any in the nation in breadth, seriousness, and tone.

These are crucial developments for assessing the adequacy of southern political institutions. A broadening of legitimate participants and ideas unquestionably strengthens them, if only because of the added texture and richness they provide. In conjunction with their ability to promote greater levels of equality and their enhanced public accountability, the broader legitimacy of southern political and governmental institutions makes a tremendous difference in the importance and significance of politics for citizens in the South. It suggests that political institutions can operate on their behalf, not against them, as so often occurred in this century.

More fundamentally, however, they suggest that southern political institutions have moved closer toward those of American democratic norms and ideals. Like all American political institutions, they have a long way to go. But they are far more democratic, and therefore more adequate to carrying out the public's business, than they formerly were. No doubt V.O. Key, like many other critics of southern politics, would wish progress toward achieving democratic goals had been even greater. But there can be no doubt that southern governmental and political institutions are far stronger and far more democratic than they were when he wrote more than forty years ago.

Southern Political Change

In each of the chapters on party development, black political participation, and gubernatorial leadership, we sought to outline the bases of political change during this century. Let us now look more broadly, however, at the question of change. Why have southern politics and political institutions undergone such a substantial modification during this century? Why, in particular, has change occurred as rapidly as it has in the last twenty-five to thirty years?

The early impetus for change came from outside the South. That it did so is not surprising, given that dominant cultural forces in the region were resistant to change of any kind, including political change. But unless a culture is wholly isolated from the outside world, eventually external influences will be felt.[21] As early as the 1930s, the initial stirrings of change in southern politics could be felt through the impact of needed New Deal programs. The World War II years saw further influence, as military bases were located in the South and the war effort forced a more open door policy on the part of southerners to the rest of the nation. These trends were further underscored by regional demographic changes that began before the war but mushroomed after it.

A number of outside forces have proven to be especially important as instruments of political and social change in the South. Migration literally changed the face of the region, as millions of blacks moved out, to be replaced by whites. The effect was to lessen the pressures that a huge underclass of poor blacks exerted on the region's politics. In-migration also provided the basis for a new, white middle class that found traditional extremist southern racial views unacceptable. It is also of interest that the 1980s saw the beginnings of a remigration of blacks to the South. It has continued into the 1990s and has even seen a return of blacks to rural areas of the South.[22] The potential impact on regional politics of the black return South—especially given that a good percentage of those returning are middle class—will assuredly be substantial.

Economic change also provided an impetus for political change. As the tenant-sharecropper system gave way to agribusiness and commercial and industrial development in the South proceeded in earnest following World War II, the colonial status of the region was transformed into a much more self-sufficient economy. The rapid urbanization and metropolitanization of the South helped improve job opportunities for southerners and fostered reallocations of political, as well as economic, resources. In many cases outside investment in the South provided an impetus for change, as many businesses declined to come South until conditions in race relations, education, and transportation facilities improved. In some instances new businesses actually acted as change agents in the communities where they settled.

An array of diffusions from other parts of the nation also had a profound effect on the region's politics.[23] Some of these were primarily economic and technological spillovers from the rise of a postindustrial economy in the nation resting heavily on such high-tech industries as petrochemicals, aerospace, and electronics; the political impact of the Research Triangle in North Carolina, Cape Kennedy in Florida, and Huntsville, Alabama, has gone well beyond their local communities.

Other changes have been created by diffusion through the media. The growth of television in the South permitted southerners to view the rest of the country from a less isolated perspective. Likewise, the way the South has been portrayed by television, newspapers, and Hollywood seems to have had a profound, if undocumented, effect on regional thinking and behavior. Even the entertainment and sports industries have affected southern life and politics, as auditoriums, stadiums, and athletic teams were forced to desegregate to maintain competitive schedules and attract visible (and financially rewarding) teams as well as performing groups and artists.

National political trends have been powerful forces for change in the South. We have in several places noted the consequences for southern politics of the shift in the national Democratic Party on civil rights issues. A conservative shift in the national Republican Party during the mid-1960s and throughout the 1980s well into the 1990s helped reorient, if not fully realign, southern politics. The difficulty Democratic presidential nominees have had in capturing the White House has proven a further impulse toward an abandonment of traditional southern political ways in favor of a more dynamic, competitive party system.

Finally, action by the federal government produced great change from without the region. We already alluded to the impact of the New Deal and World War II years. Later a host of Supreme Court decisions recast southern politics forever. Presidential action and such legislative landmarks as the 1964 Civil Rights Act and 1965 Voting Rights Act (including the 1982 revisions of Section 2) also served to alter the regional political landscape permanently.

Indeed, we have seen in this book that the role of the federal government, especially the president and Congress, in bringing political change to the South has often been erratic. Federal courts have been much more consistent in this regard. But it is also true that without federal involvement, and especially federal intervention, it is doubtful that the political changes that occurred in the South would have been as substantial as they were.

Not all political changes in the region resulted from outside forces. Some were indigenous. Although there were quite a few, let us mention only the two most important. The first was restlessness from the southern black population. Opponents of black civil rights in the South often ascribed the movement to outside agitators. There was outside help. But the historical record unequivocally shows that the initial impetus toward civil rights and political equality for blacks came from southern blacks themselves. Much of the burden of civil rights activity between 1955 and 1965 was borne by southern blacks alone. Without this indigenous political muscle, political change in the South would have been much less significant or consequential.

A second internal force for political change in the South was the moderate white community. For decades, it had been stilled. Those who sought to speak out, such as the Percy family of Mississippi, or journalists such as Harry Golden and Ralph McGill, and jurists such as Frank Johnson in Alabama, were often targets of derision, even persecution. The extremism and violence of many white southerners and the ability of such groups as White Citizens Councils, the Ku Klux Klan, Daughters of the Confederacy, and other such organizations to dominate the political agenda prevented moderate, accommodationist voices to be heard for much of this century.

Eventually, of course, it was the violence of the extremists in the face of civil rights pressures that brought about their own downfall. But moderate voices eventually saw the necessity and gained the courage to speak out.

Especially important in this regard were members of the southern business community. They were not forces for radical change. Rather they were forces for stability and order. They recognized that the violence and polarization of southern life would damage the future of the region, certainly economically but in political and social terms as well. Their ultimate rejection of extremism permitted and encouraged political and social change to occur, gradual though it may have been.

Continuities in Southern Politics

Not everything has changed in southern politics, of course. Much of the style and traditional flavor of southern politics remains. Modern southern political campaigns may have all the accoutrements of campaigns elsewhere, such as slick media work, sophisticated polling, and high-priced strategic consultants. The candidates themselves may wear Brooks Brothers or Italian designer suits instead of red galluses.

But even Ivy League educations do not cover up the traditional regional accents of the candidates. And woe is it to the north Florida candidate who fails to include some fish fries during his campaign, the North Carolina and Texas candidates who miss an important barbecue while on the campaign trail, or the Tennessee gubernatorial candidate who does not include a bluegrass band during his campaign stops east of Knoxville.

The persistence of these events is not cited to deny the changes that have occurred or to say that the modern South is just a spruced-up version of the old South. They do suggest, however, that the roots of southern politics are deep, and while the faces, vocabulary, even issues of politics may change, some cultural features remain. Consider: in some poor, rural, agricultural areas of the South the Democratic Party is still the only "real" political game. While the Democratic Party has changed, it continues to dominate the region at the executive level below the governorship and in the legislature. Racism and inequalities persist, even white supremacist candidates such as David Duke in Louisiana and Charles Davidson in Alabama, who in the spring of 1996 put forward as a centerpiece of his congressional campaign the notion that there was a biblical justification for slavery. And of course purely stylistic features of southern politics remain, such as the fish fries, barbecues, rallies in the courthouse squares of small towns, and hillbilly bands, in spite of the omnipresence of television and radio and the almost universal media-oriented, candidate-centered campaigns,[24] even for local offices.

Why do these features of southern politics persist in the light of the revolutionary changes since 1960? Several possible explanations present themselves. The most obvious, of course, is cultural inertia. Certain political styles and behaviors, such as the fish fries, become so encrusted with tradition as to achieve ritual status. Citizens are used to them and expect them; candidates and officeholders are forced to engage in the necessary rituals or risk offending large segments of voters, even when they seem to serve little or no purpose beyond obedience to tradition. These ritualistic cultural impulses do not die easily.

It is also true that cultural change is erratic and discontinuous. In areas such as cities and metropolitan areas where in-migration is rapid and there is a continuous introduction and mix of new cultural energies, changes are likely to occur rapidly. In older, more traditional areas of the South, heavily rural, agricultural, and off the beaten track of major in-migration patterns, cultural change is likely to be slower or even resisted by citizens. Thus it is no accident that much of the heart of southern Republican growth is in the white-collar suburbs of new cities and metropolitan areas, while small, more traditional villages and rural communities still remain Democratic.

In the same vein, some cultural elements may change more quickly than others, given the same time period. For example, a decade may have been sufficient to overthrow the more overt forms of racial discrimination in the South, especially given the impact of federal legislation and changes in state and local political practices. But it might not be long enough to root out more subtle forms of discrimination that are based in long-held attitudes and traditions. These indeed may take generations, or longer, to change.

Raymond Gastil has noted that while we normally think of individuals affecting culture (such as a flood of in-migrants might do), it is also true that culture affects individuals, including recent arrivals.[25] People need to learn to adapt, to fit in, to their new surroundings, and thus they assume a number of cultural elements, ranging from the type of clothes worn and food eaten to predominant political attitudes, styles, and behaviors.

Moreover, as John Shelton Reed points out, southerners as a group work hard at retaining their sense of identity and distinctiveness.[26] They want to keep as much of their history and traditions alive as possible, even in the face of rapid social change and an apparent homogenization of American life. Thus the conscious choice by southerners to keep their ways alive helps explain the perpetuation of earlier political patterns, especially uniquely southern behaviors, styles and rituals.[27]

Other factors could also be mentioned. For example, economic constraints among the southern states act as a brake on cultural change: it costs money to change, money that often has not been available. In combination, these forces have served to underscore and reinforce, rather than undermine, some of the more unique behavioral features of southern political life.

Future forecasting is always risky, but it is a good bet that many of these distinctive features will still be present as the new century dawns. The fact that, in spite of the obvious incongruities, southerners drive to political fish fries and barbecues in their Volvos, BMWs, and Hondas, or southern expatriates gather in bleak northern cities on New Year's Day to eat black-eyed peas, is evidence of their desire to maintain southern traditions as long as possible.

Southern Politics and Southern Diversity

V.O. Key showed that in spite of a common political heritage and major similarities in political culture, there was actually a great deal of diversity among the southern states. Does this diversity continue today, or has the South become increasingly homogenized, and subregional variations fewer?

The most basic subregional distinction has been between the deep South states and the rim states. It may well be that this dichotomy is less important than it once was. True, the origins of two-party politics in the South began in the rim states. A relaxing of racial tensions, and the movement toward more vigorous, Pragmatist and Policymaker gubernatorial leadership (see chapter 10) also began earlier in these states than in the deep South states.

On the other hand, by the mid- to late-1980s, deep South states in most cases had essentially caught up to the rim South on these measures. South Carolina and Mississippi rival Virginia and Florida in the degree of Republican penetration. We have seen that, in terms of presidential politics, both subregions are about equal in the degree to which they support Republican candidates.

There may be more areas of the deep South where traditional racial patterns can be found than in the border South. Blacks may continue to receive less than an equal share of services in old South areas, and while these are not exclusively in the deep South states, most of them are. It is also true that racial incidents continue to occur in both areas. More positively, politicians in both regions abjure racial rhetoric as a means of attracting support. And race as a political issue finds only an occasional place on the political agenda, usually following racial incidents, as citizens and public officials turn their attention toward other concerns.

Deep South states have also begun to have their share of Pragmatist and Policymaker governors. Jimmy Carter in Georgia, William Winter in Mississippi, and Richard Riley in South Carolina were the first in these states. But the elections of Buddy Roemer in Louisiana, Ray Mabus in Mississippi, and Carroll Campbell in South Carolina suggest that voters in the deep South states are as attuned to policy concerns as their neighbors in the rim

South. Even some of the modern Businessmen governors of the deep South—Kirk Fordice of Mississippi and Guy Hunt of Alabama, for example—have shown interest in public policy formation.

Do these changes mean that the rim South–deep South distinction no longer holds? Not necessarily. Stylistically, differences remain, if only in terms of the state and local political rituals public officials are expected to observe. The movement toward two-party politics has not proceeded uniformly across the region: Louisiana, Georgia, and Arkansas continue to look and behave more like traditional southern one-party states than the others. Moreover, the weight of southern political history and tradition may continue to be felt more strongly among the magnolias of Mississippi, Louisiana, and Alabama than in the large urban centers of Texas and Virginia, the mountains of eastern Tennessee, or the tourist centers and fast-growing suburbs of Florida.

Ultimately, perhaps most crucially, the deep South states remain significantly poorer than the rim states. The one exception is Arkansas, where poverty is as widespread as in some of the deep South states. The economic advantage held by the other rim states, especially Texas, Florida, and Virginia, may provide them with resources to cope with urgent problems that the other states lack. Indeed, it may well be that the future distinctions and variations among the southern states rest more on economic grounds—haves versus have-nots[28]—than they do on geographic considerations.

Moreover, sectional differences within the states continue to exist, creating differing political styles and issues across the entire region. Floridians, for example, continue to emphasize north-south distinctions in their politics, as voters in Tennessee continue to regard east-central-west differences. In Texas, the western plains, hill country counties, the valley, and metropolitan centers of east Texas all have very different political styles and agendas. In Mississippi, the delta–up-country political cleavage can still be felt, if not over racial issues then over such matters as economic development and state fiscal policy.

Another major force that acts to prevent the complete homogenization of southern politics is urban-rural-suburban splits. Indeed, suburban-rural alliances in state legislatures hostile to metropolitan interests, coupled with sectional differences, have replaced delta–up-country cleavages as a major force in the politics of the region. Even urban areas have acquired a diversity that, politically, was lacking: older metropolitan areas such as Birmingham, Atlanta, New Orleans, and Richmond have little in common, politically, with the new, growth-oriented, white-collar cities of Dallas, Orlando, and Charlotte.

Thus those who worry that southern politics has achieved a gray sameness are probably mistaken. True, many of the colorful rustic elements and rough edges of traditional southern politics have been replaced by a media-conscious, "blow-dried" veneer of sophistication. But there continue to be a richness, texture, and diversity within southern politics that are not likely to disappear. Indeed, the opposite is likely to occur: as more interests are articulated on the southern political stage through a stronger two-party system, greater levels of political participation by blacks and other groups, and more substantive and imaginative political leadership, that diversity is likely to be enhanced.

Southern Politics and National Affairs

For much of this century, as many observers have noted, southerners exerted great political power in Washington. At the presidential level, both Woodrow Wilson and Lyndon Johnson were southerners themselves. Franklin Roosevelt was sympathetic to many southern concerns, for both political and personal reasons. But southern influence was felt most especially in the halls of Congress, where southern senators and representatives built up vast levels of seniority during the first six decades of this century; the one-party system of the South ensured that they could return as long as they wished. As committee chairs, southerners in Congress were able to direct the flow of much national, even international, legislation.

Eventually the actuarial tables, as well as changing congressional politics, caused a modification of the southern influence in Congress. Is it therefore the case that southern influence has disappeared, or that the southern voice will not be a major one in Washington decision centers? Three factors suggest that the southern voice will continue to be heard.

First, between the 1970s and mid-1990s, a number of southern senators and representatives established themselves as major fixtures in the congressional landscape. While southerners may not have built up the astonishing level of seniority that existed prior to 1960, some have nevertheless achieved levels of prominence and prestige sufficient to carry major weight in decision making. While an exhaustive list is not possible, several examples illustrate the point well. In the Senate, Georgia's Sam Nunn became perhaps the leading specialist on defense policy; Jim Sasser of Tennessee headed the Senate Budget Committee; and Republican Jesse Helms of North Carolina became probably the leading conscience of conservatism in the Senate. In the House, such southern Representatives as Walter Jones of North Carolina and the late Claude Pepper of Florida exercised considerable power, either by virtue of position or longevity, for decades.

A second, and perhaps even more important, way in which the South will continue to exercise power in Washington is through presidential politics.

Except for Bill Clinton, no president since Richard Nixon in 1968 has entered the White House without carrying a majority of the southern states, and both the 1968 and 1992 elections were unusual because of the looming presence of George Wallace and Ross Perot. Leaving aside these two elections, Dwight Eisenhower's 1952 presidential victory was the last time a candidate won without also securing a majority of southern electoral votes.

It may well be in the future that the role of the South in determining the outcome of the presidential contest will increase; certainly, with demographic changes, reapportionment will increase the South's percentage in the Electoral College at the expense of other parts of the country.[29] Indeed the South will undoubtedly play a major role in the selection of nominees for each party, especially the Republicans, since the core of Republican support—and therefore the winning edge for the GOP—has shifted to the South. Finding a candidate politically acceptable to the region will help ensure the GOP's popular vote and Electoral College support. As long as the South continues to exert this kind of influence over presidential elections, as well as in Congress, it will continue to exercise significant strength in national politics.

Third, the growing Republican presence in Congress will ensure a powerful southern voice in Washington. Even before Republicans took over the U.S. Congress in 1994, a number of southern Republicans had achieved considerable prominence in the party and in Congress. After the Republican surge of 1994, southerners occupied key leadership roles. Newt Gingrich of Georgia became Speaker of the House, and Dick Armey of Texas was named majority leader. In the Senate, two Mississippi Republicans, Trent Lott and Thad Cochran, vied for the role of majority leader once Bob Dole stepped down in spring 1996 to concentrate on his presidential campaign. Other Republican congressmen and senators from the South also vaulted into positions of leadership, either as committee or subcommittee chairs or through other types of posts. How long Republicans will retain control of Congress is anybody's guess. To the extent they do, however, it is fair to say that the southern voice in Congress will continue to be prominent.

The South as a Region

Can we continue to talk about the South as a distinct region? Critics of the South have long looked forward to the time when it would become more like the rest of the country. Even sympathetic writers, such as Henry Grady, would not be unhappy to see some of the more excessive aspects of southern politics and culture melt away in favor of more seemly behaviors and attitudes. Has the "plasticization" and enfranchisement of the South so engulfed the region's culture, as well as its politics, so that it is unrecognizable as a separate region anymore?

If one walks through southern shopping malls or downtown streets at rush hour, the stores look, and the people behave, like those in Boston, Indianapolis, or Tacoma. Driving Alfa Romeos, Nissans, and Mercedes-Benzes is common even in smaller southern cities and communities, and gentrification of blighted, older downtown areas is a common phenomenon. Movies and television programs in the South are identical to those elsewhere; while Scotch whiskey may be in low demand at neighborhood southern taverns and roadhouses, the wine cellars and menus in chic southern restaurants are as sophisticated as their counterparts elsewhere in the nation.[30] And while H.L. Mencken used to complain about "the Sahara of the Bozart," leading musical artists, dance companies, and art exhibits are as likely to find their way to southern museums, concert halls, civic centers, and university campuses as they are anywhere else outside the New York–Boston–Chicago–San Francisco cultural axis.

And yet cultural distinctiveness persists. On one level, southern speech patterns and accents show few signs of diminishing and are even adopted by in-migrants (or, at least, their children). Magazines such as *Southern Living*, which extol and proselytize the virtue of southern life and culture, are popular and profitable.[31]

Southerners and in-migrants continue to eat a unique cuisine based, in part, on the impoverished meals of their grandparents; indeed, the opening of expensive restaurants featuring southern cooking in a number of metropolitan areas around the country has been greeted enthusiastically by food critics and the fashionable set alike. Southern manners are still courtly and formal; young children are taught to say "yes, sir" and "no, ma'am," even today, and the Christmas cotillion and debutante party are still among the high points of the social season for many traditional southerners.

There continues to be a uniquely southern style and manner of dress: the baseball cap, tee shirt, and old jeans are the approved fashion for both the blue-collar worker and high-priced southern lawyer working on his car (although now it is more likely to be in a garage than on blocks in the front yard). In much of the South a pickup truck with gun rack is still *de rigueur* as the appropriate mode of transportation; the fact that it may have an umbrella or fishing rod on the rack instead of a shotgun, and be made in Japan rather than Detroit, is amusing but beside the point. Country music is still widely heard on southern radio stations and appreciated in local bars, even as its popularity ebbs and flows elsewhere.

There is a more fundamental point: southerners have consciously not abandoned their ties to the past. Southern history is kept very much alive through school curricula and family gatherings, monuments and statues placed in parks and courthouse squares, and the willingness (some might say obsession) of southerners to think and talk about their past and their traditions. Indeed, these concerns are precisely what is meant by southerners' well-developed sense of time and place. Southerners possess a remarkable tenacity to maintain what is uniquely theirs—a history, a sense of values and customs, an identity.

It may be that H. Brandt Ayres and Thomas Naylor are right: southerners really can't eat magnolias.[32] But they can tend and nourish and admire the tree that produces them: southerners worry about the past, and they persist in conjuring up their heritage and traditions as they convey them to their children. They can also adapt them to modern conditions and to their own lifestyles. The modern southern restaurant may have a tablecloth and take credit cards, but there is no mistaking the collard greens and corn bread on the plate.

In politics, too, distinctiveness continues in spite of the enormous changes. The conditions of politics partially determine distinctiveness: as long as racism and poverty persist in the South as serious, chronic problems, it is likely that they will continue to occupy a major portion of the southern political agenda. They also will color and flavor the style and texture of southern politics, and while these may be different from the racism and poverty of the past, the ultimate influence they have on political activity and behavior is not.

Beyond this connection, however, is the fact that culture dies hard, and the ghosts of politics past—unpleasant though some of them may be—appear more often than just on Christmas Eve. Because of their insistence on bringing up the past, southerners virtually ensure that a distinctive style and even content will continue to permeate the region's politics, just as the weather and geography unmistakably underscore features of the region that are distinctively southern.

The position of politics in southern life is clearly different now from its position a generation ago. It is more central, more meaningful, more open, more important to more citizens. Nonetheless, to the extent that southerners want the past to play a role in their lives and to the degree that traditional regional problems and conditions persist, it is likely that we will continue to talk about southern politics as a significant part of the American political landscape.

The New South

After this survey of twentieth-century southern politics, we can specifically answer the questions with which we began: Is there a new South? Is there a new southern politics?

In both cases, the answer is yes, of course. In a sense, to respond to the first question, we need only visit Atlanta's airport, stand in the lobby of a Little Rock or Charlotte skyscraper, or drive along Interstate 4 in Florida between Daytona Beach and Tampa, and compare them to what was there twenty-five years ago. Atlanta was host to the 1996 Olympic Games, something unthinkable a generation ago, and it is no overstatement to say that the entire region has taken pride in the selection of this southern capital for this honor and responsibility.

To answer the second, we need only look at the election of a black governor of Virginia, black gubernatorial candidates in Georgia and Louisiana, as well as other blacks in public office; at the growth and power of a still-maturing Republican Party and a newly resurgent Democratic Party; and the impressive array of gubernatorial leadership in the region. A generation ago these developments would have seemed impossible. Now they are the rule.

But a troubling matter remains. What might Henry Grady and his new South industrialists have thought of these changes? And what about the Vanderbilt agrarians, those staunch defenders of the traditional South?

Undoubtedly these southern promoters would be happy to see the meaner aspects of southern life decline, even disappear: the bigotry, the ignorance, the disease, the authoritarianism, the hopelessness and despair. But they would also recognize that the cost of this progress has been high. For along with the money and skyscrapers and international airports have come a new host of problems for southerners to cope with: urban decay, environmental destruction, persistent inequalities of resources, and a resurgence of segregation that might prove more intractable than the first one.

Indeed, it is well past the time when southerners and nonsoutherners alike should worry about whether there is a new South and a new politics. These questions can finally be laid to rest. They should be replaced by ones that force southerners to address the region's critical issues: How can what is best about the South be maintained in the face of rapid and inevitable change? How can racism and poverty finally be reduced, even eradicated? How can southern politics play a greater role in making this change happen? Indeed, how can southern politics be made still more open and democratic for all citizens? Most fundamentally, as the new century looms, what kind of new South do southerners really want?

Notes

Chapter 1. Introduction: Seeking the New South

1. On Henry Grady, see Joel Chandler Harris, *Henry Grady* (New York: Cassell, 1890); and Raymond V. Nixon, *Henry W. Grady: Spokesman of the New South* (New York: Knopf, 1943). See also C. Vann Woodard, *Origins of the New South, 1877–1913* (Baton Rouge: Louisiana State University Press, 1951); Paul Gaston, *The New South Creed* (New York: Knopf, 1970); and Dewey Grantham, *Southern Progressivism* (Knoxville: University of Tennessee Press, 1983).

2. The state of Florida in recent years has sought to abolish its Department of Commerce, an executive agency charged in part with attracting and recruiting new business and industry to the state. It would be replaced by Enterprise Florida, an Orlando-based organization grounded in a public-private sector partnership. The purpose of this move, according to the governor, secretary of commerce, and others, is to allow the state more freedom and flexibility to move quickly and create attractive packages designed to appeal to national and international business concerns interested in investing in or moving to Florida. Their thinking was that the state agency was too limited by state laws and regulations to perform this function in a way that could compete effectively with other southern states. It is of interest that the Republican Senate and marginally Democratic House of Representatives, both probusiness, for some time resisted making the change requested by the governor and secretary. The reason apparently rested on the fact that the Florida legislature preferred to continue micromanaging executive agencies rather than bow to the wishes of the governor, secretary of commerce, and major business leaders, and thus lose control of a major state activity. In 1996, however, it accepted the governor's proposal.

3. V.O. Key Jr., *Southern Politics in State and Nation* (New York: Knopf, 1949).

4. Alexander Heard, *A Two-Party South?* (Chapel Hill: University of North Carolina Press, 1952); Donald Strong, *Urban Republicanism in the South* (University: Bureau of Public Administration, University of Alabama, 1960).

5. William C. Havard, ed., *The Changing Politics of the South* (Baton Rouge: Louisiana State University Press, 1972); Neal Peirce, *The Border South States of America* (New York: Norton, 1974) and *The Deep South States of America* (New York: Norton, 1974); Jack Bass and Walter DeVries, *The Transformation of Southern Politics* (New York: Basic Books, 1976); Alexander Lamis, *The Two-Party South* (New York: Oxford University Press, 1984); Earl Black and Merle Black, *Politics and Society in the South* (Cambridge, Mass.: Harvard University Press, 1987); Robert H. Swansborough and

David M. Brodsky, eds., *The South's New Politics* (Columbia: University of South Carolina Press, 1988); and Earl Black and Merle Black, *The Vital South* (Cambridge, Mass.: Harvard University Press, 1992).

6. For examples of how the U.S. Bureau of the Census uses this categorization of the South, see U.S. Bureau of the Census, *Statistical Abstracts of the United States, 1987,* 107th ed. (Washington, D.C.: U.S. Bureau of the Census, 1987).

7. See Kirkpatrick Sale, *Power Shift* (New York: Vintage Books, 1976); and Joel Garreau, *The Nine Nations of North America* (New York: Avon, 1982). In a somewhat different vein, see Editorial Research Reports, *American Regionalism* (Washington, D.C.: Congressional Quarterly, 1980).

8. See especially Peirce's two volumes, *Border South States of America* and *Deep South States of America,* on this point.

9. See John Shelton Reed, *The Enduring South* (Lexington, Mass.: Lexington Books, 1972), *One South* (Baton Rouge: Louisiana State University Press, 1982), and *Southerners* (Chapel Hill: University of North Carolina Press, 1983).

10. See especially Reed's *One South* for a detailed treatment of this issue.

11. Raymond Gastil, *Cultural Regions of the United States* (Seattle: University of Washington Press, 1975). See also *The Disappearing South?* ed. Tod A. Baker, Laurence W. Moreland, and Robert P. Steed (Tuscaloosa: University of Alabama Press, 1990); Daniel J. Elazar, *American Federalism: A View from the States,* 3d ed. (New York: Harper and Row, 1984); Richard J. Ellis, *American Political Cultures* (New York: Oxford University Press, 1993); and Daniel J. Elazar, *The American Mosaic* (Boulder, Colo.: Westview Press, 1994), for treatments of political culture and their persistence over time.

12. C. Vann Woodward, *The Burden of Southern History,* rev. ed. (Baton Rouge: Louisiana State University Press, 1968); for a useful commentary on Woodward's thesis, see I.A. Newby, *The South: A History* (New York: Holt, Rinehart and Winston, 1978), particularly chap. 1.

13. The May 1991 mayoral race in Jacksonville, Florida, the state's most populous city, was a classic internecine battle within the Democratic Party. Even at that late date the GOP had no candidate on the ballot. In 1995, however, the Republican candidate for mayor won the citywide election.

14. Many southerners felt that "federal interference" during the civil rights movement of the 1960s constituted a "second Reconstruction," during which a northern "army of occupation" essentially returned to the region. Opinion varies on this point, but it forms the title of a provocative book on this period by Numan V. Bartley and Hugh D. Graham, *Southern Politics and the Second Reconstruction* (Baltimore: Johns Hopkins University Press, 1975).

15. See Woodward, *Origins of the New South* (1951), and more to the point, his *Strange Career of Jim Crow,* rev. 3d ed. (New York: Oxford University Press, 1974), esp. pp. 80–81. See also, on this period, J. Morgan Kousser, *The Shaping of Southern Politics* (New Haven: Yale University Press, 1974). Newby, *The South,* and Grantham, *Southern Progressivism* are also accessible texts useful for those seeking a greater understanding of the origins of the one-party South. See also, and more recently, John B. Boles, *The South through Time* (Englewood Cliffs, N.J.: Prentice-Hall, 1995), for accessible historical overviews of this period.

Chapter 2. Race and Poverty in the Twentieth-Century South

1. United States National Emergency Council, *Report on Economic Conditions of the South* (1938; reprint, New York: Da Capo Press, 1972).

2. The following facts are from ibid., pp. 18, 21, 26–27, 29–36, 45–48, and 49–64.

3. These bare-bones statements are movingly portrayed in human terms in James Agee and Walker Evans, *Let Us Now Praise Famous Men* (Boston: Houghton Mifflin, 1969).

4. This observation is not new. Important works that treat this major problem include Howard Odum, *Southern Regions of the United States* (Chapel Hill: University of North Carolina Press, 1936); Odum and Harry Moore, *American Regionalism* (New York: H. Holt and Company, 1938); Rupert Vance, *Human Geography of the South* (Chapel Hill: University of North Carolina Press, 1935); and Vance, *All These People* (Chapel Hill: University of North Carolina Press, 1946). More recently see Charles Roland, *The Improbable Era* (Lexington: University of Kentucky Press, 1975); and Gavin Wright, *Old South, New South* (New York: Basic Books, 1986).

5. Quoted in Peirce, *Deep South States of America,* p. 38.

6. See Newby, *The South,* esp. pts. 3–6, for an overview of these developments. See also James C. Cobb, *The Selling of the South* (Baton Rouge: Louisiana State University Press, 1982); and Cobb, *Industrialization and Southern Society* (Lexington: University of Kentucky Press, 1984).

7. Vance, *Human Geography of the South,* discusses these issues at length. See also George Brown Tindall, *The Emergence of the New South* (Baton Rouge: Louisiana State University Press, 1967), esp. chaps. 8–18. These matters are also touched upon by Black and Black, *Politics and Society in the South.*

8. See *Fortune Magazine* 64 (July 1961): 167ff. The largest southern corporations were Burlington, a textile firm in Greensboro, North Carolina, ranked number 48, and R.J. Reynolds Tobacco, Winston-Salem, North Carolina, number 52. By the mid-1980s, more than 65 of the "Fortune 500" firms were in the southern states, and by the mid-1990s, 108 were located in the South, with Texas having a third of those (36); however, each southern state had at least one "Fortune 500" company headquartered in it. See *Fortune Magazine* 131 (May 15, 1995): F31–F42.

9. Emergency Council, *Report,* sec. 12, has a detailed discussion of this point.

10. Ibid., p. 59.

11. Roland, *Improbable Era,* p. 4.

12. Calculated from U.S. census data. Comparable figures for the whole United States are 1900, 40 percent; 1930, 56 percent; 1960, 69 percent. Only Texas and Florida have exceeded the U.S. average, and then beginning only in 1950.

13. Roland, *Improbable Era,* p. 3. See also Henri Pirenne, *Medieval Cities,* trans. Frank Halsey (Princeton: Princeton University Press, 1948); Jane Jacobs, *The Death and Life of Great American Cities* (New York: Random House, 1961); and Lewis Mumford, *The City in History* (New York: Harcourt, Brace and World, 1961).

14. See Tindall, *Emergence of the New South,* esp. chap. 7; and Newby, *The South,* chap. 12, for analyses of southern progressivism. See also George Mowry, *The Progressive Era* (Washington, D.C.: American Historical Association, 1972); and Grantham, *Southern Progressivism.*

15. Data are derived from U.S. Bureau of the Census, Population Division, decennial census; see also *Florida Statistical Almanac,* published by the Bureau of Economic and Business Research, University of Florida, Gainesville (1994 ed.), table 1.12, p. 6.

16. Data in these discussions are derived from U.S. Bureau of the Census materials. See esp. *Almanac of the States,* 1996, ed. Edith Hornor (Palo Alto: Information Publications, 1996). See also U.S. Bureau of the Census, *Statistical Abstract of the United States, 1995,* 115th ed. (Washington, D.C.: U.S. Bureau of the Census, 1996).

17. The figures are derived from census data as well as from Wesley C. Calef and Howard J. Nelson, "Distribution of Negro Population in the United States," *Geographi-*

cal Review 41 (January 1956): 82–97; and C. Horace Hamilton, "The Negro Leaves the South," *Demography* 1, no. 1 (1964): 273–95.

18. Ray Marshall and Virgil L. Christian Jr., eds., *Employment of Blacks in the South* (Austin: University of Texas Press, 1978), pp. 239, 241.

19. Calculated from data presented in U.S. Department of Commerce, *Personal Income, 1929–1982* (Washington, D.C.: U.S. Bureau of Economic Analysis, 1982).

20. See Emergency Council, *Report*, pp. 21–23; and Vance, *All These People*, esp. pts. 2 and 3. For detailed discussions of the characteristics of southern agriculture and its consequences for the lives of southerners, see, among other works, Vance, *Human Geography of the South*, Frederick Law Olmsted, *The Cotton Kingdom* (1861; reprint, New York: Knopf, 1953); James H. Street, *The New Revolution in the Cotton Economy* (Chapel Hill: University of North Carolina Press, 1957); Harold D. Woodman, *King Cotton and His Retainers* (Lexington: University of Kentucky Press, 1968); Gavin Wright, *The Political Economy of the Cotton South* (New York: Norton, 1978); Walter Ebeling, *The Fruited Plain* (Berkeley: University of California Press, 1979); and Gordon C. Fite, *Cotton Fields No More* (Lexington: University of Kentucky Press, 1984).

21. Vance, *All These People*, p. 215.

22. The figure for the entire United States was 35 percent.

23. Vance, *All These People*, pp. 225–30.

24. Street, *New Revolution*, p. 29.

25. For a fascinating, if fictional, account of how this happened, see Flannery O'Connor's famous short story, "The Displaced Person."

26. See Luther Tweeten, *Foundations of Farm Policy* (Lincoln: University of Nebraska Press, 1970); Monroe Billington, *The Political South in the Twentieth Century* (New York: Scribner's, 1975); and Virgil L. Christian and Carl C. Erwin, "Agriculture," and F. Ray Marshall and Virgil L. Christian, "Economics of Employment Discrimination," both in *Employment of Blacks in the South*, ed. Marshall and Christian, esp. pp. 40–50, 235.

27. See esp. Street, *New Revolution;* Wright, *Political Economy of the Cotton South;* and Fite, *Cotton Fields No More*.

28. Ebeling, *Fruited Plain*, p. 137.

29. Street, *New Revolution*, chap. 3. See also Claudius T. Murchison, *King Cotton Is Sick* (Chapel Hill: University of North Carolina Press, 1930).

30. F. Ray Marshall and Virgil L. Christian Jr., "Human Resource Development in the South," in *You Can't Eat Magnolias*, ed. H. Brandt Ayres and Thomas H. Naylor (New York: McGraw-Hill, 1972), pp. 234–36.

31. For moving accounts of the impact of cotton's collapse on people, see Vance, *Human Geography of the South*, chaps. 8, 16; and Vance, *All These People*, pt. 2.

32. This oft-heard and frequently quoted remark has no readily identifiable source and may be apocryphal. Nonetheless, the sentiments it evokes encapsulate the frustration of the modern small southern farmer in trying to make an economic success of his enterprise.

33. For helpful analyses of this proposition, see Street, *New Revolution*, chap. 2; Don Paarlberg, *American Farm Policy* (New York: John Wiley, 1964); Tweeten, *Foundations of Farm Policy;* Jim Hightower, *Hard Tomatoes, Hard Times* (Cambridge, Mass.: Schenkman, 1978); and Ebeling, *Fruited Plain*.

34. Tweeten, *Foundations of Farm Policy*, p. 131.

35. This point is one of the major themes of Hightower's *Hard Tomatoes, Hard Times*.

36. Street, *New Revolution*, p. 34 and chaps. 4–8.

37. Calculated from The Census of Agriculture, 1982.

38. The southern figure was $36 billion; Texas, $10 billion.

39. The U.S. figure was $43,618; in the South, $34,680.

40. Comparable figures for the United States were 37 percent and 65 percent, respectively.

41. The national figure was $84,459; the southern average, $73,591.

42. The change in scale was made both to take account of inflation rates and because of a small change in the way agricultural sales were reported by the 1992 Agricultural Census.

43. I am indebted to Professor Steven Sanderson of the University of Florida for this observation.

44. Emergency Council, *Report,* pp. 61–64.

45. The figures in this sentence are from 1929.

46. Emergency Council, *Report,* pp. 21–23. See also Vance, *All These People,* esp. pts. 2 and 3, for analyses of social and economic conditions in the South prior to World War II.

47. Data for 1993 are from the *Statistical Abstract, 1995* (115th ed.), table 713.

48. In 1994 the gaps between the United States and Mississippi, Arkansas, Louisiana, Alabama, South Carolina, and Tennessee were, respectively, $5,971, $4,911, $4,158, $3,799, $4,114, $2,327. The source of recent per capita income data is U.S. Bureau of the Census, *Statistical Abstract, 1995* (115th ed.), table 713.

49. The figures are absolute and do not control for inflation.

50. Marshall and Christian, "Introduction," pp. 11–13. See also Wright, *Old South, New South,* for a recent analysis of historical black-white wage differentials in the South.

51. $3,690 for blacks; $7,179 for whites.

52. Mississippi: $2,833 for blacks, and $6,484 for whites; Tennessee: $3,884 for blacks, and $6,657 for whites.

53. Data are from 1989 and are calculated from Bureau of the Census, 1990, *Census of the Population,* Social and Economic Characteristics, tables 92 and 93 for each state (Washington, D.C.: Bureau of the Census, 1993). Southern white income in 1989 reached 93 percent of the national figure ($15,627 and $16,746, respectively), while southern black income was only 80 percent of national per capita black income ($7,400 compared to $9,177).

54. The Mississippi figures in 1989 were $14,088 for whites and $5,615 for blacks; in Texas they were, respectively, $15,391 and $8,314.

55. It should be noted that only in Virginia did both white and black income figures exceed national norms in 1989. Whites in Virginia earned $19,090 per capita, and blacks $9,868.

56. Carl N. Degler, *Place over Time* (Baton Rouge: Louisiana State University Press, 1977), p. 16.

57. In 1981, for a household of four, the poverty line was $9,287; in 1984, $10,609. See Leonard Beeghley, *Living Poorly in America* (New York: Praeger, 1983), pp. 18–20. See also *MS Magazine,* April 1986, p. 47.

58. Data in this paragraph are from U.S. Bureau of the Census, *Statistical Abstract, 1995* (115th ed.), tables 749 and 751. The census South, as we noted in chapter 1, is somewhat different from the South as defined in this text.

59. These figures do not represent "functional illiteracy," for which hard data are difficult to assemble. A reasonable assumption, however, is that functional illiteracy in the South, especially among its older and black populations, is significantly higher than it is elsewhere in the nation. Data are compiled from Bureau of the Census, *Statistical Abstracts,* 1903–1995.

60. Data on health are derived from *Vital Statistics of the United States* (Washington, D.C.: Bureau of the Census, 1937–1992). It is of interest that as late as 1975

southern black rates of death from syphilis were reported as 204 percent those of whites. A public health official interviewed for this study who requested anonymity indicated that much of this differential was a result of racial discrimination: many white deaths from syphilis were unreported, or attributed to other causes, whereas deaths of blacks from syphilis were not covered up.

61. In 1990, the white southern infant mortality rate was 8.1, compared to 7.7 nationally; the 1992 figures were 7.3 and 6.9, respectively. U.S. Bureau of the Census, *Statistical Abstracts, 1995* (115th ed.), table 123.

62. In 1990, infant mortality rates among southern blacks averaged 16.8, while the national average was 18.0. In 1992, the figures were, respectively, 15.8 and 16.8. U.S. Bureau of the Census, *Statistical Abstracts, 1995* (115th ed.), table 123.

63. U.S. Bureau of the Census, *Statistical Abstracts, 1995* (115th ed.), table 170.

Chapter 3. Race, Democrats, and Old Style Southern Politics

1. Dewey Grantham, *The Regional Imagination* (Nashville: Vanderbilt University Press, 1979).

2. There is no agreed-upon definition of political culture. In general, it is the fundamental set of attitudes, beliefs, norms, and values that citizens hold about government and politics. Political culture is the basics on which governmental institutions and behaviors rests. It also defines the place government and politics occupy in society and the role they play in the lives of citizens. There is a vast literature on political culture. For useful and accessible overviews, see Lucian W. Pye, "Political Culture," in *International Encyclopedia of the Social Sciences,* ed. David L. Sills, vol. 12 (New York: Macmillan Company and Free Press, 1968), pp. 218–24; Elazar, *American Federalism;* Walter A. Rosenbaum, *Political Culture* (New York: Praeger, 1975); Gabriel Almond and Sidney Verba, *The Civic Culture Revisited* (Boston: Little, Brown, 1980); Michael Brint, *A Genealogy of Political Culture* (Boulder, Colo.: Westview Press, 1991); Ellis, *American Political Cultures;* and Elazar, *American Mosaic.*

3. Woodward, *Strange Career of Jim Crow;* Gunnar Myrdal, *An American Dilemma* (1944; reprint, New York: Pantheon, 1975).

4. The term "Jim Crow" refers to a stock black character in minstrel shows and carnivals during the nineteenth century.

5. A classic discussion of the different types of rules to which southerners adhered concerning black-white relations can be found in William Alexander Percy, *Lanterns on the Levee* (New York: Alfred A. Knopf, Inc., 1941; reprint, Baton Rouge: Louisiana State University Press, 1973). The Percy family demonstrated the paternalistic view of how blacks should be treated; in this view, blacks were regarded as slow children who had to be watched, taught, restrained, and not trusted but not treated badly either. The family had little use or sympathy for the vicious racism of their neighbors or the violence others frequently directed against blacks.

6. The modern reader might find this point of view difficult to credit. To illustrate how prevalent it was, the following quotation, from a governor of Georgia early in this century, is offered. It represents his explanation for the problems of southern agriculture. The fact that the state's chief executive engaged in rhetoric of this kind should convince the modern reader of the breadth and depth of southern racial attitudes at that time and of the willingness of demagogues and other politicians to exploit them:

We have not diversified our crops because the Negro has not been willing to diversify. We have not used improved machinery on our farms thereby economizing expenses because the Negro is not willing to use such implements. We have not improved our soil because the Negro is not willing to grow crops to be incorporated into the soil, nor leave his cotton seed to be returned to the fields that he has denuded of humus and all possible traces of fertility. Because he is unwilling to handle heavy plows we have permitted him to scratch the land with his scooter just deep enough for all the soil to be washed from the surface, leaving our fields practically barren and wasted. We have not raised stock on the farm because the Negro is cruelly inhuman and starves the work animals we put in his hands for his personal support. We have accepted his thriftless and destructive methods simply because under our present system we have not been able to do without him. If this be true our present system in this relation is absolutely ruinous and it will not invite the residence of intelligent settlers from the outside.

Quoted in Vance, *Human Geography of the South,* p. 192.

7. See chapter 2 for a discussion of southern agriculture, the tenant-cropper system, and the role of race in it.

8. Woodward, *Strange Career of Jim Crow;* Myrdal, *American Dilemma.*

9. John Hope Franklin, *From Slavery to Freedom* (New York: Vintage, 1969), pp. 439–40. Some of these lynchings occurred outside the South.

10. See Anne Firor Scott, *The Southern Lady* (Chicago: University of Chicago Press, 1970); and Florence King, *Southern Ladies and Gentlemen* (New York: Stein and Day, 1975). For a jaundiced view of the upbringing and role of the traditional southern woman, see Rosemary Daniell, *Fatal Flowers* (New York: Holt, Rinehart and Winston, 1980).

11. Key, *Southern Politics,* p. 74; William D. Miller, *Mr. Crump of Memphis* (Baton Rouge: Louisiana State University Press, 1964). See also Alfred B. Clubok, John M. DeGrove, and Charles D. Farris, "The Manipulated Negro Vote," *Journal of Politics* 26 (February 1964): 112–29.

12. Quoted in Key, *Southern Politics,* p. 232.

13. Franklin, *From Slavery to Freedom,* p. 342.

14. Key, *Southern Politics,* chap. 1.

15. Ibid., pp. 3–12. See also Kousser, *Shaping of Southern Politics.*

16. This last point is significant. Southern white discrimination against blacks is well known. But it has not been as widely recognized that up-country whites were also victimized by delta elites. The fact that the latter held most of the region's economic resources gave them additional leverage against white dirt farmers and townspeople, especially on such matters as farm, home, and shop mortgages and loans, road construction, and market accessibility for farm products. This position, of course, simply increased the likelihood of political manipulation and exploitation.

17. William Alexander Percy's autobiography, *Lanterns on the Levee,* shows the extent of internecine conflicts between genteel whites and "white trash" on issues of race, and other matters.

18. Following the Depression years, because of their devastating impact on southern agriculture and particularly on black tenants and sharecroppers, black migration out of the South reached torrential proportions; it increased still more during World War II, as blacks left the South in search of jobs. More than 4 million blacks are thought to have left the deep South states alone by 1960. See Peirce, *Deep South States of America,* p. 15. See also chapter 2 of this volume.

19. In 1900 the deep South states were 47 percent black; in 1970, 25 percent.

20. E.E. Schattschneider, *The Semisovereign People* (Hinsdale, Ill.: Dryden Press, 1975).

21. To understand how opposition was diffused, see T. Harry Williams, *Huey Long* (New York: Bantam, 1969); A.J. Liebling, *The Earl of Louisiana* (Baton Rouge: Louisiana State University Press, 1970); William Anderson, *The Wild Man from Sugar Creek* (Baton Rouge: Louisiana State University Press, 1975); Marshall Frady, *Southerners* (New York: New American Library, 1980); and Glen Jeansonne, *Messiah of the Masses* (New York: Harper Collins, 1993).

22. See Elazar, *American Federalism;* Elazar, *American Mosaic;* and Black and Black, *Politics and Society in the South,* chaps. 1 and 2.

23. See, for example, Degler, *Place over Time; Why the South Will Survive* (Athens: University of Georgia Press, 1981); John P. East, *The American Conservative Movement* (Chicago: Henry Regnery, 1986); George M. Curtis III and James J. Thompson Jr., eds., *The Southern Essays of Richard Weaver* (Indianapolis: Liberty Press, 1987); Eugene Genovese, *The Southern Tradition* (Cambridge, Mass.: Harvard University Press, 1994).

24. Key, *Southern Politics,* chaps. 1, 14. Key's view reflects his normative position concerning the role parties play in American politics; it represents the most abstract level proposed in *Southern Politics* (see chapter 1 above). Other representative and accessible views on American political parties can be found in Samuel Eldersveld, *Political Parties in Modern Society* (New York: Basic Books, 1982); Frank J. Sorauf and Paul Allen Beck, *Party Politics in America* (Glenview: Scott Foresman, 1988); Malcolm E. Jewell and David M. Olson, *American State Political Parties and Elections,* 3d ed. (Homewood: Dorsey Press, 1988); Larry Sabato, *The Party's Just Begun* (Glenview, Ill.: Scott Foresman, 1988); Martin Wattenberg, *The Decline of American Political Parties* (Cambridge, Mass.: Harvard University Press, 1990).

25. Key, *Southern Politics,* p. 16.

26. The term is from the late Lee Atwater, prominent national Republican strategist of the 1980s. Political scientists generally use another term, "umbrella organizations," to describe the broad coalitions that make up political parties in the United States. Atwater's term is more graphic and probably more accurate, since it implies the circuslike atmosphere characteristic of the internal politics of modern political parties.

27. See, for example, Austin Ranney, "Parties in State Politics," in *Politics in the American States,* ed. Herbert Jacob and Kenneth N. Vines, 2d ed. (Boston: Little, Brown, 1971), pp. 82–121. See also Joseph A. Schlesinger, "The Politics of the Executive," in ibid., pp. 211–16, 228. See also John F. Bibby and Thomas M. Holbrook, "Parties and Elections," in *Politics in the American States,* ed. Virginia Gray and Herbert Jacob, 6th ed. (Washington, D.C.: CQ Press, 1996), chap. 3; and Stephen A. Salmore and Barbara G. Salmore, "The Transformation of State Electoral Politics," in *The State of the States,* ed. Carl E. Van Horn, 3d ed. (Washington, D.C.: CQ Press, 1996), chap. 4.

28. Robert Sherrill, *Gothic Politics in the Deep South* (New York: Grossman, 1968).

29. Robert Penn Warren, *All the King's Men* (New York: Harcourt, Brace, 1946). See also Jack Temple Kirby, *Media Made Dixie,* rev. ed. (Athens: University of Georgia Press, 1986).

30. Key, *Southern Politics,* chap. 14.

31. Other statewide offices could be used, but as Key and other political observers have long noted, the presence of an incumbent in an election for major state office, such as U.S. senator or perhaps state attorney general, can discourage possible challengers. Thus incumbency partially masks the extent of factionalism present in a state. An open seat, however, in a statewide office allows it to be used for examining the extent of factionalism.

32. Key, *Southern Politics,* chap. 2.

33. See Allen Sindler, *Huey Long's Louisiana* (Baltimore: Johns Hopkins University

Press, 1956); and C. Vann Woodward, *Tom Watson, Agrarian Rebel,* 2d ed. (Savannah: Beehive Press, 1973). See also the citations in note 21, above.

34. Chapter 9 will deal specifically with demagogues in southern politics.

35. Sectional cleavages were also important in Tennessee, as the state seemed to divide into three regions: delta (western Tennessee, centered around Memphis); the piedmont (the central portion of the state, centered around the capital, Nashville); and mountain (eastern Tennessee, including Knoxville). Edward Crump took full advantage of these sectional tensions in building and maintaining his machine.

36. For a discussion of Georgia's county unit system, see Key, *Southern Politics,* pp. 117–24. The U.S. Supreme Court eventually ruled the county unit system unconstitutional as part of its attack on legislative malapportionment. See *Gray v. Sanders,* 372 U.S. 368 (1963).

37. See Sherrill, *Gothic Politics;* see also Marshall Frady, *Wallace* (New York: World Publishing Co., 1968); Dan T. Carter, *George Wallace, Richard Nixon, and the Transformation of American Politics* (Waco, Tex.: Markam Press Fund, 1992); and Carter, *The Politics of Rage* (New York: Simon and Schuster, 1995).

38. See Tindall (1967); Newby, *The South;* and esp. Grantham, *Southern Progresssivism.* See also Boles, *South through Time.*

39. Some unique features of North Carolina politics will be dealt with in Chapter 8.

40. Key, *Southern Politics,* chap. 5. See also David R. Colburn and Richard K. Scher, *Florida's Gubernatorial Politics in the Twentieth Century* (Tallahassee: University Presses of Florida, a Florida State University Book, 1980), esp. chap. 3.

41. All of the southern states required that the winners of statewide elections receive a majority (50 percent +1) vote. This requirement was in contrast to states elsewhere, where it was possible to be victorious in a statewide contest just by getting the most votes, even if less than a majority. Two principal reasons prompted the majority requirement in the South. The first was to ensure that no black candidate would win; in the unlikely event a black candidate emerged, and in the even more unlikely event significant numbers of blacks voted, it was nonetheless possible for a black candidate to emerge victorious (although with a minority of votes) if there were a half dozen or so whites in the race who split the rest of the vote. The majority vote requirement was an insurance policy against this unlikely development. The second reason was that it was much more difficult for a populist or other fringe candidate to win when there was a majority vote requirement; other dominant but conservative factions would, at least temporarily, coalesce to stop such an occurrence. It did happen, of course, on occasion, but the likelihood is that the majority vote requirement kept it from happening more often than it did.

42. We shall pursue these issues further in Chapter 10. See William Havard and Loren Beth, *The Politics of Mis-Representation* (Baton Rouge: Louisiana State University Press, 1962); Sherrill, *Gothic Politics;* Earl Black, *Southern Governors and Civil Rights* (Cambridge, Mass.: Harvard University Press, 1976); Colburn and Scher, *Florida's Gubernatorial Politics;* and Larry Sabato, *Goodbye to Goodtime Charley,* 2d ed. (Washington, D.C.: CQ Press, 1983).

43. By the 1980s, the situation had changed somewhat, although many southern states, including the relatively wealthy border states of Texas and Florida, still ranked very low on per-capita expenditures in many crucial areas of state policy. For comparative figures, see "Yardsticks: State Government Spending Patterns Are Shifting," *Governing* 1, no. 3 (December 1987): 56–57.

44. There is a large literature on this point. Representative works include Thomas R. Dye, *Politics, Economics, and the Public* (Chicago: Rand McNally, 1966); and Ira Sharkansky and Richard Hofferbert, "Dimensions of State Politics, Economics and Pub-

lic Policy," *American Political Science Review* 63 (February 1971): 112–32. See, more recently, Robert S. Erikson, John P. McIver, and Gerald C. Wright, "State Political Culture and Public Opinion," *American Political Science Review* 81, no. 3 (September 1987): 797–813; and Gerald C. Wright, Robert S. Erikson, and John P. McIver, "Public Opinion and Policy Liberalism in the American States," *American Journal of Political Science* 31, no. 4 (November 1987): 980–1001.

45. *Plessy v. Ferguson,* 163 U.S. 537 (1896).

46. On this point, see Barbara Hinckley, *The Seniority System in Congress* (Bloomington: Indiana University Press, 1971); Randall Ripley, *Congress,* 2d ed. (New York: Norton, 1978), pp. 63–69; and Barbara Hinckley, *Stability and Change in Congress,* 3d ed. (New York: Harper and Row, 1983), chap. 1.

47. James T. Patterson, *Congressional Conservatism and the New Deal* (Lexington: University of Kentucky Press, 1967), pp. 329–30; W. Wayne Shannon, "Revolt in Washington: The South in Congress," in *Changing Politics of the South,* ed. Havard, pp. 665–73; and Steven S. Smith and Christopher J. Deering, *Committees in Congress* (Washington, D.C.: CQ Press, 1984), p. 24.

48. *Brown v. Board of Education,* 347 U.S. 483 (1954).

Chapter 4. Out of the Closet: Southern Republicans and Presidential Elections

1. "Republicanism" is a vague term deliberately chosen to convey a number of possibilities: the actual presence of genuine Republicans (few in number though they might have been); a demonstrable Republican vote; the willingness of citizens to identify with Republicans or Republican issues (even if they were nominal Democrats); the presence of Republican Party organization or activity; the presence of Republican candidates for office; even the secret sigh of relief among some, especially middle-class, southerners that Republicans had won the White House.

2. See, for example, M. Margaret Conway, *Political Participation in the United States,* 2d ed. (Washington, D.C.: CQ Press, 1991).

3. Newby, *The South,* pp. 253–54.

4. Ibid. See also Woodward, *Origins of the New South* and *Strange Career of Jim Crow.*

5. Democrats active in the "redemption" process were called "Redeemers."

6. Newby, *The South,* p. 270.

7. Key, *Southern Politics,* esp. chap. 13.

8. Ibid., chap. 13.

9. Ibid., p. 278.

10. Ibid., p. 279; Colburn and Scher, *Florida's Gubernatorial Politics,* p. 94.

11. For example, in Georgia no Republican candidate for governor appeared on the ballot between 1900 and 1962; the first to do so was Bo Callaway in 1966, who beat Lester Maddox in the popular vote, but because the election was contested and thrown into the Georgia House of Representatives, Maddox (Democratic) was chosen.

12. Key, *Southern Politics,* p. 280.

13. Ibid., pp. 282–83.

14. Ibid., p. 281; Heard, *Two-Party South?*

15. Key, *Southern Politics,* p. 286.

16. Ibid., p. 286.

17. Besides the older, established black Republicans just noted, there is a small but growing group of conservative middle-class blacks emerging in the South. Intensely

conservative and buying fully into the national Republican "Contract with America" in the manner in which Alan Keyes did during his 1995–96 bid for the Republican presidential nomination, some have proven to be, like Keyes, formidable candidates. An example is Marc Little, a prominent conservative black radio talk show host from Jacksonville. He opposed Congresswoman Corinne Brown (Florida District 3) in 1994, and while he lost in an overwhelmingly Democratic (and majority black) district, he emerged as a credible and attractive candidate. In April 1996, a federal court declared Brown's district illegal, and it had to be redrawn with a smaller black population. Little chose not to run again in 1996, but speculation continues that his political career is just beginning. However, other conservative black Republicans have not fared quite as well. For example, Arthur Teele, a prominent black attorney, ran for mayor of Miami as a Republican in 1987. He finished a distant third behind two Hispanic candidates. Teele was subsequently elected to the Dade County Commission.

18. Heard, *Two-Party South?*, pp. 38–49.
19. Ibid., pp. 51–53.
20. Ibid., p. 53.
21. Strong, *Urban Republicanism.*
22. Ibid., esp. pp. 56–59.
23. The Blacks' recent works, along with those of several others, also emphasize the role of disaffected whites and the middle class in the rise of the southern Republican Party. These recent studies, however, note an important point that Key, Heard, and Strong could not foresee: because of disaffection with the Democratic Party, many blue-collar white southern males became Republican or became swing voters tending to vote for Republicans when they perceived Democratic candidates as weak and/or uncommitted to "traditional" American values such as patriotism, strong defense, families, law-and-order, etc., or not sufficiently hostile to welfare cheats, drug pushers, abortion, homosexuals, etc. On the other hand, many of these blue-collar white southerners retain certain liberal views on pocketbook economic issues, such as medical insurance, unemployment and workman's compensation, and tax policy. See Black and Black, *Politics and Society in the South* and *Vital South.*
24. Tables 4.1 and 4.2 show the percentage of the southern popular vote for Republican presidential nominees between 1900 and 1992. To make the data more accessible, they are divided into 1900–60 (Table 4.1) and 1964–1992 (Table 4.2), and arranged by deep South and border South states. Several accessible texts that provide helpful interpretive discussions of presidential elections are Arthur M. Schlesinger, ed., *History of Presidential Elections* (New York: Chelsea, 1971); Eugene Roseboom, *A History of Presidential Elections* (New York: Macmillan, 1979); and Nelson W. Polsby and Aaron Wildavsky, *Presidential Elections,* 6th ed. (New York: Scribner's, 1984).
25. The significance of these percentages will be reviewed in chapter 5; for now, they are descriptive only.
26. Key, *Southern Politics,* p. 375.
27. Newby, *The South,* pp. 389–90.
28. See Alan Fried, "'And We'll All Be Free: The Role of the Press in the Integration of the United States Army" (Ph.D. diss., College of Journalism, University of Florida, 1994).
29. See, for example, John Hope Franklin, *From Slavery to Freedom,* 4th ed. (New York: Knopf, 1974); Billington, *Political South in the Twentieth Century.*
30. Key, *Southern Politics,* p. 375.
31. Key, *Southern Politics,* pp. 335–38.
32. It is arguable that in the long run, the Republicans did exactly this: in 1980, Ronald Reagan ran what was at least partially a states' rights campaign, and wholly "against Washington." This position proved popular nationally as well as in the South and was reinforced in the Republican campaigns of 1984, 1988, and even in 1992. In 1992 the

Democrats finally hopped on the states' rights–anti-Washington-gridlock bandwagon in the person of Governor Bill Clinton of Arkansas. As the 1996 campaign dawned, some of the fervor found in both parties to run against Washington waned, but it by no means disappeared. The Dixiecrats may well have lost the 1948 election, but their message was still powerful nearly fifty years later and influenced both parties, especially the GOP, strongly.

33. *Brown v. Board of Education,* 347 U.S. 483 (1954).

34. Besides Newby, *The South,* see generally Numan Bartley, *The Rise of Massive Resistance* (Baton Rouge: Louisiana State University Press, 1969). For the Florida experience, see David R. Colburn and Richard K. Scher, "Race Relations and Florida Gubernatorial Politics after *Brown,*" *Florida Historical Quarterly* 76 (October 1976): 153–69.

35. Dwight Eisenhower received 4.1 million votes in 1952, 4.2 million in 1956; Adlai Stevenson received 4.4 million in 1952, and 4.1 million in 1956. Underscoring our point is the fact that Eisenhower "won" the southern popular vote in 1956 by about 100,000 votes, while capturing five of the states. Ike's Electoral College totals in the South distort the extent of Republican strength, because three of the five states he won—Texas, Florida, and Virginia—were among the most populous.

36. See, on the 1960 election, Theodore White, *The Making of the President, 1960* (New York: Atheneum, 1961); William Manchester, *The Glory and the Dream* (Boston: Little, Brown, 1974); and White, *America in Search of Itself* (New York: Harper and Row, 1982).

37. Kennedy received 51 percent of the vote in deep South states to Nixon's 36 percent. However, 39 percent of Mississippi's electors remained unpledged. Leaving Mississippi out of the calculations, Kennedy received 55 percent of the vote. In the border South, Kennedy got 49 percent, and Nixon 50 percent. See Table 4.1.

38. Nixon received 50+ percent of the vote in the border South states, but only 41 percent in the five deep South states. In terms of the popular vote, Nixon received 1 million in the deep South states, and Kennedy 1.5 million. The border South states were, and are, far more populous than the deep South states.

39. See Doris Kearns, *Lyndon Johnson and the American Dream* (New York: Harper and Row, 1976); and Robert A. Caro, *The Years of Lyndon Johnson* (New York: Knopf, 1982). See also Bartley and Graham, *Southern Politics and the Second Reconstruction.*

40. Theodore White, *The Making of the President, 1968* (New York: Atheneum, 1969); Frady, *Wallace;* Garry Wills, *Nixon Agonistes* (Boston: Houghton Mifflin, 1970); David Halberstam, *The Best and the Brightest* (New York: Random House, 1972); Manchester, *Glory and Dream;* White, *America in Search of Itself.* On Wallace, the best recent work is Carter, *The Politics of Rage.*

41. See, for example, Arthur M. Schlesinger, *The Imperial Presidency* (Boston: Houghton Mifflin, 1973); and William Safire, *Before the Fall* (Garden City, N.Y.: Doubleday, 1975). Scarcely anyone had paid attention to a few articles in the *New York Times* and *Washington Post* during the summer 1972 about an obscure break-in at the Watergate Hotel in Washington, D.C. It played no role in the fall campaign or election.

42. Theodore White, *The Making of the President, 1972* (New York: Atheneum, 1974); Manchester, *Glory and Dream;* White, *America in Search of Itself.*

43. The best work on the 1976 election and Jimmy Carter's pursuit of the nomination and election is Jules Witcover, *Marathon* (New York: Viking, 1977). See also Gerald Pomper, *The Election of 1976* (New York: D. McKay, 1977); and White, *America in Search of Itself.*

44. See Gerald Pomper, *The Election of 1980* (Chatham, N.J.: Chatham House, 1981); White, *America in Search of Itself;* and Polsby and Wildavsky, *Presidential Elections.* It is of interest that once inaugurated, Reagan pursued a number of policies at odds with the campaign promises that appealed to southerners, especially on budget deficits, and refused to propose protectionist economic policies on farm products and manufactured goods.

45. See Gerald Pomper, *The Election of 1984* (Chatham, N.J.: Chatham House, 1985).

46. *Congressional Quarterly Week,* 46, no. 46 (November 12, 1988): 3241–44. See also Gerald Pomper, *The Election of 1988* (Chatham, N.J.: Chatham House, 1989).

47. The importance of the South for electing Republican presidents is detailed in Black and Black, *Vital South.*

48. On the 1992 presidential campaign, see, for example, Jack Germond and Jules Witcover, *Mad as Hell* (New York: Warner, 1993); Hunter S. Thompson, *Better Than Sex* (New York: Random House, 1994); Matthew Robert Kerbel, *Edited for Television* (Boulder, Colo.: Westview Press, 1994); Mary Matalin and James Carville, *All's Fair* (New York: Random House, Simon and Schuster, 1994).

49. For another view, see Gerald Pomper, *The Election of 1992* (Chatham, N.J.: Chatham House, 1993).

50. See, for example, James L. Guth, "God's Own Party," in *Christian Century,* 110 (February 17, 1993): 172; John F. Persinos, "Has the Christian Right Taken Over the Republican Party," *Campaigns and Elections,* 15 (September 1994): 20; and Mark J. Rozell and Clyde Wilcox, eds., *God at the Grassroots* (Lanham, Md.: Rowman and Littlefield, 1995). I am indebted to Professor Ken Wald, University of Florida, for this observation and his assistance with citations.

51. The 1992 election is an anomaly in this regard. It remains to be seen whether the 1996 election will show a return to the earlier pattern in which the South votes like the rest of the nation, or whether it again bucks the trend. If the latter, it may be that a new phase of presidential electoral politics has started, in which the South and the rest of the nation are, in terms of presidential elections, out of sync.

52. As measured by the percentage of the vote given the Republican candidate. Leaving 1912 aside as an anomaly (Teddy Roosevelt ran as a Bull Moose, splitting the Republican vote and handing the election to Woodrow Wilson), the figure rises to 36 percent.

53. For example, see Louis Seagull, *Southern Republicanism* (New York: Holsted Press, 1975). Most of these voters, in Seagull's view, are white males, predominantly blue collar and lower-middle-class white collar; more recent studies have corroborated this conclusion, for example, Black and Black, *Vital South.* A good deal of media attention has also been paid to what is often rudely and unfairly called "the Bubba vote." In fact, of course, the angry voter extends to males in lower-middle-class white collar positions and to women as well. In the 1994 Republican surge, media attention focused heavily on "the angry male," found not just in the South but nationally as well. The evidence presented suggested that women were angry, too.

54. For more elaborate discussions of this point, see Seagull, *Southern Republicanism;* and Black and Black, *Politics and Society* and *Vital South.* Bob Dole, a moderate Republican who was the 1996 GOP presidential nominee, moved early in his primary campaign to shore up his strength on the right wing of the party. He campaigned early and often in the South, recognizing his need to run strongly in the region if he were to unseat President Clinton. The conservative tone and message he adopted seemed at least in part designed to be a modern version of the Republican southern strategy.

Chapter 5. Johnnies Come Lately: Southern Republicanism in State and Local Politics

1. Tip O'Neill, former Speaker of the U.S. House of Representatives, noted this point in his pithy comment, "All politics is local." See Christopher Matthews, *Hardball* (New York: Summit Books, 1988), chap. 2.

2. In many parts of the South, notably Arkansas, political debate in campaigns

centered on qualifications for office. Often "qualifications" was a surrogate term for the candidate's family pedigree, educational and professional background, factional membership, and section of residence.

3. For general discussions on state and local elections, see, for example, David Saffell, *State and Local Government* (New York: McGraw-Hill, 1993); David Berman, *State and Local Politics,* 7th ed. (Madison, Wis.: Brown and Benchmark, 1994); Robert Lorch, *State and Local Politics,* 5th ed. (Englewood Cliffs, N.J.: Prentice-Hall, 1995); Ann Bowman and Richard Kearney, *State and Local Government,* 3d ed. (Boston: Houghton Mifflin, 1996); W.B. Stouffer, Cynthia Opheim, and Susan Bland Day, *State and Local Politics,* 2d ed. (New York: Harper Collins, 1996). For more detailed information, see Bibby and Holbrook, "Parties and Elections"; and Salmore and Salmore, "Transformation of State Electoral Politics."

4. Figures can be found in the case study chapters of Key, *Southern Politics.* Key notes that in Virginia, turnouts in gubernatorial primaries between 1925 and 1945 averaged under 10 percent, allowing the Byrd machine to dominate the selection process. Even today, in aggregate, southerners register and vote at lower rates than do citizens in other parts of the country. See Harold W. Stanley and Richard G. Niemi, *Vital Statistics on American Politics* (Washington, D.C.: CQ Press, 1988), pp. 66–67. There are exceptions. In 1990 (a nonpresidential election year), in Florida the governor's race generated great statewide interest; some 58 percent of Floridians voted, a higher figure than sometimes turns out for presidential contests in Florida and elsewhere.

5. See Tindall, *Emergence of the New South,* p. 166.

6. Data for senatorial elections can only begin in 1914; prior to that time, senators were not popularly elected but were selected by state legislatures. Likewise, data for state legislatures will begin in the mid-1930s. The Council of State Governments began to collect data on state legislatures during this decade. Prior to then, data on the partisan composition of state legislatures in the South are sketchy and unreliable. For example, some of the southern states did not even bother to keep accurate records of the party affiliations of members. The overwhelming majority, of course, were Democrats, so perhaps it did not matter. However, as one longtime participant in and observer of Georgia politics told the author by telephone, some representatives from northern counties may well have been Republicans but declared themselves to be independent, even Democrats, in order to be seated. Thus there is no sure way, prior to the mid-1930s, to tell exactly how many Republicans may actually have been members of southern state legislatures.

7. Readers must not assume that nonpartisan local elections necessarily represented a breech in the solid wall of the Democratic South. The southern version of the progressive movement included provisions for nonpartisan elections at the local level. However, while the Democratic Party often did not officially take part in these elections (and in some instances was legally forbidden from doing so), partisanship did not just disappear. In fact, sometimes the local (and state) party played a behind-the-scenes role in locating candidates and running campaigns. Democratic county officials were firmly in control of election machinery. And even though the elections were nominally nonpartisan, especially in smaller communities the party affiliation of candidates was well known anyway: virtually everyone was a Democrat. Thus nonpartisan local elections constituted very little if any threat to dominant Democratic organizations and elites.

8. See, for example, Richard F. Fenno, *Home Style* (Boston: Little, Brown, 1978); Glenn R. Parker, ed., *Studies of Congress* (Washington, D.C.: CQ Press, 1985); and Parker *Homeward Bound* (Pittsburgh: University of Pittsburgh Press, 1986).

9. There is a large literature on interparty competition. For an excellent survey of the theory and methodology of this literature, see John F. Bibby, Cornelius P. Cotter, James

L. Gibson, and Robert J. Huckshorn, "Parties in State Politics," in *Politics in the American States,* ed. Virginia Gray, Herbert Jacob, and Kenneth N. Vines, 4th ed. (Boston: Little, Brown, 1983), pp. 59–96; see also Bibby and Holbrook, "Parties and Elections"; and, for another critique, Warren Heyman, "Constraints to Republican Development: The Deep South States, 1960–1986" (Ph.D. diss., Department of Political Science, University of Florida, Gainesville, 1993).

10. To pursue the point a bit further, party affiliation and registration are inadequate measures of Republican penetration because those figures do not show the willingness of non-Republicans (Democrats and independents) to vote for a GOP candidate. In fact, in some states, such as Florida, North Carolina, Tennessee, and at times Alabama, Texas, and Georgia, there was a substantial crossover vote. That is, non-Republicans would support a GOP candidate, possibly even providing a winning margin of victory. Thus we must focus on electoral outcomes, not party registration, to get a truer picture of Republican penetration.

11. For convenience, the discussion will be divided into pre- and post-1960 periods. Too much should not be made of this division; mainly it is to make the discussion easier to follow. On the other hand, as we saw in the last chapter, 1960 was the last hurrah of Democratic presidential politics in the South. Moreover, by 1960 some changes in southern life and politics that began after World War II could be felt; the civil rights movement, for example, was well under way by then. Thus, while 1960 was not a watershed year, it is a convenient way of marking the division between an old-style southern electoral politics and something new that was just starting to emerge.

12. For example, in 1916 Sidney Catts of Florida, a Democrat, appeared on the ballot as a candidate for governor but was not the real candidate of the party. He was in fact the candidate of the Prohibition Party. Catts won the election.

13. It should be remembered that each state elects two senators, who serve non-congruent terms. No separation of the seats will be made in this analysis, even though the politics of one senate seat might vary from the other. For example, in southern states where sectionalism was well developed, a tradition emerged in which each senate seat belonged to a particular part of the state, even though competition for it occurred statewide.

14. See Patterson, *Congressional Conservatism and the New Deal.*

15. These figures represent the total number of victories in each state. Obviously, then, they include repeats,—that is, seats won frequently if not continually by GOP candidates.

16. There were any number of forces at work that served as nationalizing forces on the South. The impact of television and the media generally brought the nation to the South, and vice versa; by the early 1960s television was common in the urban and metropolitan South and could even be found in some remote areas. Other nationalizing influences at this time included school textbooks (and federal pressures for national standards in education), sports, and aspects of popular culture, such as books, movies, magazines, even fast food places such as McDonald's and Burger King. See Fred Powledge, *Journeys through the South* (New York: Vanguard: 1979), esp. chap. 20.

17. Although table 5.4 stops in 1994, it should be noted that in 1995 a Republican won the governorship of Louisiana, against an African American Democratic candidate.

18. A significant number of both figures came in the 1994 Republican landslide, which was felt in the South as strongly as it was elsewhere in the nation.

19. Data on elections in which the Democrats failed to contest for House seats were not collected for this study. On a purely impressionistic basis, however, it is clear that this is not an uncommon occurrence. For example, in the 1994 House elections in Florida, four Republican congressmen faced no Democratic opposition, and an addi-

tional three Republicans faced only write-in candidates in contests in which the Democratic Party made no nomination. Thus, essentially seven of Florida twenty-three House seats (30 percent) were uncontested by Democrats. While this percentage may be somewhat higher than in other southern states, evidence gathered on Republicans indicated that in other southern states there were also House seats held by Republicans uncontested by Democrats during the 1990s.

20. There has been speculation that because of the 1994 Republican landslide even more safe Republican House seats have been created. Perhaps so. It should be noted, however, that reapportionment and redistricting of congressional seats in the early 1990s were probably more important in creating safe GOP seats than was the avalanche of 1994.

21. In 1994, Florida's Cabinet (see chapter 9) became 50 percent Democratic, 50 percent Republican; because of the Democratic governor, however, Democrats have a voting (but not always functional) majority.

22. In fact, changes in some states were so dramatic that the percentages shown in table 5.7 have to be questioned. In Tennessee, for example, a Republican governor and two Republican senators were chosen on election day, 1994, replacing a Democratic governor and two Democratic senators. On the other hand, in Florida and Georgia popular Democratic governors resisted the Republican tide—in both cases by the skin of their teeth. And in Florida all incumbent Democratic House members seeking reelection won, nationally a rarity on that day.

23. This statement might be questioned because Republicans won the governorship in 1995. Most observers interpreted the election as more a matter of racial than partisan politics; the Democratic nominee was an African American, and many white Louisiana Democrats were unwilling to vote for him. With the exception of this election, Republicans in Louisiana have not generally been able to mount many successful campaigns.

24. This figure does not include the 1995 gubernatorial election.

25. In Florida, Republican candidates regularly appear on the ballot and generally run well. They have had more trouble winning elections, however, than their counterparts in North Carolina, South Carolina, and Virginia. Texas appears to be similar to Florida in this regard; given the number of GOP candidates and the strength they seem to get at the polls, one would expect them to have captured more offices.

26. For this analysis we leave off down ticket executive positions and local offices. These are not trivial, by any means. But data on governorships and U.S. Senate and House seats are sufficient to make the point.

27. Includes 1995 Louisiana election.

28. Data are from Michael Barone, Grant Ujifusa, and Douglas Matthews, *Almanac of American Politics* (New York: E.P. Dutton, 1996).

29. Data on the partisan composition of southern legislatures prior to 1939 are available but unreliable. The Council of State Governments began to report data on the political makeup of state legislatures in the late 1930s. All data used in the table are taken from the council's authoritative series, *The Book of the States*.

30. *Almanac of the States*, 1996, ed. Hornor.

31. See Harold W. Stanley, "Southern Partisan Changes: Dealignment, Realignment, or Both?" *Journal of Politics* 50 (February 1988): 64–88.

32. For example, one survey of voters in Fairfax County, Virginia, prior to the gubernatorial election on November 7, 1989, revealed that three of four were born outside the state. See "Virginia Candidates Redouble Efforts," *New York Times,* November 6, 1989, p. 12.

33. See the detailed and elegant treatment of this point in Black and Black, *Politics and Society in the South* and *Vital South.* See also Peirce, *Deep South States of America* and *Border South States of America,* and Lamis, *Two-Party South.*

34. See Paul Cohen, "The Florida Poll," *Gainesville Sun,* January 18, 1976. See also Gregory Lee Baker, "Intra-Party Factionalism: The Florida Republican Party" (M.A. thesis, Department of Political Science, University of Florida, 1976).

35. Federal Reserve Bank of Atlanta, *Economic Review* 67, no. 6 (June 1982): 36.

36. The pathbreaking work on this subject is Seagull, *Southern Republicanism.* See also Lamis, *Two-Party South;* and Black and Black, *Politics and Society in the South* and *Vital South.*

37. See Black and Black, *Politics and Society in the South.* See also Cobb, *Selling of the South* and *Industrialization and Southern Society.*

38. See Seagull, *Southern Republicanism;* and Black and Black, *Politics and Society in the South* and *Vital South.* For earlier analyses, see Key, *Southern Politics;* Alexander Heard, *Two-Party South?;* and Strong, *Urban Republicanism in the South.*

39. Sherrill, *Gothic Politics.* See also Sale, *Power Shift.*

40. In 1988, the southern protest vote seemed to originate from dissatisfaction with the Democratic nominee (Governor Michael Dukakis of Massachusetts), patriotic issues, and concerns about drugs and crime, all of which were overtly exploited by the George Bush campaign, directed by the late Lee Atwater, a native of South Carolina. Perhaps nowhere was this exploitation better demonstrated than in a Republican commercial criticizing Dukakis for Massachusetts's prisoner-release program and featuring frightening pictures of Willie Lee Horton, a convicted black rapist and murderer. See also Black and Black, *Politics and Society in the South* and *Vital South.*

41. Ibid.; Seagull, *Southern Republicanism.* See also Thomas Edsall, *Chain Reaction* (New York: Norton, 1991).

42. The late Ed Gurney in Florida, for example, is credited with running the first media-oriented, candidate-centered campaign for the U.S. Senate in 1968, when he beat Democrat LeRoy Collins.

43. Congressional and state legislature reapportionment are carried out by state legislatures following the decennial census, which generally is reported in the spring of the year following the count. Most states, therefore, wrestle with redistricting and reapportionment by the fall, winter, and following spring.

44. The strategy, known as "divide and conquer," was thought to have originated in the Republican National Committee, specifically by the late Lee Atwater, during the late 1980s.

45. The rationale for creating so-called black access (majority-minority) and influence districts (which have less than a majority but still sizable minority population) came from changes to Section 2 of the Voting Rights Act in 1982, its accompanying Senate report, and *Thornburg v. Gingles,* 478 U.S. 30 (1986). See Richard K. Scher, Jon L. Mills, and John Hotaling, *Voting Rights and Democracy: The Law and Politics of Redistricting* (Chicago: Nelson-Hall, 1996), for a detailed examination of the issues leading to access districts.

46. In Georgia, for example, all of the white congressional districts following 1992 redistricting became Republican; only the black districts remained Democratic. Ben Ginzburg, former chief counsel to the Republican National Committee, stated any number of times that, from a Republican standpoint, the Georgia redistricting was the most successful in the South.

47. See David Bositis, *Redistricting and Representation: The Creation of Majority-Minority Districts and the Evolving Party System in the South* (Washington, D.C.: Joint Center for Political Studies, 1995).

48. *Miller v. Johnson,* 115 S.Ct. 2475 (1995); *Johnson v. Mortham,* 1996 U.S. Dist. Lexis 5859.

49. On the other hand, in Florida the state legislature passed a new congressional

districting plan following a federal court's finding that Congressional District 3 (a majority-minority district) was illegal; the new plan made significant geographic and racial changes in Florida's northeastern quadrant congressional districts but few changes in their partisan composition.

50. George Mowry, *Another Look at the Twentieth Century South* (Baton Rouge: Louisiana State University Press, 1973).

51. The 1992 presidential election has been characterized as one in which the Democrats were thought to have offered a better economic alternative to voters than the Republicans. On the other hand, the 1994 midterm elections can best be interpreted as an attack on Democratic incumbents and Washington gridlock rather than a vote of confidence for Republican economic and other policies. Readers are reminded that the Republican "Contract with America" was unveiled very late in the 1994 campaign, played little or no role in its outcome, and only later became a major force in national politics.

52. Buddy Roemer of Louisiana became a Republican in 1991. Buddy MacKay ran unsuccessfully for the U.S. Senate in 1988, losing to Republican Connie Mack in a squeaker. He was elected lieutenant governor in 1990, running on a ticket with former U.S. Senator Lawton Chiles; they were reelected in 1994.

53. Examples include the reelection in 1994 of Democratic Governors Lawton Chiles in Florida and Zell Miller in Georgia. Both faced attractive Republican candidates, and while both barely won, they bucked the massive Republican tide of that year.

54. It is of interest that the Republican-black coalitions created for southern congressional and state legislative redistricting had no lasting or staying power, and there is little evidence of increasing concerns for African American issues within the various southern Republican Parties.

55. Lawton Chiles in Florida and Zell Miller in Georgia owe their successful gubernatorial reelection bids in part to substantial African American support.

56. See Heyman, "Constraints to Republican Development." The recent texts by Black and Black, *Politics and Society in the South* and *Vital South*, place somewhat less emphasis on the impact of the black voter than does this book, but nonetheless even they recognize the balance of power black voters can have over the outcome of southern elections, especially in the deep South.

57. Key, *Southern Politics*, chap. 13.

58. Warren Heyman, "Development of a Two-Party System in Georgia?" (M.A. thesis, Department of Political Science, University of Florida, 1985).

59. This statement is based on an examination of electoral outcomes for the governorship, Senate, U.S. House of Representatives, and state legislature between 1960 and 1994. See ibid. and Heyman, "Constraints on Republican Development."

60. Richard K. Scher, "The Incumbent Wins," in *Re-Electing the Governor*, ed. Thad Beyle (Lanham, Md.: University Presses of America, 1986), pp. 89–111. Readers are reminded that both Graham and Chiles have waged successful reelection bids during the 1990s against attractive Republicans.

61. They held this seat in 1994, in spite of a massive Republican campaign on behalf of Ollie North.

62. The lieutenant governor in Florida is not a member of the executive cabinet.

63. The literature on party realignment, dealignment, and decomposition is substantial. Accessible works include Samuel Eldersveld, *Political Parties in American Society* (New York: Basic Books, 1982), and Frank Sorauf, *Party Politics in America*, 5th ed. (Boston: Little, Brown, 1984). For more specialized studies with special reference to the South, see V.O. Key, "Secular Realignment and the Party System," *Journal of Politics* 21 (May 1959): 198–210; George Brown Tindall, *The Disruption of the Solid South* (Athens: University of Georgia Press, 1972); Paul Allen Beck, "Partisan Dealignment in

the Postwar South," *American Political Science Review* 71 (June 1977): 477–96; Bruce A. Campbell, "Change in the Southern Electorate," *American Journal of Political Science* 21 (February 1977): 37–64; Campbell, "Patterns of Change in the Partisan Loyalties of Native Southerners, 1952–1972," *Journal of Politics* 39 (August 1977): 730–61; Melissa P. Collie, "Incumbency, Electoral Safety and Turnover in the House of Representatives, 1952–1976," *American Political Science Review* 75 (March 1981): 119–31; David W. Brady, "A Reevaluation of Realignments in American Politics: Evidence from the U.S. House of Representatives," *American Political Science Review* 79 (March 1985): 28–49; Richard Scammon and James A. Barnes, "Republican Prospects: Southern Discomfort," *Public Opinion* 8 (October/November 1985): 14–17; John R. Petrocik, "Realignment: The South, the New Party Coalitions and the Elections of 1984 and 1986," in *Where's the Party?* ed. by Warren Miller and John R. Petrocik (Washington, D.C.: Center for National Policy, 1987); Petrocik, "Realignment: New Party Coalitions and the Nationalization of the South," *Journal of Politics* 49 (May 1987): 347–75; and Edward G. Carmines et al., "Unrealized Partisanship: A Theory of Dealignment," *Journal of Politics* 49 (May 1987): 376–400.

64. It is of interest that the "motor-voter" law has significantly aided independent registration, as well as that for Republicans. Whether these motor-voter registrants will actually vote, however, remains to be seen. See Sandra Mortham, Secretary of State, "The Impact of the National Voter Registration Act of 1993 on the State of Florida." This document can be obtained from the Secretary of State in Tallahassee, and is available on the Internet at http://election.dos.state.fl.us/reform/nv.

65. For a different view, see Tod Baker et al., *Political Parties in the Southern States* (New York: Praeger, 1990).

Chapter 6. "I Have a Dream": Toward the Civil Rights Movement

1. Steven F. Lawson, *Black Ballots* (New York: Columbia University Press, 1976), chap. 1.

2. See, for example, Key, *Southern Politics,* chap. 4; C. Douglas Price, *The Negro and Southern Politics* (New York: New York University Press, 1957); Alfred B. Clubok, John M. DeGrove, and Charles D. Farris, "The Manipulated Negro Vote," *Journal of Politics* 26 (February 1964): 112–29; and Donald R. Matthews and James W. Prothro, *Negroes and the New Southern Politics* (New York: Harcourt, Brace and World, 1966).

3. Lawson, *Black Ballots,* chap. 1. A typical example occurred in Mississippi during the 1950s when two men, the Reverend George W. Lee of Belzoni and Lamar Smith of Brookhaven, were lynched after trying to register. See Howell Raines, *My Soul Is Rested* (New York: Penguin, 1983), pp. 131–32.

4. For representative discussions of both of these points, see Matthews and Prothro, *Negroes and the New Southern Politics;* William Keech, *The Impact of Negro Voting* (Chicago: Rand McNally, 1966); Lawson, *Black Ballots;* and James Button and Richard Scher, "Impact of the Civil Rights Movement: Perceptions of Black Municipal Service Changes," *Social Science Quarterly* 60 (December 1979): 497–510.

5. Quoted in Harvard Sitkoff, *The Struggle for Black Equality* (New York: Hill and Wang, 1981), pp. 63–64.

6. *Plessy v. Ferguson,* 163 U.S. 537 (1896).

7. The case was *Brown v. Board of Education,* 347 U.S. 483.

8. Quoted in Thomas R. Brooks, *Walls Come Tumbling Down* (Englewood Cliffs, N.J.: Prentice-Hall, 1974), p. 104.

9. See esp. Raines, *My Soul Is Rested,* bk. 1. It is ironic that dark-skinned foreign

visitors dressed in native clothes would often be treated more politely than southern blacks. On the other hand, there were incidents in which dark-skinned foreigners—including diplomats—were mistreated. For an interesting account of a white man who dyed his skin dark and dressed in a variety of ways while traveling throughout the South, see John Howard Griffin, *Black Like Me,* 2d ed. (Boston: Houghton Mifflin, 1961, 1977).

10. An interesting example of this is the doubt expressed by the wife of E.D. Nixon, one of the leaders of the 1955 Montgomery bus boycott, that he could secure the cooperation of the black community in not riding the buses. See Brooks, *Walls Come Tumbling Down,* p. 96; and Raines, *My Soul Is Rested,* pp. 44–45.

11. Sitkoff, *Struggle for Black Equality,* p. 15. See also Doug McAdam, *Political Process and the Development of Black Insurgency, 1930–1970* (Chicago: University of Chicago Press, 1982), pp. 94–98.

12. Brooks, *Walls Come Tumbling Down,* chaps. 2–4; Sitkoff, *Struggle for Black Equality,* pp. 10–18.

13. Quoted in Brooks, *Walls Come Tumbling Down,* p. 24.

14. Ibid., p. 30; Sitkoff, *Struggle for Black Equality,* p. 12.

15. Myrdal, *American Dilemma.*

16. For a moving account of the role of the black church in rural Arkansas, see Maya Angelou, *I Know Why the Caged Bird Sings* (New York: Random House, 1970).

17. For a fascinating look at the role of the urban black church, see the early chapters of Taylor Branch's magisterial *Parting the Waters* (New York: Simon and Schuster, 1988).

18. McAdam, *Political Process,* pp. 98–100. See also the standard work, Samuel S. Hill, ed., *Encyclopedia of Religion in the South* (Macon, Ga.: Mercer University Press, 1984).

19. McAdam, *Political Process,* p. 100; Raines, *My Soul Is Rested,* pp. 37–70.

20. See Aldon D. Morris, *The Origins of the Civil Rights Movement* (New York: Free Press, 1984), chap. 3.

21. See the discussion of the Montgomery black community in Branch, *Parting the Waters;* see also Brooks, *Walls Come Tumbling Down,* pp. 95–96; Sitkoff, *Struggle for Black Equality,* pp. 51–57; Raines, *My Soul Is Rested,* pp. 37–137; Morris, *Origins of the Civil Rights Movement,* pp. 40–63; Juan Williams, *Eyes on the Prize* (New York: Penguin Books, 1987), chap. 3. *Eyes on the Prize* is also the name of a major series on the civil rights movement created for and shown on PBS.

22. See Pat Watters and Reese Cleghorn, *Climbing Jacob's Ladder* (New York: Harcourt, Brace and World, 1967), esp. chaps. 2, 3. See also Pat Watters, *Down to Now* (New York: Pantheon, 1971), esp. pt. 2; Sitkoff, *Struggle for Black Equality,* chap. 3; and Raines, *My Soul Is Rested,* pp. 75–108.

23. *Missouri ex rel. Gaines v. Canada,* 305 U.S. 337 (1938).

24. McAdam, *Political Process,* pp. 154–55.

25. Sitkoff, *Struggle for Black Equality,* p. 169.

26. Watters and Cleghorn, *Climbing Jacob's Ladder,* p. 70, n. 2.

27. Ibid., pp. 141–42.

28. August Meier and Elliot Rudwick, *CORE* (New York: Oxford University Press, 1973), chap. 1; Brooks, *Walls Come Tumbling Down,* pp. 48–51.

29. Meier and Rudwick, *CORE,* chap. 1; Sitkoff, *Struggle for Black Equality,* p. 97; McAdam, *Political Process,* pp. 154–56; Raines, *My Soul Is Rested,* pp. 27–34.

30. King was regarded as the leader of the civil rights movement by blacks and whites and often acted as its spokesman. But while he dominated many of the headlines through the force of his personality, political skill, intellectual and oratorical brilliance, and moral fervor, he was never more than the movement's titular head because of

continuing rivalries and jealousies among other leaders and the inability of the Council of Federated Organizations to act as a coordinating body. See especially Branch, *Parting the Waters,* for a detailed discussion of the relationship between King and the SCLC, on the one hand, and the rest of the civil rights movement on the other. Readers unfamiliar with King's career, or his impact, are urged to examine Branch, *Parting the Waters;* and David J. Garrow, *Bearing the Cross* (New York: William Morrow, 1986). Other useful, accessible sources on King include David L. Lewis, *King: A Critical Biography* (New York: Praeger, 1970); John Alfred Williams, *The King God Didn't Save* (New York: Coward-McCann, 1970); Hanes Walton, *The Political Philosophy of Martin Luther King, Jr.* (Westport, Conn.: Greenwood Publishing Corporation, 1971); Lenwood Davis, *I Have a Dream: The Life and Times of Martin Luther King, Jr.* (Westport, Conn.: Negro Universities Press, 1973); Lerone Bennett, *What Manner of Man: A Biography of Martin Luther King, Jr.,* 4th rev. ed. (Chicago: Johnson Publishing Company, 1976); and Stephen B. Oates, *Let the Trumpet Sound* (New York: Harper and Row, 1982). Brief but helpful biographical material on King is found in Brooks, *Walls Come Tumbling Down,* pp. 101–5.

31. Sitkoff, *Struggle for Black Equality,* pp. 64–65; Morris, *Origins of the Civil Rights Movement,* chaps. 4–6.

32. Quoted in Sitkoff, *Struggle for Black Equality,* p. 65.

33. Quoted in Brooks, *Walls Come Tumbling Down,* pp. 152–53.

34. Watters, *Down to Now,* pp. 300–1; Sitkoff, *Struggle for Black Equality,* pp. 209–18; McAdam, *Political Process,* pp. 183–85, 210–11, 272n.

35. The Reverend Joseph Lowry, one of the earliest civil rights activists, noted that since blacks were accustomed to shortages of money, operating civil rights organizations and conducting protest activity on shoestring budgets did not cause any out-of-the-ordinary problems. See Raines, *My Soul Is Rested,* p. 68.

36. McAdam, *Political Process,* pp. 98–100, 125–42.

37. The following analysis is from ibid. p. 135; and Raines, *My Soul Is Rested,* pp. 68–70.

38. Raines, *My Soul Is Rested,* p. 69.

39. William H. Chafe, *Civilities and Civil Rights* (New York: Oxford University Press, 1981), pp. 60–64.

40. Lester M. Salamon and Steven Van Evera, "Fear, Apathy and Discrimination: A Test of Three Explanations of Political Participation," *American Political Science Review* 67 (December 1973): 1288–1306.

41. Brooks, *Walls Come Tumbling Down,* pp. 95–100; Sitkoff, *Struggle for Black Equality,* pp. 41–50; Raines, *My Soul Is Rested,* pp. 37–39, 43–51.

42. Watters and Cleghorn, *Climbing Jacob's Ladder,* app. 1; Raines, *My Soul Is Rested,* pp. 249–55; Kay Mills, *This Little Light of Mine: The Life of Fanny Lou Hamer* (New York: Dutton, 1993).

43. See James Farmer's recollection of the desegregation of the Jack Sprat restaurant in Chicago, in Raines, *My Soul Is Rested,* pp. 29–32.

44. Sitkoff, *Struggle for Black Equality,* pp. 61–62. For a more detailed explanation, see Walton, *Political Philosophy of King;* Garrow, *Bearing the Cross;* and Branch, *Parting the Waters.*

45. David Garrow, *Protest at Selma* (New Haven: Yale University Press, 1978); also "The Political Evolution of Martin Luther King Jr.," a public address given by David Garrow, September 4, 1985, at the University of Florida in Gainesville.

46. Raines, *My Soul Is Rested,* p. 48.

47. *Smith v. Allwright,* 321 U.S. 649 (1944); *Brown v. Board of Education,* 347 U.S. 483 (1954).

48. Raines, *My Soul Is Rested,* pp. 58–70.

49. References to the labor strife of the 1930s and to Hoovervilles can be found in virtually any standard American history text. For the general reader, two of the most accessible and helpful discussions of this period can be found in Frederick Lewis Allen, *The Big Change* (New York: Harper and Row, 1952), pp. 148–54; and Manchester, *Glory and Dream*, pp. 3–4, 10, 154–55.

50. See Chafe, *Civility and Civil Rights.*

51. Watters, *Down to Now*, p. 51; Sitkoff, *Struggle for Black Equality*, p. 67.

52. Quoted in Raines, *My Soul Is Rested*, p. 99.

53. All quoted in McAdam, *Political Process*, p. 107.

54. Ibid., p. 84.

55. Brooks, *Walls Come Tumbling Down*, pp. 60–61.

56. Quoted in ibid., p. 86.

57. See, for example, Stephen E. Ambrose, *Rise to Globalism*, 4th rev. ed. (New York: Penguin Books, 1985).

58. Bartley, *Rise of Massive Resistance.*

59. Michael Harrington, *The Other America* (New York: Macmillan, 1962).

Chapter 7. "We Shall Overcome": The Politics of the Civil Rights Movement

1. This is the title of Thomas Brooks's study of the civil rights movement, *Walls Come Tumbling Down.* For a provocative look at the origins of the civil rights movement, see Morris, *Origins of the Civil Rights Movement*, the interpretation of which is rather different from the discussion presented in this chapter. See also Williams, *Eyes on the Prize*, and the accompanying PBS documentary series of the same name for a good overview of major events in the civil rights movement.

2. *Brown v. Board of Education*, 347 U.S. 483 (1954). Two useful studies of the *Brown* decision are Daniel Berman, *It Is So Ordered* (New York: Norton, 1966); and Richard Kluger, *Simple Justice* (New York: Knopf, 1976).

3. Berman, *It Is So Ordered*, p. 14.

4. *Plessy v. Ferguson*, 163 U.S. 537 (1896).

5. In fact, NAACP litigation on public education was limited and not especially promising. See, for example, *Gong Lum v. Rice*, 275 U.S. 78 (1927).

6. *Missouri ex. rel. Gaines v. Canada*, 305 U.S. 337 (1938).

7. *Sipuel v. University of Oklahoma*, 332 U.S. 631 (1948).

8. *McLaurin v. Oklahoma State Regents*, 339 U.S. 637 (1950); and *Sweatt v. Painter*, 339 U.S. 629 (1950).

9. *Brown v. Board of Education*, 347 U.S. 483 (1954).

10. Brooks, *Walls Come Tumbling Down*, pp. 104–5; Sitkoff, *Struggle for Black Equality*, p. 23.

11. *Brown v. Board of Education*, 349 U.S. 294 (1955).

12. Bartley, *Rise of Massive Resistance*, discusses this possibility but does not adopt it. But Berman, *It Is So Ordered*, pp. 121–26, strongly suggests that the Court's tentativeness did contribute to massive resistance.

13. Brooks, *Walls Come Tumbling Down*, pp. 95–96.

14. See esp. Williams, *Eyes on the Prize*, chap. 1.

15. Brooks, *Walls Come Tumbling Down;* 95–96; Sitkoff, *Struggle for Black Equality*, pp. 51–57; Williams, *Eyes on the Prize*, chap. 3.

16. See the interview with E.D. Nixon in Raines, *My Soul Is Rested*, pp. 37–39, 43–51.

17. Brooks, *Walls Come Tumbling Down*, pp. 95–96; Raines, *My Soul Is Rested*, pp. 41–44; Williams, *Eyes on the Prize*, chap. 3. Parks in later years indicated that she was no more tired that day than any other work day, nor did her feet hurt worse than usual. But, she said, the combination of fatigue and disrespectful treatment by the bus driver were more than she could take; she said she had simply had enough.

18. Brooks, *Walls Come Tumbling Down*, pp. 95–96; Raines, *My Soul Is Rested*, pp. 41–44; Williams, *Eyes on the Prize*, chap. 3.

19. Sitkoff, *Struggle for Black Equality*, pp. 52–53; Williams, *Eyes on the Prize*, chap. 3.

20. See Morris, *Origins of the Civil Rights Movement*, chap. 3.

21. Sitkoff, *Struggle for Black Equality*, pp. 54–57; Raines, *My Soul Is Rested*, pp. 131–37; Williams, *Eyes on the Prize*, chap. 3.

22. Reported in Brooks, *Walls Come Tumbling Down*, p. 119. See the original article, "Bus Integration in Alabama Calm," in *New York Times*, December 22, 1956, pp. 1, 11.

23. Bartley, *Rise of Massive Resistance*. See also Newby, *The South*, chap. 1.

24. See Bartley, *Rise of Massive Resistance*, for a full discussion of the southern reaction to *Brown*. See also Colburn and Scher, "Race Relations and Florida Gubernatorial Politics."

25. See Bartley and Graham, *Southern Politics and the Second Reconstruction*. There were other reasons why southerners felt besieged after *Brown*, some of which suggest the presence of regional delusions: the South was a victim of foreign plots; communists had infiltrated the Supreme Court; and there was an international communist-Zionist conspiracy to promote miscegenation and thereby weaken America through genetic transformations.

26. Bartley, *Rise of Massive Resistance*, p. 201.

27. Quoted in ibid., p. 192. This type of activity by white citizens councils continued well into the 1960s. See, for example, Florence Mars, *Witness in Philadelphia* (Baton Rouge: Louisiana State University Press, 1977). For other examples, see Elizabeth Jacoway and David R. Colburn. eds., *Southern Businessmen and Desegregation* (Baton Rouge: Louisiana State University Press, 1982). Even judges were not exempt; see Robert Francis Kennedy Jr., *Judge Frank M. Johnson: A Biography* (New York: Putnam, 1978).

28. Journalists and editors such as Harry Golden of the *Carolina Israelite* and Ralph McGill of the *Atlanta Constitution*, who sought to project the voice of moderation and reason into political debate, were hounded by southern zealots. Neither caved in.

29. Quoted in Sherrill, *Gothic Politics*, p. 314; Bartley, *Rise of Massive Resistance*, p. 287. See also Frady, *Wallace;* and Carter, *Politics of Rage*.

30. Quoted in Bartley, *Rise of Massive Resistance*, p. 201.

31. The county unit system was a unique apparatus designed to ensure rural domination of statewide elections by declaring winners on the basis of weighted scores determined by the population of counties. It was somewhat analogous to the Electoral College system used to elect the president. See Key, *Southern Politics*, pp. 117–24. The U.S. Supreme Court declared the county unit system unconstitutional in *Gray v. Sanders*, 372 U.S. 368 (1963).

32. Quoted in Colburn and Scher, *Florida's Gubernatorial Politics*, pp. 76–77.

33. Quoted in Bartley, *Rise of Massive Resistance*, p. 116, and reprinted in the *New York Times*, March 12, 1956, pp. 1, 19. The original text of the manifesto was inserted in the *Congressional Record*, March 12, 1956.

34. Bartley, *Rise of Massive Resistance*, p. 131.

35. One authoritative study of the Klan is David Chalmers, *Hooded Americanism* (New York: F. Watts, 1981).

36. Bartley, *Rise of Massive Resistance*, p. 207.

37. Ibid., p. 200.

38. See Elizabeth Jacoway, "Taken by Surprise: Little Rock Business Leaders and Desegregation," in *Southern Businessmen and Desegregation*, ed. Jacoway and Colburn, pp. 15–41. Standard works on the Little Rock story, besides the Jacoway chapter, include *Crisis in the South: The Little Rock Story*, compiled by the editors of the *Arkansas Gazette* (Little Rock: Arkansas Gazette, 1959); and Corinne Silverman, *The Little Rock Story*, rev. ed. (University: University of Alabama Press, 1959). See also Williams, *Eyes on the Prize*, chap. 4.

39. Sherrill, *Gothic Politics*, p. 106; Sitkoff, *Struggle for Black Equality*, pp. 29–30; Jacoway, "Taken by Surprise," p. 21; Williams, *Eyes on the Prize*, chap. 4.

40. Jacoway, "Taken by Surprise," pp. 39–40.

41. See Bartley, *Rise of Massive Resistance*, pp. 320–22; Colburn and Scher, *Florida's Gubernatorial Politics*, chap. 8.

42. The standard text on the civil rights struggle in Greensboro is Chafe, *Civilities and Civil Rights*. See also Morris, *Origins of the Civil Rights Movement*, chap. 9; and Williams, *Eyes on the Prize*, chap. 5.

43. Chafe, *Civilities and Civil Rights*, pp. 79–83; Sitkoff, *Struggle for Black Equality*, pp. 69–70.

44. Accounts of the exact language used at the lunch counter differ somewhat. But there is general agreement on the sequence of events that occurred. See Chafe, *Civilities and Civil Rights*, p. 83.

45. Ibid., pp. 83–98.

46. Brooks, *Walls Come Tumbling Down*, p. 147; Watters, *Down to Now*, p. 83; McAdam, *Political Process*, pp. 138–40.

47. Brooks, *Walls Come Tumbling Down*, pp. 155–56; Williams, *Eyes on the Prize*, pp. 140–47.

48. See the interviews in Raines, *My Soul Is Rested*, p. 110; and Williams, *Eyes on the Prize*, pp. 144–46.

49. *Morgan v. Virginia*, 328 U.S. 373 (1947); *Boynton v. Virginia*, 364 U.S. 354 (1960).

50. Sitkoff, *Struggle for Black Equality*, pp. 97–101; Raines, *My Soul Is Rested*, pp. 111–12; and Williams, *Eyes on the Prize*, chap. 5.

51. Brooks, *Walls Come Tumbling Down*, p. 161; Sitkoff, *Struggle for Black Equality*, p. 101; Raines, *My Soul Is Rested*, pp. 113–15; Williams, *Eyes on the Prize*, chap. 5.

52. Brooks, *Walls Come Tumbling Down*, pp. 161–62; Raines, *My Soul Is Rested*, pp. 115–16; Williams, *Eyes on the Prize*, chap. 5.

53. Brooks, *Walls Come Tumbling Down*, p. 163; Raines, *My Soul Is Rested*, pp. 116–21; Williams, *Eyes on the Prize*, chap. 5.

54. Brooks, *Walls Come Tumbling Down*, p. 164; Sitkoff, *Struggle for Black Equality*, pp. 107–8; Raines, *My Soul Is Rested*, pp. 122–25; Williams, *Eyes on the Prize*, chap. 5.

55. Quoted in Sitkoff, *Struggle for Black Equality*, p. 109.

56. Ibid., p. 110.

57. At some state universities in the South, violence and ugly racial turmoil were absent during desegregation. In Florida, for example, moderate Governor LeRoy Collins and University of Florida President J.Wayne Reitz managed to keep desegregation efforts orderly and relatively peaceful. In this they were aided by on-campus student leaders, who seemed to accept desegregation as inevitable and who wanted to avoid the kind of incidents that marked massive resistance elsewhere in the South. See Richard R. Alexander, " 'A Smooth Transition': Racial Integration at the University of Florida" (M.A. thesis, Department of History, University of Florida, May 1991).

58. Brooks, *Walls Come Tumbling Down*, pp. 187–89.

59. Raines, *My Soul Is Rested*, pp. 325–27. See also "'96 in Congress Open Drive to Upset Integration Ruling," *New York Times*, March 12, 1956, p. 1.

60. Quoted in Sitkoff, *Struggle for Black Equality*, p. 156. See also Frady, *Wallace;* and Carter, *Politics of Rage.*

61. Brooks, *Walls Come Tumbling Down*, p. 211; Sitkoff, *Struggle for Black Equality*, pp. 157–58. Although it is difficult to document conclusively, there is reason to think that the Athletic Department at the University of Alabama played a role in the desegregation of the university. Department staff felt that if they could not recruit quality black athletes, they could not continue to be competitive in major college sports. The possibility further existed that the powerhouse northern and western teams Alabama liked to play, especially in football, to achieve a high national ranking might choose to drop the Crimson Tide from their schedules if the university remained segregated. The actual assault on segregated athletics probably began in 1956, when Georgia Tech under Coach Bobby Dodd played a desegregated Pittsburgh team in the Sugar Bowl in New Orleans. Dodd and Tech were bitterly criticized in the South for taking this step. See "The Gray Fox," *New York Times*, November 10, 1987, p. D31.

62. Williams, *Eyes on the Prize*, pp. 197–206.

63. Useful and accessible sources on the Albany campaign include Howard Zinn, *Albany, A Study in National Responsibility* (Atlanta: Southern Regional Council, 1962); Watters and Cleghorn, *Climbing Jacob's Ladder*, esp. pp. 52–57; Watters, *Down to Now;* Brooks, *Walls Come Tumbling Down*, pp. 174–90; Garrow, *Protest at Selma*, esp. pp. 2–3, 221–27; Sitkoff, *Struggle for Black Equality*, pp. 125–27; and Williams, *Eyes on the Prize*, chap. 6.

64. Civil rights leaders sometimes became possessive, even jealous, of "their" territory. For King to move into an area without first being invited would have been considered an affront. Chronologies of the Birmingham campaign can be found in Brooks, *Walls Come Tumbling Down*, and Sitkoff, *Struggle for Black Equality*, but the oral history in Raines, *My Soul Is Rested*, pp. 139–85, is extremely helpful and revealing. See also the account of Birmingham in Frady, *Wallace;* Morris, *Origins of the Civil Rights Movement*, chap. 10; Williams, *Eyes on the Prize*, chap. 6; and the brief but insightful examination in U.S. Commission on Civil Rights, *Twenty Years after Brown* (Washington, D.C.: U.S. Commission on Civil Rights, 1975), pp. 20–23.

65. This point, in fact, is one of the major themes of Garrow's *Protest at Selma*. See also the public lecture given by Garrow, "Political Evolution of King." A somewhat different view of King's political evolution is given in Charles Sager, *Selma, 1965* (New York: Scribner's, 1974).

66. Quoted in Raines, *My Soul Is Rested*, p. 145.

67. See Raines's interview with Shuttlesworth, ibid., pp. 154–61, for an account of the relationship between the two ministers. Shuttlesworth avoided direct criticism of King but did feel that King might have been too willing to trust the good faith of Birmingham officials.

68. Brooks, *Walls Come Tumbling Down*, chap. 10.

69. James Silver, *Mississippi: The Closed Society*, new ed. (New York: Harcourt, Brace and World, 1966).

70. See Howard Zinn, *SNCC* (Boston: Beacon Press, 1964). Brooks, *Walls Come Tumbling Down* and Sitkoff, *Struggle for Black Equality* have useful discussions of freedom summer, but the oral history in Raines, *My Soul Is Rested*, pp. 233–90, and Williams, *Eyes on the Prize*, chap. 7, are most helpful.

71. Robert Penn Warren, *Who Speaks for the Negro?* (New York: Random House, 1965); see also Brooks, *Walls Come Tumbling Down*, p. 243.

72. Quoted in Brooks, *Walls Come Tumbling Down*, p. 244.

73. Ibid., pp. 245–46.

74. Florence Mars provides a firsthand account of events in Neshoba County during the period of the slayings. She herself was harassed by fellow southerners, and her story is characteristic of what happened to moderate whites in the deep South who tried to speak out against the violence and hatred. See *Witness in Philadelphia*. The men were later convicted on other charges related to the murders. The incident also became the subject of a 1988 movie, *Mississippi Burning*, a dramatic if fictionalized account of civil rights activity in Mississippi.

75. Williams, *Eyes on the Prize*, chap. 7.

76. See the remarks by Dave Dennis in Raines, *My Soul Is Rested*, p. 278.

77. It was during the convention that the nation "met" Fannie Lou Hamer and came to know of the horrors she and fellow civil rights activists faced at Winona. For a transcript of Hamer's account, see Watters and Cleghorn, *Climbing Jacob's Ladder*, pp. 363–75. See also Raines, *My Soul Is Rested*, pp. 249–55.

78. Lawson, *Black Ballots*, p. 299.

79. Accounts of the Selma campaign can be found in Watters and Cleghorn, *Climbing Jacob's Ladder;* Watters, *Down to Now;* Brooks, *Walls Come Tumbling Down;* Sitkoff, *Struggle for Black Equality;* Raines, *My Soul Is Rested;* and Williams, *Eyes on the Prize*, chap. 8. The standard texts on this crucial episode are Fager, *Selma;* and Garrow, *Protest at Selma*. See also Garrow, *Bearing the Cross;* and Branch, *Parting the Waters*.

80. For a horrifying account of the demonstration and Jackson's murder, see Raines, *My Soul Is Rested*, pp. 190–93.

81. King undoubtedly had his reasons for absenting himself from Selma and for taking his chief aide, the Reverend Ralph Abernathy, with him. He was not enthusiastic about the march. He was also conscious of not offending Johnson, who was thought to be jealous of King. Many people were later critical of King for leaving the march, but this largely came later, after it turned out that March 7 was one of the most critical days in the long civil rights struggle.

82. Quoted in "Johnson Urges Congress at Joint Session to Pass Law Insuring Negro Vote," *New York Times*, March 16, 1965, pp. 1, 30–31; see also Williams, *Eyes on the Prize*, chap. 8.

83. Public support for a vigorous federal role in promoting desegregation declined sharply between 1965 and 1969. The drop was especially noticeable among whites outside the South. For example, in a Gallup Poll survey on the question of whether the federal government was moving too fast on school desegregation, the percentage of non-southern whites agreeing that it was jumped from 28 percent in April 1965 to 42 percent in August 1969. See *The Gallup Poll, 1935–1971*, vol. 3, *1959–1971* (New York: Random House, 1972), pp. 1933, 2210–11.

Chapter 8. "Free at Last"? The Civil Rights Movement in Retrospect

1. Slave revolts were usually isolated incidents that had little lasting impact on the status of blacks in the South. Black political involvement during Reconstruction was almost wholly at the behest of carpetbaggers, northern Republicans, and the army of occupation.

2. In 1950, the nonwhite population (the vast majority of which was black) of the city of Montgomery was 42,555, representing 40 percent of the total of 106,525; in the

urbanized area of Montgomery, 42,754 nonwhites lived, or 39 percent of the total of 109,468. The total standard metropolitan statistical area (SMSA) of Montgomery contained 138,965 people, of whom about 61,000 were nonwhite. The boycott was thought to be about 90 percent effective. Extrapolating to 1955, regardless of which figures are used, suggests conservatively that tens of thousands of Montgomery blacks participated in the Montgomery boycotts. Not all of these individuals normally rode the buses, of course, but those who did not supported those who did, including arranging other means of transportation. Data come from *1950 Census of the Population,* vol. 2, *Characteristics of the Population,* pt. 2, *Alabama* (Washington, D.C.: U.S. Bureau of the Census, 1952), table 33, "General Characteristics, Age by Color and Sex, for Standard Metropolitan Statistical Areas, Urbanized Areas, and Urban Places of 10,000 or More, 1950," pp. 249–51.

3. Data supporting these figures can be found in the citations listed for these events in chapter 7.

4. See Watters and Reese Cleghorn, *Climbing Jacob's Ladder.*

5. David R. Colburn, *Racial Change and Community Crisis: St. Augustine, Florida, 1877–1980* (New York: Columbia University Press, 1985).

6. In theoretical terms, King and other civil rights leaders sought to expand the scope of conflict, yet at the same time control its direction. See Schattschneider, *Semisovereign People;* Garrow, *Protest at Selma.*

7. The figures that follow all come from *The Gallup Poll,* vols. 2 and 3 (New York: Random House, 1972). These data come from a poll dated July 12, 1954, 2: 1249.

8. June 23, 1961, ibid., 3:1723.

9. June 21, 1961, ibid., p. 1724; *Boynton v. Virginia,* 364 U.S. 354 (1960).

10. June 28, 1961, *Gallup Poll,* 3:1724.

11. February 2, 1964, ibid., p. 1863.

12. May 24, 1964, ibid., p. 1881; April 11, 1965, ibid., p. 1933; April 14, 1965, ibid., p. 1933.

13. Jacoway and Colburn, eds., *Southern Businessmen and Desegregation.* See also the letter written by James W. Button and Richard K. Scher, in *New Perspectives* (journal of the U.S. Commission on Civil Rights) 18, no. 1 (Winter/Spring 1986): 47–48.

14. It is of interest that some students of civil rights feel that by the mid-1990s, the Supreme Court began leading a retreat in some areas of civil rights, especially on affirmative action, minority set-aside contract programs, minority scholarships, and civil rights. A discussion of the latter possibility can be found in Scher, Mills, and Hotaling, *Voting Rights and Democracy.*

15. Having said this, it would be naive to assume the Court does not in some measure reflect contemporary political trends, although there may be either a lead or lag time in how it does so. Other, less charitable, observers of the Court also remind us that individual justices of the U.S. Supreme Court are known to read newspapers and follow political events and thus are not insensitive to contemporary political realities.

16. On July 25, 1989, the National Public Radio program "All Things Considered" aired a story about a small town in South Carolina, Saluda, where black youths from a Methodist camp who were helping to rebuild homes for the poor were denied the right to swim at a local pool, although white youngsters from the camp were let in. See also "Blacks Found Lagging Despite Gains," *New York Times,* national ed., Friday, July 28, 1989, p. 6.

17. Useful sources on the 1964 Civil Rights Act include U.S. Commission on Civil Rights, "A Summary of the Civil Rights Act of 1964," *Civil Rights Digest,* special bulletin (Washington, D.C.: U.S. Commission on Civil Rights, August 1964); U.S.

Commission on Civil Rights, *Federal Civil Rights Enforcement* (Washington, D.C.: U.S. Commission on Civil Rights, 1971); and U.S. Commission on Civil Rights, *Twenty Years after Brown.*

18. For other examples and requirements, see the *Civil Rights Digest* (1964).

19. James Coleman, *Equality of Educational Opportunity* (Washington, D.C.: U.S. Department of Health, Education and Welfare, Office of Education, 1966). This massive volume became popularly known as the "Coleman Report."

20. Evidence for this statement rests on inferences from the public opinion data cited earlier; southern white opposition to desegregation began to decrease, and support for civil rights began to increase, by this time.

21. See Lawson, *Black Ballots,* chaps. 1–3; and Richard Scher and James Button, "Voting Rights Act: Implementation and Impact," in *Implementation of Civil Rights Policy,* ed. Charles S. Bullock III and Charles M. Lamb (Monterey: Brooks Cole, 1984), pp. 21–22.

22. *Smith v. Allwright,* 321 U.S. 649 (1944).

23. Scher and Button, "Voting Rights Act," p. 23. See also Harrell R. Rodgers and Charles S. Bullock III, *Law and Social Change* (New York: McGraw Hill, 1972), pp. 23–28; and Lawson, *Black Ballots,* pp. 179–249.

24. Scher and Button, "Voting Rights Act," p. 24.

25. A date just prior to the 1964 presidential election.

26. *South Carolina v. Katzenbach,* 383 U.S. 301 (1966), quoted in Scher and Button, "Voting Rights Act," p. 26.

27. For a detailed discussion of the implementation of the Voting Rights Act, see Scher and Button, "Voting Rights Act." See also Steven F. Lawson, *In Pursuit of Power* (New York: Columbia University Press, 1985).

28. See the brief discussion of the impact of Section 2 changes in the South in chapter 5, above. For a longer discussion, see Scher, Mills, and Hotaling, *Voting Rights and Democracy.*

29. See *Shaw v. Reno,* 113 S.Ct. 2816 (1993); and *Miller v. Johnson,* 115 S. Ct. 2475 (1995). A brief overview of these issues can be found in Richard K. Scher, John L. Mills, and John Hotaling, "Voting Rights after *Shaw v. Reno,*" in *Studies in Southern Parties and Elections,* ed. Robert P. Steed, Laurence W. Moreland, and Tod A. Baker (Tuscaloosa: University of Alabama Press, forthcoming), chap. 1.

30. Garrow, *Protest at Selma,* p. xi; Scher and Button, "Voting Rights Act," p. 21.

31. Scher and Button, "Voting Rights Act," p. 41.

32. The reader should be reminded that after 1982, all states were covered by the Voting Rights Act; the term applies to the original group of border South states not initially covered by the triggering mechanism of Section 5.

33. Data on voter turnout by race for nonpresidential elections are difficult to obtain, but evidence suggests that turnout for these contests is usually less than for presidential elections, sometimes by as much as 20 percent or more.

34. See Bositis, *Redistricting and Representation.*

35. A fourth issue has been articulated in recent years: the creation of majority-minority districts could actually depress black turnout. Using controlled statistical methods, however, Bositis, *Redistricting and Representation,* demonstrates that lower turnout in these districts is not the independent result of these districts but rather the product of other, often unique and probably temporary, forces.

36. In 1982, a black candidate for the U.S. House of Representatives from a majority-black district in Mississippi lost to a white candidate, indicating an anomaly in expected voting outcomes. In Gretna, Florida, a small, majority-black town west of Tallahassee, black voters helped elect a white mayor over a black candidate.

37. Salamon and Van Evera, "Fear, Apathy and Discrimination."

38. Colburn and Scher, *Florida's Gubernatorial Politics*, pp. 81–82.

39. Peirce, *Deep South States*, p. 23.

40. "Wallace Captures 4th Term as Governor of Alabama," and "Stennis Easily Re-Elected, Winning 7th Term," *New York Times*, November 3, 1982, p. A22; "The South Democrats Gain on All Fronts," *New York Times*, November 4, 1982, p. A24.

41. "Vote Is a 'Miracle' in Mississippi," *Miami Herald*, November 17, 1986, p. 1.

42. Fowler in turn was defeated in 1992 by a Republican.

43. In the spring of 1996, an Alabama Republican state senator running for Congress announced in the middle of his campaign that, in his judgment, the Bible permitted slavery. There was an immediate furor, heard most loudly from black Democrats, but his critics included Republicans as well. The candidate subsequently withdrew from the race. The senator, named Charles Davidson, later put a copy of his controversial speech on the Internet. See http://www.dixienet.org/Slpapers/davidson.html.

44. The appointment of blacks to public office is also important, but it will not be treated in this text.

45. See James W. Button and Richard K. Scher, "The Election and Impact of Black Officials in the South," in *Public Policy and Social Institutions*, ed. Harrell Rodgers, Jr. (Greenwich: JAI Press, 1984), pp. 183–218. See also James W. Button, *Blacks and Social Change* (Princeton: Princeton University Press, 1989), pp. 226–27.

46. An overview of these arguments can be found in Scher, Mills, and Hotaling, *Voting Rights and Democracy*.

47. Newby, *The South*, pp. 262–63.

48. The early figures are from the annual Survey of Black Elected Officials complied by the Joint Center for Political Studies, Washington, D.C.; the 1993 figures are from U.S. Bureau of the Census, *Statistical Abstracts, 1995*, 115th ed., table 455.

49. U.S. Bureau of the Census, *Statistical Abstracts, 1995*, 115th ed., table 455.

50. Douglas Wilder was elected governor of Virginia in November 1989. In summer 1990, Andrew Young, mayor of Atlanta, was a major candidate for governor of Georgia but lost the Democratic nomination in a runoff to a white candidate, Zell Miller. In 1995 a Democratic African American candidate for governor of Louisiana lost to a Republican.

51. Charles S. Bullock III, "The Election of Blacks in the South: Preconditions and Consequences," *American Journal of Political Science* 19 (November 1975): 737–38; Button and Scher, "Election and Impact of Black Officials," p. 190; "JCPS Roster of Black Elected Officials, 1987," *Focus* (monthly newsletter of the Joint Center for Political Studies) 15 (October 1987): 5.

52. It should be noted, however, that during the 1970s and 1980s blacks became mayors of some of the South's most prominent cities, including Atlanta, New Orleans, Birmingham, Charlotte, Baltimore, and Washington, D.C., as well as a host of smaller cities. This trend continued into the 1990s.

53. U.S. Commission on Civil Rights (1971), pp. 12–15; Button and Scher, "Election and Impact of Black Officials," p. 192; and "JCPS Roster."

54. James David Campbell and Joe Feagin, "Black Politics in the South: A Descriptive Analysis," *Journal of Politics* 37 (February 1975): 139–49; Button and Scher, "Election and Impact of Black Officials," p. 192.

55. There is a large literature on these two points. See the representative citations at the end of the Button and Scher, "Election and Impact of Black Officials," p. 192.

56. *Gomillion v. Lightfoot*, 364 U.S. 339 (1960).

57. How this attention is to be accomplished created enormous controversy throughout the South during the reapportionment-redistricting cycle of 1991–92. Based on

1982 changes to Section 2 of the Voting Rights Act as well as *Thornburg v. Gingles* (1986), pressures were felt in southern state legislatures to create minority access and influence districts that aggregated minority groups (African Americans and Hispanic Americans) to enhance the likelihood of their electing a candidate of choice. The creation of these districts was and remains highly controversial. See Scher, Mills, and Hotaling, *Voting Rights and Democracy,* for analysis of the legal and political issues involved during this cycle.

58. These suits were filed largely on the basis of the 1982 changes to Section 2 of the Voting Rights Act and *Thornburg v. Gingles* (1986).

59. See Paige Alan Parker and Larry R. Johnson, "The Southern Black Candidate in At-Large City Elections: What Are the Determinants of Success?" (paper presented at the annual meeting of the Southern Political Science Association, Atlanta, November 1982).

60. Peter Eisinger, "Black Employment in Municipal Jobs: The Impact of Black Political Power," *American Political Science Review* 76 (June 1982): 380–81; Peter Sellers, *Being There,* a United Artists film released in 1979.

61. Button and Scher, "Election and Impact of Black Officials," pp. 201–10; a comprehensive study of this issue is in Button, *Blacks and Social Change.*

62. Button and Scher, "Election and Impact of Black Officials," p. 208.

63. Perhaps nowhere are the problems of southern black officials more clearly, and poignantly, shown than in Melissa Fay Greene's brilliant book *Praying for Sheetrock* (Reading, Mass.: Addison-Wesley, 1991).

64. See, for example, Campbell and Feagin, "Black Politics in the South"; Thomas R. Dye, *Politics, Economics, and the Public;* Keech, *Impact of Negro Voting;* Watters and Cleghorn, *Climbing Jacob's Ladder;* Wirt, *Politics of Southern Equality;* Button and Scher, "Impact of the Civil Rights Movement"; and most recently Button, *Blacks and Social Change.*

65. Button and Scher, "Impact of the Civil Rights Movement," p. 508.

66. James W. Button, *Black Violence* (Princeton: Princeton University Press, 1978). Button's conclusions are based on national, not purely southern, research. See also his recent volume on the relationship between civil rights strategies and political outcomes, *Blacks and Social Change.*

67. The reader might well recall the quotation from Dr. Martin Luther King's famous "Give Us the Ballot" speech delivered in 1957, cited above in chap. 6. See also Matthews and Prothro, *Negroes and the New Southern Politics.*

68. Greene's *Praying for Sheetrock* is an excellent account of the ambiguous relationship that exists between whites and blacks in the modern South.

69. Chet Fuller, *I Hear Them Calling My Name* (Boston: Houghton Mifflin, 1981). See also "Most Will Honor Dr. King, but Some Still Dispute the Holiday," *New York Times,* national ed., January 18, 1987, p. 11.

70. The senator's speech can be found on the Internet; see note 43.

71. In a provocative and insightful book, Carol Stack portrays a number of southern blacks who have moved back to rural areas of the South as a place where they feel more comfortable than elsewhere and that in some measure they can call their own, at least insofar as it represents their past. See *Call to Home* (New York: Basic Books, 1996).

72. Examples are numerous. Representative examples can be found in "Is the Death Penalty Only for Killers of Whites?" *Washington Post,* October 12, 1986, p. D1; and Greene, *Praying for Sheetrock.*

73. See "EEOC Probes Racism in North Carolina Town," *Washington Post,* October 22, 1986, p. A10. The recession of 1990–91 seemingly hit blacks harder than whites, both in the South and elsewhere. Moreover, there seems little doubt that the late 1980s and 1990s witnessed a retrenchment by the Supreme Court on affirmative action for

blacks. It need hardly be pointed out that affirmative action in both public and private employment continues to be highly controversial.

74. Ironically, in a major voting rights case, *Miller v. Johnson*, 115 S. Ct. 2475 (1995), the U.S. Supreme Court took the Voting Rights Section of the Department of Justice to task for going too far in insisting on creating black congressional districts above and beyond what the Voting Rights Act required.

75. "Blacks Challenge Administration View of Voting Rights Act," *Gainesville Sun*, December 7, 1986, p. 5A. See also "Wider Power Due in Voting Act," *New York Times*, national ed., January 6, 1987, p. A14.

76. U.S. Bureau of the Census, *Characteristics of the Population*, vol. 1 (Washington, D.C.: U.S. Bureau of the Census, 1960). Volume 1 is actually a multivolume series encompassing summary data for the United States and individual states. Data were collected from the eleven southern states volumes, table 133 in each volume, which reports median income by race and sex.

77. These data come from U.S. Bureau of the Census, *Census of the Population, Detailed Population Characteristics*. United States Summary Section B: *Regions* (Washington, D.C.: U.S. Bureau of the Census, March 1984), vol. 2, tables 330 and 332, pp. 897–908, and 999–1000. These data reflect the federal government's definition of the South and include Washington, D.C., Kentucky, West Virginia, Maryland, Delaware, and Oklahoma in addition to the traditional eleven southern states.

78. Ibid., Regional Summary (March 1984), vol. 1, tables 316 and 321, pp. 95–99, 325–27; and vol. 2, table 338, pp. 1334–41. These figures also reflect the federal definition of the South.

79. Readers are again referred to *Praying for Sheetrock* as a moving and insightful portrayal of black-white economic gaps in the South and the failure of the civil rights movement to address key structural problems that keep the black-white economic gap from narrowing.

Chapter 9. Steering the Ship of State: The Southern Governorship

1. The problem of traditional southern leadership is discussed in Key, *Southern Politics*, pp. 3–4, 180–82, 302–10.

2. Implicit in this statement is a set of assumptions about gubernatorial leadership. These will be explained in the next chapter.

3. Some useful references on the historical evolution of the office of governor include Leslie Lipson, *The American Governor: From Figurehead to Leader* (Chicago: University of Chicago Press, 1939); Coleman Ransone, *The Office of Governor in the South* (University: University of Alabama Press, 1951); Ransone, *The Office of Governor in the United States* (University: University of Alabama Press, 1956); Joseph E. Kallenbach, *The American Chief Executive* (New York: Harper and Row, 1966); Ransone, *The American Governorship* (Westport, Conn.: Greenwood Press, 1982); and Sabato, *Goodbye to Goodtime Charley*. Helpful and accessible treatments of the modern governor include Thad Beyle, "Governors," in *Politics in the American States*, ed. Virginia Gray, Herbert Jacob, and Robert B. Albritton, 5th ed. (Glenview, Ill.: Scott, Foresman/Little Brown, 1990), chap. 6; Thad Beyle, "Governors: The Middlemen and Women in Our Political System," in *Politics in the American States*, ed. Gray and Jacob, chap. 6; Thad L. Beyle, "Being Governor," in *State of the States*, ed. Van Horn, chap. 5.

4. Quoted in Sabato, *Goodbye to Goodtime Charley*, p. 4.

5. For additional material on the post-Reconstruction southern governorship, see

Key, *Southern Politics*; Woodward, *Origins of the New South*; and Tindall, *Emergence of the New South.*

6. Woodward, *Origins of the New South,* pp. 375, 402, 405. A good deal of reference material for the preceding statements comes from Robert Sobel and John Raimo, eds., *Biographical Directory of the Governors of the United States* (Westport, Conn.: Meckler, 1978). See also Colburn and Scher, *Florida's Gubernatorial Politics,* esp. chap. 3.

7. LeRoy Collins, *Forerunners Courageous* (Tallahassee: Colcade Press, 1971).

8. See Tindall, *Emergence of the New South*; Woodward, *Origins of the New South*; and Newby, *The South,* for occasional references to gubernatorial behavior in this same vein. For details on the Florida experience, see Colburn and Scher, *Florida's Gubernatorial Politics.*

9. Woodward, *Origins of the New South*; Tindall, *Emergence of the New South*; and Newby, *The South,* all deal with southern progressivism. The most thorough text, however, is Grantham, *Southern Progressivism.* See esp. Grantham's helpful bibliographic essay for further readings.

10. Woodward, *Origins of the New South,* has considerable detail on the Aycock administration; see also the Aycock entry in Sobel and Raimo, eds., *Bibliographical Directory of Governors.*

11. Hunt was elected governor again in 1992.

12. For a broader look at reforms in governor's office, see Lipson, *American Governor*; Ransone, *Office of Governor in the South, Office of Governor in the United States,* and *American Governorship;* Sabato, *Goodbye to Goodtime Charley*; and the recent Beyle pieces, "Governors: Middlemen and Women" and "Being Governor."

13. Schlesinger, "Politics of the Executive," p. 229. Schlesinger's bibliography is useful for those wanting specifics on individual states.

14. See Colburn and Scher, *Florida's Gubernatorial Politics*; and Sabato, *Goodbye to Goodtime Charley,* for discussions of the importance of gubernatorial appointments.

15. Council of State Governments, *The Book of the States, 1960–1961* (Lexington: Council of State Governments, 1961), p. 123.

16. Schlesinger, "Politics of the Executive," p. 225.

17. The method of calculation was the same as above. Council of State Governments, *The Book of the States, 1988–1989* (Lexington: Council of State Governments, 1988), pp. 53–57.

18. Douglas St. Angelo and Bill O. Gibson, "Administrative and Functional Agencies," in *Florida's Politics and Government,* ed. Manning J. Dauer, 2d ed. (Gainesville: University Presses of Florida, A University of Florida Book, 1984), p. 125. In fact, by the mid-1990s the Florida legislature began to take a close look at some of the state's major "superagencies," especially Health and Rehabilitative Services (HRS), the state's largest agency, on the grounds that it had become too large, too unwieldy, and too unaccountable. The lieutenant governor led a successful reorganization effort of HRS, but members of the legislature were still unsatisfied. The latest plan was to split HRS into two or more agencies (Health, in particular, would be moved into a new one). In part the goal was simply to create a more viable and workable state agency; but the legislature's other objective was to allow more opportunity for it to micromanage state functions, for which it is justifiably known.

19. Discussions of the Florida Cabinet can be found in Havard and Beth, *The Politics of Mis-Representation*; Manning J. Dauer, "Florida: The Different State," in *Changing Politics of the South,* ed. Havard, pp. 92–164; Colburn and Scher, *Florida's Gubernatorial Politics,* esp. chaps. 4, 5; and Richard Scher and David Colburn, "The Governor and His Office," in *Florida's Politics and Government,* ed. Manning J. Dauer, 2d ed. (Gainesville: University Presses of Florida, A University of Florida Book, 1984),

pp. 105–23. See also Richard K. Scher, "The Governor and Cabinet: Executive Policy-Making and Policy Management," in *The Policy Management System: Discontinuity and Reform in Florida*, ed. Richard Chackerian (Tallahassee: Askew School of Public Administration and Policy, Florida State University, and the Florida Center for Public Management, 1994), chap. 4; and Richard K. Scher, "Administrative Reform and Executive Policy Making," in *Reinventing Government in Florida*, ed. Jamil Jreisat and Frank P. Sherwood (Tallahassee: Florida State University and Florida Center for Public Management, Publication Number 81094, 1994), chap. 5.

20. Florida will begin a process of constitutional revision in 1997. In preparation for this activity, a former governor headed a blue-ribbon study commission designed to look into the possibility of reforming, even abolishing, the Cabinet. It is not clear whether or not the results of this study commission will have any bearing on constitutional revision; continuation of the Florida Cabinet seems virtually as certain as death and taxes.

21. Colburn and Scher, *Florida's Gubernatorial Politics*, p. 121.

22. See, on this point, the classic works by Peter Bachrach and Morton Baratz, "Two Faces of Power," *American Political Science Review* 56 (1962): 947–52; Bachrach and Baratz, "Decisions and Non-Decisions," *American Political Science Review* 57 (September 1963): 632–42. See also Schattschneider, *Semisovereign People*.

23. See Cortez Ewing, *Primary Elections in the South* (Norman: University of Oklahoma Press, 1953).

24. Modern readers are reminded that incumbency was not regarded as a major political albatross until the elections of 1994, or possibly the preceding one in 1992. Whether it will continue to be so viewed by the electorate remains to be seen.

25. See Liebling, *Earl of Louisiana*.

26. See Carter, *Politics of Rage*.

27. See David R. Colburn and Richard K. Scher, "Florida Gubernatorial Politics: The Fuller Warren Years," *Florida Historical Quarterly* 53 (April 1975): 389–408; also, Colburn and Scher, *Florida's Gubernatorial Politics*, esp. pp. 134–39.

28. Colburn and Scher, *Florida's Gubernatorial Politics*, p. 97.

29. Some accessible works on budgeting, including materials on state budgeting, are Allen Schick, *Budget Innovation in the States* (Washington, D.C.: Brookings Institution, 1971); Edward A. Lehan, "Public Budgeting," in *Essays in Public Finance and Financial Management*, ed. John Petersen and Catherine Spain (Chatham, N.J.: Chatham Publishers, 1980); Lance LeLoup, *Budgetary Politics*, 2d ed. (Brunswick, Ohio: King's Court, 1980); and Robert Lee and Ronald Johnson, *Public Budgeting Systems*, 3d ed. (Baltimore: University Park Press, 1983).

30. I am indebted to Professors Lynn Leverty, University of Florida, and Clifton McCleskey, University of Virginia, for their helpful insights on gubernatorial budget authority in these and other states.

31. Council of State Governments, *Book of the States, 1960–1961*, p. 123. See also Lipson, *American Governor*; and Ransone, *Office of Governor in the South* and *Office of Governor in the United States*, for discussion of the budgetary powers of southern governors early in this century. Colburn and Scher, *Florida's Gubernatorial Politics*, detail the Florida experience.

32. Ransone, *Office of Governor in the United States*, pp. 162–63.

33. Discussions of the limited impact which the governor can have on the budget can be found in ibid., pp. 289–91; and Ransone, *American Governorship*, p. 129. See also Colburn and Scher, *Florida's Gubernatorial Politics*, pp. 149–52. More general discussions can be found in Kallenbach, *American Chief Executive*; Schlesinger, "Politics of the Executive"; Thad Beyle and J. Oliver Williams, *The American Governor in Behavioral Perspective* (New York: Harper and Row, 1972); Sabato, *Goodbye to Good-*

time Charley; and Beyle, "Governors: Middlemen and Women" and "Being Governor." The budget crunch of the early 1990s underscores the governor's continuing budget weaknesses. In Florida, for example, the existence of special earmarked funds forced new Governor Lawton Chiles to scramble to balance the budget and required his calling a special legislative session to gain approval to use the interest on some trust accounts to cover budget deficits.

34. Ransone, *Office of Governor in the South*, p. 199; Ransone, *Office of Governor in the United States*, p. 344; Sabato, *Goodbye to Goodtime Charley*, p. 85. See also Lipson, *American Governor*, for an early discussion of the problem of gubernatorial staffing; he provides a number of southern examples.

35. The bibles of this line of thinking were David E. Osborne, *Reinventing Government* (Reading Mass.: Addison-Wesley, 1992); and Philip K. Howard, *The Death of Common Sense* (New York: Random House, 1995).

36. Only in North Carolina and Georgia, under Governors Jim Hunt and Zell Miller, respectively, did there seem to be any evidence that government could do something other than downsize (or "rightsize," as it became known). To some extent this could also be said of Texas under Governor Ann Richards, although she lost her 1994 reelection bid partially as a result of her desire to keep state government alive and vital.

37. See Charles Lindblom, "The Science of Muddling Through," *Public Administration Review* 19 (Spring 1959): 79–88. A reasonable question can be asked, although it transcends this study, about whether the latest budgeting techniques (or, less charitably, gimmicks) actually enhance budgetary control either by the legislature or governor. There is at least anecdotal evidence that the basic "political football" character of state budgets has in no basic way been altered by introduction of new budgeting methods and that in fact they might have become primarily an excuse for ever greater levels of micromanagement of both state and local services by these institutions of state government.

38. See, for example, Frank Prescott, "The Executive Veto in the American States," *Western Political Quarterly* 3 (1950): 98–112; Thad Beyle, "The Governor's Formal Powers," *Public Administration Review* 28 (1968): 540–45; Schlesinger, "Politics of the Executive," pp. 229–30; and Charles Wiggins, "Executive Vetoes and Legislative Overrides in the American States," *Journal of Politics* 42 (November 1980): 1110–17.

39. Prescott, "Executive Veto," p. 112.

40. In Florida, the culinary metaphor has been changed, and local pet projects are called "turkeys."

41. In 1988, Florida Governor Bob Martinez item-vetoed so many projects that the Speaker of the House and other state officials sued him. They argued that he had exceeded his authority and had in fact vetoed (hence eliminated) the state budget. While the State Supreme Court found on behalf of the governor, legislative rankling against him could still be felt in the next legislative session.

42. Prescott, "Executive Veto," p. 112.

43. Some useful sources on the weakness of the traditional southern legislature include Alexander Heard, ed., *State Legislatures in American Politics* (Englewood Cliffs, N.J.: Prentice-Hall, An American Assembly Book, 1966); Malcolm Jewell, *The State Legislature*, 2d ed. (New York: Random House, 1968); Donald Herzberg and Alan Rosenthal, eds., *Strengthening the States* (Garden City, N.Y.: Doubleday, 1971); Alan Rosenthal, *Legislative Performance in the States* (New York: Free Press, 1974); Samuel C. Patterson, "Legislators and Legislatures in the American States," in *Politics in the American States*, ed. Gray, Jacob, and Vines, pp. 135–79; and Alan Rosenthal and Maureen Moakley, eds., *The Political Life of the American States* (New York: Praeger, 1984).

44. Wiggins, "Executive Vetoes and Legislative Overrides," p. 111.

45. It is of interest that even the Republican state senate in Florida voted to sustain the governor's veto of the tobacco liability repeal. While several Republican senators

voted with the governor purely as a statement about tobacco use, others may well have been courted by the governor in order to ensure their votes.

Chapter 10. Red Galluses No More: The Leadership of Southern Governors

1. It is impossible to list even a representative sample of works on the many political characters who have been seen on the southern political stage. Two accessible works that provide useful vignettes into some of them are Sherrill, *Gothic Politics,* and Frady, *Southerners.* For readers wishing to examine a particular colorful southern politician in detail, the following is a list of superb, easily accessible biographies: Dewey Grantham, *Hoke Smith and the Politics of the New South* (Baton Rouge: Louisiana State University Press, 1958); Frady, *Wallace;* Williams, *Huey Long;* Liebling, *Earl of Louisiana;* Woodward, *Tom Watson;* Wayne Flynt, *Cracker Messiah* (Baton Rouge: Louisiana State University Press, 1977); Jeansonne, *Messiah of the Masses;* and Carter, *Politics of Rage.*

2. Models of leadership include those presented by Alexander George and Juliette George, *Woodrow Wilson and Colonel House* (New York: John Day, 1956); Clinton Rossiter, *The American Presidency,* 2d ed. (New York: Time, Inc., 1963); Alexander George, "Assessing Presidential Character," *World Politics* 26 (January 1974): 234–82; James David Barber, *The Presidential Character,* 2d ed. (Englewood Cliffs, N.J.: Prentice-Hall, 1977); and James McGregor Burns, *Leadership* (New York: Harper and Row, 1979). See also Manning J. Dauer, David R. Colburn, and Richard K. Scher, "A Typology of Executives" (paper presented at the annual meeting of the Southern Political Science Association, Gatlinburg, Tennessee, November 2, 1979); and Colburn and Scher, *Florida's Gubernatorial Politics,* pp. 1–8.

3. This point has been a criticism of the George and Barber approaches to leadership. However, there are far more data available for presidents than for southern governors; and of course the number of presidents is far more manageable than of southern chief executives.

4. Political scientists have developed a substantial literature to try to show how economic forces and conditions influence political activity. See Dye, *Politics, Economics, and the Public.*

5. Gastil, *Cultural Regions of the United States.* See also *Disappearing South?* ed. Baker, Moreland, and Steed; Elazar, *American Federalism;* Ellis, *American Political Cultures;* and Elazar, *American Mosaic,* for treatments of political culture and their persistence over time.

6. The terms "passive" and "active" are used here somewhat less behaviorally than they are in Barber, *Presidential Character.* They are the attitudes and beliefs that incumbents had toward the governorship and what they regarded as appropriate behavior for the office. The assumption is that these attitudes and beliefs would guide behavior.

7. This point is developed fully in Richard Neustadt, *Presidential Power* (New York: Wiley, 1976).

8. On this point, see both Key, *Southern Politics;* and Black, *Southern Governors and Civil Rights.*

9. Recent discussions of this point include Sabato, *Goodbye to Goodtime Charley;* Beyle, Governors," "Governors: Middlemen and Women," and "Being Governor."

10. Rossiter, *American Presidency.*

11. See Cobb, *The Selling of the South* and *Industrialization of Southern Society.*

12. Colburn and Scher, *Florida's Gubernatorial Politics,* p. 128.

13. Ibid., pp. 128–53.

14. See Morton Grodzins, *The American System,* ed. Daniel Elazar (Chicago: Rand McNally, 1966); and Elazar, *American Federalism.*

15. Havard and Beth, *Politics of Mis-Representation.*

16. The figure is derived from an examination of the universe of southern governors in office from 1900 to 1994. It should be considered more a measure of relative proportion than an exact percentage because disputes are possible about the categorization of individual governors. Nonetheless, the evidence is incontrovertible that the number of Businessmen southern governors approaches two-thirds of the total. Sources examined for the assessment include individual biographies, histories of the South, and the helpful Sobel and Raimo, eds., *Biographical Directory of the Governors.*

17. See Merlin Cox, "David Sholtz: New Deal Governor of Florida," *Florida Historical Quarterly* 64, no. 2 (October 1964): 142–52; Colburn and Scher, *Florida Gubernatorial Politics,* p. 242.

18. The sobriquet is, of course, common; but in this instance it comes from Sabato, *Goodbye to Goodtime Charley.*

19. Perhaps the best treatment of the political aspects of southern populism and the imposition of legalized forms of discrimination is in Woodward, *The Strange Career of Jim Crow.* See also Woodward, *Origins of the New South;* Kousser, *Shaping of Southern Politics;* and Newby, *The South.*

20. Key, *Southern Politics,* chapters 2–14.

21. See Frady, *Wallace,* and Carter, *Politics of Rage,* for the differences in the "two" George Wallaces.

22. Key, *Southern Politics,* chap. 8.

23. A common populist-style bumper sticker in the South reads, "If you are not completely outraged, you are not paying attention."

24. Frady, *Wallace;* Carter, *Politics of Rage.*

25. See Frady, *Southerners,* pp. 326–58.

26. Perhaps the best example is Robert Penn Warren's classic *All the King's Men,* a novel whose main character showed similarities to Huey Long. The film version, starring the late Broderick Crawford as the demagogic Willie Stark, is also a powerful political drama. See also Kirby, *Media Made Dixie.*

27. See Sherrill, *Gothic Politics,* and Frady, *Southerners,* for profiles of many of these figures.

28. See Williams, *Huey Long,* pp. 432–39; see also Liebling, *Earl of Louisiana;* Frady, *Wallace,* pp. 6–43, and Jeansonne, *Messiah of the Masses.* Another useful book, although not strictly a biography, is Allan P. Sindler, *Huey Long's Louisiana* (Baltimore: Johns Hopkins Press, 1956).

29. The attitudes that Clayton Williams of Texas expressed toward women in his 1990 gubernatorial campaign may have qualified him, in some minds, as demagogic. He was defeated by a woman, Ann Richards. See Sue Tallerson-Rinehart, *Claytie and the Lady* (Austin: University of Texas Press, 1994). I am indebted to Professor Lynn Leverty, University of Florida, for her helpful insights on Texas gubernatorial politics.

30. See Percy, *Lanterns on the Levee,* and Mars, *Witness in Philadelphia.* See also Sherrill, *Gothic Politics.*

31. Askew is a fascinating example of a combination of Populist and Policymaker types. It is an interesting speculation about the possibility of future southern governors also embodying these two different approaches.

32. The term "moderate progressivism" is not original, but its application to southern gubernatorial politics may be. Classic southern progressivism, despite its name, was frequently a very conservative force in the region. The term, as meant here, suggests a much more forward-looking, policy-centered approach to public issues than did the

classic southern progressives.

33. See W.J. Cash, *The Mind of the South* (New York: Vintage, 1969); Degler, *Place over Time;* Genovese, *Southern Tradition.*

34. Colburn and Scher, *Florida's Gubernatorial Politics,* p. 231.

35. Sabato, *Goodbye to Goodtime Charley.*

36. The exception may be David Duke in Louisiana, but as of this writing, while he has been a frequent candidate for statewide office, he has yet to win.

37. Black, *Southern Governors and Civil Rights.*

38. See Schlesinger, "Politics of the Executive," p. 229. See also Robert Goldwin, *A Nation of States* (Chicago: Rand McNally, 1963); Elazar, *American Federalism;* and Beyle, "Governors" and "Governors: Middlemen and Women."

Chapter 11. The New South

1. Peirce, *Deep South States of America.*

2. The late Harry Golden, editor of the *Carolina Israelite,* frequently wrote about how much more easily desegregation occurred if participants were standing, rather than sitting, together.

3. It is true that in the 1990s race relations in the South may have taken a more abrasive turn than they had shown a decade earlier. Whether this phenomenon is transitory remains to be seen; it may be that the 1990s will see consolidation in the South following rapid changes in the 1970s and 1980s, not only in race relations but in leadership as well. Our point for the moment, however, is that even in the 1990s, race relations in the South are not what they were in the 1960s, or earlier.

4. It is of interest that, in the spring of 1996, when a Republican state senator in Alabama, Charles Davidson, revealed that he found a biblical justification for slavery, his critics included white Republicans as well as African Americans. See chapter 8.

5. See, for example, David C. Perry and Alfred Watkins, eds., *The Rise of the Sunbelt Cities* (Beverly Hills, Calif.: Sage, 1977).

6. Emergency Council, *Report.* It would, however, conclude that it is the poorest region.

7. "50–Year Trend Reversed as U.S. Regions Grow Apart Economically," *New York Times,* August 23, 1987, p. 18. Chapter 2 of this volume shows data for the 1990s indicating that the previous pattern continues.

8. For a cogent recent overview of the effectiveness of welfare programs, see, for example, Harrell Rodgers, *Poor Women, Poor Families* (Armonk, N.Y.: M.E. Sharpe, 1986). See also "Does Our Welfare System Hurt the Poor?" in *Taking Sides,* ed. George McKenna and Stanley Feingold (Guilford, Conn.: Dushkin Publishing Group, 1987), pp. 228–43.

9. In the 1990s, criticism of welfare programs became virtually an article of faith for all candidates and officeholders, in the South and elsewhere. Some states began significant efforts to reform welfare. In the summer of 1996 Congress passed, and the president signed, a controversial, hard-edged welfare reform bill. It must be noted, however, that this bill, as well as other reforms, was actually punitive in nature; relatively few seemed designed, like the experiments in Florida, to foster self-sufficiency.

10. On farm problems, for example, see Hightower, *Hard Tomatoes, Hard Times.*

11. See John F. Bibby, Cornelius P. Cotter, James L. Gibson, and Robert J. Huckshorn, "Parties in State Politics," in *Politics in the American States,* ed. Gray, Jacob, and Albritton, chap. 3. See also Bibby and Holbrook, "Parties and Elections."

12. This is a major theme in much of Key's writing. See, in addition to *Southern Politics,* his *Politics, Parties and Pressure Groups,* 4th ed. (New York: Crowell, 1958),

and *The Responsible Electorate* (Cambridge, Mass.: Belknap Press, 1966). See also American Political Science Association, Committee on Political Parties, "Toward a More Responsible Two-Party System," *American Political Science Review* 44, suppl. (September 1950); and Austin Ranney, *The Doctrine of Responsible Party Government* (Urbana: University of Illinois Press, 1962).

13. There are many such models. See, besides Key, such works as Schattschneider, *Semisovereign People;* Matthews and Prothro, *Negroes and the New Southern Politics;* Peter Bachrach, *The Theory of Democratic Elitism* (Boston: Little, Brown, 1967); Roger W. Cobb and Charles D. Elder, *Participation in American Politics* (Boston: Allyn and Bacon, 1972); and Button, *Blacks and Social Change.*

14. See, for example, Rossiter, *American Presidency;* Neustadt, *Presidential Power;* Barber, *Presidential Character;* Burns, *Leadership;* and Colburn and Scher, *Florida's Gubernatorial Politics.*

15. See, for example, *The Federalist Papers* (New York: Viking Penguin, 1987); John Dewey, *Democracy and Education* (1916; reprint, New York: Macmillan, 1961); and Schattschneider, *Semisovereign People,* as models of normative democratic theory.

16. See, for example, Bachrach, *Theory of Democratic Elitism;* and Cobb and Elder, *Participation in American Politics.*

17. See, for example, the *Declaration of Independence;* Dewey, *Democracy and Education;* Thomas Dye, *The Politics of Equality* (Indianapolis: Bobbs-Merrill, 1971); Christopher Jencks, *Inequality* (New York: Basic Books, 1972); Herbert Gans, *More Equality* (New York: Vintage, 1973); Leonard Reissman, *Inequality in American Society* (Glenview, Ill.: Scott, Foresman, 1973); and Beeghley, *Living Poorly in America.*

18. There is concern in the mid-1990s South that elimination or severe curtailment of affirmative action programs in education might significantly limit African American opportunities to enroll in the region's leading institutions of higher education.

19. Seagull, *Southern Republicanism;* Black and Black, *Politics and Society in the South* and *Vital South.*

20. Black, *Southern Governors and Civil Rights.*

21. An excellent movie illustrating this point is *The Gods Must Be Crazy* (1981).

22. See Stack, *Call to Home.*

23. See Jack Walker, "The Diffusion of Innovations among the American States," in *American Political Science Review* 63 (September 1969): 880–99. See also his "Innovation in State Politics," in *Politics in the American States,* ed. Jacob and Vines, chap. 10.

24. Stephen A. Salmore and Barbara G. Salmore, *Candidates, Parties and Campaigns,* 2d ed. (Washington, D.C.: CQ Press, 1985).

25. Gastil, *Cultural Regions of the United States.*

26. See, for example, Reed, *One South* and *Whistling Dixie* (Columbia: University of Missouri Press, 1990).

27. In this vein see also Degler, *Place over Time;* and Genovese, *Southern Tradition.*

28. Haves–have-nots is, of course, the great dichotomy Key felt characterized and motivated southern politics at midcentury.

29. See Black and Black, *Vital South.*

30. A 1996 survey of one hundred top restaurants in America by *Wine Spectator* magazine included a very large percentage in the South; the most extensive wine list of any American restaurant may well be found at Bern's, in Tampa.

31. There are a host of spinoffs, including magazines on southern gardens and southern architecture and interiors.

32. Ayres and Naylor, eds., *You Can't Eat Magnolias.*

Select Bibliography

This bibliography is highly selective. It is limited to readily accessible books and is designed to guide readers to other materials on twentieth-century southern politics. Additional references on specific topics can be found in the notes to each chapter.

Agee, James, and Walker Evans. *Let Us Now Praise Famous Men.* Boston: Houghton-Mifflin, 1969.

Angelou, Maya. *I Know Why the Caged Bird Sings.* New York: Random House, 1970.

Ayres, H. Brandt, and Thomas Naylor, eds. *You Can't Eat Magnolias.* New York: McGraw Hill, 1972.

Baker, Tod, Charles Hadley, Robert Steed, and Laurence Moreland, eds. *Political Parties in the Southern States.* New York: Praeger, 1990. *Note:* Baker, Steed, and Moreland are editors of a long series of books stemming from The Citadel Symposium on Southern Politics. While only this volume is listed here, references in the text list a number of others. All are worth consulting, whether the reader is a generalist or specialist.

Bass, Jack, and Walter DeVries. *The Transformation of Southern Politics.* New York: Basic Books, 1976.

Bartley, Numan. *The Rise of Massive Resistance.* Baton Rouge: Louisiana State University Press, 1969.

Bartley, Numan, and Hugh D. Graham. *Southern Politics and the Second Reconstruction.* Baltimore: Johns Hopkins University Press, 1975.

Beeghley, Leonard. *Living Poorly in America.* New York: Praeger, 1983.

Billington, Monroe. *The Political South in the Twentieth Century.* New York: Scribner's, 1975.

Black, Earl. *Southern Governors and Civil Rights.* Cambridge, Mass.: Harvard University Press, 1976.

Black, Earl, and Merle Black. *Politics and Society in the South.* Cambridge, Mass.: Harvard University Press, 1987.

————. *The Vital South.* Cambridge, Mass.: Harvard University Press, 1992.

Branch, Taylor. *Parting the Waters.* New York: Simon and Schuster, 1988.

Brooks, Thomas R. *Walls Come Tumbling Down.* Englewood Cliffs, N.J.: Prentice-Hall, 1974.

Button, James W. *Blacks and Social Change.* Princeton: Princeton University Press, 1989.

Carter, Dan T. *The Politics of Rage.* New York: Simon and Schuster, 1995.

Cash, W.J. *The Mind of the South.* New York: Vintage, 1969.

Chafe, William H. *Civilities and Civil Rights.* New York: Oxford University Press, 1981.

Chalmers, David. *Hooded Americanism.* New York: F. Watts, 1981.

Cobb, James C. *Industrialization and Southern Society.* Lexington: University of Kentucky Press, 1984.

———. *The Selling of the South.* Baton Rouge: Louisiana State University Press, 1982.

Colburn, David R., and Richard K. Scher. *Florida's Gubernatorial Politics in the Twentieth Century.* Tallahassee: University Presses of Florida, a Florida State University Book, 1980.

———. *Racial Change and Community Crisis: St. Augustine, Florida, 1877–1980.* New York: Columbia University Press, 1985.

Conti, Joseph. *Challenging the Civil Rights Establishment.* Westport, Conn.: Praeger, 1993.

Daniel, Pete. *Standing at the Crossroads.* New York: Hill and Wang, 1986.

Degler, Carl. *Place over Time.* Baton Rouge: Louisiana State University Press, 1977.

Editorial Research Reports. *American Regionalism.* Washington, D.C.: Congressional Quarterly, 1980.

Ewing, Cortez. *Primary Elections in the South.* Norman: University of Oklahoma Press, 1953.

Fite, Gordon C. *Cotton Fields No More.* Lexington: University of Kentucky Press, 1984.

Frady, Marshall. *Southerners.* New York: New American Library, 1980.

Franklin, John Hope. *From Slavery to Freedom,* 4th ed. New York: Knopf, 1974.

Fuller, Chet. *I Hear Them Calling My Name.* Boston: Houghton Mifflin, 1981.

Garreau, Joel. *The Nine Nations of North America.* New York: Avon, 1982.

Garrow, David. *Bearing the Cross.* New York: William Morrow, 1986.

———. *Protest at Selma.* New Haven: Yale University Press, 1978.

Gastil, Raymond. *Cultural Regions of the United States.* Seattle: University of Washington Press, 1975.

Gaston, Paul. *The New South Creed.* New York: Knopf, 1970.

Genovese, Eugene. *The Southern Tradition.* Cambridge, Mass.: Harvard University Press, 1994.

Grantham, Dewey. *The Regional Imagination.* Nashville: Vanderbilt University Press, 1979.

———. *Southern Progressivism.* Knoxville: University of Tennessee Press, 1983.

Griffin, John Howard. *Black Like Me,* 2d ed. Boston: Houghton Mifflin, 1961, 1977.

Havard, William C., ed. *The Changing Politics of the South.* Baton Rouge: Louisiana State University Press, 1972.

Havard, William C., and Loren Beth. *The Politics of Mis-Representation.* Baton Rouge: Louisiana State University Press, 1962.

Heard, Alexander. *A Two Party South?* Chapel Hill: University of North Carolina Press, 1952.

Hill, Samuel S., ed. *Encyclopedia of Religion in the South.* Macon, Ga.: Mercer University Press, 1984.

Jacoway, Elizabeth, and David R. Colburn, eds. *Southern Businessmen and Desegregation.* Baton Rouge: Louisiana State University Press, 1982.

Keech, William. *The Impact of Negro Voting.* Chicago: Rand McNally, 1966.

Key, V.O., Jr. *Southern Politics in State and Nation.* New York: Knopf, 1949.

Kluger, Richard. *Simple Justice.* New York: Knopf, 1976.

Kousser, J. Morgan. *The Shaping of Southern Politics.* New Haven: Yale University Press, 1974.

Lamis, Alexander. *The Two Party South*. New York: Oxford University Press, 1984.

Lawson, Stephen F. *Black Ballots*. New York: Columbia University Press, 1976.

————. *In Pursuit of Power*. New York: Columbia University Press, 1985.

Mars, Florence. *Witness in Philadelphia*. Baton Rouge: Louisiana State University Press, 1977.

Marshall, Ray, and Virgil L. Christian Jr., eds. *Employment of Blacks in the South*. Austin: University of Texas Press, 1978.

Matthews, Donald R., and James W. Prothro. *Negroes and the New Southern Politics*. New York: Harcourt, Brace and World, 1966.

McAdam, Doug. *Political Process and the Development of Black Insurgency, 1930–1970*. Chicago: University of Chicago Press, 1982.

Meier, August, and Elliot Rudwick. *CORE*. New York: Oxford University Press, 1973.

Morris, Aldon D. *The Origins of the Civil Rights Movement*. New York: Free Press, 1984.

Mowry, George. *Another Look at the Twentieth Century South*. Baton Rouge: Louisiana State University Press, 1973.

Murchison, Claudius T. *King Cotton Is Sick*. Chapel Hill: University of North Carolina Press, 1930.

Myrdal, Gunnar. *An American Dilemma*. 1944. Reprint, New York: Pantheon, 1975.

Newby, I.A. *The South: A History*. New York: Holt, Rinehart and Winston, 1978.

Odum, Howard. *Southern Regions of the United States*. Chapel Hill: University of North Carolina Press, 1936.

Odum, Howard, and Harry Moore. *American Regionalism*. New York: H. Holt and Company, 1938.

Olmsted, Frederick Law. *The Cotton Kingdom*. 1861. Reprint, New York: Knopf, 1953.

Patterson, James T. *Congressional Conservatism and the New Deal*. Lexington: University of Kentucky Press, 1967.

Peirce, Neal. *The Border South States of America*. New York: W.W. Norton, 1974.

————. *The Deep South States of America*. New York: W.W. Norton, 1974.

Percy, William Alexander. *Lanterns on the Levee*. New York: Knopf, 1941. Reprint, Baton Rouge: Louisiana State University Press, 1973.

Perkins, Joseph, ed. *A Conservative Agenda for Black Americans*. Washington, D.C.: The Heritage Foundation, 1990.

Powledge, Fred. *Journeys through the South*. New York: Vanguard, 1979.

Price, C. Douglas. *The Negro and Southern Politics*. New York: New York University Press, 1957.

Raines, Howell. *My Soul Is Rested*. New York: Penguin, 1983.

Ransone, Coleman. *The Office of Governor in the South*. University: University of Alabama Press, 1951.

Reed, John Shelton. *The Enduring South*. Lexington, Mass.: Lexington Books, 1972.

————. *One South*. Baton Rouge: Louisiana State University Press, 1982.

————. *Southerners*. Chapel Hill: University of North Carolina Press, 1983.

Rodgers, Harrell R., and Charles S. Bullock III. *Law and Social Change*. New York: McGraw Hill, 1972.

Roland, Charles. *The Improbable Era*. Lexington: University of Kentucky Press, 1975.

Sabato, Larry. *Goodbye to Goodtime Charley*, 2d ed. Washington, D.C.: CQ Press, 1983.

Sale, Kirkpatrick. *Power Shift*. New York: Vintage, 1976.

Scott, Anne Firor. *The Southern Lady*. Chicago: University of Chicago Press, 1970.

Seagull, Louis. *Southern Republicanism*. New York: Holsted Press, 1975.

Sherrill, Robert. *Gothic Politics in the Deep South*. New York: Grossman, 1968.

Silver, James. *Mississippi: The Closed Society,* new ed. New York: Harcourt, Brace and World, 1966.

Sitkoff, Harvard. *The Struggle for Black Equality.* New York: Hill and Wang, 1981.

Stack, Carol. *Call to Home.* New York: Basic Books, 1996.

Street, James. *The New Revolution in the Cotton Economy.* Chapel Hill: University of North Carolina Press, 1957.

Strong, Donald. *Urban Republicanism in the South.* University: Bureau of Public Administration, University of Alabama, 1960.

Swansborough, Robert H., and David M. Brodsky, eds. *The South's New Politics* Columbia: University of South Carolina Press, 1988.

Tindall, George Brown. *The Disruption of the Solid South.* Athens: University of Georgia Press, 1972.

————. *The Emergence of the New South, 1913–1945.* Baton Rouge: Louisiana State University Press, 1967.

United States National Emergency Council. *Report on Economic Conditions of the South.* 1938. Reprint, New York: Da Capo Press, 1972.

Vance, Rupert. *All These People.* Chapel Hill: University of North Carolina Press, 1946.

————. *Human Geography of the South.* Chapel Hill: University of North Carolina Press, 1935.

Warren, Robert Penn. *Who Speaks for the Negro?* New York: Random House, 1965.

Watters, Pat. *Down to Now.* New York: Pantheon, 1971.

Watters, Pat, and Reese Cleghorn. *Climbing Jacob's Ladder.* New York: Harcourt, Brace and World, 1967.

Wheeler, Marjorie Spruill. *New Women of the South.* New York: Oxford University Press, 1993.

Wilson, Charles R. *Judgment and Grace in Dixie.* Athens: University of Georgia Press, 1995.

Wirt, Frederick. *Politics of Southern Equality.* Chicago: Aldine, 1970.

Woodman, Harold D. *King Cotton and His Retainers.* Lexington: University of Kentucky Press, 1968.

Woodward, C. Vann. *The Burden of Southern History,* rev. ed. Baton Rouge: Louisiana State University Press, 1968.

————. *Origins of the New South, 1877–1913.* Baton Rouge: Louisiana State University Press, 1971.

————. *The Strange Career of Jim Crow,* rev. 3d. ed. New York: Oxford University Press, 1974.

Wright, Gavin. *Old South, New South.* New York: Basic Books, 1986.

————. *The Political Economy of the Cotton South.* New York: Norton, 1978.

Zinn, Howard. *SNCC.* Boston: Beacon Press, 1964.

Index

About the Author

Richard K. Scher (Ph.D., Columbia, 1972) is professor of political science at the University of Florida, Gainesville, where he won the Teacher of the Year Award in 1992–93. He is co-author of *Florida's Gubernatorial Politics in the Twentieth Century* and principal author of *Voting Rights and Democracy: The Law and Politics of Districting.* He is currently completing *The Modern Political Campaign.* Dr. Scher is an active political consultant and a frequent commentator on regional politics.